Reading
Architectural Plans

About the Author

Ernest R. Weidhaas received his Bachelors and Masters degrees in Mechanical Engineering from New York University. His professional achievements include the positions of Assistant Dean for Commonwealth Campuses, College of Engineering; Head of the General Engineering Department; and Professor of Engineering Graphics at The Pennsylvania State University. He has been a registered professional engineer in the Commonwealth of Pennsylvania for over 25 years.

Professor Weidhaas has served as a Director of the American Society for Engineering Education, Director of the Engineering Graphics Division of the American Society for Engineering Education, and Chairman of both the Engineering Technology Division and the Technical College Council of that society and has designed residential, commercial, industrial, agricultural, and military buildings and equipment.

Reading
Architectural Plans

For Residential And
Commercial Construction

Third Edition

Ernest R. Weidhaas

Professor Emeritus of Engineering Graphics
The Pennsylvania State University

ALLYN AND BACON   Boston   London   Sydney   Toronto

Library of Congress Cataloging in Publication Data

Weidhaas, Ernest R.
    Reading architectural plans for residential and commercial
construction/Ernest R. Weidhaas.—3rd ed.
        p.   cm.
    Includes index.
    1. Architecture, Domestic—Designs and plans.   2. Commercial
buildings—Designs and plans.   3. Architecture—Details.   I. Title.
NA7115.W44   1989   89-68
728'.022'3—dc19   CIP
ISBN 0-205-11890-9

Printed in the United States of America

10   9   8   7   6   5   4   3   2   1   94   93   92   91   90   89

Contents

Appendix

Figure 1. Metric plot plan of the M residence.
Figure 2. Metric basement plan of the M residence.
Figure 3. Metric floor plan of the M residence.
Figure 4. Metric front elevation of the M residence.
Figure 5. Metric rear elevation of the M residence.
Figure 6. Metric section A of the M residence.
Figure 7. Plot plan of the Z residence.
Figure 8. Floor plans of the Z residence.
Figure 9. Elevations of the Z residence.
Figure 10. Interior elevations of the Z residence.
Figure 11. Sections of the Z residence.
Figure 12. Electrical plan and details of the Z residence.
Figure 13. Drawing No. 1. Index of the South Hills Office Building.
Figure 14. Drawing No. 2. Plot plan of the South Hills Office Building.
Figure 15. Drawing No. 3. Foundation plan of the South Hills Office Building.
Figure 16. Drawing No. 4. Footing details of the South Hills Office Building.
Figure 17. Drawing No. 5. Plaza floor plan of the South Hills Office Building.
Figure 18. Drawing No. 6. First-floor plan of the South Hills Office Building.
Figure 19. Drawing No. 7. South elevation of the South Hills Office Building.
Figure 20. Drawing No. 8. North elevation of the South Hills Office Building.
Figure 21. Drawing No. 9. East and west elevations of the South Hills Office Building.
Figure 22. Drawing No. 10. Interior elevations of the South Hills Office Building.
Figure 23. Drawing No. 11. Longitudinal section of the South Hills Office Building.
Figure 24. Drawing No. 12. Typical sections of the South Hills Office Building.
Figure 25. Drawing No. 13. Typical details of the South Hills Office Building.
Figure 26. Drawing No. 14. Room schedules of the South Hills Office Building.
Figure 27. Drawing No. 15. Door and window schedules of the South Hills Office Building.
Figure 28. Drawing No. El. Electrical plan of the South Hills Office Building.
Figure 29. Drawing No. H1. Heating-cooling plan of the South Hills Office Building.
Figure 30. Drawing No. P1. Water supply plan of the South Hills Office Building.
Figure 31. Drawing No. P2. Sanitary plan of the South Hills Office Building.
Figure 32. Drawing No. S1. First-floor structural plan of the South Hills Office Building (second-, third-, and fourth-floor structural plans similar).
Figure 33. Drawing No. S2. Roof structural plan of the South Hills Office Building (using "old" steel designations).
Figure 34. Drawing No. S3. Structural section and column schedule of the South Hills Office Building.
Figure 35. Drawing No. S4. Structural details of the South Hills Office Building.
Figure 36. Drawing No. S5. Concrete slab plan of the South Hills Office Building (first, second, third, and fourth floors).

Exercises appear as a separate shrink-wrapped package.

Preface

Nearly everyone will, at some time, need to read and understand a set of architectural plans. Persons in technical occupations have a continuing need to interpret commercial plans, but even nontechnical persons such as home owners have occasion to refer to residential plans. This book, then, is designed for use in architectural plan reading courses, but it is also intended as a guide to be easily followed by any individual who wishes to learn how to understand building plans.

An attempt has been made to present the text in an interesting and easy-to-read manner. The illustrations have been carefully drawn to provide maximum clarity and accuracy. To improve realism, pictorials are shown in perspective. A variety of photographs taken from all over the country are included to illustrate regional differences in building practices. Chapters are short and as self-contained as possible so that they can be rearranged or omitted according to the requirements of each reader or class. Lumber sizes conform to the American Softwood Lumber Standard PS 20-70, and structural steel designations conform to the latest revisions recommended by the American Institute of Steel Construction. A special effort was made to emphasize the need for safety awareness on the part of everyone associated with a building project.

The chapters in this book are grouped into three major sections. The first seven chapters provide a general introduction to architectural plan reading. Plans for a split-level house (the M residence) dimensioned in a modular system are included near the end of this first section, and fold-out plans for this same building dimensioned in metric units are in the Appendix.

The second section of fifteen chapters is concerned with *residential* plan reading. Because most persons are more familiar with houses than with any other structure, this seems to be the best introduction to such a vast field. To provide continuity, the plans for a two-story traditional house (the A residence) are included in the appropriate chapters of this section. The last chapter of the second section describes and illustrates a contemporary house (the Z residence). Complete fold-out plans for this building are in the Appendix. A comprehensive set of eight exercises on the Z residence plans can be used to confirm progress to this point.

The final section of ten chapters provides the information needed to read the plans of *commercial* and other nonresidential buildings. The last chapter of this third section describes and illustrates a five-story commercial building of bolted and welded steel construction together with photographs of it being erected. Complete fold-out plans for the building are in the Appendix. A set of eleven exercises for this commercial building can be completed by advanced students.

Exercises are shrinkwrapped separately and three-hole punched for easy insertion in a binder. Students using this text in a formal course should complete and submit their exercises according to the instructions of their instructor.

This third edition includes expanded sections on computer-aided drafting and construction documents. New sections have been added including metal framing, fiber glass shingles, membrane roofing, flat roof ponding, superinsulation, low-E glass, home computer centers, and balcony railing standards. The plan reading exercises have been revised and increased to over 1700 questions.

It is hoped that the reader will enjoy this book as much as the author enjoyed preparing it. The author would be most grateful to receive suggestions for improvement and to correspond with readers.

Ernest R. Weidhaas

Illustration
Acknowledgments

Chapter 1. *Figure 1*—residence, Rolscreen Company; office building, photos by Bill Hedrich, Hedrich-Blessing (Manufacturers and Traders Trust Building, Buffalo, N.Y., Minoru Yamasaki & Associates, architects). *2*—Keuffel & Esser Company. *3–4*—Computervision Corporation—International Business Machines Corporation. *7*—Gruen Associates, Architects • Engineers • Planners. *8*—Perkins & Will, architects (photo by Bill Hedrich of Hedrich-Blessing). *9–11*—Bruning Division of Addressograph-Multigraph. **Chapter 4.** *Figures 1 and 2*—Frederick Post Company. **Chapter 5.** *Figure 2*—The Construction Specifications Institute. **Chapter 6.** *Figure 3*—United States Steel Corporation. *8–10*—Professor M. Isenberg, The Pennsylvania State University. **Chapter 8.** *Figure 25*—Timber Engineering Company. *32 and 33*—California Redwood Association. *39*—Rolscreen Company. *41–43*—American Iron and Steel Institute (Ziegelman & Ziegelman, architects; Samuel V. Tarenit, structural engineers). **Chapter 10.** *Figure 2*—Professor M. Isenberg, The Pennsylvania State University. *4*—Mr. and Mrs. M. C. Mateer (Philip F. Hallock, architect). *5*—Scholz Homes, Inc. **Chapter 11.** *Figures 4 and 5*—Bethlehem Steel Corporation. *6 and 7*—Forest Products Promotion Council. *8*—Callaway Gardens, Pine Mountain, Ga. *9*—California Redwood Association (Thomas Babbitt, architect). *10*—Eliot Noyes & Associates, architects. *11*—Rolscreen Company (Good Shepherd Methodist Church, Park Ridge, Ill.; Stade-Dolan Associates, architects; Vern Bengston, builder; Hedrich-Blessing, photo). *14*—Union Tank Car Shop, Baton Rouge, La. *15 and 16*—Copper Development Association. **Chapter 12.** *Figure 1*—Rolscreen Company (G. C. Hann residence, Minneapolis, Minn.; Newt Griffith, Peterson, Clark & Griffin, Inc., architect; Johnson & Jasper, builder). **Chapter 13.** *Figure 1*—Anderson Corporation; Rolscreen Company; Bill Hedrich of Hedrich-Blessing. *2–5, 7, 11, and 12*—Anderson Corporation. *6*—Rolscreen Company (Irving Robinson, architect; Avery Construction Company, builder). *10*—Rolscreen Company. **Chapter 14.** *Figure 1*—Educational Facilities Laboratories (photo Randal Partridge). *2*—Rolscreen Company. *3*—Rolscreen Company (Penninsula Golf Club, San Mateo, Calif.). *7*—Morgan Company. *8*—Scholz Homes, Inc. *9*—Frantz Manufacturing Company. **Chapter 16.** *Figures 2 and 3*—

Armstrong Cork Company. *4*—United States Steel Corporation. *11*—Julius Blum & Co., Inc. *12*—Mr. and Mrs. Donald W. Hamer. **Chapter 17.** *Figures 8 and 9*—Vega Industries, Inc. *11*—Acorn Fireplaces, Inc. *12*—Condon-King Division of the Majestic Company. **Chapter 18.** *Figure 1*—Armstrong Cork Company. **Chapter 19.** *Figures 5 and 6*—Professor M. Isenberg, The Pennsylvania State University. **Chapter 20.** *Figures 29–32*—Mr. Peter Hollander. *34*—Professor M. Isenberg, The Pennsylvania State University. *36 and 37*—United States Steel Corporation. **Chapter 21.** *Figures 6 and 7*—American Iron and Steel Institute (Vincent G. Kling, architect; Oliver and Smith, associated architects; Fraioli-Blum-Yesselman, structural engineers; Kling-Leopold, Inc., mechanical-electrical engineers). **Chapter 22.** *Figures 1–12*—Mr. and Mrs. Donald W. Hamer. **Chapter 23.** *Figure 1*—American Institute of Timber Construction. *8*—Timber Engineering Company. *13 and 14*—Weyerhaeuser Company. *15, 18, 21, and 22*—American Plywood Association. **Chapter 24.** *Figures 4–7, 9, 14, and 15*—Portland Cement Company. *18 and 19*—Structural Clay Products Institute. *22*—Indiana Limestone Company. *23*—Vermont Marble Company (Manufacturers & Traders Trust Company Building, Buffalo, N.Y.; Minoru Yamasaki & Associates, architects). *25*—Pittsburgh Corning Corporation. **Chapter 25.** *Figures 1 and 2*—United States Steel Corporation. *3*—Western Wood Products Association. *7–9 and 11–13*—Gateway Building Products. *33*—Department of the Air Force. **Chapter 26.** *Figure 4*—United States Steel Corporation. *6 and 7*—Republic Steel Corporation. *8*—Bethlehem Steel Corporation. *9*—The James F. Lincoln Arc Welding Foundation. **Chapter 27.** *Figure 13*—United States Steel Corporation. **Chapter 28.** *Figures 2–4*—Timber Engineering Company. *7, 8–10, 13, 14, and 16*—Bethlehem Steel Corporation. *11, 12, 15, and 17*—Ceco Steel Products Corporation. *26 and 27*—American Institute of Steel Construction. **Chapter 31.** *Figures 1–8*—The Construction Specifications Institute. **Chapter 32.** All illustrations and drawings of South Hills Office Building courtesy of Jack W Risheberger & Associates, Registered Architects and Engineers. **Exercise 39.** Portland Cement Company. **Exercise 40.** Jack W Risheberger & Associates, Registered Architects and Engineers.

Reading
Architectural Plans

I

Introduction to Architectural Plans

1

Architectural Plans

Wherever you are at this moment, look around. The building you are in and all the other buildings you can see were planned on paper before they were actually built. Large and small buildings: office buildings, industrial structures, public buildings, and private residences (Figure 1)—all were completely described by architectural plans before their foundations were started. And after the architectural plans were finished, the plans were "read" by all sorts of persons: contractors, owners, suppliers, engineers, surveyors, bankers, and inspectors, for a building is a complex project involving many different construction trades and professions. Actually, it is likely that *everyone* will at some time need to read and understand a set of architectural plans.

Early Plans

Architectural plans have been used over the centuries to help design and describe proposed buildings. Plans were used even before the invention of paper. For example, one of the oldest existing architectural plans, several thousand years old, describes a Babylonian temple designed by an architect-ruler named Gudea. This plan was engraved with a metal

stylus upon a stone tablet which is now on display at the Louvre.

Early architectural plans were drawn on wax tablets, papyrus, or vellum, and later on paper. Papyrus (from which the word *paper* derives) was manufactured from strips of papyrus reeds that grew in the Nile. The strips were laid in cross-grained layers and then pressed together. The oldest known papyrus, dating to 3500 B.C., is in the National Library in Paris. Vellum was a thin paper made from fine animal skin. It was used as early as 1400 B.C. Paper made from wood was invented in China in A.D. 105, replacing silk and bamboo.

Pencils also have a long history. Early engraving tools, called *styli*, were made of horn, ivory, wood, or metal. Pliny described his silver stylus in A.D. 77. To draw (rather than

Residence

Figure 1. Architectural plans for these buildings were prepared before construction.

Office building (*Manufacturers and Traders Trust building, New York*)

3

engrave) lines, hard lead styli were used and we still call a graphite pencil a "lead" pencil. The graphite pencil is a comparatively recent invention, first manufactured in England about 1600.

Engraved lines were erased by smoothing over a line with the blunt end of the stylus. A sharp knife was used to erase lead and graphite lines before the discovery of india rubber in 1770. Other drafting instruments, such as the straightedge and compass, have been found illustrated on the walls of tombs dating back to 4000 B.C.

Contemporary Plans

Today most architectural plans are drawn on high-quality tracing paper using mechanical drafting pencils. The tracing

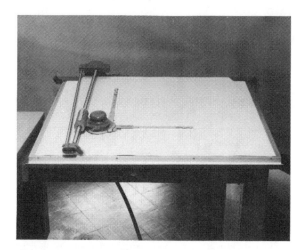

Figure 2. Drafting machine.

Figure 3. Light pen and oscilloscope.

paper is usually printed with borders and title blocks to save drafting time. Drafting machines for horizontal, vertical, and inclined lines (Figure 2), and templates for circular arcs are used. In addition, a variety of computer-assisted drafting equipment is commonly available in architectural drafting rooms. For example, an architectural drafter can "draw" on an oscilloscope (Figure 3) with a photoelectric device called a *light pen*. Using the control panel, the drafter can level or revolve lines and draw circular arcs. Lines can be erased or moved to new positions by "picking them up" with the light pen. Upon command the computer will store a finished drawing electronically for later recall and provide a clear scope to work on. One computer-aided system, widely used by architectural firms for many of the traditional drafting and design tasks, is shown in Figure 4.

Regardless of the method of drafting, however, architectural plans themselves will not greatly change in appearance in the near future. And the ability to read these plans will still be a valuable skill for everyone.

Reading Plans

Reading an architectural plan means understanding the symbols and other conventions used by the draftsman to describe the building design. The following chapters will introduce you to the conventions used in *residential plans* and to the great majority of those used in *commercial plans*. Most people are more familiar with home construction than with the heavier construction of office buildings, schools, and other "commercial" structures. This makes residential plans easier to read, so they are introduced first.

An architectural plan is not drawn to the same size as the proposed building, of course. It is reduced to a smaller, more convenient size, called a *scaled drawing*. For example, a house 40′ long may be shown on paper as only 10″ long. However, this 10″ drawing would still be an accurate representation of important features of the house. Obviously, many insignificant or self-evident features must be omitted to prevent overcrowding the drawing. For example, fasteners such as nails and mortar and hardware such as doorknobs and hinges are not shown. As you learn to read plans, your common sense will help you fill in such missing details.

Many features on architectural plans[1] are shown by accepted *conventions* rather than by showing how they really look. For example, a straight line and circular arc are used to show the plan[1] view of a door and the direction of its swing—consequently the placement of its hinges. Although there are hundreds of such conventions, they are usually not difficult to learn. In fact, after you learn to read architectural drawings, you'll wonder why they previously looked so strange.

One suggestion on how to use this book to learn to read plans: remember this is a textbook, not a novel. Steady reading is therefore not desirable. Rather, you should *study* new or difficult sections and *skim* or entirely skip sections of no use to you. For example, if you can already read mechanical drawings, skip Chapter 2 (Projections), but if you are unfamiliar with, say, building construction methods, concentrate on Chapter 8 (Light Framing), including visits to con-

---

1. The word *plan* has several different meanings. It can mean the top of a building (*plan view*) or it can mean any drawing of a building (*architectural plan*).

struction sites. The exercises associated with each chapter should nearly all be completed and corrected to give you confidence in your progress.

Creating Plans

Buildings are designed by architects using *sketches* and then *preliminary drawings*. The *working drawings* used for construction are developed from preliminary drawings by architectural drafters, and technical *specifications* are assembled by a specifications writer. For larger projects, *shop drawings* may also be needed. *Presentation drawings* or models may be created to help explain the project. The entire process may vary somewhat but usually consists of these steps:

1. Preliminary sketches
2. Presentation drawing
3. Preliminary drawings
4. Working drawings and specifications
5. Shop drawings

Preliminary Sketches. The architect designs a building by making a number of preliminary sketches on grid paper, often called *thumbnail sketches*. These are purposely drawn small to avoid getting bogged down with details at this early stage. Preliminary plan and elevation sketches of the Z residence are shown in Figures 5 and 6. The working drawings for this residence are included in the Appendix.

Presentation Drawings. Presentation drawings are pictorials used for presentation to nonprofessionals who in all likelihood cannot read architectural plans. One of the chief purposes of presentation drawings or models is to "sell" the design to the prospective owner. A presentation rendering in tempera (poster paint) is shown in Figure 7, and an architectural model is shown in Figure 8.

Preliminary Drawings. Using the preliminary sketches as a guide, preliminary drawings are drawn with drafting instruments. Preliminary drawings are further refinements of the sketches, and at this stage the architect begins to coordinate the many structural, mechanical, and electrical details.

Working Drawings. The working drawings are the finished construction drawings that will be reproduced for use by the contractor and subcontractors who erect the building. A complete set of working drawings usually includes a plot plan, foundation and floor plans, elevations, sections, details, schedules, structural plans, mechanical plans, and electrical plans. In addition to working drawings, written technical specifications are prepared to give detailed instructions on materials, finishes, and workmanship—all grouped by building trades. Copies of the working drawings and specifications are provided to potential contractors for their use in estimating the building cost and submitting a competitive bid. Fold-out working drawings of the Z residence and fold-out working drawings of the South Hills Office Building are in the Appendix. Typical specifications are in Chapter 31.

Shop Drawings. Shop drawings are specialized drawings prepared by the suppliers of commercial building components. For example, the structural steel fabricator would

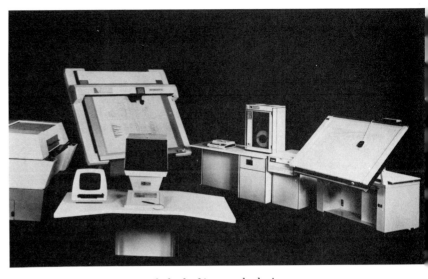

Figure 4. A computer-aided drafting and design system.

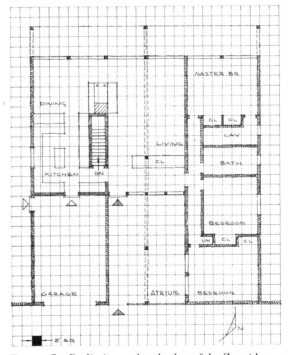

Figure 5. Preliminary sketch plan of the Z residence.

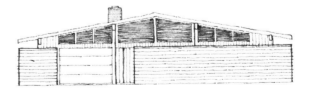

Figure 6. Preliminary elevation sketch of the Z residence.

5

Figure 7. A presentation rendering.

Figure 8. A presentation model.

prepare shop drawings that detail each required steel beam. Shop drawings are submitted to the architect and contractor for approval before the steel is cut to shape.

Reproducing Plans

Working drawings are drawn on translucent tracing paper so that prints can be made easily.

Blueprints

An early reproduction process produced prints having white lines on a dark blue background. They were called *blueprints*. Although this process has been largely replaced by the whiteprint process, the term *blueprint* is now used to refer to any type of print.

Whiteprints

Whiteprints are reproductions having dark lines on a white background. Most whiteprints are reproduced using the *diazo* process, often called *Ozalid*, a trade name formed from *diazo* (a chemical compound) spelled backwards. There are two basic steps in the diazo process (Figure 9).

1. Exposing. The translucent tracing is placed over a sheet of diazo-coated paper, and both are fed into a machine that exposes them to light. Where light passes through the tracing, the coating on the print paper is deactivated and will be white; where light is prevented by a pencil line from reaching the print paper, the coating will remain as an exact image of the line.

2. Developing. The print paper, separated from the tracing, is exposed to ammonia vapor to develop the images into dark lines. The darkness of any printed line depends upon the darkness of the tracing line and the length of exposure time.

The ammonia developer requires venting to the outside for

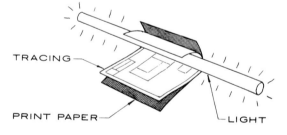

1) EXPOSING

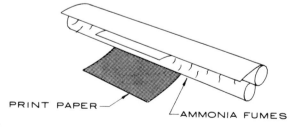

2) DEVELOPING

Figure 9. Whiteprinting process (courtesy Bruning– Division of Addressograph-Multigraph).

Figure 10. A whiteprinter that requires no venting (courtesy Bruning–Division of Addressograph-Multigraph.

Figure 11. A microfiche display unit (courtesy Bruning–Division of Addressograph-Multigraph).

safety, but several patented developers now available require no venting. Such a whiteprinter is shown in Figure 10.

Microforms

Plans or prints may be stored flat in drawers or rolled and placed in tubes. For a large architectural office, this requires considerable storage space, so the plans may be reproduced

to a size smaller than a postage stamp, called a *microcopy* or *microfilm*. For viewing, the microcopy is used to project a magnified image onto a screen (Figure 11), or a full-size reproduction can be made. A microcopy can be mounted in a hole in a keypunch card called an *aperture card*. This permits information to be located using a sorting machine. A number of microcopies can also be reproduced on one sheet called a *microfiche*.

2

Projections

The ability to communicate complex ideas is one of the talents that distinguish humans from other forms of life. The first formal methods of communication were spoken languages and picture languages. Picture languages have developed through the years into a great number of written languages and into one universally accepted graphic language. This universal graphic language is based on a theory of *projections*. That is, it is assumed that imaginary sight lines, called *projectors*, extend from the eye of the observer to the object being described. If a transparent surface is placed between the eye and the object, the projectors can be assumed to transmit an image of the object on that intervening surface. In the theory of projections, the transparent surface is called a *picture plane*, and the image is called a *projection* of the object.

Types of Projection

Perspective Projection

When the projectors all converge at a point—the observer's eye, as shown in Figure 1—the resulting projection of the object on the picture plane is called a *perspective projection*. Perspective projections are often used by architects to present a realistic picture of a proposed building.

Parallel Projection

When the projectors are all parallel to each other, as if the observer had moved to infinity, the resulting projection is called a *parallel projection*. For most architectural drafting, the projectors are also assumed to be perpendicular to the picture plane, resulting in an *orthographic projection* (*ortho* is a Greek prefix meaning "at a right angle"). There are two kinds of orthographic projection, depending on the relation of the object to the picture plane. These are called *multiview projection* (Figure 2a) and *axonometric projection* (Figure 2b).

Multiview Projection. In a multiview projection, the object is positioned so that its principal faces are parallel to the picture planes. This is the type of projection most useful to architects because principal lines and faces appear in true size and shape on the picture plane. It is called *multiview* projection because more than one view is required to show all three principal faces (*multi* is a Latin prefix meaning "many").

Axonometric Projection. In axonometric projection, the object is tilted in respect to the picture plane so that all faces and axes are visible but not in true shape (*axono* is a Greek prefix meaning "axis"). Axonometric projections are often used because they are easier to draw than perspectives.

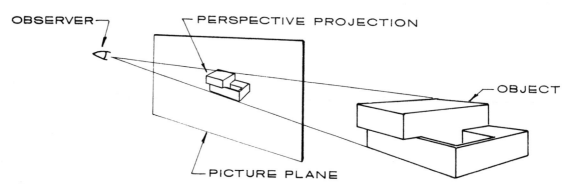

Figure 1. Perspective projection.

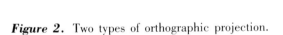

MULTIVIEW PROJECTION

FACE PARALLEL TO
PICTURE PLANE

AXONOMETRIC PROJECTION

FACES TILTED TO
PICTURE PLANE

Figure 2. Two types of orthographic projection.

Figure 3 and Table I illustrate the different features of each type of projection.

Multiview Projections

The Glass Box

The easiest way to understand multiview projection is to imagine the object placed inside a glass box so that all six faces (front, rear, plan, bottom, and both ends) face different sides of the glass box. This is illustrated in Figure 4, where an object (a clay model of a building) has been surrounded by imaginary transparent planes. If projectors were dropped perpendicularly from the object to each face of the glass box, a number of projection points would be obtained which could then be connected to give a true-size and -shape projection of the six principal faces of the object.

If the glass box is then unfolded, as shown in Figure 5, all six faces can be illustrated on a single sheet of paper, as shown in Figure 6. Note the terms *height, width,* and *depth*: height is vertical distance, width is end-to-end distance, and depth is front-to-rear distance.

Study Figure 6 and notice that all adjacent views are in projection, for example.

1. The front view is in projection with the rear and end views. These four views have the same *height* and are

often called *elevations* (such as front elevation, rear elevation, right-end elevation, and left-end elevation).
2. The front view is in projection with the plan and bottom views, since these views have the same *width*.
3. Also notice that four views (plan, bottom, and both ends) have a common element of *depth*.

In architectural drafting, views of an entire building are often so large that each view requires an entire sheet of paper. In such cases, titles or other identifications are used to clarify the relationships between views.

Number of views. Six views are seldom shown. A simple architectural detail is usually described in two or three views, but a complex building might be described with a great number of views in addition to sections and details. Partial views may also be included.

Quadrants. The frontal and horizontal planes of the glass box in Figure 4 can be extended to divide space into four sectors known in geometry as *quadrants* (Figure 7). The object can be placed in any quadrant and projected to the projection planes. The horizontal plane is folded clockwise into the frontal plane, as shown by the arrows in Figure 7. This results in four arrangements of views called first-, second-, third-, and fourth-angle projection.

Third-angle projection produces the relationship between

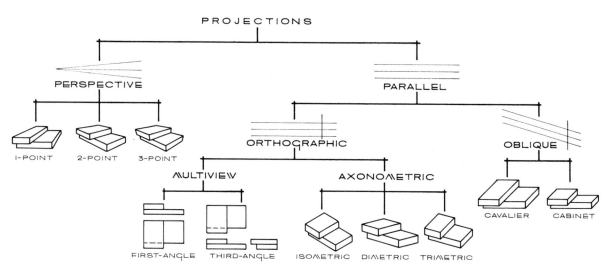

Figure 3. Types of projections.

Table I. Types of projections

		Type	Relation of Projectors to:		Relation of Object Faces to Picture Plane
			Each Other	*Picture Plane*	
Perspective		One-point	Converging	Many angles	One face parallel
		Two-point	Converging	Many angles	Vertical faces oblique
		Three-point	Converging	Many angles	All faces oblique
Parallel	Orthographic — Multiview	First-angle	Parallel	Perpendicular	Parallel
		Third-angle	Parallel	Perpendicular	Parallel
	Axonometric	Isometric	Parallel	Perpendicular	Three equally oblique
		Dimetric	Parallel	Perpendicular	Two equally oblique
		Trimetric	Parallel	Perpendicular	Three unequally oblique
	Oblique	Cavalier	Parallel	Oblique	45°
		Cabinet	Parallel	Oblique	Arc tan 2

views of the glass box described previously in which the plan view is *above* the front elevation.

First-angle projection produces a slightly different relationship between views in that the plan is *below* the front elevation. In first-angle projection, the picture plane is beyond the object rather than between the object and observer.

Third-angle projection is used for most architectural and technical drafting in the United States. Occasionally, however, first-angle projection is used in architectural drafting when it is more convenient to place a plan below an elevation. In Chapter 17 the plan and front elevation of each fireplace in Figure 4 is in first-angle projection, and the front and end elevations are in third-angle projection.

Second- and *fourth-angle* projections produce overlapping views and are not used.

Language of Lines

Eight types of lines constitute the basic "alphabet" of architectural plans. They are illustrated in Figure 8. Notice that these lines were drawn using five different line weights. *Line weight* refers to the blackness and thickness of a line and ranges from an extremely heavy cutting plane line to barely visible construction lines and guide lines (see Figure 9).

Outline. Outlines, also called *visible lines* are heavy lines that describe the visible shape of an object, including its edges, edge views of planes, and contours of curved surfaces.

Invisible Line. Invisible lines, also called *hidden lines*, are outlines that cannot be seen by the observer because they are covered by portions of the object that are closer to the observer. The locations of such invisible edges are indicated when necessary to describe the object accurately. Invisible lines are indicated by dashed lines of medium weight.

Cutting Plane Line. The cutting plane line represents the edge view of a cutting plane sliced through an object to reveal inner features. The cutting plane is shown as the heaviest-weight line so that the location of a section can be easily identified.

Section Line. Section lines indicate any cut portion of an object. A number of sectioning symbols are shown in Figure 1 of Chapter 3. Section, center, dimension, and extension lines are all the same light weight.

Center Line. Center lines indicate axes of symmetry. Most center lines are shown by alternating short and long dashes. In small-scale drawings, a continuous lightweight line may be used.

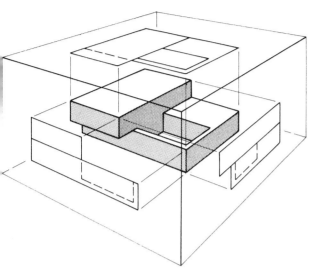

Figure 4. The glass box.

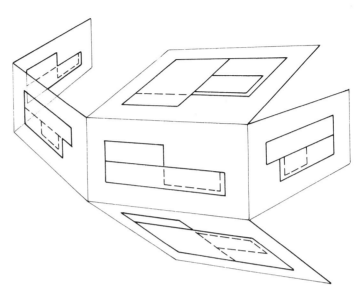

Figure 5. Opening the glass box.

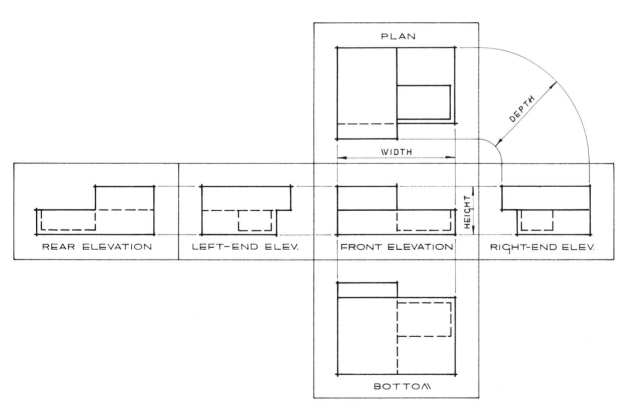

Figure 6. Standard arrangement of the principal views.

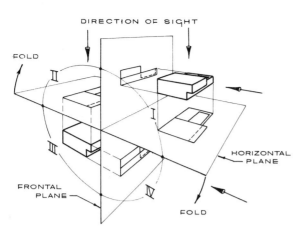

Figure 7. The four quadrants.

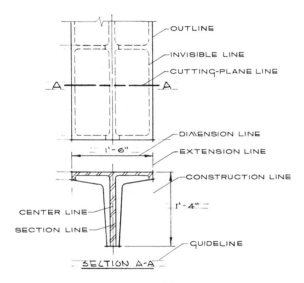

Figure 8. The language of lines.

CUTTING PLANE LINE

OUTLINE

INVISIBLE LINE

SECTION, DIMENSION, AND
CENTER LINES

CONSTRUCTION AND GUIDE LINES

Figure 9. Architectural line weights.

Dimension Line.   Dimension lines are used to indicate the direction and limits of a dimensioned feature. Some types of arrowheads used with dimension lines are illustrated in Chapter 4, Figure 7.

Extension Line.   Extension lines serve as an extension of a feature on the object so that dimensions can appear next to a view rather than be crowded on the view.

Construction and Guide Lines.   Very light construction and guide lines are useful to the draftsman when laying out and lettering a drawing. Although often still visible on the whiteprints, they have no usefulness in reading a drawing.

Reading Multiview Projections

In addition to reading the conventions and symbols used on architectural plans, you should learn to read multiview projections. That is, given multiview projections of an object, you should be able to visualize its shape and features. The following hints may help.

First, the same features are always in projection in adjacent views. Consequently, a point or line in one view may be projected to and read in an adjacent view to help understand what it represents.

Read views simultaneously rather than one at a time. Staring at a single view usually will not be particularly helpful. Your eyes should project a feature back and forth between views until you are able to visualize the feature and eventually the entire object.

Finally, there is a useful rule, called the *rule of configuration*, which states that the configuration (shape) of a plane remains about the same in all views, unless the plane appears in its edge view. For example, a five-sided surface will always have five sides—not four or six—unless it appears on edge.

Sectioning

Architectural components are seldom solid objects as discussed in the preceding sections. Rather, they consist of complex assemblies that require sectional views to describe them adequately. A section is an imaginary cut through a component (part) or assembly of components. All the material on one side of the cut is removed so the interior can be studied. Sections are often cut through entire structures, walls, floors, roofs, foundations, structural assemblies, stairs, and fireplaces. The scale of sectional views is often increased to further clarify the details. Cutting plane lines are used only when needed to show where the cut was taken. Arrows are added to the ends of cutting plane lines when needed to show the direction of sight.

Full Section.   A full section is a cut through the entire building or component as shown in Figure 22 in the Appendix. A vertical cut through the long dimension of a building is called a *longitudinal section*, and a cut through the short dimension of a building is called a *transverse section*. Both are helpful in analyzing the building's structure and detailing.

Half-section.   A half-section is a cut to remove only one-quarter of a symmetrical component. Thus both the exterior and interior can be read in one view, as indicated in Figure 10.

Offset Section. The cutting plane can be *offset* (bent) to permit it to cut through all necessary features. For example, although a horizontal cutting plane through an entire building is usually assumed to be at a height about 4′ above floor level, it would be offset *upward* to cut through a high strip window, and offset *downward* to cut through a lower level of a split-level house. Usually such offsets need not be indicated by a cutting plane line.

Broken-out Section. A broken-out section is used to show the most critical area for sectioning and still present the exterior appearance of the component all in one view (see Figure 11).

Revolved Section. A revolved section is a section that has been revolved 90° and placed on the exterior view of a component. As with a broken-out section, this permits the showing of a greater amount of information in a small space (see Figure 12). *Revolved partial sections* are used to indicate the sectional profile of a special column, jamb, or molding (see Figure 13).

Removed Section. A removed section is simply a revolved section removed to another location. This is often drawn to a larger scale. A cutting plane is given to indicate where this sectional cut was taken.

Auxiliary Views

Occasionally in architectural drafting, a view is required that is not a principal view. Such views are called *auxiliary views* and may show the true size and shape of an inclined or oblique surface or the true length of an inclined or oblique edge. Auxiliary views are classified as *primary* auxiliary views and *secondary* auxiliary views. A *primary auxiliary view* is perpendicular to one of the three principal planes of projection and is inclined to the other two. A *secondary auxiliary view* is obtained by projection from a primary auxiliary view.

Primary Auxiliary Views

A primary auxiliary view is projected from a principal view. Common examples in architectural drafting are views needed to show the true size and shape of each face of a building having walls or wings that are not at 90° angles to each other. An example is shown in Figure 14. Points 1, 2, 3, and 4 in Figure 14 were located in the auxiliary elevation view by transferring distances from the front elevation.

Secondary Auxiliary Views

A secondary auxiliary view is projected from a primary auxiliary view. Although not commonly used in architectural drafting, secondary auxiliary views are occasionally required for accurate shape description or to solve structural problems. An example is shown in Figure 15, which illustrates the procedure to find the true size and shape of face 1-2-3 of

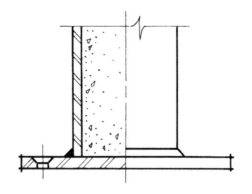

Figure 10. A half-section of a welded steel column.

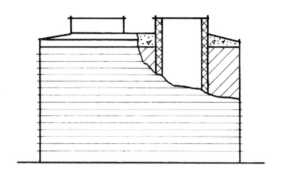

Figure 11. A broken-out section of a chimney cap.

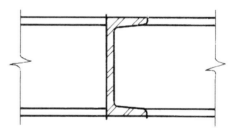

Figure 12. A revolved section of a steel channel.

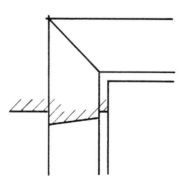

Figure 13. A revolved partial section of door trim.

the geodesic dome so that a pattern can be made. Two auxiliary views are required, because the draftsman needed to draw an edge view of face 1-2-3 before finding the true-size and -shape view.

Pictorial Projections

Pictorial projections are often used by architects because they describe the actual appearance of an object better than most other types of projection. All three principal faces of an object can be shown in one view. Such pictures are easily understood by persons not trained in reading multiview projections.

Pictorial projections can be classified as *parallel* and *perspective*. Parallel projections are easier to draw, but perspective projections are more realistic. Parallel pictorial projections are classified as *axonometric* and *oblique*, as follows.

Axonometric Projection

As in orthographic projection, the projectors in axonometric projection are parallel to each other and perpendicular to the picture plane. But the object has been tilted in

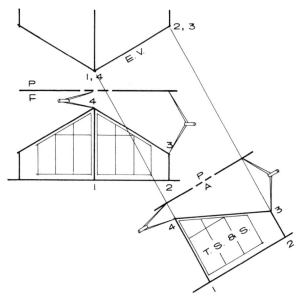

Figure 14. A primary auxiliary view.

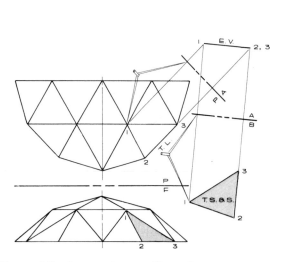

Figure 15. A secondary auxiliary view.

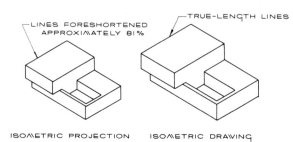

Figure 16. Comparison of isometric projection and isometric drawing.

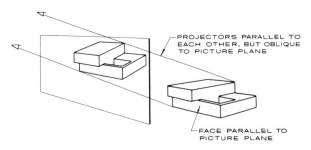

Figure 17. Oblique projection.

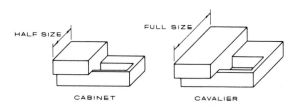

Figure 18. Comparison of cabinet and cavalier drawings.

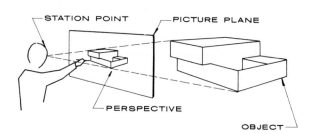

Figure 19. Perspective projection.

respect to the picture plane so that all three principal faces are seen in one view, although they are not in true size or true shape. When the object is tilted so that all three principal faces are equally inclined to the picture plane, the axonometric projection is called an *isometric projection*. When only two faces are equally inclined to the picture plane, a *dimetric projection* results. When no two faces are equally inclined, a *trimetric projection* results. A form of isometric projection, called *isometric drawing*, is by far the most popular pictorial method.

Isometric Drawing. Isometric drawing differs from isometric projection in that the principal edges in an isometric drawing are drawn true length rather than foreshortened (Figure 16). Therefore, isometric drawings can be drawn directly and quickly. The principal edges appear as vertical lines or as lines making an angle of 30° to the horizontal.

Oblique Projection

An oblique projection (Figure 17) is obtained by parallel projectors that are oblique rather than perpendicular to the picture plane. The projectors can be assumed to be at any angle to the picture plane, but it is most common to project them to produce receding lines that will appear at an angle of 45° to the horizontal. Usually these 45° lines slant to the right.

The angle of the projectors also determines the amount of foreshortening of the receding lines. For example, the receding lines can be reduced to half size (called a *cabinet drawing*) or drawn to full scale (called a *cavalier drawing*, Figure 18). The proportions of two-thirds and three-quarters are also used.

Perspective Projection

A perspective projection shows exactly how the building will appear to the eye or to a camera. The illustrator in Figure 19, drawing on a window with a wax pencil, will obtain the same perspective as a camera—as long as the relative positions of the observer, object, and picture plane are identical. If the picture plane is placed parallel to one face of an object, the resulting perspective is called a *one-point perspective* because receding lines appear to vanish at *one vanishing point* (abbreviated "VP" in Figure 20). If it is placed parallel to a set of lines (usually vertical lines) without being parallel to an entire face, the resulting perspective is called a *two-point* perspective because two vanishing points are used. When the picture plane is not parallel to any of the object's lines and faces, a *three-point* perspective results (see Figure 20).

The two-point perspective is more commonly used than either the one-point or three-point perspective. For example, nearly all the perspectives in this book were drawn in two-point perspective. A one-point perspective of a building's exterior is unsatisfactory for most purposes, since it looks very much like a standard elevation drawing. Room interiors, however, may be drawn in one-point perspective, as shown in Figure 21. A three-point perspective of a building exterior is not often used, since it means that the observer must be looking *up* at the building ("worm's-eye" view) or *down* on the building ("bird's-eye" view), as in Figure 22. Obviously, neither of these is considered a normal line of sight.

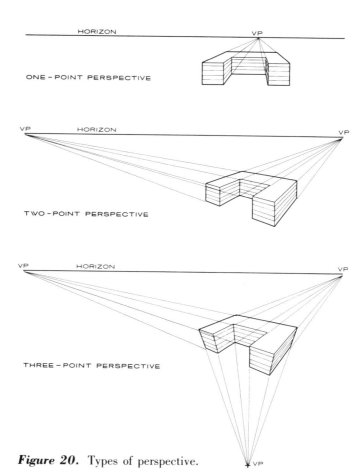

Figure 20. Types of perspective.

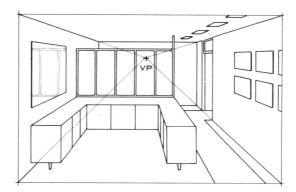

Figure 21. One-point interior perspective.

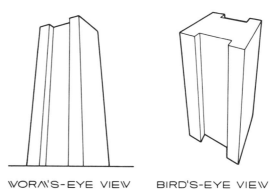

WORM'S-EYE VIEW   BIRD'S-EYE VIEW

Figure 22. Three-point perspective.

15

3

Architectural Symbols

A system of architectural symbols to indicate commonly used materials and features has developed through the years. To read an architectural plan readily, you must be so familiar with these symbols that you can understand them without referring to a legend or textbook. About seventy-five of these symbols are shown in Figures 1–7. Study these until you can identify the meaning of each without looking at the words. Confirm your progress by covering the names under the row of symbols with a sheet of paper. Then write in the name of each symbol and check your answers with the correct names.

Symbol Conventions

Figure 1 shows the symbols most often used on architectural sections, and Figure 2 shows those used on architectural elevations. Notice that most materials have different symbols for section views than are used in elevation views. Also notice that all section and elevation symbols appear lighter than the outlines.

Figure 3 shows some common structural steel shapes used on architectural plans. Both the W shape and S shape beams are commonly used for house girders. The W shape beam is often used as a column in industrial buildings, but pipe columns are used on residences. Angle sections are used to support masonry over wall openings; they may be obtained with equal or unequal legs. Both angle and channel sections are generally used as elements of built-up sections for commercial structures. Steel is also obtainable in round bar shapes, square bar shapes, and rectangular plates.

Wall symbols are shown in Figure 4, together with the accepted dimensioning practices: to the outside face of the studs for frame walls, and to the outside of the masonry for masonry walls (see Chapters 4 and 5 for more information on dimensioning). The absence of any wall section symbol indicates a frame wall. A wood symbol or *poché* (darkening of wall by shading or light lines) is occasionally used.

All fixed equipment supplied by the builder would be included in the plans, but equipment furnished by the owner would be omitted. Figure 5 shows an assortment of symbols that are used to denote equipment and appliances. A dashed line may represent an invisible object (like the dishwasher

shown built in under the counter) or a high object (like the wall cabinets that are above the plane of the section).

The conventions used to indicate windows and doors in a frame wall are shown in Figure 6. Although the doors are shown opened a full 90°, an angle of 30° is often used instead (see the alternate symbol in Figure 6). These same window and door conventions may appear in other kinds of walls, as shown in Figure 7.

Architectural Techniques

The "alphabet of lines" shown in Chapter 2 (Figure 9) is the approved line convention for all architectural and engineering drawings. However, many architectural drafters and architectural offices have developed their own styles of linework. Some of the most commonly used styles of line techniques are illustrated in Figure 8 and are described in the following. You will not find all of these techniques used simultaneously because drafters try to be consistent in use of symbols and techniques within each set of plans.

Cutting Plane Technique.   This technique is used for section views. The lines formed by the cutting plane are darkened.

Distance Technique.   It is possible to show depth in an architectural drawing by emphasizing the lines closest to the observer. Even if the plan in Figure 8 had been omitted, you would be able to visualize the shape of the building by this technique.

Silhouette Technique.   The silhouette is emphasized by darkening the outline. One of the oldest techniques, it is still used today.

Shadow Technique.   Recessions and extensions can be shown by darkening the edges away from the light source. The light is usually assumed to be coming from the upper left.

Major-Feature Technique.   This is a common technique. The major elements are outlined, and the elements of lesser importance are drawn in with finer lines. The diagrams in this book were drawn using this technique.

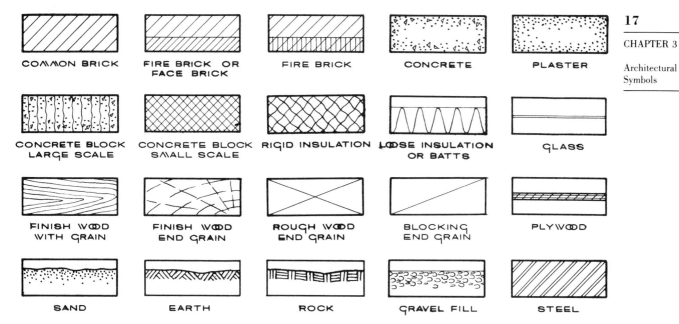

Figure 1. Architectural symbols in section view.

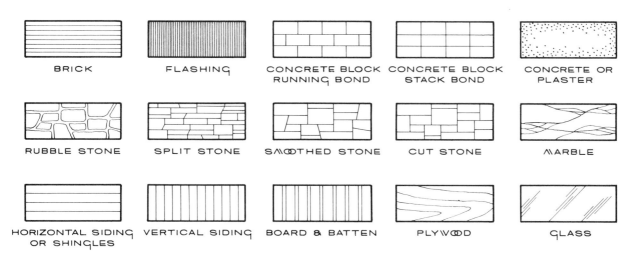

Figure 2. Architectural symbols in elevation view.

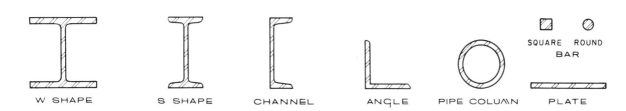

Figure 3. Structural steel shapes.

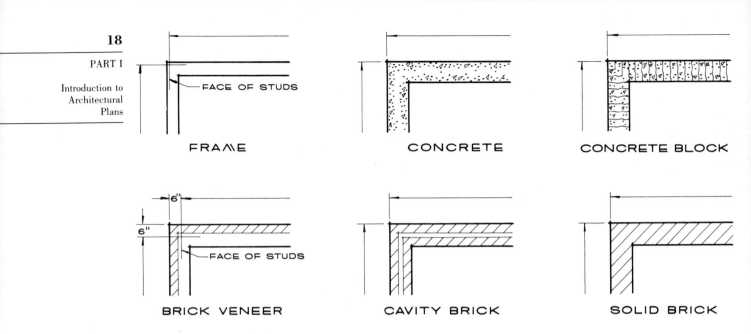

Figure 4. Wall symbols.

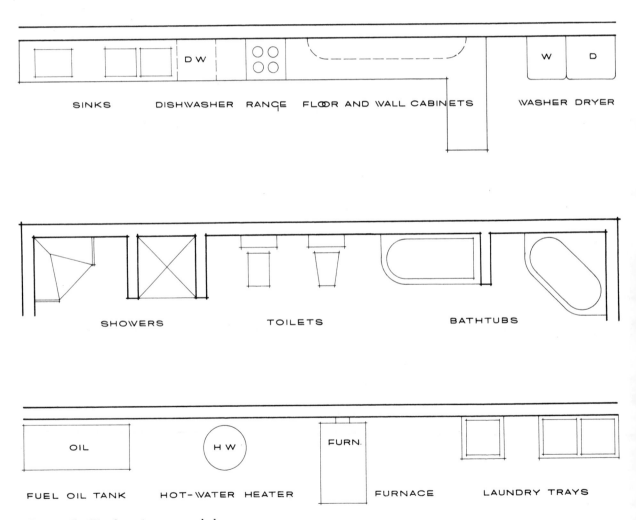

Figure 5. Fixed equipment symbols.

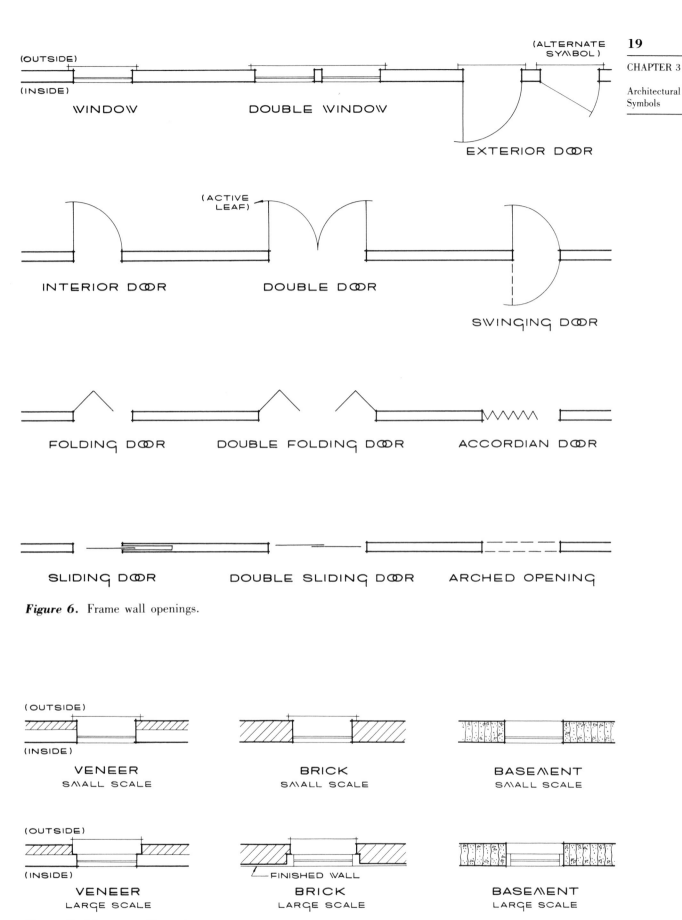

Figure 6. Frame wall openings.

Figure 7. Masonry wall openings.

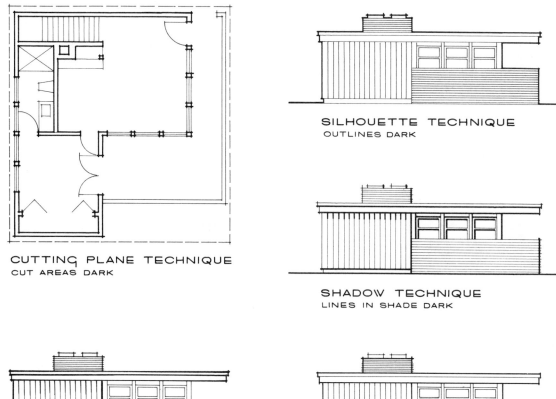

CUTTING PLANE TECHNIQUE
CUT AREAS DARK

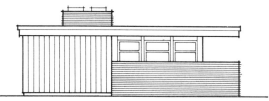

SILHOUETTE TECHNIQUE
OUTLINES DARK

SHADOW TECHNIQUE
LINES IN SHADE DARK

DISTANCE TECHNIQUE
NEAR LINES DARK; FAR LINES LIGHT

MAJOR-FEATURE TECHNIQUE
MAJOR ELEMENTS DARK

Figure 8. Common techniques.

4

Architectural Dimensions

To read architectural plans, you must become familiar with the graphic language used in two different professions: architecture and surveying. The architect uses architectural drawing to provide the instructions for constructing a building, and the surveyor uses topographical drawing to describe the plot of land occupied by the building. The dimensioning practice in each of these fields differs slightly. Let's look at both.

Architect's Scale

The drawing of a building and most of its components must be reduced in size (*scaled down*) to fit on tracing paper. For this purpose, architects and architectural drafters normally use an *architect's scale*. Any of three types—triangular, two-bevel, or four-bevel scales—are chosen according to preference (Figure 1). The architectural scales are:

$$12'' = 1' \text{ (full scale)}$$

$$6'' = 1'$$

$$3'' = 1'$$

$$1\ 1/2'' = 1'$$

$$3/4'' = 1' \qquad 1'' = 1'$$

$$3/8'' = 1' \qquad 1/2'' = 1'$$

$$3/16'' = 1' \qquad 1/4'' = 1'$$

$$3/32'' = 1' \qquad 1/8'' = 1'$$

$$1/16'' = 1'$$

Notice that there are really *two* architectural scale systems. The one shown in the left-hand column is based on the full scale and proceeds to smaller scales; the other (the right-hand column) is based on a $1/16'' = 1'$ scale and proceeds to larger scales.

Use of Scale

An architect's scale is used to show a building scaled down on a plan without having to make any calculations. For example, an architect's scale of $1/8'' = 1'$ would be used to show each foot of building as $1/8''$ long on a plan. Although this is a reduction of 96 to 1, no calculations are needed to make the drawing or to read it, for the architect's scale is calibrated to read the building size directly. In Figure 2 notice that the dimension of $28'\text{-}6''$ can be immediately read on the scale as $28'\text{-}6''$. This is easier than measuring $3\ 9/16''$ on a full scale and then multiplying by 96 to obtain $28'\text{-}6''$!

Full scales are usually *fully divided*, but architect's scales are usually *open divided*. Fully divided scales have all basic units subdivided into smaller units. Open divided scales have only the first basic unit subdivided. For example, the $1/8'' = 1'$ scale in Figure 2 shows inches at one side of the zero mark and feet on the other side. Although awkward at first, open divided scales are easier to read when one becomes familiar with them.

To double the number of different scales shown on each face, scales are often *overlapped*. For example, the $1/8''$ and $1/4''$ scales of Figure 3 are overlapped by starting each from opposite ends. As you study these scales, you will notice that the foot numerals also overlap each other.

Architectural Plan Dimensions

Architectural dimensioning practices vary, depending on the method used to construct the building. The masonry portion

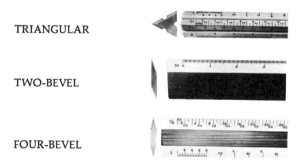

TRIANGULAR

TWO-BEVEL

FOUR-BEVEL

Figure 1. Scales.

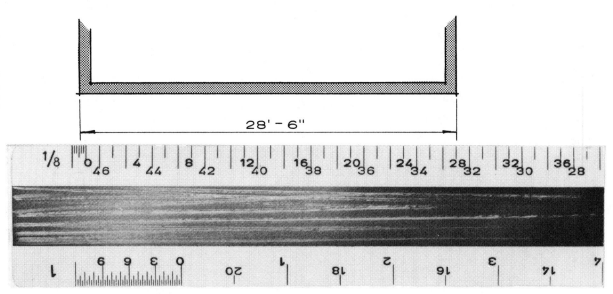

Figure 2. Use of the architect's scale.

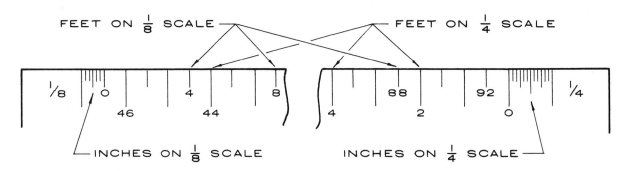

Figure 3. Overlapping scales.

of a building is dimensioned quite differently from the frame or veneered portion. For example, in masonry construction the widths of window and door openings are shown, since these dimensions are needed to lay up the wall. Openings in a frame wall, however, are often dimensioned to their center lines to simplify locating the window and door frames.

In masonry construction, dimensions are given to the faces of the walls. In frame construction, overall dimensions are given to the outside faces of studs because these dimensions are needed first. Masonry partitions are dimensioned (measured) to their faces, whereas frame partitions are usually dimensioned to their center lines. The thicknesses of masonry walls and partitions are found on the plan, but frame wall thicknesses are found on detail drawings, where construction details are shown to a larger scale.

Masonry veneer on a wood frame wall is dimensioned as a frame wall would be (to the outside faces of the studs), since the wood frame is constructed before the veneer is laid up. Figures 4–6 illustrate these differences.

Here are some additional features of architectural dimensioning:

1. Often three lines of dimensions are given on each wall: a line of dimensions close to the wall locating windows and doors, a second line locating wall offsets, and, finally, an overall dimension.

2. No *usable* dimension is omitted even though the dimension could be obtained by addition or subtraction of other dimensions. Included are overall dimensions, any change in shape of outside walls, all rooms, halls, window locations, and exterior door locations.

3. All obvious dimensions *are* omitted. For example:
   a. Interior doors at the corner of a room.
   b. Interior doors centered at the end of a hall.
   c. The widths of both identical side-by-side closets.

4. Columns and beams are located by dimensions to their center lines.

5. To free the plan from excessive dimensions, the sizes of windows and doors will be found in window and door schedules.

6. All dimensions over 12″ are given in feet and inches (to the nearest 1/16″). The symbols for feet (′) and inches (″) are used except for zero inches. For example.

   6″, not 0′- 6″
   1′- 0, not 1′- 0″
   1′- 6″, not 1′- 6

7. Dots, small circles, triangles, perpendicular lines, or diagonal lines (as shown in Figure 7) may be used in place of arrowheads to indicate ends of dimension lines. Dots are nearly always used in tight spaces.

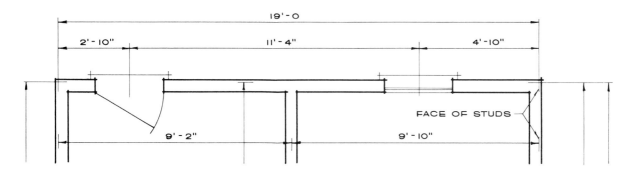

Figure 4. Dimensioning masonry construction (concrete, concrete block, solid brick, and cavity brick).

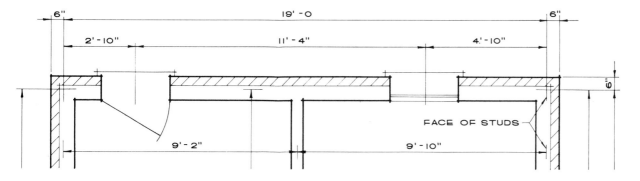

Figure 5. Dimensioning frame construction.

Figure 6. Dimensioning veneer construction.

8. House drawings are usually made to a scale of 1/4″ = 1′- 0. Larger buildings are usually drawn to a scale of 1/8″ = 1′- 0. Details are drawn to larger architectural scales. You will find an indication of the scale near the drawing or in the title block.

Refer to the plan dimensions of the A residence in Chapter 9 for a complete example of dimensioning practices.

Elevation Dimensions

Of many different methods of indicating elevation dimensions, finish dimensions and construction dimensions are most often used.

Finish Dimensions. This method indicates the actual dimension of the inside of the room when completely finished; thus the distance between the *finished floor* and the *finished ceiling* is specified. This method is often used by designers, since they can quickly specify a desired room height: 8′- 0 is often used for the first floor and 7′- 6″ for the second floor.

Construction Dimensions. This method indicates the dimensions actually needed by the contractor when framing a building. Thus, in platform framing, the distance between the *top of the subflooring* and the *top of the plate* indicates the exact height to construct the sections of walls and partitions. This method is preferred by builders. The National Lumber Manufacturers Association recommends a first-floor height of 8′- 1 1/2″ and a second-floor height of 7′- 7 1/2″. These

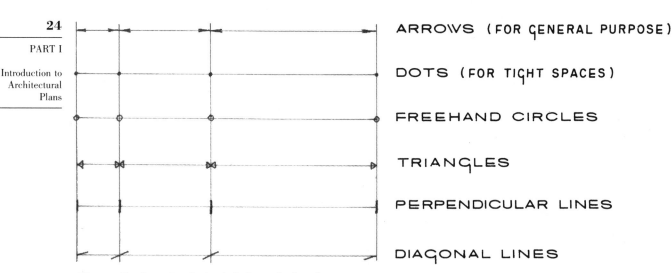

ARROWS (FOR GENERAL PURPOSE)

DOTS (FOR TIGHT SPACES)

FREEHAND CIRCLES

TRIANGLES

PERPENDICULAR LINES

DIAGONAL LINES

Figure 7. Arrowheads (and their equivalents).

dimensions will result in 8′- 0 and 7′- 6″ room heights after the finished floor and ceiling have been added.

Refer to the elevation dimensions of the A residence in Chapter 12 for a complete example.

Sectional Dimensions

Materials and sizes not shown on the plans and elevations are specified on sectional views. Since sectional views are drawn to a larger scale than are the plans and elevations, more detailed dimensions are shown in sectional views. The dimensions, material, and location of all members are given, leaving nothing to the builder's imagination.

Nominal ("name") sizes are used for rough material, but actual sizes are used for finish material as in:

- 1″ × 8″ subflooring (nominal dimensions)
- 3/4″ × 7″ fascia (actual dimensions)

Some offices attempt to show rough material by omitting the inch marks from nominal dimensions. Thus 2″ × 4″ would indicate finished lumber, measuring 2″ × 4″, but 2 × 4 would indicate rough lumber, measuring 1 1/2″ × 3 1/2″. See the A residence sections in Chapter 12 for examples of the dimensions used on sectional views.

Topographical Dimensions

A complete study of topographical drawing and dimensioning would be quite lengthy. Fortunately, we are interested only in the areas of topography related to the plot plan.

The boundaries of a plot are described by dimensions given in hundredths of a foot (two places beyond the decimal point), such as 151.67′. However, the surveyor will, whenever possible, lay out plots using even lengths (such as 100′). When this is done, the dimension is given simply as 100′ rather than 100.00′. Bearings (such as N 5° 10′ 15″ E) are also given to show the compass direction of the boundaries. The bearings are given starting at one corner of the plot and proceeding around the perimeter until the starting point is again reached. Thus two opposite and parallel sides of a plot have opposite bearings (such as N 30° E and its opposite, S 30° W).

Contour lines are dimensioned by indicating their elevation above sea level or some other datum plane like a street or the floor of a nearby building. Elevations of the land at the corners of the plot and at the corners of the building are also shown.

An engineer's scale is used rather than an architect's scale, 1″ = 20′ being quite common. The plot plan of the A residence in Chapter 10 shows these dimensions.

5

Metric Dimensions

Architectural plans in most industrialized countries are dimensioned in metric units. Great Britain adopted the metric system in 1975, and the United States is following on a voluntary but steady basis. Consequently more and more plans will be dimensioned in metric units each year rather than in our present (English) units.

The metric system was conceived over three hundred years ago by Gabriel Mouton, a Frenchman who designed a decimal system based upon the circumference of the earth. The unit of length was called the *meter*, from the Greek *metron* ("measure"). In 1960 the meter was internationally redefined in terms of the wavelength of a specific color of light.

SI Metric System

The SI (Système International) metric system is based on seven units of interest to the architect and builder, shown in the list that follows. Multiples and submultiples are expressed by a decimal system, making the arithmetic of measuring much easier than with our present system.

1. Length: meter (m)
2. Time: second (s)
3. Mass: kilogram (kg)
4. Temperature: Kelvin (K)
5. Electric current: ampere (A)
6. Luminous intensity: candela (cd)
7. Amount of substance: mole (mol)

Prefixes are used to eliminate insignificant digits and decimals. For example, 3 mm (3 millimeters) is preferred to 0.003 m (0.003 meter). Some metric prefixes are shown in Table I.

Wherever possible, multiple and submultiple prefixes representing steps of 1000 are used. For example, length is

Portions of this chapter courtesy The Construction Specifications Institute.

shown in millimeters, meters, and kilometers. Use of the centimeter and decimeter is avoided. A period is not used after an SI symbol except when it occurs at the end of a sentence (for example, 2 mm not 2 mm.). To assist in reading numbers with four or more digits and to eliminate the confusion caused by the European use of commas to express decimal points, digits are placed in groups of three separated by a space, without commas, starting both to the left and right of the decimal point (for example, 12 625, not 12,625). This space is optional with a four-digit number, however (for example, either 1500 or 1 500). An example of architectural plan dimensioned in metric units is shown in Figure 1.

Reading SI Units on Architectural Drawings

Working Drawings

On working drawings scaled between 1:1 and 1:100, you will usually find that the millimeter is the preferred SI measurement unit. The symbol (mm) will be deleted, but look for the note "All dimensions in millimeters except as noted." On drawings of large structures scaled between 1:200 and 1:2000, the preferred measurement unit is usually the meter, taken to three decimal places (for example, 8.500). Again, the symbol (m) will be deleted, but look for the note "All dimensions in meters except as noted."

Table I. Metric prefixes.

Prefix	SI Symbol	Multiplication Factor
mega	M	10^6 (1 000 000)
kilo	k	10^3 (1 000)
hecto	h	10^2 (100)
deka	da	10^1 (10)
deci	d	10^{-1} (0.1)
centi	c	10^{-2} (0.01)
mili	m	10^{-3} (0.001)
micro	μ	10^{-6} (0.000 001)

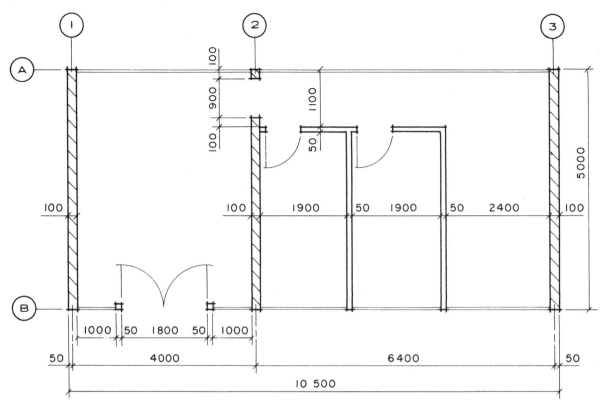

Figure 1. A plan dimensioned in metric units (millimeters).

Plot Plans

Surveyors indicate land distances on plot plans in meters (and on maps in kilometers). Surveyors normally measure to an accuracy of about 1 cm, and therefore you will find such distances on plot plans shown as meters taken to two decimal places (for example, 8.50). Contour lines are usually established at 0.5-m intervals, 1-m intervals, 2-m intervals, or 5-m intervals. The 0.5-meter interval is shown in Figure 1 in the Appendix.

Angles

According to the National Bureau of Standards,[1] plane angles will be specified in three ways. The SI unit (the radian) will be used in calculations. Engineers will specify angles in degrees with decimal submultiples (for example, 11.25°) on engineering and construction drawings. Surveyors will continue to specify angles in degrees, minutes, and seconds (for example, N 10° 12′ 30″ E) on plot plans.

Lumber

Rough Lumber

Although U.S. standards for softwood lumber have not yet been established, it is expected they will be patterned after

the ISO standards.[2] ISO is the International Organization for Standardization and consists of standards organizations in each country such as the American National Standards Institute, the British Standards Institution, and the Canadian Standards Association. ISO standards for lumber include a rough thickness of 50 mm (2″) and rough widths of 100 mm (4″), 150 mm (6″), 200 mm (8″), 250 mm (10″), and 300 mm (12″). The smaller sizes of 100 mm and 150 mm are also available in a thickness of 38 mm (1 1/2″). Strapping is commonly available in 19 mm (3/4″) by 75 mm (3″) and 100 mm (4″) as well as 25 mm (1″) by 100 mm (4″) and 150 mm (6″).

On metric drawings joist and rafter spacings of 16″ oc and 24″ oc are shown as spacings of 400 mm and 600 mm.

Finish Lumber

Finish (dressed) lumber is commonly available in metric countries in 12-mm (approximately 1/2″) and 19-mm (approximately 3/4″) thicknesses. Dressed widths are 5 mm smaller than rough widths.

Panels

Sheets of plywood, fiberboard, and hardboard will be available in a 1200 × 2400-mm size. Some thicknesses of plywood available in metric countries are 12 mm (1/2″), 16 mm (5/8″), 19 mm (3/4″), and 25 mm (1″).

1. *Recommended Practice for the Use of Metric (SI) Units in Building Design and Construction*, U.S. Department of Commerce/National Bureau of Standards, reprinted with corrections June 1977.

2. These examples of the modular sizes of building materials should be considered tentative until standards are established and manufacturing changeovers are announced.

Table II. Brick sizes

	Nominal Metric Dimensions			Nominal English Dimensions		
		3-course			*3-course*	
	Width	*Height*	*Length*	*Width*	*Height*	*Length*
Modular brick	100 mm	200 mm	200 mm	4″	8″	8″
Roman brick	100 mm	150 mm	300 mm	4″	6″	12″
Norman brick	100 mm	200 mm	300 mm	4″	8″	12″
SCR brick	150 mm	200 mm	300 mm	6″	8″	12″

Masonry

Concrete Masonry

Concrete masonry units, usually called *concrete blocks*, are manufactured in modular sizes based upon the 4″ module. The 8″ × 8″ × 16″ stretcher unit is most often used. The actual size of such a block is 7 5/8″ × 7 5/8″ × 15 5/8″ to allow for 3/8″ mortar joints. Converted to metric, these units are 200 × 200 × 400 mm nominally. Actual size is 190 × 190 × 390 mm to allow for 10-mm mortar joints.

Brick Masonry

Four common types of modular brick are shown in Table II. Actual sizes are 10 mm smaller than nominal sizes to allow for mortar joints.

Steel Beams

Complete ("hard") conversion of steel beams to metric sizes is expected to occur only during the last stages of conversion. Some ("soft") conversion tables, however, are now available. These "soft" conversion tables give the properties of customary beams in metric terms. For example, a W 6 × 15.7 (a W shape beam sized 6″ by 6″ weighing 15.7 lb./ft.) is converted to 152 mm by 152 mm having a mass (weight) of 23 kg/m.[3]

Metric Scales

Common metric scales used in architectural drawing are listed in Table III together with their equivalent English scales.

For an example of plans dimensioned in metric units, see the M residence, Figures 1–6 in the Appendix. Study these plans giving particular attention to the 100-mm module. Make a note of any questions and check with your instructor at the first opportunity.

Dual Dimensioning

Architectural offices with practice limited to the United States do not normally use metric units. However, when a

3. *Weight* is a commonly used term, but in technical work it is correct to use the term *mass* to indicate quantity of matter.

Table III. Common architectural scales

Metric Scale	Approx. Equivalent English Scale	Used for
1:1	12″ = 1′-0 (1:1)	Full-scale patterns
1:5	3″ = 1′-0 (1:4)	Detail sections
1:10	1 1/2″ = 1′-0 (1:8)	Wall sections
1:20	1/2″ = 1′-0 (1:24)	Structural sections
1:50	1/4″ = 1′-0 (1:48)	Large-scale plans and elevations
1:100	1/8″ = 1′-0 (1:96)	Small-scale plans and elevations
1:200	1″ = 20′ (1:240)	Large-scale plot plans
1:500	1″ = 50′ (1:600)	Small-scale site plans

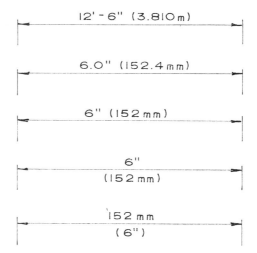

Figure 2. Dual dimensioning systems (courtesy The Construction Specifications Institute).

component manufactured to metric sizes is required to mate with a component manufactured to English sizes, *dual dimensioning* may be used. Dual dimensions or metric dimensioning is also used by architectural offices that practice in foreign countries. Dual dimensioning is simply the placing of the metric counterpart after the English dimension, for example, 1″ (25.4 mm). Dual dimensioning may be shown by any of the methods illustrated in Figure 2.

A number of countries are now using a metric system that varies slightly from the SI metric system. For projects in such countries, the architectural drafter determines what metric system is used, then gives dual dimensioning using that country's metric units and SI metric units. Particularly involved are building components or prefabricated assemblies that are manufactured under one dimensioning system but are mated with components from another system.

English-Metric Conversions

Conversions from the English to the SI metric system can be made with the help of Table IV. Retain, in all conversions, the number of significant digits so that accuracy is neither sacrificed nor exaggerated. Conversion is quite easy using a pocket calculator: $1\ 1/16'' = 1.0625 \times 25.4 = 27$ mm. Building site or plot plans are generally dimensioned in decimals, such as $101.24'$. Conversion of these dimensions is simple: $101.24' = 101.24 \times 0.3048 = 30.858$ m.

Table IV. English-metric conversions (accurate to parts per million)

1 inch = 25.4 millimeters
1 foot = 0.304 8 meter
1 yard = 0.914 4 meter
1 mile = 1.609 34 kilometers
1 quart (liquid) = 0.946 353 liter
1 gallon = 0.003 785 41 cubic meter
1 ounce (avdp) = 28.349 5 grams
1 pound (avdp) = 0.453 592 kilogram
1 horsepower = 0.745 700 kilowatt
1 millimeter = 0.039 370 1 inch
1 meter = 3.280 84 feet
1 meter = 1.093 61 yards
1 kilometer = 0.621 371 mile
1 liter = 1.056 69 quarts (liquid)
1 cubic meter = 264.172 gallons
1 gram = 0.035 274 0 ounce (avdp)
1 kilogram = 2.204 62 pounds (avdp)
1 kilowatt = 1.341 02 horsepower

6

Modular Coordination

Module (from the Greek word for "measure") means a standard unit of measurement. A modular system is a system of construction in which most materials are equal in size to an established module or a multiple of that module. Such a system is called *modular coordination* because the materials fit together (coordinate) without cutting.

Advantages

At present about 20 percent of American architectural firms use modular dimensioning. These are the firms that specialize in masonry or precut lumber buildings. Modular coordination has some definite advantages:

1. It reduces cutting and fitting.
2. It reduces building costs.
3. It standardizes sizes of building materials.
4. It reduces drafting errors by reducing fractional dimensions.

A simple example can illustrate these advantages. An open barbecue pit is to be built of 8″ × 8″ × 16″ concrete blocks[1] with inside dimensions approximately 3′ square. If this pit were designed without giving thought to the size of the blocks, we would find that the four corner blocks in each course must be cut down from 16″ to 12″ (Figure 1). If, however, an 8″ module were planned as shown in Figure 2, no cutting would be required and a larger barbeque pit would be obtained without using additional blocks.

Size of Module

Any convenient size of module is used in modular coordination. An 8″ module was used in the preceding example. A 4′

1. The actual size of an 8″ × 8″ × 16″ block is 7 5/8″ × 7 5/8″ × 15 5/8″. When laid up with a 3/8″ mortar joint, however, the blocks fit in an 8″ module.

planning module is used in layout work. A 20′ structural module is often used in steel factory construction. The most common module, however, is 4″, since brick, block, structural tile, window frames, and door bucks are all available in multiples of 4″. Countries with metric rather than English measurements use a 100-mm module (4″ = 101.6 mm).

Example. When the U.S. Steel Building in Pittsburgh was designed, a modular system was included to simplify conversion of office spaces. For example, the reception area shown in Figure 3 can be converted into additional office space simply by rearranging the wall panels.

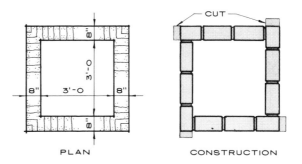

Figure 1. Nonmodular barbecue pit design.

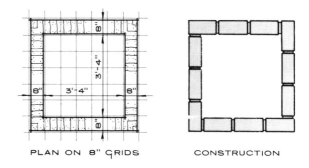

Figure 2. Modular barbecue pit design.

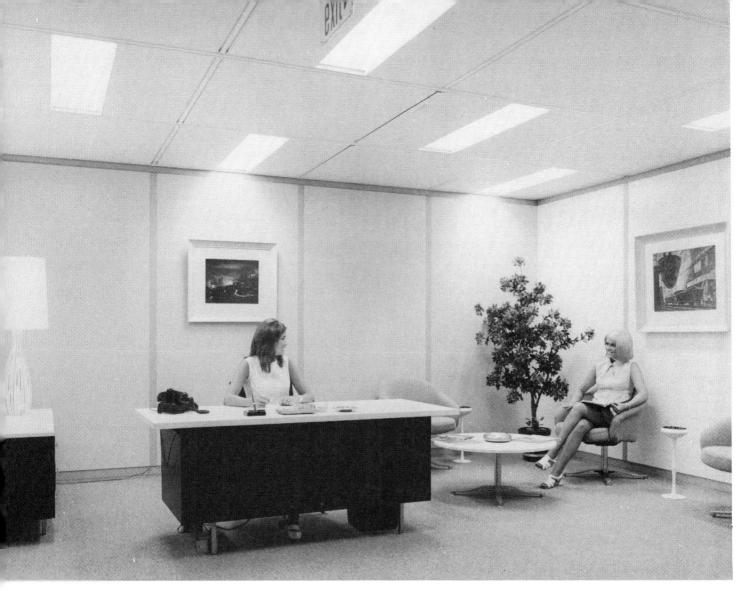

Figure 3. Interior modular design of the U.S. Steel Building, Pittsburgh (courtesy U.S. Steel Corporation).

Reading Modular Dimensions

Modular plans are easily identified by light 4″ grids on all plans, elevations, and sections drawn to a scale of 3/4″ = 1′ or larger. For smaller scales, only a 4′ planning grid is shown, since it is impractical to show 4″ grids. Whenever possible, the building parts are fitted between grid lines or centered on grid lines, as shown in Figure 4. Occasionally an *edge* arrangement is used. Study typical walls in the plan shown in Figure 6.

To indicate the location of building parts, grid dimensions (measurements from grid line to grid line) are used. Grid dimensions are identified by arrows, as shown in Figure 5. To indicate any position *not* on a grid line, dots are used in place of arrows (off-grid dimensions in Figure 5). Plans and elevations will contain mostly grid dimensions. But since many materials are not sized in 4″ modules (3 1/2″ studs, for example), these materials are related to the nearest grid line by means of location dimensions in the section views. Loca-

tion dimensions have an arrow on the grid end and a dot on the off-grid end.

The 4″ module is three-dimensional, applying to both horizontal and vertical dimensions. Elevation grids are established as follows (Figure 7):

1. The top of the subfloor in wood frame construction coincides with a grid line.
2. The top of a slab-on-ground coincides with a grid line.
3. The actual finished floor in all other types of construction is located 1/8″ below a grid line.

For plans dimensioned according to the modular system see the M residence, Figures 8–10. This same residence appears in the appendix dimensioned in metric units. Study these plans, giving particular attention to the use of arrows and dots at the end of dimension lines. Make a note of any questions and check with your instructor at the first opportunity.

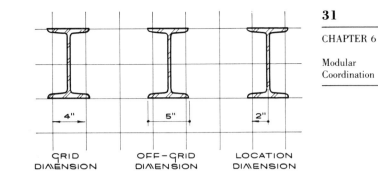

Figure 4. Relation of a stud wall to a grid line.

Figure 5. Modular grid dimensions, off-grid dimensions, and location dimensions.

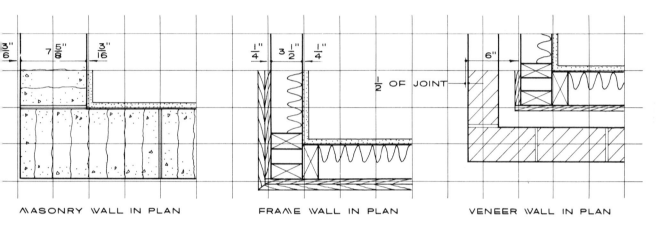

Figure 6. Modular walls in plan.

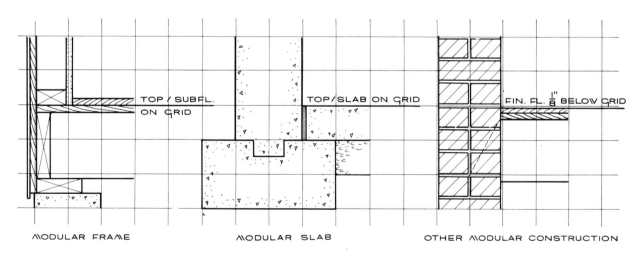

Figure 7. Modular walls in elevation.

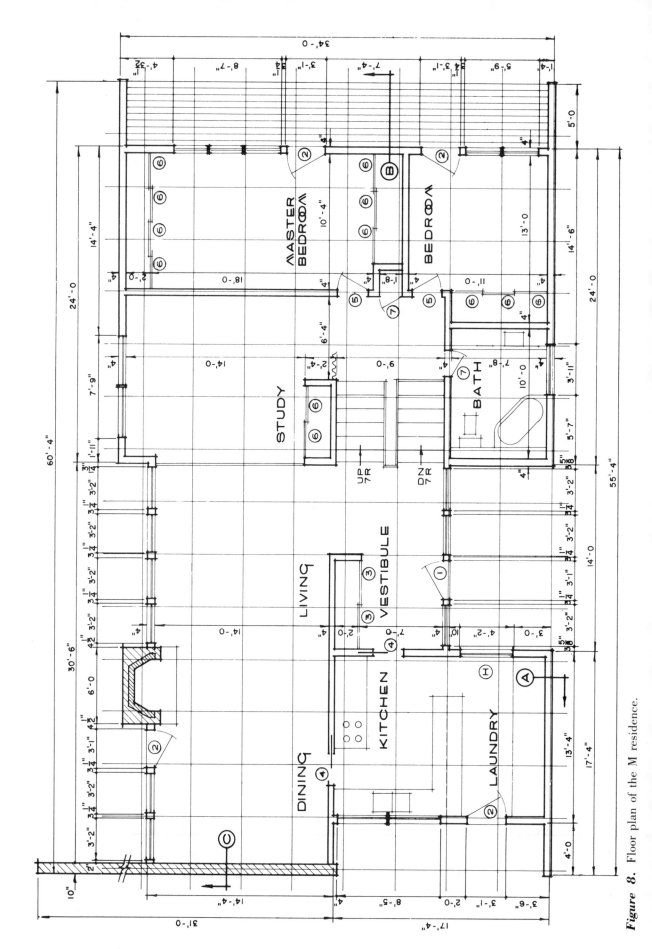

Figure 8. Floor plan of the M residence.

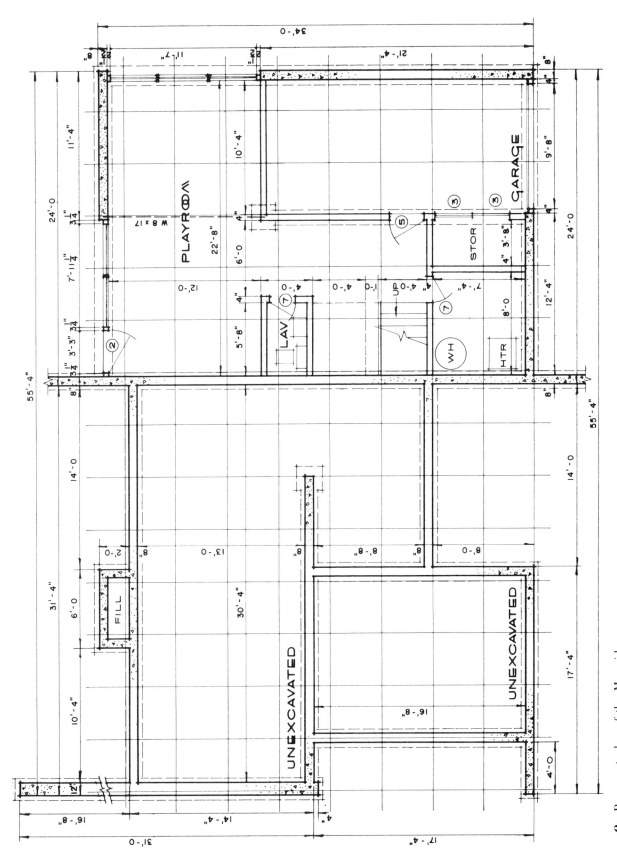

Figure 9. Basement plan of the M residence.

33

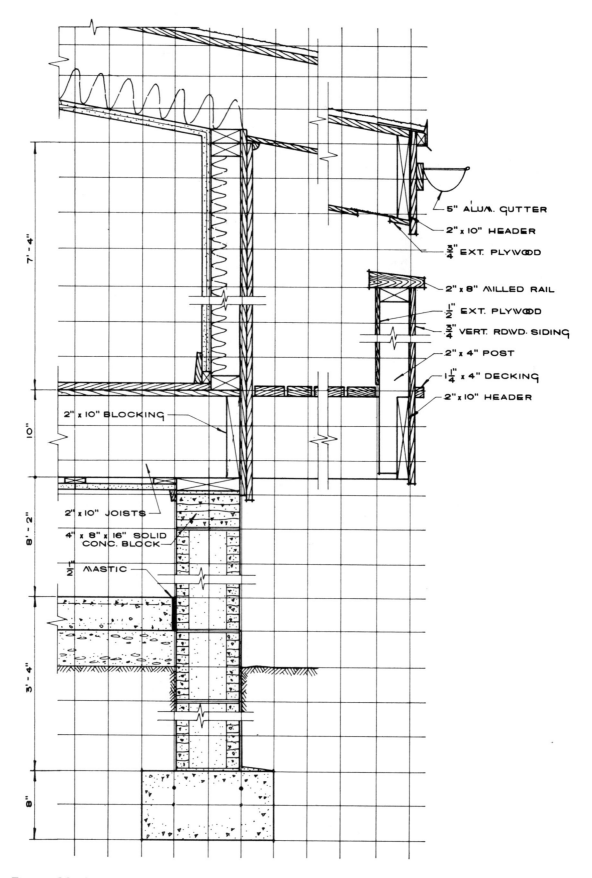

5" ALUM. GUTTER

2" x 10" HEADER

$\frac{3}{4}$" EXT. PLYWOOD

2" x 8" MILLED RAIL

$\frac{1}{2}$" EXT. PLYWOOD

$\frac{3}{4}$" VERT. RDWD. SIDING

2" x 4" POST

$1\frac{1}{4}$" x 4" DECKING

2" x 10" HEADER

2" x 10" BLOCKING

2" x 10" JOISTS

4" x 8" x 16" SOLID CONC. BLOCK

$\frac{1}{2}$" MASTIC

Figure 10. Section B through bedrooms of the M residence.

7

Architectural Calculations

Architectural calculations usually involve simple mathematical processes such as addition and multiplication, but occasionally these "simple" calculations become difficult for a variety of reasons. Let's look at examples of such problems and at ways to solve them.

Addition of Mixed Numbers

Adding dimensions given in feet and inches is not difficult, but always remember to reduce the answer to its simplest form.

Example 1   Add 8'-6", 10'-8", and 1'-3".
Solution   1. 8'-6" + 10'-8" + 1'-3"
           = 19'-17"
      2. Reduce to 20'-5".

Example 2   Add 3/4" and 5/8".
Solution   1. Convert 3/4" to 6/8" (to obtain common
          denominator).
      2. 6/8" + 5/8" = 11/8"
      3. Reduce to 1 3/8".

Example 3   Add 2'-3 1/2" and 1'-10 5/8".
Solution   1. 2'-3 1/2" + 1'-10 5/8"
           = 3'-13 9/8"
      2. Reduce to 3'-14 1/8".
      3. Further reduce to 4'-2 1/8".

Subtraction of Mixed Numbers

Subtracting dimensions given in feet and inches requires care when a larger quantity of inches must be subtracted from a smaller quantity of inches.

Example 4   Subtract 4'-10" from 18'-2".
Solution   1. Convert 18'-2" to 17'-14".
      2. 17'-14" − 4'-10" = 13'-4"

Example 5   Subtract 1'-10 7/8" from 5'-4 1/4".

Solution   1. Convert 5'-4 1/4" to 5'-3 10/8".
      2. Further convert 5'-3 10/8" into
         4'-15 10/8".
      3. 4'-15 10/8" − 1'-10 7/8"
         = 3'-5 3/8"

Multiplication of Mixed Numbers

The most appropriate way to multiply dimensions given in feet and inches is determined by the use to be made of the result. Usually the desired result is an area stated in decimal square feet. An electronic desk or pocket calculator is helpful.

Example 6   Find the area of floor tile required for a
         10'-3" × 14'-8" room.
Solution   1. Convert 10'-3" to 10.25'.
      2. Convert 14'-8" to 14.667'.
      3. 10.25' × 14.667' = 150.33675 sq. ft.
      4. Round 150.33675 to 150.4 sq. ft.

Example 7   Find the volume of concrete required for
         an 8"-thick wall that is 8'-6" high and
         120' long.
Solution   1. Convert 8" to 0.667'.
      2. Convert 8'-6" to 8.5'.
      3. Divide cubic feet by 27 to obtain cubic
         yards:

$$\frac{0.667 \times 8.5 \times 120}{27} =$$

         25.19777 cu. yd.
      4. Round to 25.2 cu. yd.

English-Metric Conversion

English units converted to metric units are usually rounded to the nearest whole millimeter. Metric units converted to English units are usually rounded to the nearest sixteenth of an inch.

Example 8   Convert 8'-6" to metric units.
Solution   1. Convert 8'-6" to 8.5'.
2. 8.5 × 304.8 = 2590.80 mm (using a conversion factor of 1' = 304.8 mm from Table IV in Chapter 5).
3. Round to 2591 mm.

Example 9   Convert 1000 mm to English units.
Solution   1. $\dfrac{1000}{25.4} = 39.370"$ (using a conversion factor of 1" = 25.4 mm from Table IV in Chapter 5).
2. $\dfrac{.370}{.0625} = 5.92$ sixteenths of an inch (using a conversion factor of 1/16" = .0625").
3. Round $\dfrac{5.92"}{16}$ to $\dfrac{6"}{16}$ and reduce to $\dfrac{3"}{8}$.
4. Reduce 39 3/8" to 3' - 3 3/8".

Lumber Measurement in Board Feet

Wood products may be specified and sold by the square foot (plywood), running foot (molding), or number of pieces (rails), but most lumber is sold by the *board foot*. A board foot is the amount of wood contained in a piece of nominal lumber 1" thick × 12" wide × 1' long. The *nominal size* is the size of rough, green lumber. After planting, the actual *finished size* is about 1/2" smaller in both thickness and width than nominal, but board foot measurement of finished lumber is always based on the nominal size. The abbreviation for board feet is BM ("board measure"). The abbreviation for 1,000 is M; consequently, 1,000 board feet is abbreviated MBM.

The board feet in any piece of lumber can be calculated as follows: BM = thickness (inches) × width (feet) × length (feet).

Example 10   Find the board feet in a 2" × 4" stud 8'-0 long.
Solution   1. Convert 4" width to 4/12 ft.
2. BM = 2 × 4/12 × 8 = 5.33333 (using a calculator).
3. Round to 5.3 BM.

Example 11   Find the board feet in 60 pieces of 2" × 10" joists 14' long.
Solution   1. Convert 10" width to 10/12 ft.
2. BM = 60 × 2 × 10/12 × 14 = 1400 BM (using a calculator).
3. Convert to 1.4 MBM.

Rafter Size

A common problem is determining the needed rafter length for a given run. This is easily done graphically by drawing the rafter to scale and measuring the required length. It can be found more accurately by calculating first the rise and then the length using the Pythagorean theorem. But make sure the calculations include all factors, such as measuring the run and rise to the ends of the rafter.

Example 12   Find the length of a rafter pitched 6 in 12 (sloped to rise 6" for each 12" of run) for a total run of 14'.
Solution   1. Calculate rise by proportion: $\dfrac{\text{rise}}{14} = \dfrac{6}{12}$; rise = 7'.
2. Calculate length by Pythagorean theorem:
length $= \sqrt{7^2 + 14^2} = \sqrt{245} = 15.7'$
3. Increase 15.7' to 16' nominal length.

II

Reading Residential Plans

8

Light Framing

It is extremely important that you become thoroughly familiar with standard construction practices. Trying to read architectural plans without a knowledge of construction would be like a contractor trying to build without being able to read blueprints. In either case, chaos would result.

Although there are many different types of acceptable construction in use today, we will study in detail the most commonly used type: the *platform frame*. This will be done step by step, starting with the site survey and excavation and working up to the roof and finish materials—as though we were actually building. Later we will look at other kinds of construction to see how they differ from the platform frame.

Preparing the Site

Survey

Before starting construction, the house lot is surveyed by a registered surveyor who will accurately locate the property lines. The property corners are marked with 30″-long galvanized iron pipes driven almost completely into the ground. The surveyor may also stake out the corners of the house, checking the local building ordinances for requirements on minimum setback from the road and minimum side and rear yards. The ordinance may state that the front of the building must align with buildings in adjacent lots.

If there are trees on the site, the house would usually be placed to save a maximum number. As a rule, all trees within 5′ of the proposed building are cut down, since the excavation will disturb their roots so much that they will die.

The surveyor will also establish correct elevations, usually using the adjoining road or house as a reference. All this information is placed on a survey map which will be the basis of the plot plan. Figure 1 shows a survey map for the A residence.

Staking

Although the surveyor may stake out the house foundation, this is more often done by the building contractor. The

builder locates the future outside corners of the foundation and marks these points with tacks in small stakes. Then, since these stakes will be disturbed by the excavation, larger 2″ × 4″ stakes are driven 4′ beyond the foundation lines, three at each corner. Figure 2 shows 1″ × 6″ batter boards nailed to these stakes so that all their tops are at the same elevation.

Using a plumb bob, the builder then stretches stout twine across the batter boards directly above the corner tacks. Saw

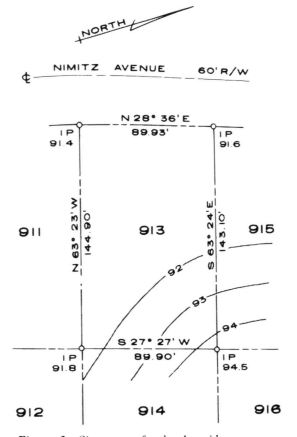

Figure 1. Site survey for the A residence.

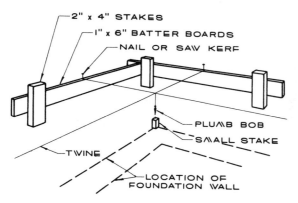

Figure 2. Staking.

cuts or nails are used to mark the batter boards where the twine touches to establish a more permanent record of the foundation lines (Figure 3). Of course, it is particularly important to check for squared corners. This may be done with surveying instruments, by measuring diagonals, or by using the principle of the 3- 4- 5 triangle (Figure 4).

Excavation

The first excavation is usually done by power equipment. First, about a foot of topsoil is removed and stored at the side of the lot to be used later in the finish grading. Then, the excavation itself is made, the depth depending on these factors:

1. On sloping land, the foundation must extend above the highest perimeter point of finished grade by:
   a. Eight inches in wood frame construction to protect the wood from rotting due to moisture.
   b. Two inches in brick construction to protect the first brick course from constant exposure to moisture which may eventually work into the joints.
2. The footing must extend below the lowest perimeter point of finished grade by the prevailing frost line

depth. This is necessary to prevent upheaval when the ground freezes. Figure 5 may be consulted for a general indication of frost line depth, but a more accurate depth for a particular area may be obtained from local architects and builders.

3. When a full foundation is to be built, a minimum of 6'- 9" is allowed from the top of the basement floor to the bottom of the floor joists, as shown in Figure 6. Remember that a girder under the joist reduces the headroom. The minimum confortable ceiling height for a habitable room is 7'- 6", and 8' is more often used for the main living areas.
4. When a crawl space (for inspection and repair) is to be built, a minimum of 18" is allowed to the bottom of the joists. Or 2'- 6" is specified for a more comfortable working height. Water is prevented from accumulating in the crawl space by:
   a. Locating the crawl space 1 1/2" above the outside finished grade.
   b. Providing a special drain to a lower elevation or storm sewer.
   c. Relying on local soil conditions which may be such that water will naturally drain from the crawl space.
5. The excavation should extend down to *unfilled* ground. Because it is so important that a good bearing surface be provided, the trench for the footings should be dug shortly before pouring the concrete to prevent softening of the bearing ground by exposure to rain and air.

Starting the Foundation

Footing

Footings increase the bearing surface of the house on the ground so that there will be less settling. Footings should be of concrete poured on undisturbed land. Average residential construction on firm land calls for footings twice as wide as the foundation wall, from 16" to 24". The depth of the footing should equal the wall thickness, ranging from 8" to 12". Side

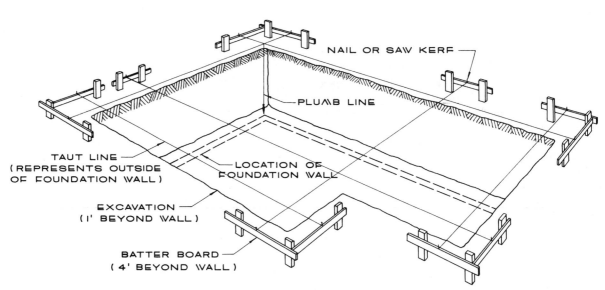

Figure 3. Excavation.

forms may be omitted if the ground permits sharply cut trenches. Reinforcing steel is used when the footing spans pipe trenches. As mentioned previously, the frost line determines the minimum depth of footing excavation; this depth varies from 1'-6" in Florida to 4'-6" in Maine.

The bottoms of footings are always horizontal, never inclined. Thus, on sloping land *stepped footings*, such as those shown in Figure 8, are used. The horizontal portion of a step footing should not be less than 32"; the vertical portion should not exceed 24". To reduce cutting when building the foundation wall, these dimensions should be in modular block units. The horizontal and vertical portions of the stepped footing should be of equal thickness, and both portions are poured at the same time.

Footings are also required for chimneys and columns. Since column footings must support as much as one-quarter of the total weight of the house, they are stepped out even farther (usually to 24" square or 30" square).

Drainage

To provide drainage around the foundation and ensure a dry basement, 4" perforated pipes are laid in the foundation excavation or footing excavation. Two types of drain pipe are available:

1. A rigid, perforated plastic pipe, 4" diameter in 10' lengths and joined by plastic fittings.
2. A flexible, perforated plastic pipe, 4" diameter in 250' rolls.

Ground fill above either type encourages drainage to the drain pipes. The drain line should slope slightly (1/16" per ft. minimum) to a catch basin, dry well, or sewer.

Foundation

Foundations may be constructed to provide a basement or crawl space (Figure 7). When a concrete floor is poured at ground level, it is called *slab construction*. This slab may be described as floating or perimeter. The *floating slab* requires reinforcing, since it is meant to "float" as an integral unit on the ground. Although this construction has been used in cold climates, it is best suited to areas where frost penetration is no problem. The *perimeter foundation*, on the other hand, provides a complete foundation wall to protect the slab from frost. The rigid insulation reduces heat loss from the house.

Materials. The two most common foundation materials are poured concrete (8" to 12") and concrete blocks (8", 10", or 12").

Poured Concrete. The poured concrete foundation is usually considered superior because it is more likely that poured concrete will be waterproof and termite-proof. A 1- 2 1/2- 5 concrete mix is often used: 1 part cement, 2 1/2 parts fine aggregate (sand), and 5 parts coarse aggregate (gravel or crushed stone). Poured concrete walls are sometimes *battered* (sloped) from 12" thickness at the bottom to 8" thickness at the top. This prevents adhesion between the walls and clay ground due to freezing and guards the wall

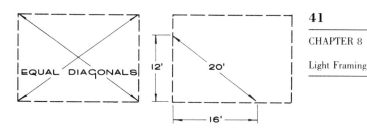

Figure 4. Methods of squaring corners.

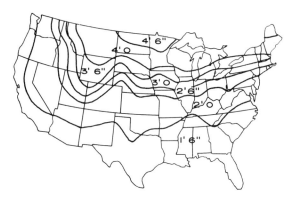

Figure 5. Footing depths in the United States.

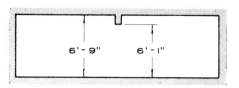

MINIMUM BASEMENT HEIGHTS

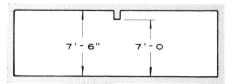

MINIMUM HABITABLE ROOM HEIGHTS

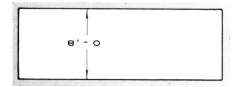

RECOMMENDED ROOM HEIGHT

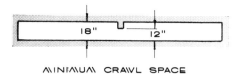

MINIMUM CRAWL SPACE

Figure 6. Minimum design heights.

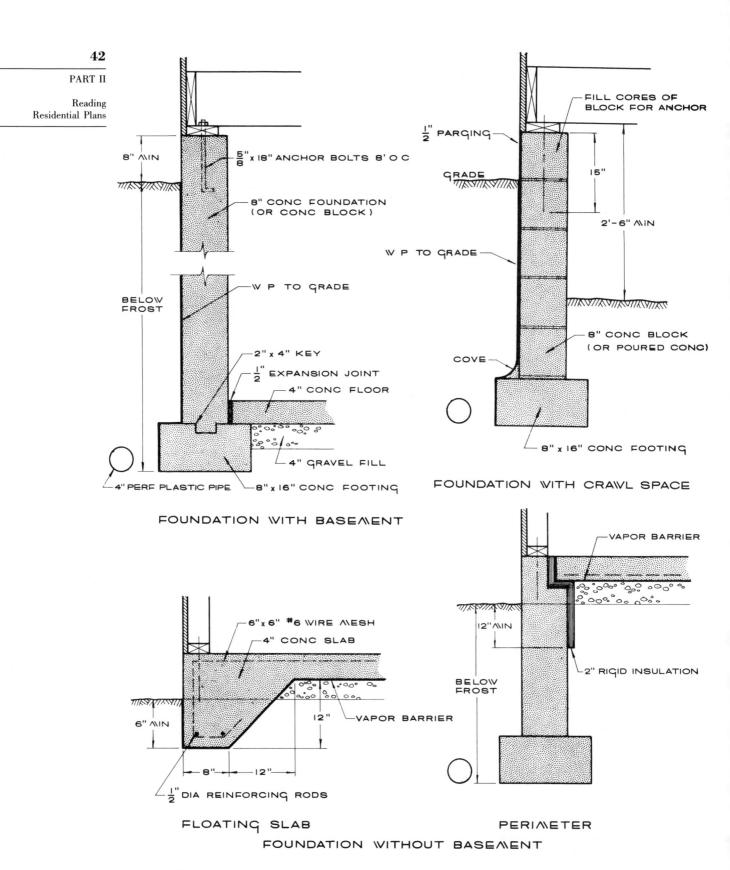

Figure 7. Foundations.

from being lifted by frost action. The outside faces of the foundation and footing are mopped with hot tar or asphalt for additional protection against water. For this purpose, emulsified or hot tar (pitch) is superior to asphalt, since asphalt in continual contact with moisture may eventually disintegrate.

Concrete Block. A 1/2″ layer of cement plaster (called *parging*) is applied to the outside block wall and covered with hot tar or asphalt waterproofing. It is good practice to fill the cores of the top course of concrete blocks with concrete to prevent passage of water or termites. Long stretches of wall are often stiffened with 8″ × 16″ pilasters every 16′, as shown in Figure 9. This is particularly important when using walls of only 8″ block.

Reinforcing Steel. Concrete has excellent strength in *compression* but is weak in *tension*. Therefore, when any portion of a concrete member is expected to be subjected to tension, steel rods or steel wire mesh are cast in that portion to resist the tension. This is called *reinforcing steel*.

In light construction, reinforcing is used in concrete bond beams, concrete lintels, and occasionally in concrete slabs and footings (see Figure 10). This reinforcing is best placed near the *bottom* of bond beams, lintels, column footings, and suspended slabs to resist the tension there. It is common

building practice also to place reinforcing near the bottom of wall footings and on-grade slabs, on the assumption that these members are similar to bond beams. However, many engineers now specify that reinforcing rods in wall footings be near the *top* to better prevent cracking that could then extend up into the wall above. Reinforcing wire mesh in slabs poured on grade is also specified near the top of the slab to control cracking that would affect the exposed floor surface.

Constructing the Platform Frame

Sill

The sill is a 2″ × 6″ plank resting directly on top of the foundation wall. Notice in the top left-hand drawing of Figure 11 that the sill is set back about an inch from the outside wall so that the sheathing, which is nailed to the sill, will be flush with the outside foundation wall in wood frame construction. Some builders allow for irregularities in the face of the foundation wall by setting the sill flush so that the sheathing projects beyond the outside of the foundation wall. This is illustrated in Figure 12 of Chapter 6.

The sill is fastened by 1/2″, 5/8″, or 3/4″ bolts spaced 8′

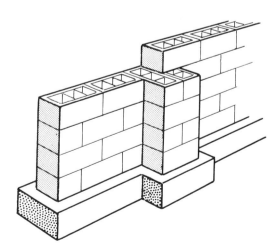

Figure 8. Stepped footing.

Figure 9. Pilaster construction.

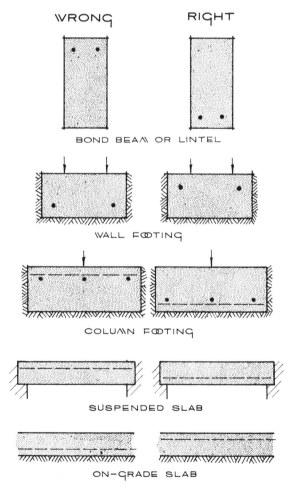

Figure 10. Placement of reinforcing steel in light construction.

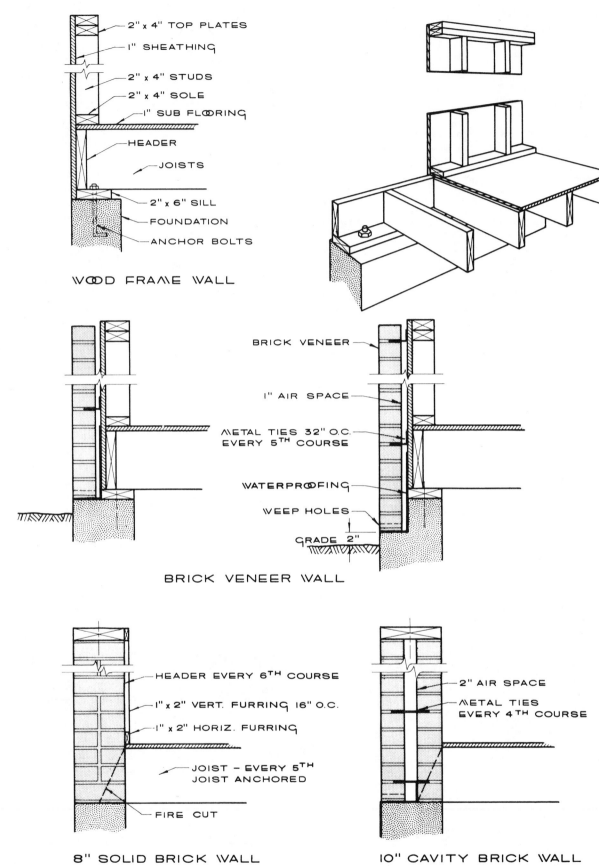

2" x 4" TOP PLATES
1" SHEATHING
2" x 4" STUDS
2" x 4" SOLE
1" SUB FLOORING
HEADER
JOISTS
2" x 6" SILL
FOUNDATION
ANCHOR BOLTS

WOOD FRAME WALL

BRICK VENEER
1" AIR SPACE
METAL TIES 32" O.C.
EVERY 5TH COURSE
WATERPROOFING
WEEP HOLES
GRADE 2"

BRICK VENEER WALL

HEADER EVERY 6TH COURSE
1" x 2" VERT. FURRING 16" O.C.
1" x 2" HORIZ. FURRING
JOIST - EVERY 5TH
JOIST ANCHORED
FIRE CUT

8" SOLID BRICK WALL

2" AIR SPACE
METAL TIES
EVERY 4TH COURSE

10" CAVITY BRICK WALL

Figure 11. Types of walls.

apart. These extend 6″ into a poured concrete foundation or 15″ into a concrete block foundation. Holes are drilled into the sill, a bed of mortar (called *grout*) is spread on the foundation, and the sill is tapped into a level position. Nuts and washers are tightened by hand. Several days later they may be wrench-tightened. The grout provides a level bed for the sill and makes an airtight joint.

Header

The principal members of the platform are joists and headers which are spiked on top of the sill. *Joists* are horizontal beams that span the foundation walls. The ends of the joists are framed into *headers*. Headers and joists are the same size lumber. The header is spiked upright to the top outside edge of the sill. Where a basement window or door breaks the foundation wall, it is good practice to let the header, rather than the sill, act as the spanning member. This is best accomplished by a ledger strip spiked to the header and extending at least 6″ beyond the opening, as shown in Figure 12. The joists are cut to rest on the ledger and are also spiked to the header. A steel angle lintel may be used instead of the ledger.

Girder

The dimensions of most houses are so great that joists cannot span the foundation walls. In that case, a wood *girder* (that is, several 2″- thick members spiked together) or a steel beam is used, as shown in Figure 13. Notice that the girder is too long to span the foundation walls and must be supported by wood or steel columns, as in Figure 14. Steel pipe columns (usually referred to by the trade name of *Lally columns*) are capped with a steel plate to increase the bearing surface with the wood girder. A 3 1/2″- diameter column is large enough for ordinary requirements.

The girder is framed into the foundation wall as shown in Figure 15 so that it bears a minimum of 4″. As a rule, it is considered good practice to provide the greatest possible bearing surface between two members. In the case of wood, the length of bearing surface should not be less than 4″ for safest construction (see Figure 16). However, to save headroom, joists are occasionally framed level with the girder using iron stirrups, ledger strips, or framing anchors. Joists may also be set "level" with a steel beam (actually, such joists are installed with their upper edges an inch above the steel beam to allow for wood shrinkage and to prevent a bulge in the floor above).

The wall pocket for a wood girder should be large enough to allow a minimum of 1/2″ air space at the sides and ends of the girder (see Figure 15). This air space allows moisture to escape and reduces the possibility of decay.

Floor Joists

Because so much material is made in 4′ lengths (4′ × 8′ plywood, plasterboard, rigid insulation, 4′ rocklath lengths, and so forth), it is desirable that floor joists, wall and partition studs, and rafters be spaced either 12″, 16″, or 24″ oc[1] (all

1. The designation *oc* is the abbreviation for *on center* and refers to the center-to-center spacing of members.

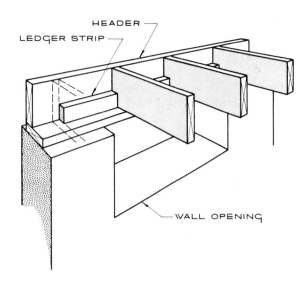

Figure 12. Use of a ledger strip.

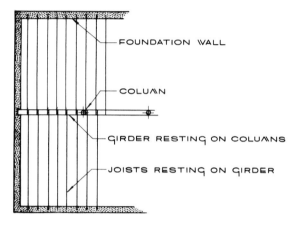

Figure 13. Use of a girder.

even divisions of 4′) to avoid cutting. Since 24″ oc is usually too weak, and 12″ oc is wasteful, 16″ oc is normally used. Joist spans are often 14′ to 16′.

Joists and headers are doubled around all openings, such as stairwells and chimneys, as shown in Figure 17. When a partition runs parallel to a joist, its entire weight must be supported by one or two joists. Since this weight may cause excessive bending, such a joist is also stiffened by doubling it. When partitions run at right angles to joists, no extra support is necessary. Joists may be spaced 12″ oc instead of the usual 16″ oc under bathrooms, and occasionally under kitchens, to allow for weakening caused by pipes set into the floor.

When joists frame into masonry walls as in Figure 11, their ends are cut at an angle (called *firecut*) to prevent the walls being pushed outward if the joists should sag (see Figure 18). Firecutting also helps prevent cracks in the masonry wall due to the joists settling.

Bridging

Bridging (Figure 19) is used to keep the joists vertical and in alignment and to distribute a concentrated load on more

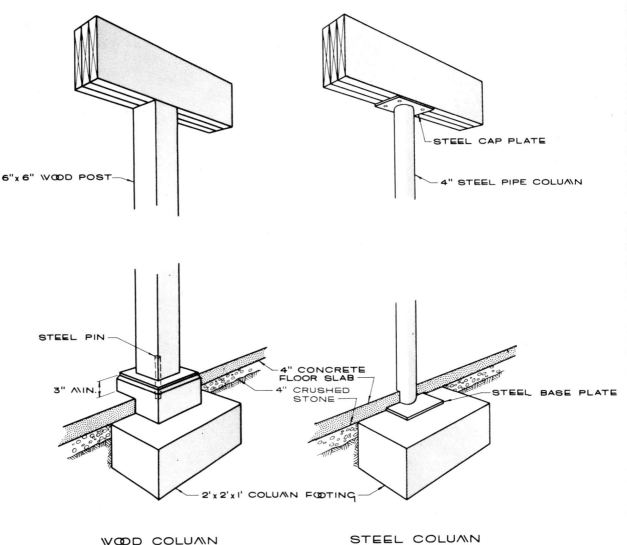

6"x 6" WOOD POST

STEEL CAP PLATE

4" STEEL PIPE COLUMN

STEEL PIN

3" MIN.

4" CONCRETE
FLOOR SLAB
4" CRUSHED
STONE

STEEL BASE PLATE

2'x 2'x 1' COLUMN FOOTING

WOOD COLUMN

STEEL COLUMN

Figure 14. Use of columns.

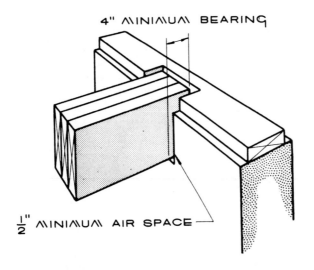

4" MINIMUM BEARING

½" MINIMUM AIR SPACE

Figure 15. Girder pocket.

than one joist. Solid wood blocking, $1'' \times 3''$ wood bridging, or metal straps may be used. Rows of bridging are spaced a maximum of $7'$ apart. Since the subflooring has a tendency to align the joist tops, the lower end of the wood and strap bridging is not nailed until the subflooring is laid.

Subflooring and Flooring

Subflooring is a wood floor of $5/8''$ plywood or $1''$ boards laid over joists to serve as a base for the finished floor. The finished floor is usually of tongue-and-grooved hardwood—oak, maple, or birch is used. When plywood or boards laid diagonally are used for subflooring, the finished flooring is laid parallel to the long dimension of the room; when boards laid perpendicular to the joists are used for subflooring, the finished flooring must be laid perpendicular to the subflooring regardless of the room proportions. Building paper is laid between subflooring and flooring as a protection against air and moisture.

Studs

The term *wall* designates an exterior wall; a *partition* is an interior wall. Partitions may be either *bearing* or *curtain* (nonbearing). A wall or partition consists of vertical members spaced 16″ oc called *studs*, a lower horizontal sole plate, and doubled top plates, as shown in Figure 11. All of these members may be 2″ × 4″ lumber. When a 4″ cast-iron soil stack is used, however, the wall is made of 2″ × 6″ lumber, to conceal it. In cold climates, studs of 2″ × 6″ lumber spaced 24″ oc are used to increase the wall thickness so that more insulation can be installed in the walls. Often an entire wall including sole and top plates is assembled horizontally on the subflooring and then raised and braced in position while the sole is spiked to the subflooring. This method avoids toenailing the stud to the sole. Sheathing serves as an additional tie between wall, header, and sill.

Window and Door Openings

The horizontal framing member above a window or door opening is called a *header*, and the horizontal framing member below the window is called the *rough sill*. All members framing an opening are doubled for greater strength and to provide a nailing surface for trim (Figure 20). The headers are laid with the long edge vertical to provide greater

strength. They must be shimmed,[2] however, to increase their 3″ (2 × 1 1/2″) thickness to 3 1/2″. The size of the headers ranges from doubled 2″ × 4″ members up to doubled 2″ × 12″ members, depending on the span and the superimposed load.

2. Shims are tapered wood strips. They are used in pairs and placed between two members to true them up as desired.

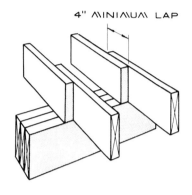

JOISTS
OVER WOOD GIRDER

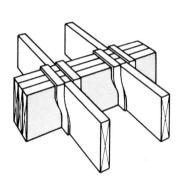

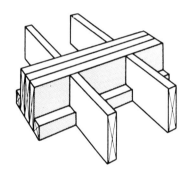

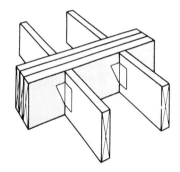

USING IRON STIRRUPS   USING LEDGER STRIPS   USING FRAMING ANCHORS

JOISTS LEVEL WITH WOOD GIRDER

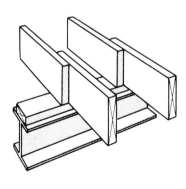

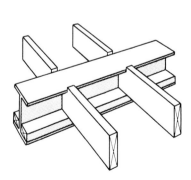

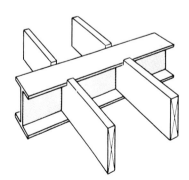

JOISTS
OVER STEEL BEAM   RESTING ON WOOD NAILERS   RESTING ON BEAM

JOISTS LEVEL WITH STEEL BEAM

Figure 16. Methods of framing joists.

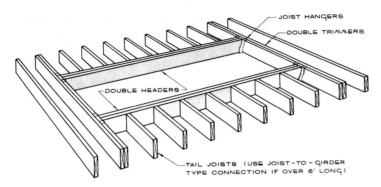

Figure 17. Stairwell framing.

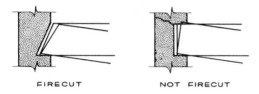

Figure 18. Use of firecutting.

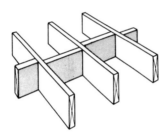

SOLID BLOCKING

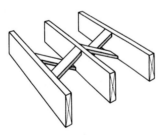

1" x 3" WOOD BRIDGING

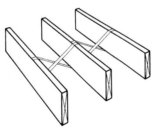

METAL STRAP BRIDGING

Figure 19. Bridging.

Corner Posts

Corner posts provide surfaces for nailing the sheathing to the outside faces of the wall at the corner and for nailing lath to both inside faces of the corner. Two methods of accomplishing this are illustrated in Figure 21.

Cantilever Framing

Figure 22 shows the method of framing for cantilevered construction, such as the second-floor overhang of a garrison house. For strength, the length of the lookouts should be at least three times the length of the overhang.

Sheathing

Sheathing is nailed to the exterior of the studs in a manner similar to that used for the subflooring. Common sheathing materials are:

1. 5/16″ minimum × 4′ × 8′ plywood.
2. 1/2″ minimum × 4′ × 8′ composition board. This has the advantage of providing some additional insulation but does not make a good base for exterior finish nailing nor does it provide the diagonal bracing strength of plywood. When composition board is used as outside sheathing, it should be asphalt-coated to prevent disintegration and to serve as a moisture barrier.
3. 1″ × 6″ boards applied diagonally. If the boards are applied horizontally, corner braces must be let into the studs to stiffen the wall.

Plywood or 1″ boards should be used for roof sheathing.

Building Paper

Building paper is asphalt-saturated felt or paper used between subflooring and finished flooring, between sheathing and finished wall covering, and between roofers and roof covering. It prevents wind and water from entering the building through the cracks, while still allowing water vapor to escape.

Constructing Roofs and Exteriors

Rafters

Rafters are usually spaced 16″ or 24″ oc. The upper end of the rafter is spiked to a 1″- or 2″-thick ridge board, the depth of which is not less than the end cut of the rafter. The lower end of the rafter is cut to obtain a full bearing on the top plate. This cut is called a *bird's mouth* (see Figure 23).

Roof Thrust

A sloping roof exerts not only a *downward* thrust on the exterior walls but also an *outward* thrust that tends to push the exterior walls apart, as shown in Figure 24. The result of this outward thrust may be prevented by the following measures:

1. Run the ceiling joists parallel to the rafters together with 1″ × 6″ or 2″ × 4″ collar beams spaced 4′ oc.

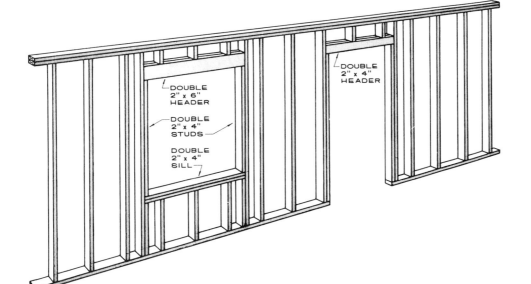

Figure 20. Rough framing of windows and doors.

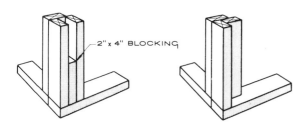

Figure 21. Methods of framing corner posts.

2. Support the rafters at the ridge by a bearing partition or beam.
3. Roof trusses or trussed rafters (Figure 25) may be used for large spans without bearing partitions, allowing great freedom in room planning. Notice, though, that a truss greatly reduces the usefulness of the attic space. Because a truss is composed of a number of small spans, the members need not be heavy. A typical trussed rafter is shown in Figure 26.

Flat Roofs

Flat roofs may be laid level to hold water on the roof (called a *water-film* roof) or, more commonly, sloped slightly to prevent water from collecting. The roof joists rest directly on the top plates and serve a double purpose: as roof rafters and as ceiling joists. When a wide overhang is desired, the roof joists are framed for cantilever framing, as shown in Figure 22. Although wood roof joists are used to frame flat roofs in residential construction, steel *open-web joists* (also called *bar joists*), as in Figure 27, are normally used in commercial construction, since they can span up to 48′. Because shingles cannot be used for a flat roof covering, a *built-up roof* finish is used. A built-up roof is constructed by

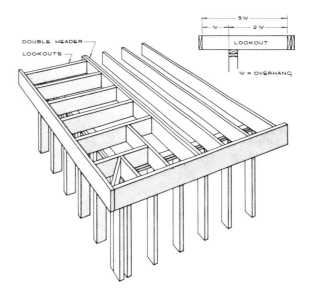

Figure 22. Cantilever framing.

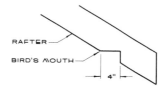

Figure 23. Bird's mouth.

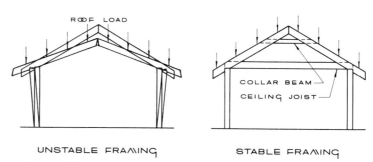

Figure 24. Framing for avoiding outward thrust.

Figure 25. Erecting trussed rafters.

laying down successive layers of roofing felt and tar or asphalt topped with roll roofing, gravel, or marble chips.

Cornices

Figure 28 shows cornice construction over a frame wall, a brick wall, and a brick veneer wall. Methods of framing various overhangs are also shown, ranging from wide overhangs to a flush cornice. The raised cornice is used to provide an additional foot of head room in the attic space or, in the case of wide overhangs, to provide more clearance above the windows beneath the cornice. Since roof gutters are often unsightly, they may be built into the roof as shown in Figure 28. Obviously, built-in gutters must be very carefully flashed.

Exterior Finishes

Exterior wall finish (Figure 29) covers the sheathing and building paper. Since the choice of finish greatly influences the final appearance and upkeep of a house, the materials should be carefully selected.

Plastic and metal siding installed over sheathing is available in horizontal clapboard and vertical V-groove styles. Plastic siding (usually vinyl) and metal siding (usually aluminum) is manufactured in a variety of colors and textures. Advantages include durability and low maintenance.

Wood siding is usually of red cedar, cypress, or California redwood because these materials have superior weather resistance. Corners may be mitered for a neat appearance, but wood or metal corners are more durable (see Figure 30). The style of the house will also influence the corner treatment.

Board-and-batten wood siding is relatively inexpensive and presents an attractive finish.

Wood shingles are also of red cedar, cypress, or redwood. Hand-split shakes may be used for a special effect. Shingles are often left unpainted and unstained to obtain a delightful weathered finish. Red cedar and California redwood weather to a dark gray color; cypress weathers to a light gray with a silver sheen. Various types of composition siding—hardboard, fiberboard, asbestos, asphalt, and so forth, in imitation of wood, brick, or stone—have certain advantages, but they must be carefully specified so as not to cheapen the appearance of the building.

Brick and stone finishes are durable, require little upkeep, and present a fine appearance. Types of brick bonds are shown in Figure 31. The word *bond* used in reference to masonry has several meanings. *Mortar bond* is the adhesion of the mortar to the brick or block units. *Structural bond* is the method of overlapping the masonry units so that the entire wall is a single structural member. *Pattern bond* is the decorative pattern formed by the use of different combinations of units. The pattern may result from the type of structural bond specified (as an 8″ solid brick Flemish bond wall

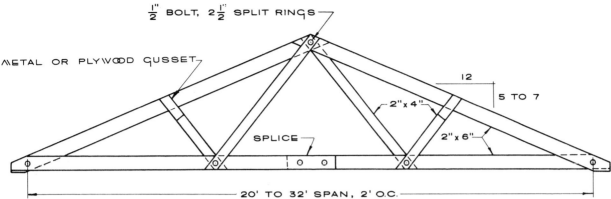

Figure 26. Typical trussed rafter.

using full brick laid as stretchers and headers) or it may be purely decorative (as a 4″ brick veneer Flemish bond wall using full- and half-brick).

The *stretcher* or *running bond* is the most popular bond. Since no headers are used, this is often used in single-wythe walls (veneer and cavity) with metal ties. The *common bond* is a variation of the running bond with a course of headers every fifth, sixth, or seventh course to tie the face wall to the backing masonry. *English bond* is laid with alternate courses of headers and stretchers, and *Flemish bond* is laid with stretchers and headers alternating in each course. The *stack bond* is a popular contemporary pattern. Because of the alignment of all vertical joints, reinforcing is needed in the horizontal joints. A masonry wall may be varied by diamond, basket-weave, herringbone, and other patterns. Also, brick can be recessed or projected for special shadow effects. Decorative variations are endless.

Concrete block lends itself well to contemporary designs. Special effects may be obtained by the bond or by the block itself, which can be specified in many textured and sculptured surfaces.

Stucco is a cement plaster that may be used on exterior walls for special effects.

Finishing the Interior

Interior Finish

Interior walls are often of plaster or dry-wall finish. Ceilings may be of the same finish or of ceiling tile. Figures 32 and 33 illustrate contemporary interiors finished in horizontal and vertical redwood planking.

Plaster. Plaster finishing is considered superior to dry-wall finish, but it has the following disadvantages:

1. It is more likely to crack.
2. Wet plaster requires many days to dry, during which all construction must be halted.
3. Wood framing is completely soaked with moisture during the drying period and may warp.

Gypsum lath measuring 3/8″ × 16″ × 4′ (usually referred to as *rocklath*) or 27″ × 8′ metal lath is nailed to the studs and joists as a base for the plaster. Notice in Figure 34 that a gypsum lath base requires strips of metal lath to reinforce the areas most susceptible to cracking: wall and

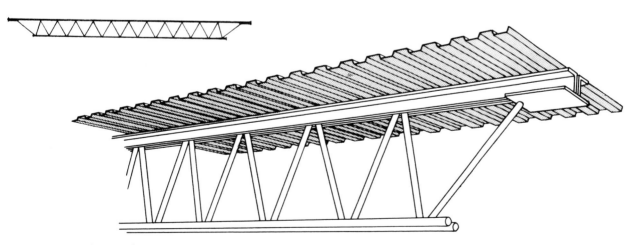

Figure 27. Open-web joist.

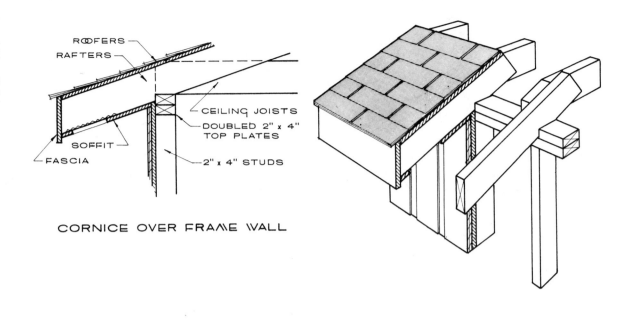

CORNICE OVER FRAME WALL

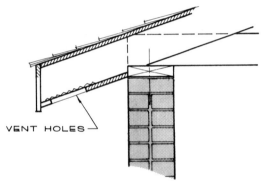

CORNICE OVER BRICK WALL

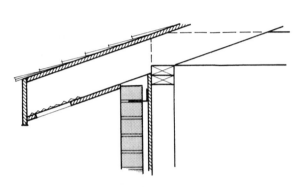

CORNICE OVER VENEER WALL

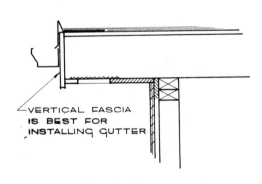

FLAT ROOF CORNICE

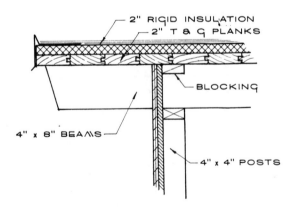

PLANK AND BEAM CORNICE

Figure 28. Cornices.

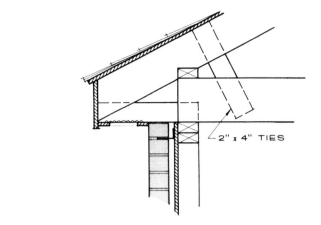

BOX CORNICE

RAISED CORNICE

2" x 4" TIES

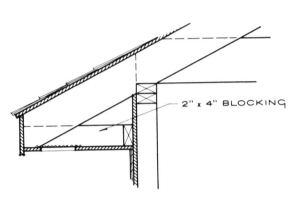

2" x 4" BLOCKING

WIDE OVERHANG

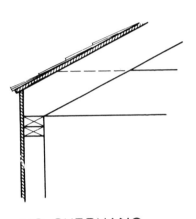

NO OVERHANG

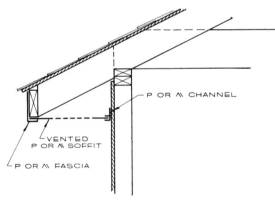

P OR M CHANNEL

VENTED P OR M SOFFIT

P OR M FASCIA

PLASTIC OR METAL CORNICE

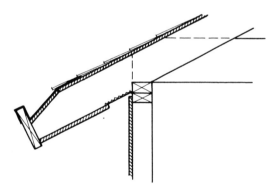

BUILT-IN GUTTER

Figure 28. continued.

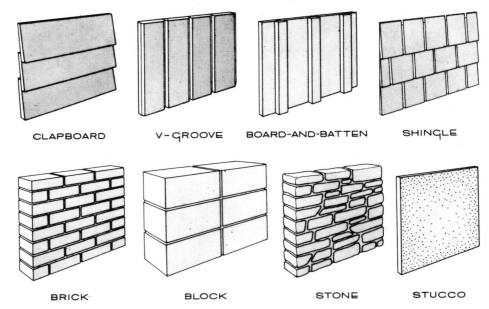

CLAPBOARD V-GROOVE BOARD-AND-BATTEN SHINGLE

BRICK BLOCK STONE STUCCO

Figure 29. Types of exterior finish.

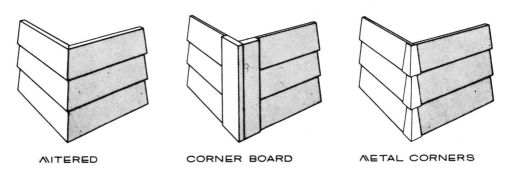

MITERED CORNER BOARD METAL CORNERS

Figure 30. Siding corner construction.

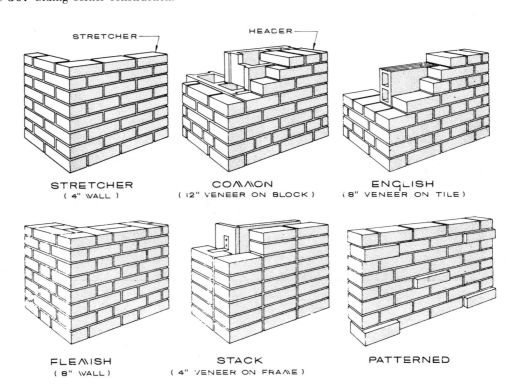

STRETCHER HEADER

STRETCHER
(4" WALL)

COMMON
(12" VENEER ON BLOCK)

ENGLISH
(8" VENEER ON TILE)

FLEMISH
(8" WALL)

STACK
(4" VENEER ON FRAME)

PATTERNED

Figure 31. Brick bonds.

Figure 32. Interior finished with horizontal planking.

Figure 33. Interior finished with vertical planking.

ceiling intersections, the upper corners of door and window openings, and other openings such as electric outlets. Wood grounds, equal in thickness to the lath and plaster, are installed around openings and near the floor. They serve as a leveling guide for the plaster and act as a nailing base for the finished trim and the baseboard. Steel edges are used on outside corners to protect edges from chipping.

Three coats of plaster—a scratch coat (so called because it is scratched to provide a rough bond with the next coat), a brown coat (which is leveled), and a finish coat—are used over metal lath. Two-coat "double-up" plaster (the scratch coat and brown coat combined) is used over rocklath. The finished coat may be a smooth, white coat which is painted or wallpapered, or it may be a textured coat (called *sand finish*), which usually has the color mixed into the plaster so that no further finishing is necessary. A moisture-resistant plaster (called *Keene's cement*) is used in kitchens and bathrooms. It is also possible to plaster with only a single 1/4″ coat of finish plaster when applied over a special 1/2″ × 4′ × 8′ gypsum lath.

Dry Wall. The most common type of dry-wall material is 3/8″ or 1/2″ gypsum board, as shown in Figure 35. When finished, this wall will look just like a plastered wall. Other kinds of dry-wall finishes, such as 1/4″ plywood panels with a hardwood veneer, are used for special effects, such as for a single bedroom wall or a fireplace wall. A den may be completely paneled. For all dry-wall finishes, it is important that the studs or joists be carefully aligned.

Gypsum Board. Gypsum board consists of a cardboard sandwich with a gypsum filler. It is installed by nailing 4′ × 8′ sheets directly to the studs or joists, and slightly setting

the nailheads. Joint cement then covers the nailheads; joint cement over perforated paper tape is applied to mask the joints. When the joint cement is sanded, a smooth wall results, ready for painting or wallpapering as with plaster walls.

Other Construction Types

Platform framing (Figure 36), in which framing studs only one story high rest on a complete platform, has been discussed in detail. Other construction types are braced framing, balloon framing, and plank-and-beam framing.

Braced Framing

Braced framed construction was used in colonial times and is still used today in modified forms (Figure 37). Braced framing utilized heavy (4″ thick) sills and corner posts. In two-story construction, the corner posts ran the full height of the building, with heavy girts let into them to support the second floor. In early braced framing, the studs served only as a curtain wall, carrying no load. Recently, a type of modular construction using corner and wall posts in a manner similar to braced framing has been gaining popularity.

Balloon Framing

The *balloon* framed house is characterized by studs resting directly on the sill and extending the full height of the stories, as shown in Figure 38. Second-floor joists rest on a ledger, which is spiked to the studs. The joists are also lapped and spiked to the studs. This type of framing has largely been replaced by platform framing, but balloon framing does have

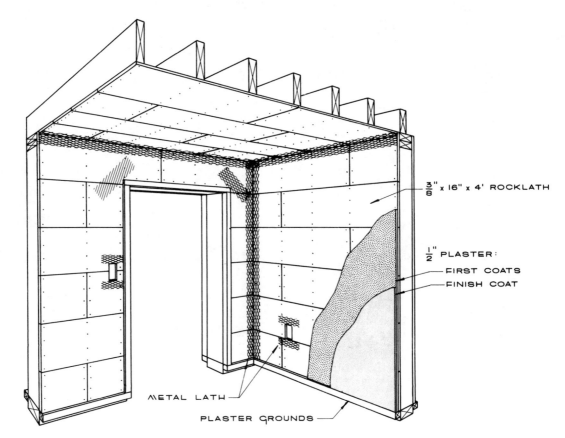

Figure 34. Plastered finish.

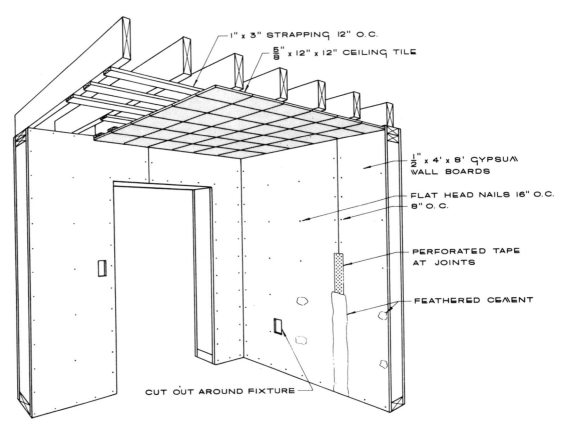

Figure 35. Dry-wall finish.

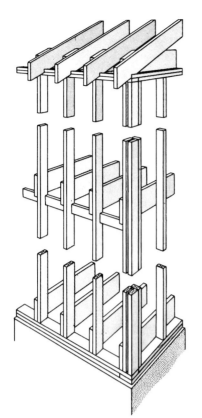

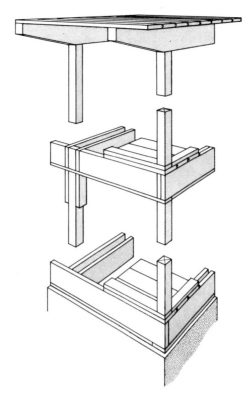

Figure 36. Platform construction.   *Figure 37.* Modern braced construction.

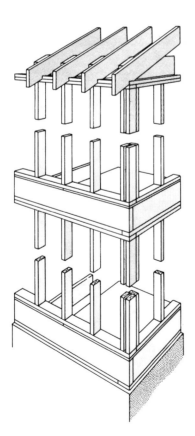

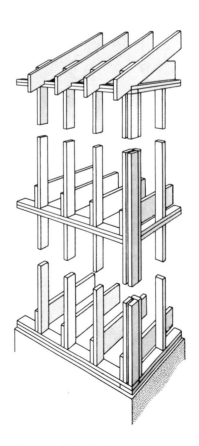

Figure 38. Balloon construction.   *Figure 39.* Plank-and-beam construction.

Figure 40. A cathedral ceiling and window walls provided by plank-and-beam framing.

the advantage of lessening vertical shrinkage, and is therefore best for two-story brick veneer or stucco construction. However, additional firestopping of 2″ blocking must be provided to prevent air passage from one floor to another. Recently, balloon framing has been used in cold climates to minimize air infiltration because balloon framing permits the vapor barrier to be installed without gaps at the top and bottom of walls.

Plank-and-Beam Framing

Plank-and-beam framing (Figure 39) is used in residential buildings and in assembly buildings such as schools and churches. It is similar to a type of framing called *mill construction* which was used for years to build factories and warehouses. Plank-and-beam framing in residential construction developed from the trend toward window walls, which made it necessary to frame a number of openings in the exterior walls (Figure 40). Plank-and-beam framing is a heavy construction using posts at least 4″ square, beams at least 4″ wide, and wood decking at least 2″ thick. The decking is usually tongue-and-grooved, continuous-span planking. Posts and beams are spaced from 4′ to 7′ oc. Construction details are similar to those shown in Chapter 23 on timber construction.

Metal Framing

Metal framing is commonly used for constructing commercial and industrial buildings; and wood framing, for residences. Wood members are widely available, easily fabricated, and economical, but they are combustible and may be weakened by decay or termites. Wood can be pressure-treated with fire-retardant chemicals or decay- and termite-resistant preservatives. Metal framing, however, is superior in many aspects of safety and durability.

Galvanized steel and aluminum components are manufactured for use as studs, sills, headers, joists, bridging, fascia, window framing, door framing, and doors. See Figure 41. Components are cut to length using a power saw with a metal cutting blade. Then they are assembled by snap-in clips, bolting, or welding. Stud depths are usually 2½″, 4″, and 6″. Joist depths are 6″, 8″, 9″, 10″, and 12″. Standard lengths of most sections are available up to 32′ long, or they can be ordered cut to special lengths at the mill. Wall and ceiling surfaces can be attached to nailable studs and joists by means of nailing grooves that hold spiral-shank nails tightly in place (Figure 42), or they can be attached

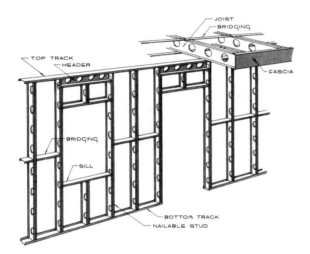

Figure 41. Metal framing components.

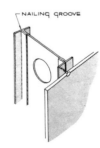

Figure 42. Nailable metal stud.

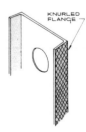

Figure 43. Screw stud with knurled flanges.

to screw studs through knurled flanges using power driven self-drilling, self-tapping, sheet metal screws (Figure 43).

Future Construction Methods and Materials

Today's methods of building construction are based mostly on lumber and nails put together in a specific way. It certainly does not take much foresight to realize that there will be revolutionary changes in building construction in the next few decades. Already many companies are manufacturing precut buildings (with lumber cut to the correct size), prefabricated ones (with entire wall sections already factory-assembled), and even entire buildings mass-produced. Assembly-line methods are not the only answer, however, since most people want custom-built homes. Other companies have made complete breaks with traditional construction, and there are still others who have launched full-scale research and development programs in the housing field.

Some mobile home manufacturers have departed from the traditional house trailer to modular units that can be connected side by side, end to end, or stacked several stories high in various combinations. Figure 44 shows a bank that was factory-built in three sections weighing 7 1/2 tons each, transported to the site (Figure 45), and bolted together. The structural system is a welded three-dimensional truss made of steel tubular beams and columns. Four lift rings are provided on the roof so that a crane can move each unit to a flatbed train or truck (Figure 46). All panels, glass, and interior finishes are installed at the factory. Final erection can be completed in three days.

Figure 44. A modular bank.

Although we can easily predict there will be changes, it is impossible to predict their exact form and direction, since they depend on future research and development. Be alert to these changes and accept them readily. For the present, though, learn all you can about current construction methods and materials.

Figure 45. Trucking modular units to the site.

Figure 46. Crane lifting modular units from a flatbed truck.

9

Floor Plans

Working Drawings

Finished drawings made by the architect and used by the contractor are called *working drawings* (Figure 1). The working drawings, together with the specifications and the general conditions, form the legal contract between owner and contractor.

In general, information on the design, location, and dimensions of the elements of a building is found on working drawings, whereas information on the quality of materials and workmanship is found in the specifications (see Chapter 31 for information on specifications). Since the working drawings constitute a major portion of the contract documents, the architect is careful that they give the contractor exactly the information needed, arranged in an orderly manner.

A fairly complete set of working drawings would include the following drawings in this order:

1. Title page and index (a perspective is often included)
2. Plot plan
3. Foundation plan
4. First-floor plan
5. Second-floor plan
6. Elevations
7. Sections
8. Typical details
9. Schedules
E1. Electrical requirements
H1. Heating and air conditioning
P1. Piping
P2. Plumbing
V1. Ventilation
S1. Floor framing plan
S2. Roof framing plan
S3. Column schedule
S4. Structural details

Usually all the working drawings are drawn to the same scale (1/8″ = 1′ or 1/4″ = 1′) with the exception of details, which are drawn to a larger scale, and the plot plan, which is drawn to an engineer's scale.

Floor Plans

Of all the different kinds of working drawings, the floor plan is the most important, since it includes the greatest amount of information. The floor plan will show the building layout and room sizes, door and window placement, bathroom and kitchen fixtures, stairway and fireplace positioning, and much more. A floor plan is actually a sectional drawing obtained by passing an imaginary cutting plane through the walls about 4′ above the floor (midway between floor and ceiling), as shown in Figure 2. The cutting plane may be offset to a higher or lower level so that it cuts through all desired features, such as a high strip window or low fireplace opening (see Figure 3). In the case of a split-level house, the cutting plane must be considerably offset, as shown in Figure 4.

Figure 1. Working drawings are required for all building construction.

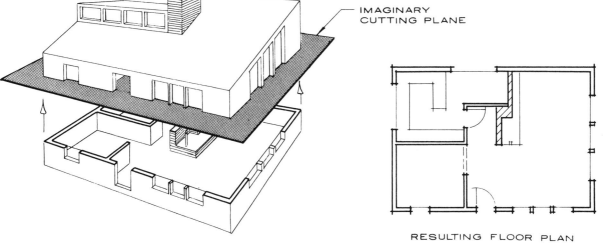

Figure 2. Imaginary cutting plane used to obtain a floor plan.

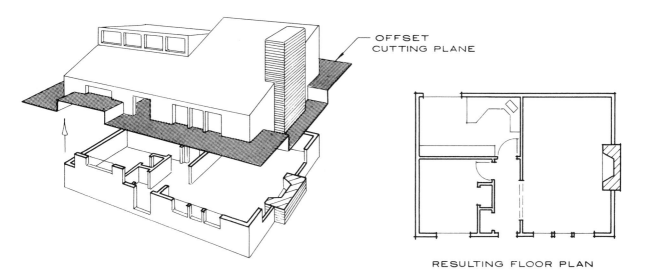

Figure 3. Cutting plane offset to show all desired features.

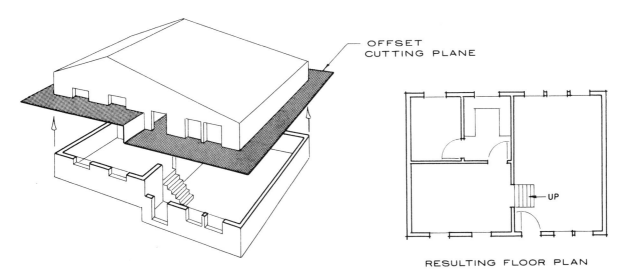

Figure 4. Cutting plane offset to obtain a floor plan of a split-level house.

To "read" a plan means to study the plan until you thoroughly understand it. To read a floor plan, proceed in the following manner:

1. Layout. First, look at the exterior walls and interior partitions to understand the general building layout and individual room placement. Check some dimensions to get a feeling for the size of the rooms. A quick comparison with a feature of known size, such as the size of a door opening, is also useful to determine approximate room sizes. Personally, I imagine myself walking in through the entrance and proceeding from room to room. This gives me a feeling for the relationship between rooms. To practice such visualization, try to read the room plans shown with furnishings in Figures 5–10. Cover the pictorials with your hand or with a piece of paper until you have formed a mental picture of each room. Then compare your mental picture with the pictorial.

2. Components. Next study (in any order) the lesser components of the building, including:

Doors. Note the placement, types, and direction of movement of doors. Much detailed information is given in the door schedules which may be placed near the floor plans. See Chapters 14 and 15 for more information.

Windows. Note the number, size, and placement of windows. The width of windows shown on the plan is that of the sash opening. Detailed information is given in the window schedules which may be placed near the elevation views. See Chapters 13 and 15 for more information.

Stairs. A complete flight of stairs is seldom illustrated. Rather, only several treads are shown to a break line. "Read" the direction of the stairs to learn if they are going up or down. See Chapter 16 for more information.

Fireplace. The fireplace section typically shows the fireplace opening, fire brick placement, hearth, ash drop, and any flues from fireplaces or furnaces at lower levels. See Chapter 17 for more information.

Equipment. Study all built-in equipment, such as bathroom fixtures (bathtub, toilet, sink, and medicine cabinet), kitchen fixtures (cabinets, sink, built-in wall ovens, counter-top burners, and built-in refrigerator or freezer), and closet fixtures (shelves and clothes rod). The location of a movable stove or refrigerator is shown even if it is not included in the contract. Notice that the wall cabinets are shown as hidden lines. A hidden (dashed) line on an architectural plan may refer to a feature (cabinet, archway, or beam) *above* the level of the imaginary cutting plane.

3. Symbols. Read all symbols, for they give much information. Wall symbols, for example, indicate if the wall is wood frame, brick, or veneer. When the meaning of a symbol is unclear, look up the legend of symbols on the title page or check in standard reference works such as *Architectural Graphic Standards* by Ramsey and Sleeper or *Time-Saver Standards* by Callendar.[1] See Chapter 3 for more information.

4. Dimensions. A properly drawn plan will include all dimensions needed to construct the building. However, some sizes must be obtained by adding or subtracting other dimensions. Also, all obvious dimensions are omitted. For example, there would be no need for the draftsman to give the location dimension of a door that is centered in the space at the end of a hall. See Chapters 4 and 5 for more information.

5. Other Information. The location of lighting or heating units may be included on the floor plan. This is done only when the plan will not become crowded. Occasionally, all furniture placement is shown.

---

1. Charles G. Ramsey and Harold Sleeper, *Architectural Graphic Standards*, 7th ed. (New York: John Wiley & Sons, 1981); John H. Callendar, *Time-Saver Standards for Architectural Design Data*, rev. 6th ed. (New York: McGraw-Hill, 1982).

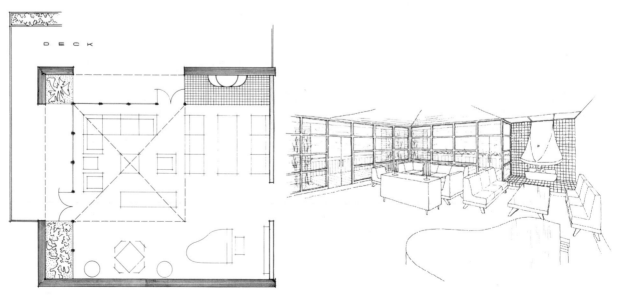

Figure 5. Practice reading a living room plan.

Figure 6. Practice reading a dining room plan.

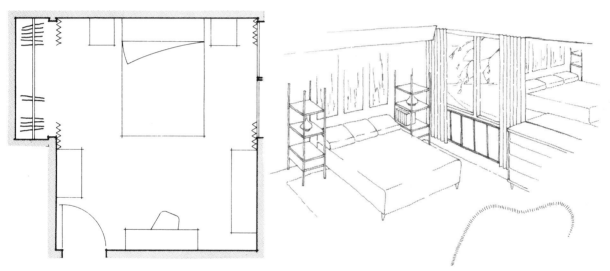

Figure 7. Practice reading a bedroom plan.

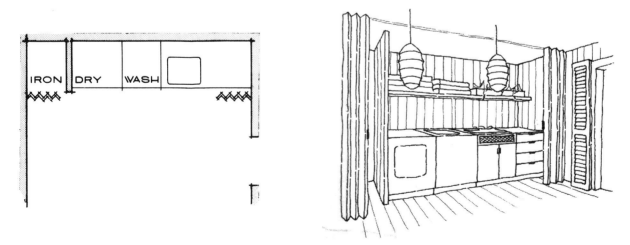

Figure 8. Practice reading a family room-laundry plan.

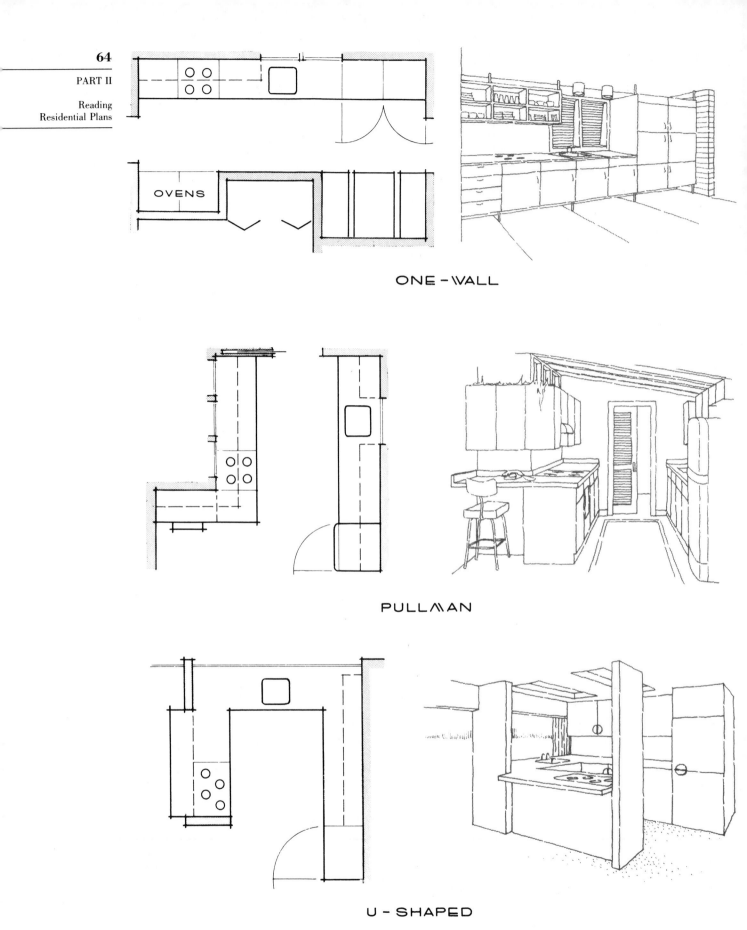

OVENS

ONE — WALL

PULLMAN

U — SHAPED

Figure 9. Practice reading kitchen plans.

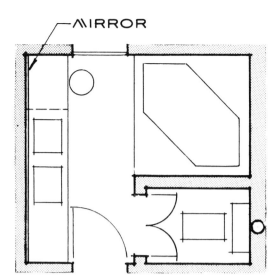

Figure 10. Practice reading a bathroom plan.

Reading the A Residence Floor Plans

The first-floor, second-floor, and basement plans of the A residence are shown in Figures 13–15. Study these plans until you understand every line and symbol. Make a note of any questions you have and check with your instructor at the first opportunity. The following comments might answer some of your questions.

A Residence First-Floor Plan

The A residence is a "center hall" plan (see Figure 13). This means that the living room and dining area are located on either side of the front vestibule. The living room of the A residence is designed with an arched piano alcove, and the dining room has an offset serving alcove. The kitchen is U-shaped with a preparation island. The peninsula counter divides the kitchen from the family room. The utility room is used for storing canned and frozen food.

A schedule mark (a number for doors and a letter for windows) is assigned to each door or window of the same size and type. The door numbers are placed within circles near the doors. The door schedule for the A residence is near the second-floor plan. Swinging doors are typically sized as follows:

Interior doors:	2'- 6" × 6'- 8" × 1 3/8"
Allow for approximately 2'- 9" rough opening	
Front door:	3'- 0" × 6'- 8" × 1 3/4"
Allow for approximately 3'- 3" rough opening	
Rear door:	2'- 8" × 6'- 8" × 1 3/4"
Allow for approximately 2'- 11" rough opening	

The quarter-curved lines show the direction of door swing. Door sills are shown only for exterior doors.

Windows are represented by lines indicating the sill and glass. Window schedule marks and the window schedule appear on the elevation views.

The notation "UP 14 R" near the stair means that the stairs

go up 14 risers to the second floor. The notation "DN 13 R" means down 13 risers to the basement.

The fireplace section shows the shape of brick work and hearth, two flues, and the fire brick.

Dimension lines are finished with small, closed dots rather than arrowheads.

See the glossary Chapter 29 for the meaning of "BIBB." See the abbreviations Chapter 30 for the meaning of "CL," "DN," "LC," "R," and "SQ."

A Residence Second-Floor Plan

Begin reading the second-floor plan by noticing that some features relate to the first-floor plan: the exterior walls, the stairway, chimney location, plumbing partition (that is, the partition behind the toilets), and some bearing partitions. Principal walls and partitions are often over one another from foundation to roof to ensure a stiff frame and to facilitate plumbing and heating installations. Also, notice that the fenestration requires that first- and second-floor windows be directly over one another.

Notice in Figure 14 that the overall depth dimension of the second-floor plan of the A residence has been increased 2'- 5", from 25'- 10" to 28'- 3", due to the 2'- 0 overhang at the front of the house and a 5" dimensional offset at the rear. This 5" dimensional offset is due to the change from brick veneer (4" brick and 1" air space) to frame construction, as shown in Figure 11. The width dimension has also increased 10", from 39'- 8" to 40'- 6", because of this same 5" dimensional offset at each side.

Notice also that some minor dimensions have been omitted for the sake of clarity. For example, the width of the bedroom closets would have to be scaled from the drawing. This is accepted practice, since the exact location of these partitions is not critical.

When reading the doors on the second-floor plan, notice that doors opening into rooms from the hall are designed to swing into the room against a wall. For closets, sliding or folding doors are often specified.

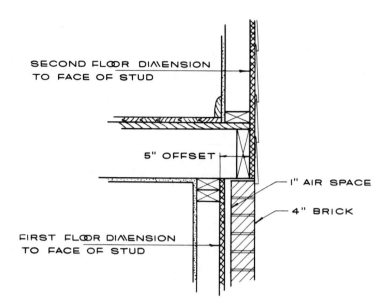

Figure 11. Second-floor 5″ offset.

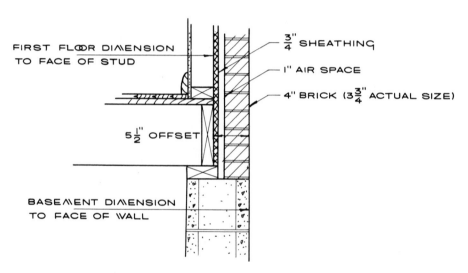

Figure 12. Basement 5 1/2″ offset.

See the abbreviations, Chapter 30, for the meaning of abbreviations "BR," "DN," "LC," and "R" used on the second-floor plan and the abbreviations "GAR," "HD," "LT," "MK," "NO," and "WP" used in the door schedule.

A Residence Basement Plan

As with the second-floor plan, begin reading the basement plan (Figure 15) by relating features with the first-floor plan: exterior walls, stairway, chimney, and bearing girder.

Foundation walls are 10″ thick with stiffening pilasters, which are needed on long, straight runs of wall. Hidden lines are used to show the foundation footings and column footings. The double-headed arrow is used to show the direction of the floor joists. Notice that the overall depth of the basement has been increased 11″, from 25′- 10″ to 26′- 9″, because of a 5 1/2″ dimensional offset. This offset can be better understood by referring to Figure 12.

The basement of the A residence has been designed for the future construction of a recreation room, game room, shop, and lavatory. This allows better planning in locating necessary utilities. Find each of the following:

1. The furnace, located near chimney flue (within 10′)
2. Provision for fuel storage, near the driveway but removed from the furnace (beyond 10′)
3. Hot-water heater
4. Water meter
5. Floor drain
6. Electrical entrance panel
7. Laundry drop

See the abbreviations, Chapter 30, for the meaning of "AMP," "COL," "D," "FURN," "GAL," "GALV," "HW," "OC," "R," and "W."

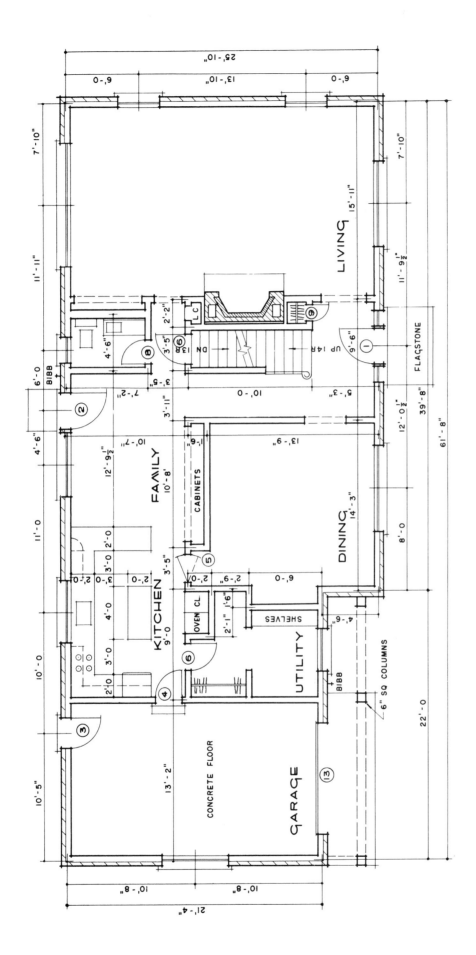

Figure 13. First-floor plan of the A residence.

67

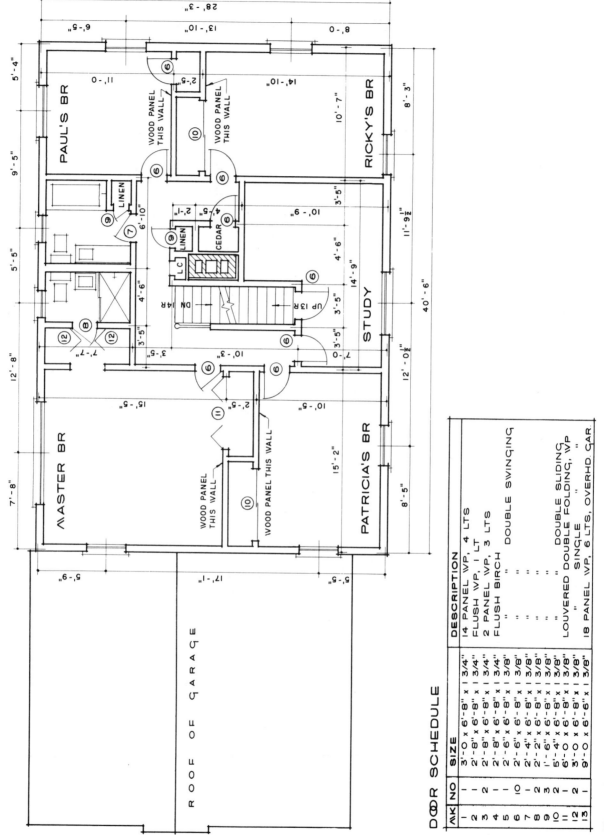

DOOR SCHEDULE

MK	NO	SIZE	DESCRIPTION
1	1	3'-0 x 6'-8" x 1 3/4"	14 PANEL WP, 4 LTS
2	2	2'-8" x 6'-8" x 1 3/4"	FLUSH WP, 1 LT
3		2'-8" x 6'-8" x 1 3/4"	2 PANEL WP, 3 LTS
4		2'-8" x 6'-8" x 1 3/4"	FLUSH BIRCH
5	10	2'-6" x 6'-8" x 3/8"	" " DOUBLE SWINGING
6	2	2'-6" x 6'-8" x 3/8"	" " "
7	1	2'-4" x 6'-8" x 3/8"	" " "
8	2	2'-2" x 6'-8" x 3/8"	" " "
9	3	1'-6" x 6'-8" x 3/8"	" " DOUBLE SLIDING
10	2	5'-4" x 6'-8" x 3/8"	LOUVERED DOUBLE FOLDING, WP
11	1	6'-0 x 6'-8" x 1 3/8"	" " SINGLE
12	2	3'-0 x 6'-6" x 1 3/8"	18 PANEL WP, 6 LTS, OVERHD. GAR.
13	1	9'-0 x 6'-6" x 1 3/8"	

Figure 14. Second-floor plan of the A residence.

68

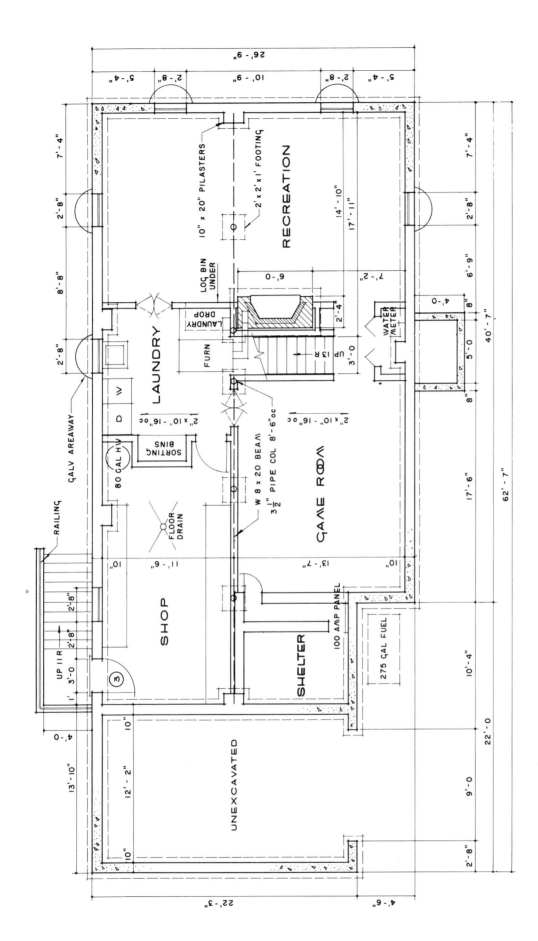

Figure 15. Basement plan of the A residence.

69

10

Plot Plans

A plot plan shows the shape and contour of a plot of land, the location of the house on the plot, and information on utilities, driveways, walks, and terraces. A roof plan or a landscaping plan also may be included.

Reading Plot Plans

To read a plot plan, follow these steps:

1. Property Lines. First, look at the shape and dimensions of the plot. Property lines are usually shown as medium-weight center lines. The plot plan is drawn to an engineer's scale (such as $1'' = 20'$) rather than to an architect's scale (such as $1/16'' = 1'- 0$). Also find an arrow that shows the direction of north.

Bearings are given to show the compass direction of the property lines. Notice in Figure 2 that the opposite and parallel property lines have opposite bearings (such as N 3° W and its opposite S 3° E) because the surveyor started at one corner and surveyed clockwise around the perimeter until reaching the starting corner again.

2. Contour Lines. Next, study the contour lines. The property lines and dimensions give you a feeling for the *shape* and *size* of the lot, and the contour lines give you a feeling for the *slope* of the lot.

A *contour line* is an imaginary line representing a constant elevation on the lot. The vertical distance between adjacent contour lines is called the *contour interval*, and is usually $1'$ for a residential lot. Contour lines are dimensioned by indicating their elevation above sea level or some other reference plane, such as a nearby street or house.

The easiest way to learn to read contour lines is to imagine that you are constructing a model of the plot. For example, a model of the small section of sloping land shown in Figure 1 could be built by cutting out cardboard sections shaped to the contour lines and then filling in the resulting terraces with modeling clay. Practice this technique by trying to read the plot plan of the M residence first described in Chapter 5. This plot plan is shown in Figure 2. First, notice that the contour lines indicate sloping ground from the northwest corner to the southeast corner. The elevations of permanent markers at these corners are 101.4′ and 89.2′, which shows that the land slopes a total of 12.2′.

When the existing land contour is not satisfactory, it must be adjusted by cutting away or filling in. This is indicated on the plot plan by showing the proposed position of the altered contour lines with a solid line; existing contours are indicated by broken lines. Figure 2 shows that the land has been filled in west of the retaining wall and cut out east of the retaining wall.

Can you form in your mind a mental model of this plot? If so, you have learned to read the most difficult part of any plot plan.

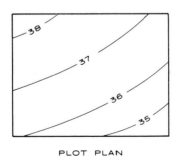 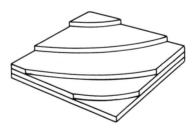 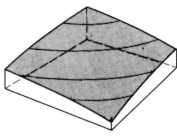

PLOT PLAN   ROUGH MODEL   FINISHED MODEL

Figure 1. Reading contour lines.

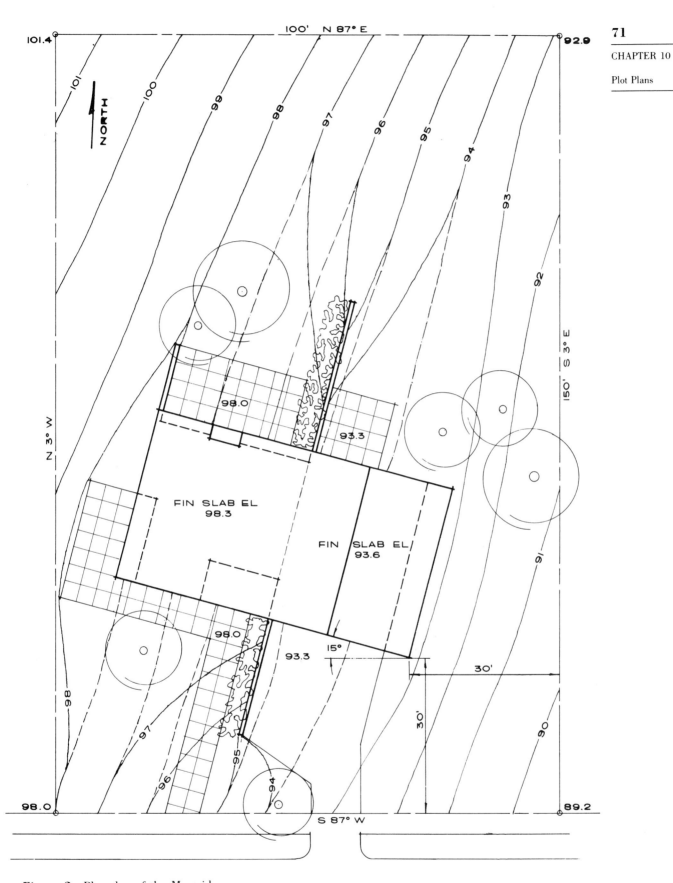

Figure 2. Plot plan of the M residence.

3. Building Location. After you have determined the shape, size, and slope of the plot, study the location of the building on the plot. The building location is specified by dimensions from the front property line and from a side property line. These dimensions are often critical because they position the building to conform to zoning regulations and to satisfy requirements of utilities, topography, solar orientation, wind orientation, and landscaping.

4. Zoning. The first known zoning law was passed in ancient Rome to prevent industries from locating too near the central forum of the city. This established the principle that private property can be restricted in favor of the general welfare. The first comprehensive zoning ordinance in the United States was passed in New York City in 1916 as a consequence of a tragic fire at the Triangle Shirtwaist factory. Over one hundred dressmakers, mostly young girls, died in that building, which was higher than firefighting equipment could reach, and which had no sprinklers and an incomplete fire escape.

Most communities now have zoning ordinances that restrict the size and location of buildings to prevent crowding and to encourage the most appropriate use of land. It is imperative that everyone associated with a building project understand and adhere to all zoning regulations and building codes. Several regulations of one community's zoning ordinance are given in Table I.

5. Utilities. Utilities such as water, sewer, electric, gas, and telephone lines are often shown on the plot plan. To prevent crowding, utilities have been removed from the plot plan of the M residence and are shown in Figure 3. The

Table I. Sample of zoning regulations

Article V. Residence District

Section 501. Each lot in this district shall comply with the following minimum requirements:

501-1. Lot area per:

One-family dwelling	10,000 sq. ft.
Two-family dwelling	12,000 sq. ft.

501-2. Lot width:

One-family dwelling	75'
Two-family dwelling	100'

501-3. Front yard depth:

Dwelling	30'
Nondwelling	40'

501-4. Side yard width:

Dwelling and accessory building	8'
Nondwelling	20'

501-5. Rear yard depth:
The rear yard depth shall be at least 20 percent of the depth of the lot measured from the front building line to the nearest point of rear lot line, but in no case shall this be less than 15'.

Section 502. The maximum height of structures in this district shall be:

502-1. Dwelling	26'	(not exceeding two stories)
502-2. Accessory building	16'	(not exceeding one story)
502-3. Nondwelling	40'	

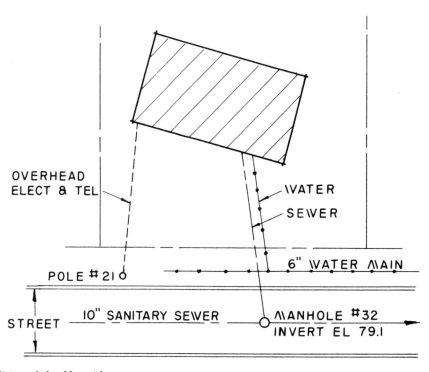

Figure 3. Utilities of the M residence.

Figure 4. Landscaping to provide both planting groups and uninterrupted lawn.

Figure 5. A terrace well integrated with the interior plan (courtesy of Scholz Homes, Inc.).

designation "INVERT EL 79.1" means that the elevation of the bottom inside of the sewer line is 79.1′ at manhole #32.

6. Other Information. Usually the building is shown on a plot plan with heavy lines representing the outside basement dimensions. Often the building is sectioned as well. Hidden lines are used to indicate roof overhang. On structures with fairly involved roof intersections, a roof plan is shown in place of a section to indicate ridges, valleys, and hips.

The elevation of the finished floor is shown, as are other details such as street names, drives, walks, terraces, and landscaping (Figures 4 and 5).

Reading the Plot Plan of the A Residence

The plot plan of the A residence is shown in Figure 6. Notice that the ground is nearly level: just a gentle rise of several feet to the northeast corner.

Existing trees have been plotted, giving the type of tree and diameter. Notice that two trees will have to be removed to make room for the building, but the curved driveway is designed to fit between trees without any being removed. Dashed lines are used to show the extent of planting.

See the abbreviations, Chapter 30, for the meaning of "EL" and "FIN." If you have any unanswered questions concerning this plot plan, check with your instructor at the first opportunity.

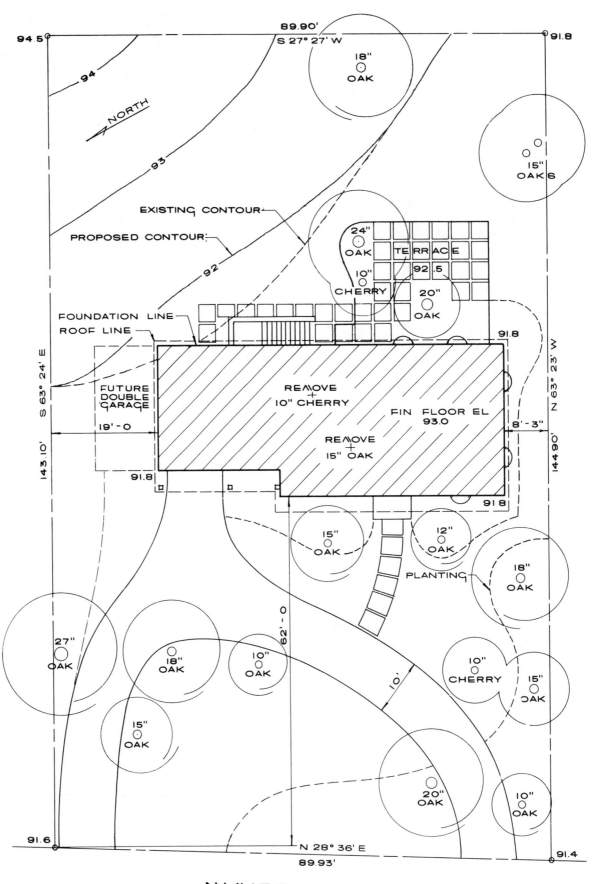

Figure 6. Plot plan of the A residence.

11

Roof Framing Plans

The roof is an important feature in the exterior appearance of a building. The shape of a roof is determined by reading the elevations, and the framing of a roof is determined by reading the framing plans. Occasionally, framing plans are omitted when sufficient information for roof framing is present in some other view.

Types of Roofs

There are a good many types of roofs. They are classified broadly into two categories: roofs used mostly on traditional houses, and roofs used mostly on contemporary houses. (*Contemporary* in this book is used to mean present-day construction of ranch, split-level, and modern styles of buildings.) Let us look at traditional and at contemporary roofs in turn.

Traditional Roof Types
(Figure 1)

Gable. The gable roof is the most common form of residential roof because it is easy to construct, is pitched for drainage, and is universally accepted as a pleasing shape. This roof is also used in contemporary designs. To be precise, the gable is the triangular portion of the end of a house, and a roof that slopes on both sides of the triangle is a *gabled roof*. Louvers are installed in the gables to allow warm air and moisture to escape.

Hip. A hip roof has sloping ends as well as sloping sides. This type is more difficult to construct than a gable, but it is still used with a low pitch on ranch houses. However, every hip or valley increases chances for leakage.

Gambrel. The gambrel roof is used on Dutch Colonial designs to increase headroom on the second floor. Since the framing is complicated, it is not widely used today. A gambrel is identified by having a steeper slope on the lower part of the roof than on the upper part.

Mansard. The mansard roof was named after the French architect who originated it. It is characterized by having two slopes at the ends as well as on the sides; like the gambrel, the lower portion of the roof has a steeper pitch than the upper portion. Mansard roofs are rarely built today, but they were extensively used on French-styled houses in the nineteenth century.

Dormer Types (Figure 2)

Gable. A dormer is a type of window used to let light into an otherwise dark area. The designer must weigh the expense of dormers against the expense of an additional story.

Shed. A shed dormer gives nearly all the advantages of a full story, without disturbing the one-floor look of the house. This dormer type is sometimes called a *dustpan*.

Dutch Colonial. A Dutch Colonial dormer might be termed a shed dormer on a gambrel roof. The second-floor wall may be set back from the first-floor wall.

French. Arched dormer tops indicate French influence.

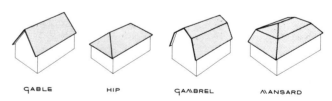

Figure 1. Traditional roof styles.

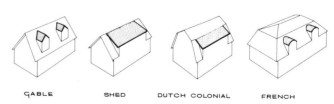

Figure 2. Dormers.

Contemporary Roof Types
(Figures 3–11)

Flat. The flat roof is the most common form of commercial roof (see Figures 4 and 5). Most roofs that appear flat actually have a slight slope of 1/4″ to 1/2″ per foot for drainage. Roofing is laid in layers (called *plies*) of tar and gravel or with membranes of plastic or other flexible material.

Some roofs are designed as perfectly flat, thus allowing water to remain on them. This is called a *water-film roof*, and the water serves as insulation from cold in winter and from heat (by reflection and evaporation) in summer. Other roofs that are designed to slope may become distorted so

that *ponding* (puddles) occur. In either case, there is a great possibility of roof leaks.

Shed. The shed roof, which has a steeper slope than a flat roof, is suited to a solar house when the high wall faces south. It also gives interesting interior effects when the beams are left exposed. Beams measuring 4″ × 10″ spaced 4′ oc might be used. This roof takes standard roofing material.

Clerestory. A clerestory (or clearstory) roof contains windows fitted between two roof planes. This roof solves the problem of introducing light into the center of a house. The clerestory may be used with a sawtooth roof as shown in Figure 3 or with other roof types.

Butterfly. As its name implies, this roof resembles a butterfly with upraised wings. The pitch and length of each side of the butterfly roof are not always equal. This roof "opens up" the house, providing plenty of light and air. Drains may be at the end of the valley or in the middle, running down through the center of the house.

Folded. Some roofs are so new that some imagination must be used to find descriptive names. As the name implies, the folded or pleated roof looks as though it were a folded sheet of paper and is quite popular in office and motel design. Roofing material may be exterior grade plywood or metal.

Parasol. The parasol roof (see Figure 8) is in the shape of an umbrella blown inside out. Round and square variations are possible. Often the material used is reinforced concrete.

Vaults and Domes. Vaults and domes have staged a comeback from Byzantine days. More often used on commercial than residential buildings, they limit the possible shapes of the floor plan.

A *geodesic dome* is framed of members nearly equal in length that are joined to form triangular patterns. The trian-

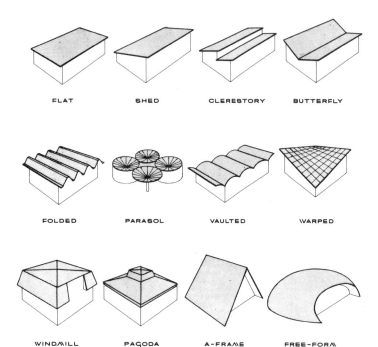

Figure 3. Contemporary roofs.

Figure 4. A flat roof on a residential design.

Figure 5. A flat roof on a commercial design.

Figure 6. A wood-shingled roof of unique design.

Figure 7. Another view of the residence shown in Figure 6.

Figure 8. A beach pavilion with parasol roofs.

Figure 9. A metal roof on an A-frame.

Figure 10. A house constructed by spraying concrete on an inflated plastic balloon.

Figure 11. A conical roof.

gles are then joined to form pyramids (tetrahedrons), giving a double-faced structure of great strength (see Figure 12). The framing members are usually straight rather than curved, which causes the geodesic dome to look like a polyhedron rather than a hemisphere. The inventor of the geodesic dome is R. Buckminster Fuller, who received patents on a number of designs, some based on shapes other than the tetrahedron. One popular system is based on the octahedron as shown in Figures 13 and 14.

Warped. Beginnings have been made in the development of warped surfaces for roofs. In most cases, the warped surface is a hyperbolic paraboloid, that is, a surface generated by a line moving so that its ends are in contact with two

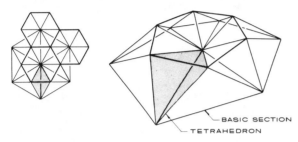

Figure 12. Detail of a tetrahedral-based geodesic dome.

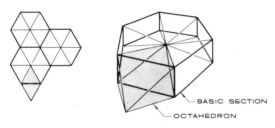

Figure 13. Detail of an octahedral-based geodesic dome.

Figure 14. Union Tank Car Shop, Baton Rouge, Louisiana.

skew lines. This produces a superior roof due to its high resistance to bending. Warped roofs have been constructed of molded plywood, reinforced concrete, and sprayed plastic.

Windmill. The windmill roof is often used on modern two-story townhouses to lend interest to an otherwise simple design.

Pagoda. The pagoda roof provides an interesting interior, as well as exterior, design. Connected clusters of pagoda-roofed rooms have been successfully designed.

A-Frame. Originally specified for low-cost summer or winter cabins, larger structures such as churches have adopted this roof form. The classic A-frame roof is a gable roof that reaches the ground on two sides. A variation is shown in Figure 9.

Free-Form. The shape of free-form roofs may depend on the method of construction (see Figure 10). Urethane foam has been sprayed on a "knit jersey" material stretched over a pipe frame. This construction has proved strong, weather-resistant, and self-insulating, but a serious disadvantage is that some forms of urethane foam are very flammable. Consequently, it should be covered by a fireproof material rather than installed exposed. Sprayed urethane foam should always be protected against any possible source of combustion.

Roofing Materials

Although several new roofing materials and methods have been mentioned, the large majority of residential roofs are constructed of built-up tar and gravel or membrane roofing when the roof is flat and of shingle when the roof slopes more than 3 in./ft.

Built-up Roofing. Built-up tar and gravel roofing is used on flat and slightly sloping roofs. This type is constructed of alternate layers of roofing felt and mopped-on hot tar or asphalt. Three to five layers (called *plies*) are used, then topped by crushed gravel or marble chips embedded in the tar. Roofing contractors will bond a three-ply economy roof for ten years and a five-ply roof for twenty years.

Membrane Roofing. Membrane roofing is rapidly replacing built-up roofing for use on flat and slightly sloping roofs. Easy to apply and repair, membrane roofing is lighter in weight and a better heat reflector than built-up roofing. Most membranes are also available in various colors. The membrane is a thin layer (about 1/8″ thick) of plastic, rubber, bitumen, or aluminum. Available in rolls or large sheets, the membrane is applied over mopped-on adhesive or may be loose-laid and covered with ballast of crushed gravel or marble chips. Joints are heat-sealed or spliced using a contact adhesive pressure-sealed by roller. Membranes also can be applied in fluid form by spray, brush, or squeegee. The membrane then hardens through chemical curing or evaporation of a solvent in the mixture. The manufacturer's bond for defective material is usually for fifteen years, but the roofer's guarantee for proper installation is usually only for two to five years.

Figure 15. Installing roofing panels of copper sheets bonded to plywood.

Figure 16. Installing crimped copper sheets over an arched roof.

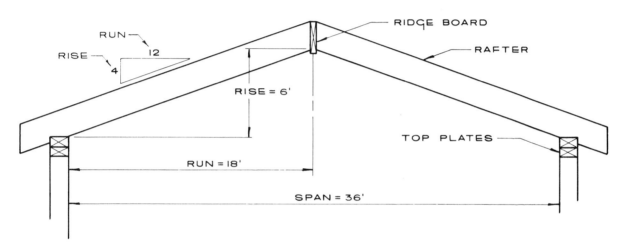

Figure 17. Roof pitch terms.

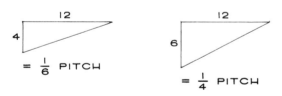
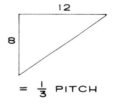
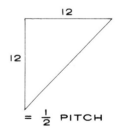

Figure 18. Alternate method of specifying pitch.

Shingles. Fiber glass shingles, consisting of a fiber glass mat saturated with asphalt, are now commonly used in house construction because they are durable and their cost is moderate. Asphalt shingles, consisting of a cellulose mat saturated with asphalt, are still available. Wood shingles and shakes are often of cedar or redwood and present a handsome appearance. Unfortunately, the fire hazard of wood shingles is great. Roofing shingles are sold by *squares*; a square is the amount of shingling needed to roof 100 sq. ft.

Slate and tile are occasionally used for roofing materials. Both are relatively heavy and expensive, however. Metal roofs of tin, copper, zinc, aluminum, and lead are often used on commercial buildings. See Figures 15 and 16.

Roof Pitch

Some roof pitch terms are shown in Figure 17. The terms *rise* and *run* are used in two ways:

1. To describe the *actual* dimensions of a roof; for example, the roof in Figure 17 has a rise of 6′, a run of 18′, and a span of 36′.
2. To describe the rise per unit of run; for example, the roof in Figure 17 has a rise of 4″ in a run of 1′.

The *roof pitch* is also described in two ways:

1. By a fraction whose numerator is the rise and denominator is the span; for example, a roof with a rise of 6′ and a span of 36′ has a 6/36 pitch, which would be reduced and shown as a 1/6 pitch.
2. By a pitch triangle on the elevations showing the rise in whole inches per 12″ of run; for example, the 4-12 pitch triangle shown in Figure 17 indicates a rise of 4″ for a run of 12″ (see Figure 18).

In general, steeper roofs are found in areas where there are heavy snowfalls, since snow is naturally shed from a steep roof.

Special steps are taken with low-pitched shingled roofs to prevent wind from lifting the tabs and allowing water to seep under them. Several solutions are possible:

1. Interlocking tab shingles
2. Self-sealing shingles that have factory-applied adhesive on the underside
3. Each tab cemented with a spot of quick-setting adhesive during installation
4. Heavyweight shingles (300#, 15″ × 36″) which are stiffer than regular shingles (210#, 12″ × 36″) and are sized for triple overlap.

Flashing

Thin sheets of soft metal are used to prevent leakage at critical points on roofs and walls. These sheets are called *flashing* and are usually of lead, zinc, copper, or aluminum. Some areas that are flashed include:

· Intersections of roof with chimney, with soil pipe, and with dormer (see Figure 6, Chapter 17)
· Roof valleys

Gutters

Gutters are used when the soil is likely to be eroded by rain dripping from the roof, or when roof overhangs are less than 12″ in a one-story structure or 24″ in a two-story structure. Downspouts conduct the water down the wall to a storm sewer (not a sanitary sewer), dry well, or splashblock (a concrete pad placed to prevent soil erosion), as shown in Figure 19. When gutters are omitted, diverters are used over entrances to the house to drain rainwater off to the sides. Guttering is made of galvanized iron, copper, aluminum, or zinc alloy, or it may be built into the roof as shown in Figure 28 of Chapter 8.

Skylights

Plastic domes are often used to light the interior of industrial buildings. Skylights have also been used in residences to

obtain specific effects. Both fixed and ventilation types are available in sizes ranging from 24″ square to 48″ square.

Reading Roof Framing Plans

Roof framing is described in Chapter 8. Figure 20 shows some common terms used in roof construction.

When unusual or difficult roof construction is necessary, a roof framing plan is included in the working drawings. Floor framing plans and ceiling joist framing plans are also included when necessary.

Figure 21 shows the roof framing plan for the roof shown in Figure 20. Notice that a single heavy line is used to indicate each rafter. Cover the pictorial (Figure 20) with a sheet of paper and practice reading the roof framing plan (Figure 21) until you can understand it without referring to the pictorial for help. Check with your instructor if you have any questions.

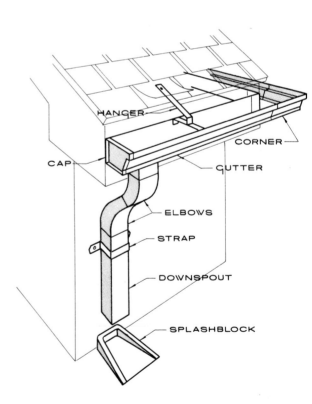

Figure 19. Guttering terms.

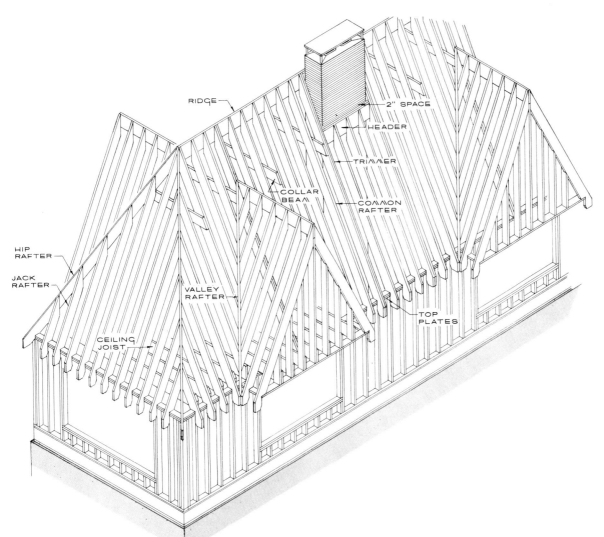

Figure 20. Roof framing terms.

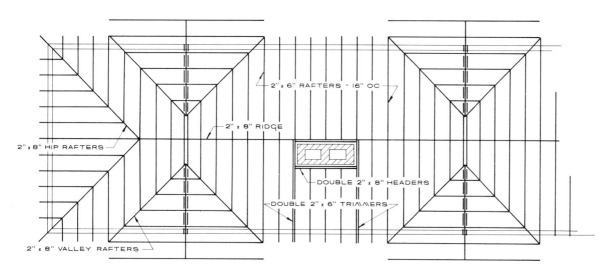

Figure 21. Roof framing plan.

12

Elevations and Sections

An architectural elevation is a view of a side of a building. When elevations show the inside of a building, they are called *interior elevations;* when they show the outside, they are called simply *elevations.*

Exterior elevations are as necessary to the satisfactory appearance of a building as the floor plan is to its satisfactory functioning (Figure 1). Normally, elevations of the four sides of a building are sufficient to describe it. In some cases, however, more than the four elevations are needed; for example, a structure built around an open court would require additional exterior elevations to show the building as seen from the court.

The scale of the elevations is usually 1/4″ = 1′ for a small residence or 1/8″ = 1′ for larger buildings. Occasionally,

one or two major elevations are drawn to the large 1/4″ = 1′ scale, and the less important elevations are drawn to the smaller 1/8″ = 1′ scale.

Reading Elevations

To read elevations, follow these steps:

1. Coordinate Elevations and Plan. First, look at *all* the elevations and compare them with the floor plan and with each other. It is best to start with the front elevation and study the position and shape of walls, windows, and doors in relation to information shown on the floor plan and end elevations. Read each elevation until you are familiar with it and understand how it relates to the other elevations and to the floor plan. If the plot is steeply sloping, you also need to study the elevations in relation to the contour lines on the plot plan.

Elevation views are often labeled to help identification. Either of two methods may be used:

1. Front elevation
   Rear elevation
   Right-end elevation
   Left-end elevation
2. North elevation
   East elevation
   South elevation
   West elevation

In the first method, the right-end elevation is the elevation to the right of the front elevation as the front elevation is viewed from the outside. In the second method, the north elevation is the elevation that faces generally northward, but it does not have to face exactly north. When an interior elevation is designated as a north elevation, this means the *outside* of the wall faces north, and the *inside* wall faces south.

2. Windows and Doors. Most architectural features are too complicated to show in detail, and therefore certain

Figure 1. A front elevation provides the first indication of the character of a building.

simplifications and conventions are used. For example, windows and doors are considerably simplified. Figure 2 shows how a door and window would appear if drawn completely, but this type of representation is never used. Figure 3 shows standard representations, with lines only for the opening, trim, and panels. Notice that even the doorknob is omitted.

A further simplification is often used: one window on an elevation is detailed, and all similar windows are merely outlined by a rectangle, as shown in Figure 3. As a general rule, windows are installed with their tops aligned with the tops of exterior doors. This simplifies construction by allowing the builder to use one size header for all normal wall openings. A front door will usually be 3'- 0 by 6'- 8" (actual size of the door), and a rear door will be 2'- 8" by 6'- 8". A single garage door averages 9'- 0 wide by 7'- 0 high, and a double garage door 16'- 0 wide by 7'- 0 high. Window sizes are chosen from manufacturers' catalogs, which offer a great variety of sizes and types. This information can be found in the window and door schedules. Windows fall into the following general types:

· Fixed
· Double-hung (slides vertically)
· Sliding (slides horizontally)
· Awning (hinged at top and swings outward)
· Hopper (hinged at bottom and swings inward)
· Casement (hinged at side and usually swings outward)
· Pivoted (hinged at center, half swings outward and half inward)
· Jalousie (many individually hinged panes)

The dashed lines in Figure 4 indicate hinged windows. The hinge is located where the dashed lines meet. Also you may want to take note of the fenestration. The term *fenestration* deals with the arrangement of windows (and doors) in a wall. Satisfactory fenestration usually includes:

1. Windows arranged symmetrically in a symmetrical elevation (Figure 5), but off center in an asymmetrical elevation (Figure 6).
2. Windows lined up on different floors. This is important for both aesthetic and structural reasons (Figure 7).
3. Types and sizes of windows minimized (Figure 8).
4. Windows arranged in groupings (Figure 9).

See Chapters 13–15 for more information.

3. Materials Representation. Like windows and doors, materials are also represented by only a few lines. Brick, for example, is indicated by several horizontal lines spaced about 3" apart (to the proper scale) rather than showing each brick and mortar joint. However, bricks are shown when laid on edge for windowsills or window and door heads. Figure 10 shows the usual representation of brick, stone, concrete block, placed (poured) concrete, clapboards, and vertical siding. Roofs are usually left blank.

4. Footings and Areawalls. Hidden lines are used to indicate the location of footings, below-grade windows, and their areawalls. An areawall is a retaining wall that holds the earth back from a below-grade opening. Common materials used for areawalls are concrete, masonry, and corrugated

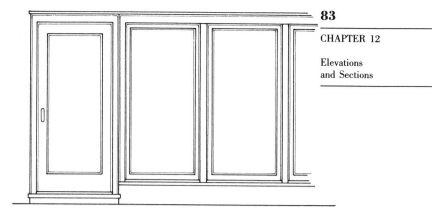

Figure 2. Actual representation (not used) of door and windows.

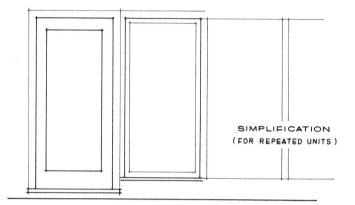

Figure 3. Standard representation of door and windows.

Figure 4. Representation of hinged windows.

sheets of galvanized iron. Take particular note of the hidden foundation and footing lines. Notice that the footing and the outside wall of the foundation are shown, but the basement floor and inside wall of the foundation are *not* shown. It is easy to read these lines: just imagine the ground has been removed and the draftsman has included only lines that you would see.

5. Dimensions. Elevation dimensions are limited mostly to vertical dimensions, since horizontal dimensions

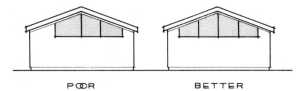

Figure 5. Symmetrical fenestration.

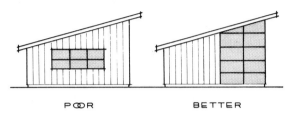

Figure 6. Asymmetrical fenestration.

Figure 7. Vertical alignment of windows.

Figure 8. Disorderly fenestration.

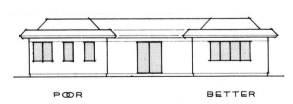

Figure 9. Orderly fenestration.

have already been shown on the floor plan. Elevation dimensions include:

a. Finished-floor-to-finished-floor heights, or finished-floor-to-finished-ceiling height for the topmost story
b. Height of roof
c. Depth of footings
d. Height of other features, such as a chimney or a masonry wall
e. Height of windows
f. Roof slope indication

Reading the A Residence Elevations

The front, rear, and end elevations of the A residence are shown in Figures 11–13. Study these elevations and coordinate them with the first-floor plan (Figure 13 in Chapter 9).

Notice that a lettered schedule mark is placed within a circle near each window. The window schedule for the A residence is near the left-end elevation.

Miscellaneous details in an elevation view vary depending on the design of the building. In the case of the A residence, find the following details:

1. Roof fascia and return
2. Roof louvers
3. Chimney and flashing
4. Lintels and drops
5. Entrance lighting fixtures
6. Weatherproof convenience outlets
7. Hose bibbs
8. Basement door areaway

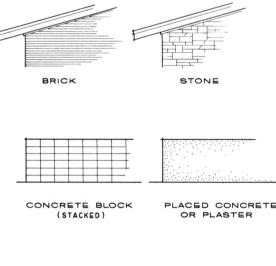

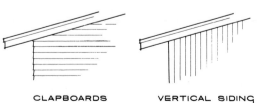

Figure 10. Representation of exterior materials.

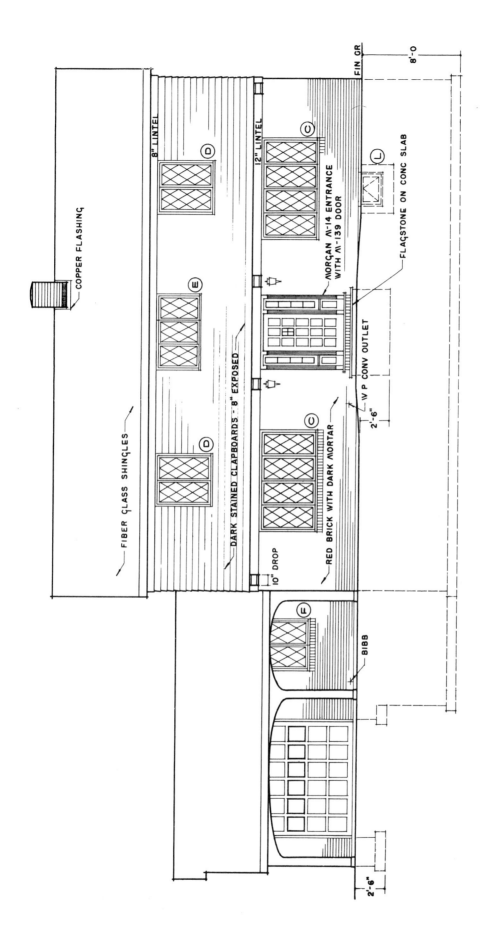

Figure 11. Front elevation of the A residence.

85

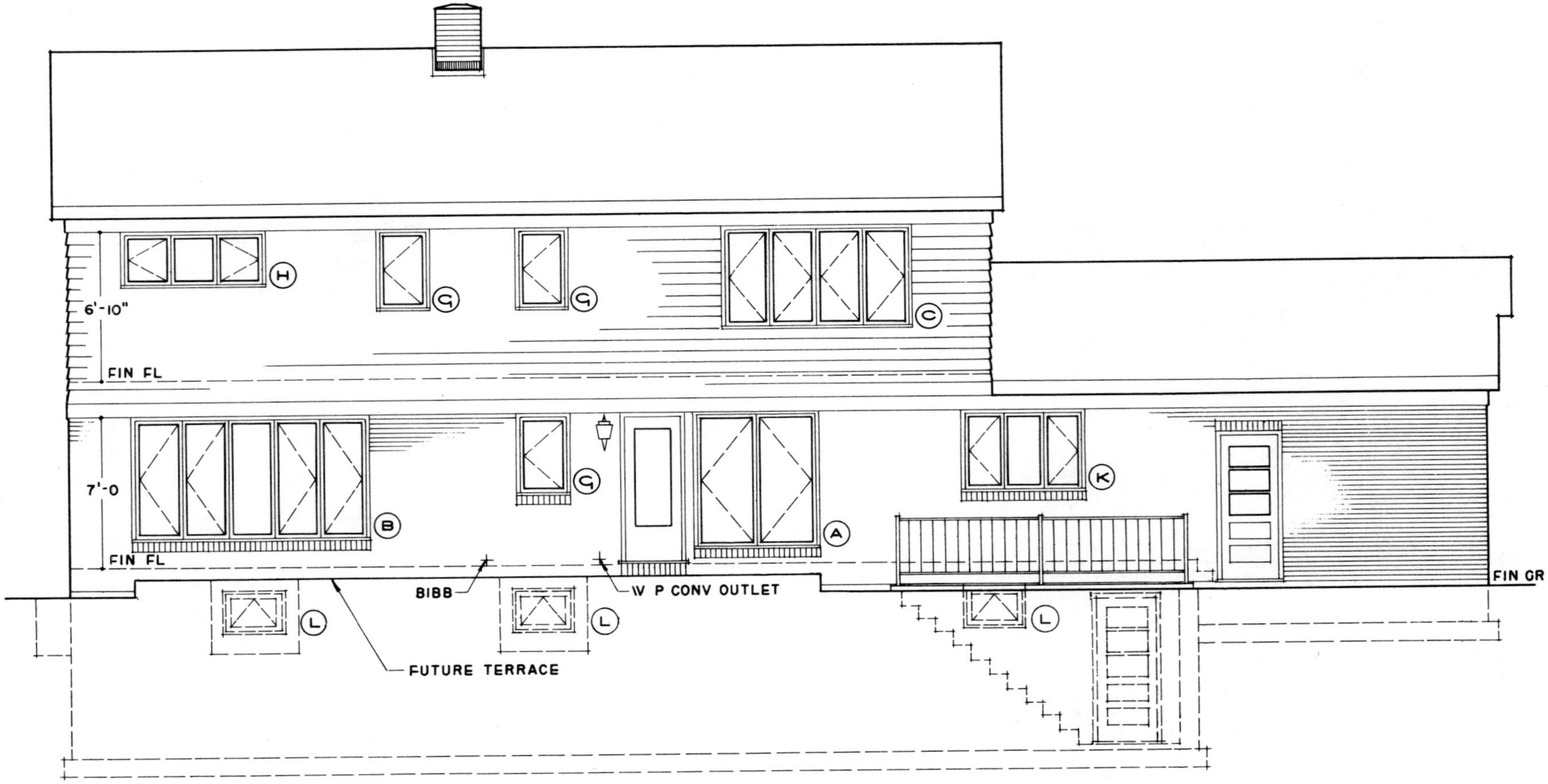

Figure 12. Rear elevation of the A residence.

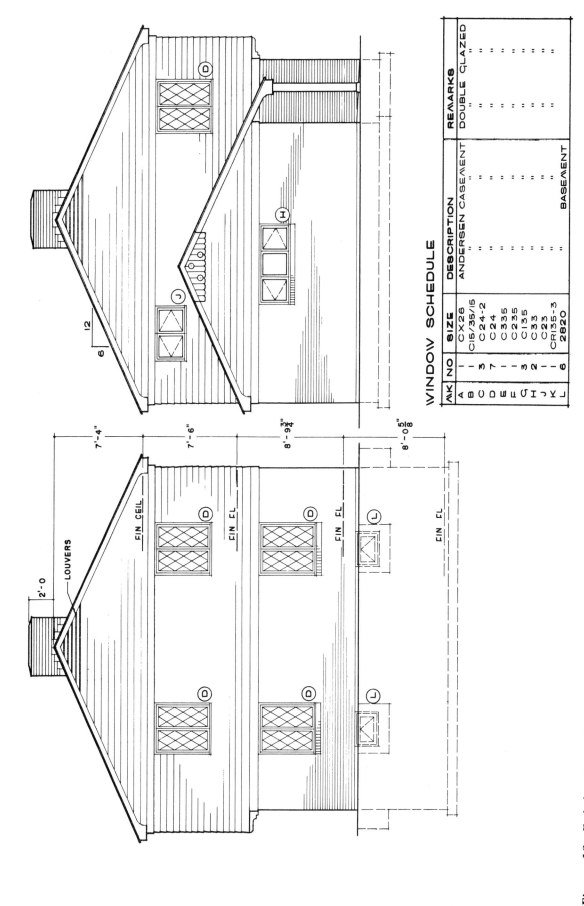

Figure 13. End elevation of the A residence.

87

Figure 14. Front view of the completed A residence, built with a double garage.

Figure 15. Patio view of the A residence.

See the abbreviations in Chapter 30 for the meaning of "CLG," "CONC," "CONV," "FIN," "FL," "GR," and "WP."

Photographs of the completed A residence are shown in Figures 14 and 15.

Reading the A Residence Interior Elevations

Interior elevations are included in a set of working drawings only when there is some special interior construction to be illustrated. This is often the case in kitchen design. Figure 16 shows the interior elevations of the kitchen of the A residence. Notice that the relation of each elevation to the plan is shown by sight arrows. A sight arrow shows the drawing number on which the detail appears. Sight arrows 1/7, 2/7, and so on are interpreted as detail #1 on drawing #7, detail #2 on drawing #7, and so on. When in doubt on how to read sight arrows, just check the legend on the cover sheet of the working drawings.

Reading Sections

Just as a floor plan is obtained by passing an imaginary horizontal cutting plane through the building, sections are obtained by passing imaginary vertical cutting planes through various parts of the building. A section through the entire building, such as in Figure 17, is a *structural section*. Structural sections are useful in showing the rigidity of framing, method of construction, and length of members. A $1/4'' = 1'$ scale is often used.

A section through just one wall of the building is a *wall section*. A wall section shows the construction of a typical wall to a larger scale than the structural section. A scale of $1\ 1/2'' = 1'$ is often used. Sizes and material specifications for both rough and finished members are shown.

Any special or unusual construction must be detailed. Sections through such special elements of the building are called *detailed sections*. These sections may be shown to a large scale—up to full size.

A complete set of working drawings contains one or more of each of these types of sectional views.

Reading the A Residence Sections

The structural section of the A residence is shown in Figure 18. Study this section until you understand the framework from foundation to roof. Notice that the basement girder is located directly under the first-floor bearing partition. Also notice that the $2'' \times 10''$ first-floor joists are reduced to $2'' \times 8''$ second-floor and ceiling joists which are further reduced to $2'' \times 6''$ roof rafters. The collar beams help prevent the rafters from bowing inward.

The wall section of the A residence is shown in Figure 19. This section is extremely important, for it shows clearly the construction of a typical exterior wall from footing to rafters. You should spend a good deal of time studying this section. Encircle or check with a red pencil all portions you don't understand. Then check with your instructor (or another student) at first opportunity so that you can completely understand this section.

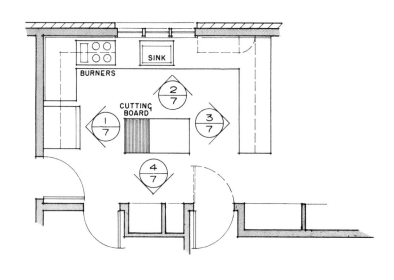

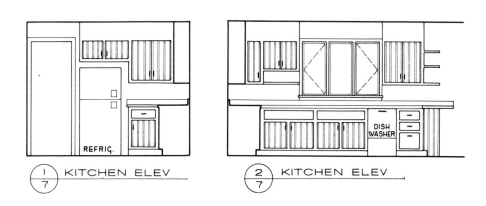

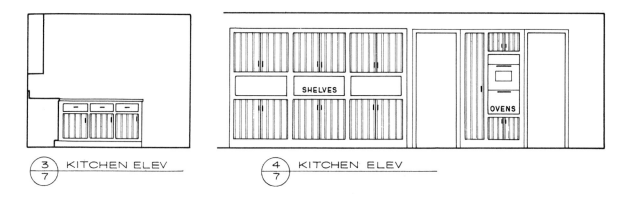

Figure 16. Interior elevations of the A residence kitchen.

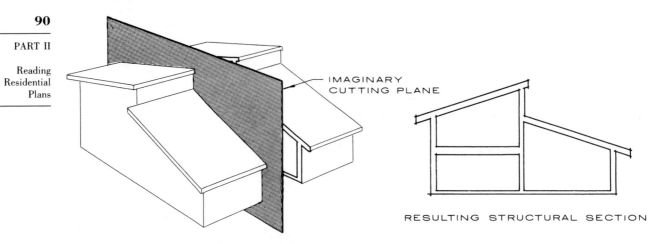

Figure 17. Imaginary cutting plane used to obtain a structural section.

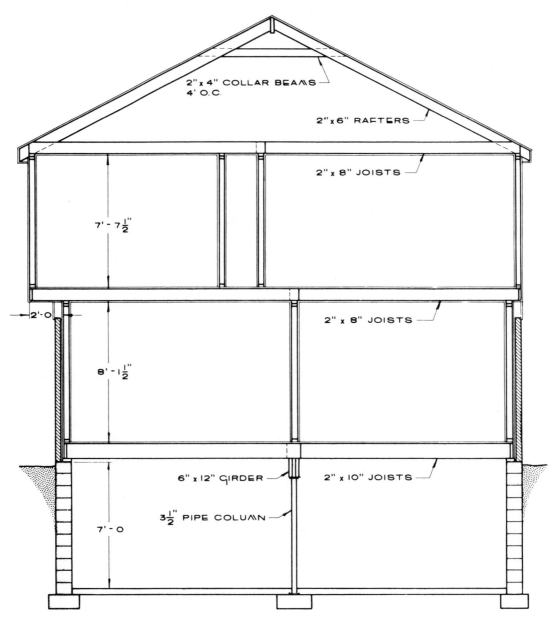

Figure 18. Structural section of the A residence.

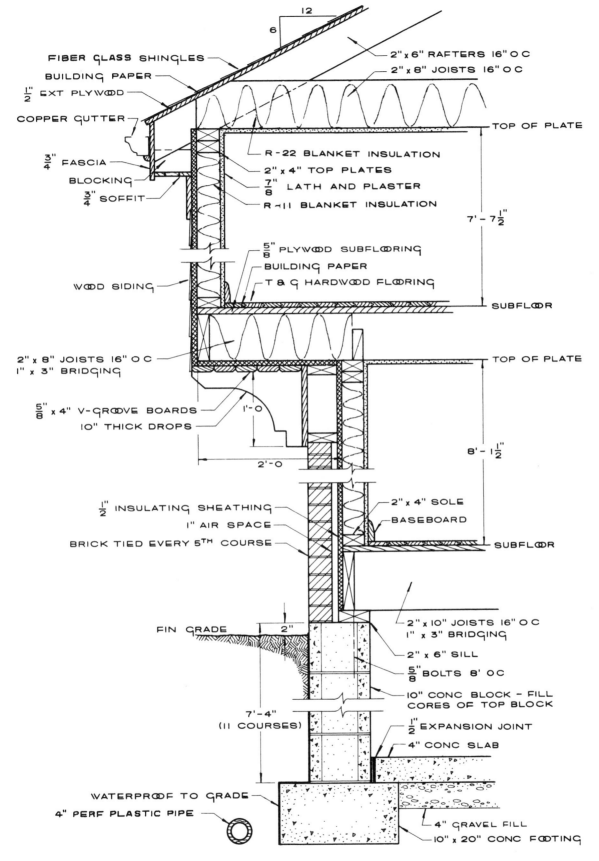

Figure 19. Typical wall section of the A residence.

13

Window Details

Many architects consider the window to be the most important single component in the successful design of a building. The proper selection and placement of windows is necessary for aesthetic as well as functional reasons. In addition to providing light and air, windows can change the interior of a room by providing framed views or window walls, and they can change the exterior of a building by the fenestration. For these reasons, then, window details are included in every set of architectural plans, and you should be able to read these details with confidence.

Types of Windows

There are many different types of windows now on the market. Some of the most commonly used are:

- Casement
- Awning
- Hopper
- Projected
- Sliding
- Double-hung
- Pivoted
- Jalousie
- Fixed

These windows can be obtained in many metals, wood, and clad wood (wood with a plastic or metal sheathing) in nearly any size ranging from small lavatory windows to entire window walls. Let us look at each in turn.

Casement. A casement window (Figure 1) is hinged at the side and usually swings outward so that the inside drapes are not disturbed. Screens therefore are hung on the inside. When more than two casement windows are installed side by side, it is often the practice to specify fixed sash for the middle windows, and a hinged sash at each end.

When the sash is hinged at the top, it is called an *awning* window (Figure 2); when the sash is hinged at the bottom, it is called a *hopper* window. To prevent rain from entering the open windows, awning windows swing outward, and hopper windows swing inward.

Projected. A projected window (Figure 3) is somewhat different from a casement window in that some form of link-

CASEMENT
SASH LOCK

CASEMENT
HINGES

Figure 1. Casement windows.

age other than the hinge is used. A projected window swings open and slides at the same time. Projected windows may also be classified as casement, awning, and hopper according to the direction of swing. Metal projected windows are commonly used on commercial buildings, and wooden casement (nonprojected) windows are commonly used on residences.

Sliding. Sliding or gliding windows (Figure 4) are designed to run on horizontal tracks in pairs. The tracks are curved so that the sash are in line when closed but will move past each other when opened. Most sliding windows contain sash that can be removed from the frame for easy cleaning. The screen is installed on the outside of the window.

Double-hung. The double-hung window (Figure 5) is usually specified for colonial-style houses. This window contains two sash that slide in vertical tracks. A spring-balance arrangement is used to counterbalance the weight of the sash and hold them in any desired position. The sash are easily removed for window cleaning. Double-hung windows may be obtained with self-storing screens and storm windows.

Pivoted. This window revolves on two pivots—one at the center of the top of the sash, and the other at the center of the bottom of the sash. Not often specified for houses, the pivoted window is common in taller buildings because of its ease of cleaning.

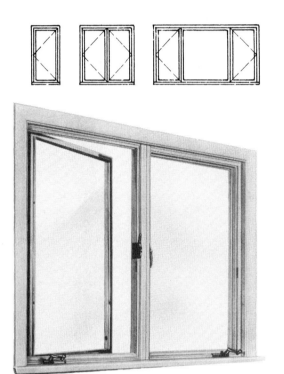

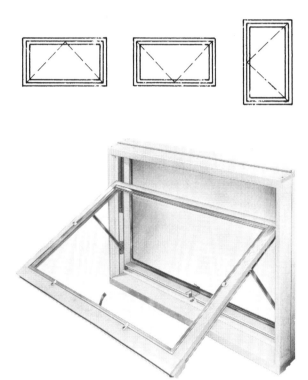

Figure 1. continued

Figure 2. A window arrangement of fixed and awning units.

Figure 3. Projected windows.

Jalousie. The jalousie window is a series of small awning panes all operated together. It has not become very popular because the view through it is interrupted by the many intersections.

Fixed. When views and light are desired without ventilation (as is often true of air-conditioned buildings), fixed windows are specified. Large fixed windows are sometimes called *picture windows*. Some fixed windows are designed so that they can be opened only by window washers for cleaning. Fixed windows are stocked in both rectangular and trapezoidal shapes (Figure 6).

Basement Windows. The most often specified basement window is a reversible awning-hopper window (Figure 7). The sash is designed so that it can be easily removed from

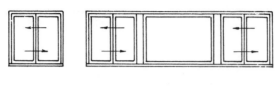

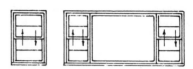

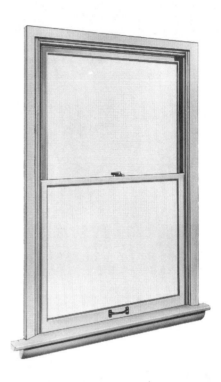

Figure 4. Sliding windows.

Figure 5. Double-hung windows.

the frame and installed to swing up (awning) or down (hopper). In both cases, the swing is toward the inside. Since a basement window is installed at the inner side of the foundation wall, there is no danger of rain entering. The screen is installed on the outside of the frame.

Installation

Before studying specifications and the detailing of windows, it is necessary to understand how a window is installed in a building wall (Figure 9). The glass and its immediate framing members are called the *sash*. Except in fixed windows, the sash is designed to be opened for ventilation or entirely removed for easy cleaning. The sash is surrounded by the *window frame*, which is permanently fastened to the rough wall (studs). The window frame has an L-shaped cross section, the outer portion of which is called the *blind stop*. The blind stop helps to properly position the frame in the rough opening.

Stock windows are obtained with the sash already installed in the frame so that the entire window unit can be set into the rough opening. The rough opening is constructed several inches larger than the window frame to allow for leveling the window. After the window is in place, exterior and interior trim are used to close the cracks between the frame and the rough opening.

Terminology

Many special terms are used to describe the various parts of a window. Figure 8 shows a cutaway pictorial of a double-hung window and the corresponding sectional details. The terms *head*, *jamb*, *rail*, and *sill* indicate that the sectional cuts were taken through the head (the upper horizontal members), jamb (side vertical members), meeting rail (middle horizontal members), and sill (lower horizontal members).

Sash. The members of the upper sash are called *top rail*, *meeting rail*, and *side rails*. The lower sash members are called *meeting rail*, *bottom rail*, and *side rails*.

Window Frame. The members of the window frame are called *top jamb*, *side jamb*, and *blind stop* (or *windbreaker*).

Interior Trim. The interior trim and apron cover the crack between the window frame and the interior finished wall.

Exterior Casing. The exterior casing (which may be called *trim*) also covers wall cracks. In addition, it serves as the frame around the *storm sash or screens*.

Drip Cap. The drip cap prevents water from seeping into the window head. Note the *drip groove* on the underside to prevent water from seeping inward underneath the drip cap. *Flashing* can be used in place of the wooden drip cap.

Double Glazing. A second glass pane may be installed in the sash, creating a dead air space to provide insulation and prevent condensation on the inside pane. In addition, the outside pane can be manufactured with a microthin transparent coating, called *low-E glass*, which reflects outside heat in summer and inside heat in winter.

Mullions and Muntins. See Figure 10. Mullions are members (usually vertical) that separate adjacent windows.

Figure 6. Trapezoidal fixed window units.

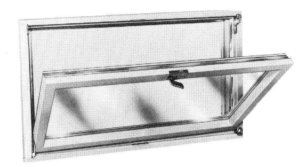

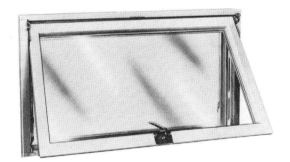

Figure 7. Basement windows.

Muntins are smaller members used to subdivide large glass areas. Many manufacturers offer removable muntins so that the windows may be subdivided to any taste. Also, these muntins may be removed for easy cleaning.

Reading Window Details

The window detail in Figure 8 is typical of the window details found on most architectural drawings, so you should study it until you have a clear picture of the window construction and installation. If you have any questions, check with your instructor at the first opportunity.

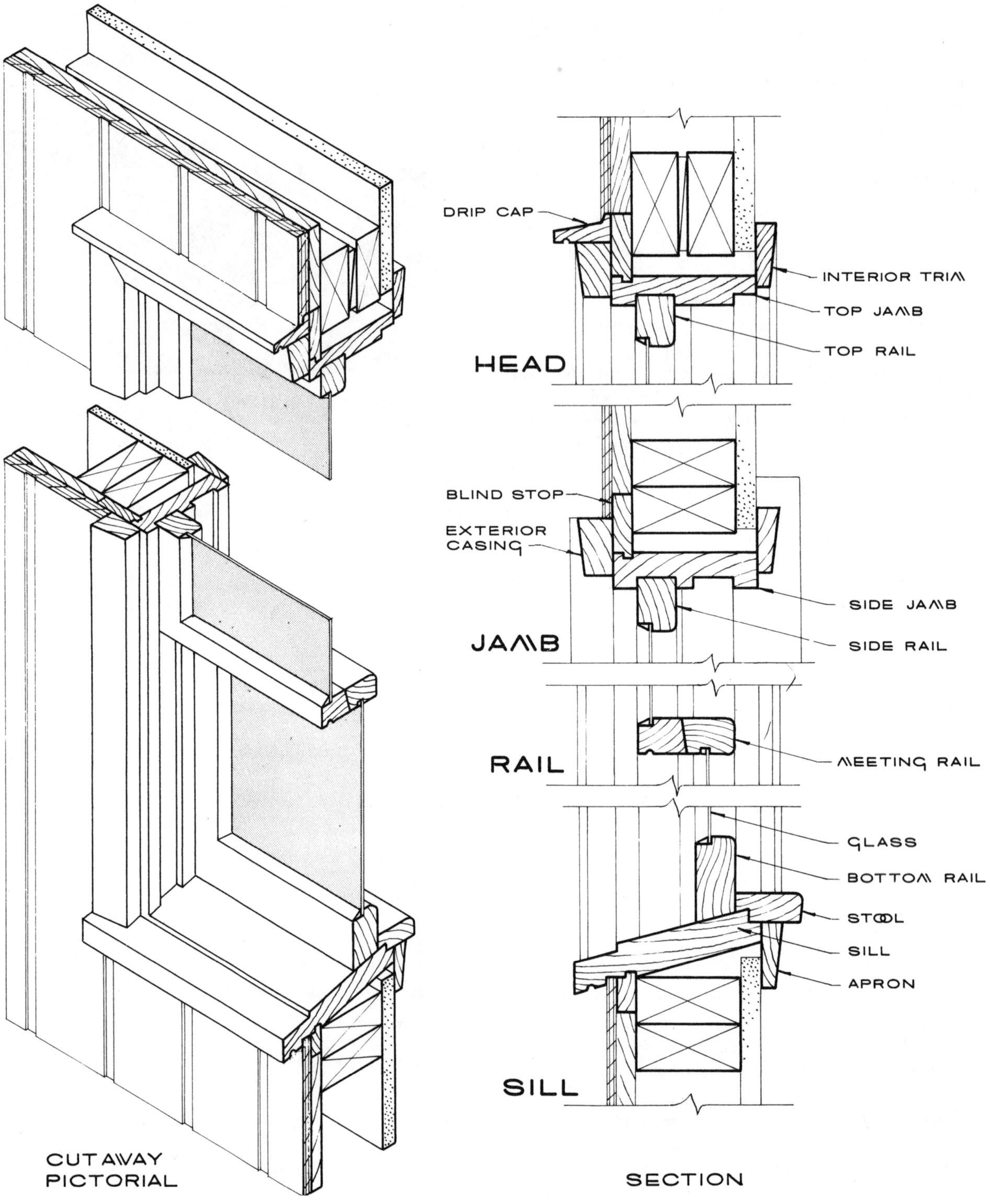

DRIP CAP

INTERIOR TRIM

TOP JAMB

TOP RAIL

HEAD

BLIND STOP

EXTERIOR
CASING

SIDE JAMB

SIDE RAIL

JAMB

RAIL

MEETING RAIL

GLASS

BOTTOM RAIL

STOOL

SILL

APRON

SILL

**CUTAWAY
PICTORIAL**

SECTION

Figure 8. Double-hung window in a wood frame wall.

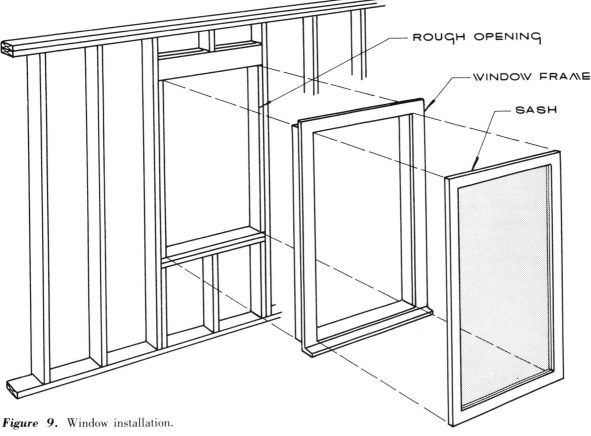

Figure 9. Window installation.

Reading Window Specifications

Each manufacturer has its own set of window sizes and catalog numbers. To simplify window specifications, tables showing these sizes and numbers may be obtained from the

manufacturers. A table for Andersen casement windows is shown in Figure 12. Six window heights are obtainable, each height recommended for a different condition. Table I and

Table I. Andersen casement window catalog numbers

Andersen Catalog Number	Rough Open Height	Recommended for
2	2'- 0 5/8″	Extreme privacy
3	3'- 0 1/2″	Lavatory, bedroom
35	3'- 5 3/8″	Kitchen
4	4'- 0 1/2″	Dining area
5	5'- 0 3/8″	Living area
6	6'- 0 3/8″	Solar wall

Andersen Catalog Number	Rough Open Width	Preferred for
CR	1'- 5 1/2″	Emphasis on vertical lines
CN	1'- 9″	General applications
C	2'- 0 5/8″	General applications
CW	2'- 4 7/8″	Wider uninterrupted view

Andersen Catalog Number	Muntins	Preferred for
N	None	Modern
H	Horizontal	Modern
D	Divided (both directions)	Traditional

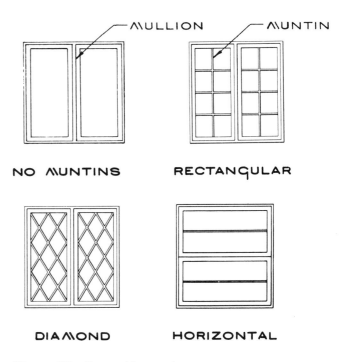

Figure 10. Removable muntins.

Figure 11 show how these different window sizes will fit into different types of rooms.

Manufacturers do not offer a large variety of window widths, since wide windows are obtained by specifying a number of individual units that are installed side by side. Andersen casements may be obtained in only four widths,

but in multiple sash units and with different muntin arrangements. For example, the Andersen catalog number CW4H35 indicates a *wide casement* of *four* sash units, *horizontal* muntins, and a *# 35* height of 3'-5 3/8". As previously suggested, make a copy of any questions and get clarification from your instructor.

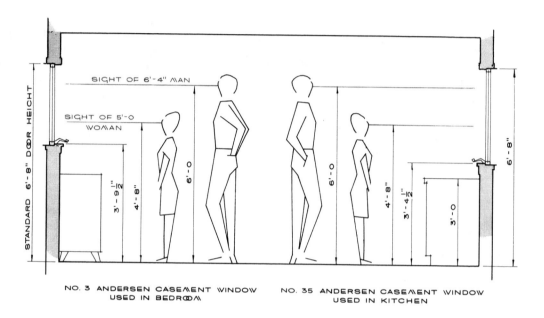

NO. 3 ANDERSEN CASEMENT WINDOW
USED IN BEDROOM

NO. 35 ANDERSEN CASEMENT WINDOW
USED IN KITCHEN

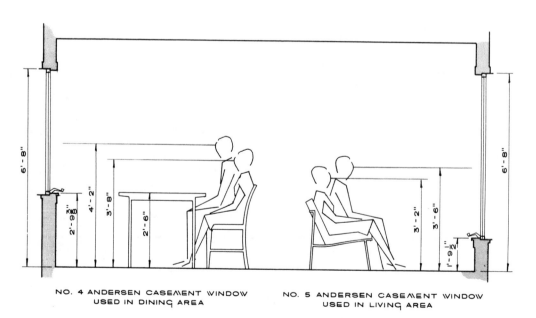

NO. 4 ANDERSEN CASEMENT WINDOW
USED IN DINING AREA

NO. 5 ANDERSEN CASEMENT WINDOW
USED IN LIVING AREA

Figure 11. Selection of window height.

NOTES

For tracing purposes we show layout with divided light sash. Omit the bars if one light sash are desired.

The first number under each unit identifies one light sash, second number identifies horizontal light sash, and the last number is for divided light sash.

All divided light sash have 8 x 12 glass, and horizontal light sash have 16-1/4 x 12 glass, except the 2-8 3/16 high sash which have 10 inch high lights.

Standard one light sash are glazed at the factory with DS glass or furnished open for glazing by others. Sash will take any type of glass up to 1/8" thick.

Sash can also be furnished with Welded Insulating Glass and on special order open for glazing by others with obscure glass, leaded glass or other special glass up to 1/2" thick.

Sash may be operating or stationary. Specify number of operating sash in each unit and how hinged as viewed from outside.

Sash opening widths are from inside face of jamb to inside face of jamb and include 1-3/4 inch mullion posts for multiple openings.

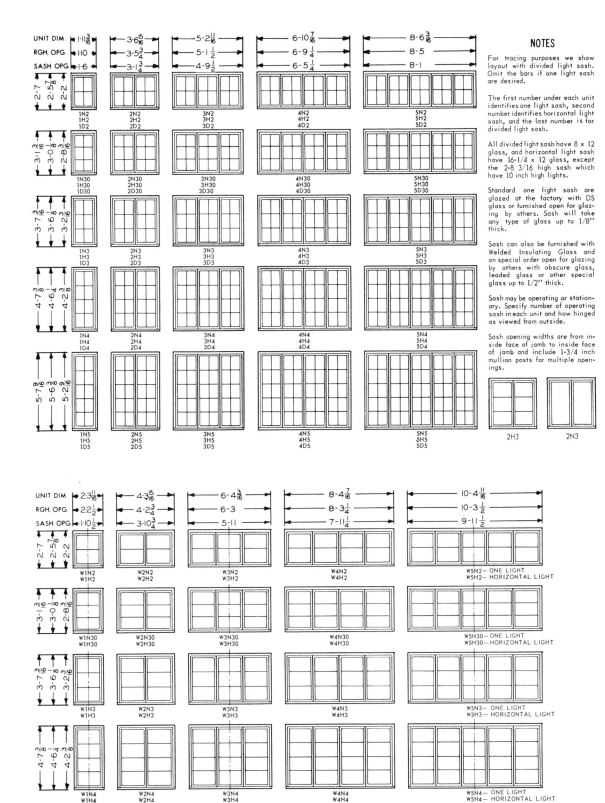

Figure 12. Andersen casement window—table of sizes.

14

Door Details

Doors, like windows, are considered to be important components in the design of a successful building. The main entrance door is particularly important since it will be the first detail experienced by visitors. The other doors are also carefully chosen; a building can be no better than its details. In many ways, reading door details is similar to reading window details.

Types of Doors

Doors are available in a wide range of types and materials. Residential doors most commonly used are *hinged*, *sliding*, *folding*, and *accordion*. These doors may be obtained in single and double units. Wood is usually used, but metal and glass doors are also popular.

Hinged. Hinged doors (Figure 1) may be flush, paneled, or louvered. The *flush door* is most popular due to

Figure 1. An office building entranceway with double glass doors.

its clean lines and low cost. It may be either *solid-core* or *hollow-core*. The solid-core flush door is constructed of solid wood covered with wood veneer and is preferred for exterior doors. The hollow-core flush door has an interior of honeycombed wood strips also covered by veneer. The most popular are mahogany and birch.

Paneled doors consist of ponderosa pine members framing wood or glass panels. The framing members are called *top rail*, *bottom rail*, and *side rails*. The midheight rail is called a *lock rail*.

Louvered doors are constructed like paneled doors, but with louvers replacing the panels. They are often used as closet doors to permit air circulation.

Hinged doors may be installed as a *double unit* (two doors, one hung on the right jamb, the other on the left) to allow a larger and more dramatic passageway. Hinged double doors with glass panels are called *French doors*. A *Dutch door*, on the other hand, is a single door that has been cut in half so that the top half can be opened for light and air without opening the bottom half. Simulated Dutch doors, which open like ordinary doors, are specified to give the appearance of a Dutch door without the function. A door hung on special hinges that permit it to swing in both directions is called a *swinging door* and is often used between kitchen and dining area to permit operation by a simple push.

Sliding. Sliding doors are used to save the floor space that is required for hinged doors. They are especially useful in small rooms. Sliding doors are hung from a metal track screwed into the door frame head. A single sliding door slides into a pocket built into the wall. Double sliding doors are usually installed so that one door slides in front of the other. This has the disadvantage of opening up only one half of the doorway space at a time. Exterior sliding doors of glass (Figure 2) serve the double purpose of a doorway and window wall.

Folding. A folding door is partially a hinged and partially a sliding door. Two leaves are hinged together, one being also hinged to the doorjamb. The other leaf has a single hanger sliding in a track. Although some floor space is

Figure 2. A window wall of sliding glass doors.

Figure 3. An accordion partition.

required for the folding door, it has the advantage of completely opening up the doorway space. Single (total of two leaves) and double (total of four leaves) units are available.

Accordion. A door that operates on the principle of the folding door, but that contains many narrow leaves, is called an accordion door. These leaves may be made of hinged wood or a flexible plastic material. Accordion or folding partitions are used to provide an entire movable wall between rooms. The folds of the retracted partition may be left exposed or hidden by a wall pocket (Figure 3).

Materials

In addition to wood doors, metal-clad wood doors (called *kalamein doors*) or hollow metal doors are used for fireproofing and strength. Metal door frames (called *door bucks*) are also available. Even all-glass doors are used. Bronze, aluminum, and glass doors are commonly used for public buildings, but wood remains the most popular choice for residential construction. Figure 4 shows how a door frame fits into the rough opening in the same way a window is installed. The door, in turn, fits into the door frame.

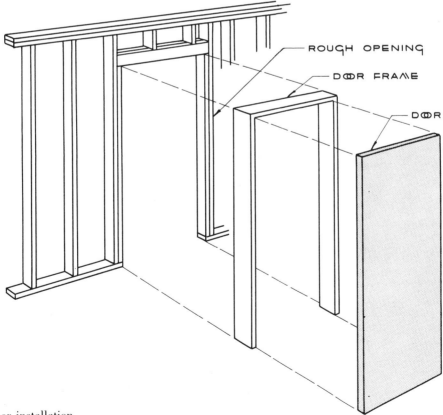

Figure 4. Door installation.

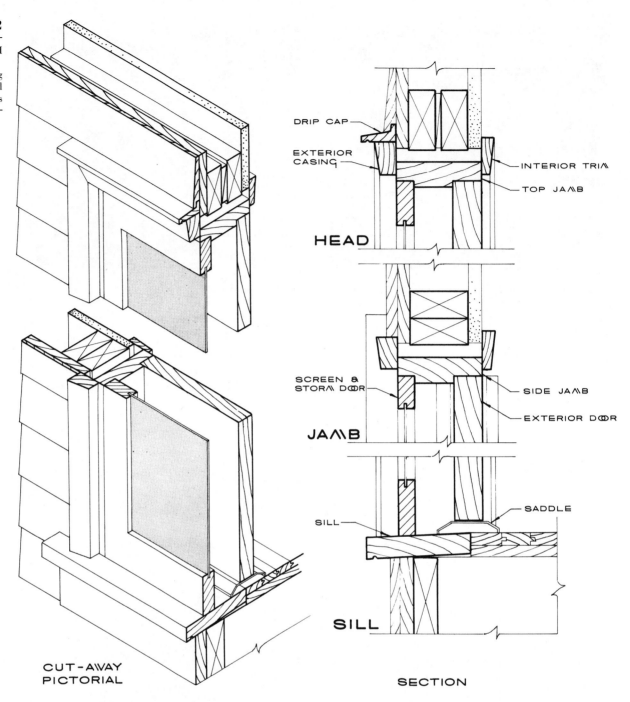

CUT-AWAY
PICTORIAL

DRIP CAP

EXTERIOR
CASING

INTERIOR TRIM

TOP JAMB

HEAD

SCREEN &
STORM DOOR

SIDE JAMB

EXTERIOR DOOR

JAMB

SILL

SADDLE

SILL

SECTION

Figure 5. An exterior door in a wood frame wall.

Terminology

Figure 5 shows a cutaway pictorial of a hinged exterior door, and the corresponding sectional details. Figure 6 shows the pictorial and details of a sliding interior door. Notice that a saddle is used to weatherproof the exterior door, but such protection is not necessary for the interior door. Carefully study both these details. Make a note of any questions you might have and check those questions with your instructor at the first opportunity.

Reading Door Details

As with windows, manufacturers supply *tracing details* for the convenience of architectural drafters. These tracing details are slipped under the tracing vellum and all applicable details are copied. Tracing details for a Morgan entrance are shown in Figure 7. These details are typical of the door details found on most architectural drawings, and so you should study them to obtain a clear understanding of door construction and installation.

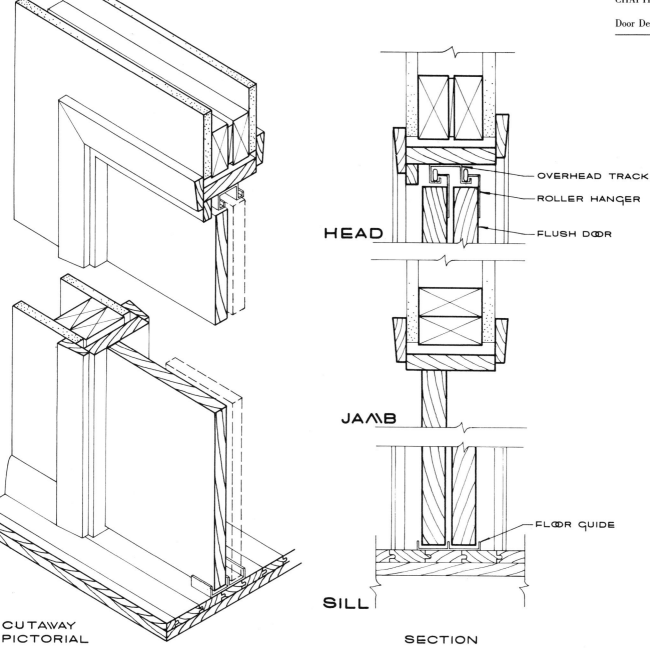

HEAD

—— OVERHEAD TRACK

—— ROLLER HANGER

—— FLUSH DOOR

JAMB

—— FLOOR GUIDE

SILL

CUTAWAY
PICTORIAL

SECTION

Figure 6. A double sliding door in an interior wall.

Reading Door Specifications

The type of door specified for each location is determined by functional and aesthetic considerations. Tables in manufacturers' catalogs are consulted for available styles and sizes. In general, exterior doors are 1 3/4″ thick and interior doors are 1 3/8″ thick. Widths from 2′- 0 to 3′- 0 in even inches are available, although some manufacturers offer doors as narrow as 1′- 6″ and as wide as 4′- 0. Residential doors are obtainable in 6′- 6″ to 7′- 0 heights in even inches. The most popular height is 6′- 8″. Typical residential door sizes for interior and exterior doors are:

· Interior doors: 2′- 6″ × 6′- 8″ × 1 3/8″
· Front entrance door: 3′- 0 × 6′- 8″ × 1 3/4″
· Other entrance doors: 2′- 8″ × 6′- 8″ × 1 3/4″

The rough opening must be considerably larger than the door sizes. The frame for a 3′- 0 × 6′- 8″ door, for instance, would require a 3′- 2 3/4″ × 6′- 11″ (top of subfloor to bottom of header) rough opening.

DIMENSIONS	6'-8" DOORS	7'-0" DOORS
Rough Opening	4'-11⅝" x 6'-11"	4'-11⅝" x 7'-3"
Width at Casing	5'-3⅛"	5'-3⅛"
Height (overall)	7'-1⅜"	7'-5⅜"
Sidelight	1'-6" x 6'-8"	1'-6" x 7'-0"

Rough opening height is taken from top of rough floor.

When Entrance is used with brick veneer or masonry walls we recommend that the entrance is set flush with plaster line on the inside for reveal on outside.

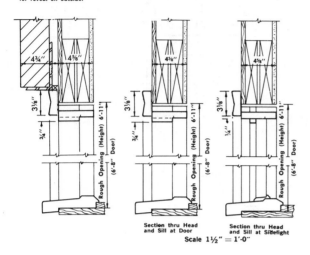

Section thru Head and Sill at Door
Section thru Head and Sill at Sidelight
Scale 1½" = 1'-0"

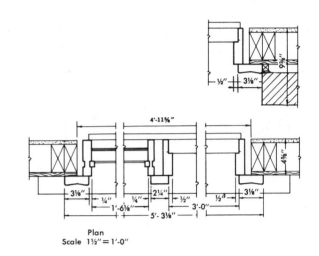

Plan
Scale 1½" = 1'-0"

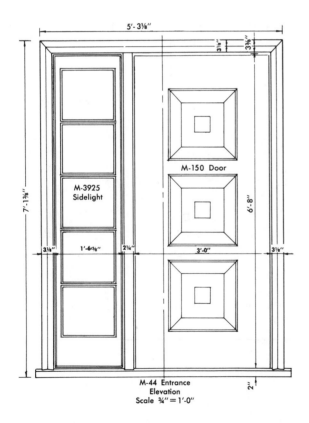

M-3925 Sidelight
M-150 Door
M-44 Entrance Elevation
Scale ¾" = 1'-0"

Figure 7. A Morgan contemporary entrance—details and sizes.

Figure 8. Double-width garage door (courtesy of Scholz Homes, Inc.).

Hardware. The hardware for doors is specified by indicating the desired manufacturer and catalog number in a hardware schedule. Some of the many hardware items are door butts (hinges), lock sets, doorstops, door checks (for public buildings), and cabinet hinges, handles, and catches.

Garage Doors. Most residential garage doors are of the overhead type (Figure 8). An overhead door is composed of several hinged sections that roll up to the ceiling on tracks. Adjustable springs are used to counterbalance the weight of the door. Headroom in the range of 3″–13 1/2″ (depending on the hardware type and door size) is required above the bottom of the header. Remote-controlled motors may be specified to operate garage doors.

Residential garage doors are usually stocked in 6′- 6″ and 7′- 0 heights by 1 3/8″ thick. Common widths for single doors are 8′-0 and 9′-0; double doors are 16′-0 to 18′-0 wide.

In addition to wood, garage doors may be obtained in aluminum and fiberglass in the same range of sizes. Fiberglass doors are also available in 18′- 0 widths. Common sizes for residential and commercial garage doors are given in Figure 9.

Air Doors. The air door (also called *air curtain*) is advantageous for commercial buildings because it invites prospective customers to enter. The air door is simply a downward air flow which serves to retard the passage of heat, cold, insects, and dirt. A "curtain" of moving air is blown down through a ceiling grating located above the entrance. The air is drawn in through a floor grating located directly below the ceiling grating. Before being heated and recirculated, it is filtered to remove dust. Air door details and specifications are usually included with the plans for heating and air conditioning.

RESIDENTIAL GARAGE DOOR
AVAILABLE FROM 8′-0″ x 6′-6″ TO 18′ x 7′

COMMERCIAL GARAGE DOOR
AVAILABLE TO 20′ x 16′

Figure 9. Garage door sizes.

15

Schedules

A building is composed of a tremendous number of parts. In fact, if all these parts were indicated on the plans, the plans would be so crowded they would not be readable. Therefore the designer includes much information in schedules on the working drawings or in the written specifications (see Chapter 31 for a discussion of specifications writing).

Door and Window Schedules

Figures 1 and 2 show typical layouts for door and window schedules. Although this information may be included on the drawings in the form of notes, it is usually considered better

practice to use schedules and keep the actual plans and elevations uncluttered. Of course, a reference mark or symbol is placed on each door in the plan and each window in the elevations. These marks are repeated in the door and window schedules with all the necessary sizes and information. A numeral is used for doors and most other scheduled items, but a letter is used for windows. A different mark is used for different sizes or types of doors and windows, but the same mark is used for similar doors and windows. Such marks are enclosed in circles, which are about 1/4″ in diameter. The usual place for the door schedule is near the floor plan, and the window schedule is often found near the elevations. Or you may find all schedules grouped on one separate sheet.

DOOR SCHEDULE

MK	NO.	SIZE	ROUGH OPENING	DESCRIPTION	REMARKS
1	1	3'-0 x 6'-8" x 1¾"	3'-2¾" x 6'-11"	14 PANEL WP, 4 LTS	
2	1	2'-8"x6'-8"x1¾"	2'-10¾" x 6'-11"	FLUSH WP, 1 LT	
3	2	2'-8"x6'-8"x1¾"	2'-10¾" x 6'-11"	2 PANEL WP, 3 LTS	
4	10	2'-6"x6'-8"x1⅜"	2'-8¾" x 6'-11"	FLUSH BIRCH	
5					
6					

Figure 1. A door schedule.

WINDOW SCHEDULE

MK	NO.	SIZE	ROUGH OPENING	DESCRIPTION	REMARKS
A	1	G65	6'-0½" x 5'-0½"	ANDERSEN GLIDING	DOUBLE GLAZED
B	1	C24-2	8'-0⅝" x 4'-0½"	" CASEMENT	" "
C	3	C23	4'-0½" x 3'-0½"	" "	" "
D					
E					

Figure 2. A window schedule.

Additional Schedules

In addition to doors and windows, other materials may be specified by the use of schedules. Figures 3–7 show the outlines of some other commonly used schedules. The plans for a large, well-detailed building might contain many other types of schedules in addition to those illustrated.

Customs and Rules of Schedules

Rather than taking the time to letter the same words many times over, the ditto mark (as in Figure 2) is used, or the note "DO" (short for *ditto*, as in Figures 6 and 7).

Abbreviations are often used to reduce the size of the schedule. Standard abbreviations are used and are listed in a table of abbreviations on the drawings. The abbreviations used on Figures 1–7 are as follows. For a more extensive list of commonly used abbreviations, see Chapter 30.

- CL   closet
- ELEV   elevation
- FIN   finish
- S   S shape beam
- LAV   lavatory
- LT   light (window glass)
- MK   mark
- NO.   number
- REINF   reinforce
- T&G   tongue-and-groove
- WP   white pine
- W/   with
- L   angle
- #   pounds or number

When spaces on the schedule do not apply to a material, they are left blank (as in the Figure 1 remarks column) or filled with a strike line (as in the Figure 6 ceiling finish column).

The desired manufacturer of a product may be specified (as in Figure 2, Andersen windows) or merely given as an example of an acceptable product (as in Figure 7, Pass & Seymour electric fixtures).

COLUMN AND BEAM SCHEDULE

MK	NO.	DESCRIPTION	LENGTH	REMARKS
1	4	3½" STEEL PIPE COLUMN W/PLATES	7'-0	
2	1	S 7 × 15.3 FLOOR GIRDER	42'-0	
3				
4				

Figure 3. A column and beam schedule.

LINTEL SCHEDULE

MK	NO.	DESCRIPTION	LENGTH	REMARKS
1	6	L 5 × 3½ × ⅜	4'-8"	
2				
3				

Figure 4. A lintel schedule.

FOOTING SCHEDULE

MK	A	B	C	ELEV	REINF	REMARKS
1	8"	1'-4"	8"	93.4'	2 #4	
2	10"	1'-6"	8"	93.4'	2 #4	
3	8"	1'-4"	8"	97.4'	NONE	
4						

Figure 5. A footing schedule.

FINISH SCHEDULE

MK	ROOM	FLOOR	FIN	WALL	FIN	CEILING	FIN	TRIM	FIN
1	LIVING ROOM	T&G OAK	VARN-ISH	SHEET ROCK	PAINT	ACOUST. TILE	—	PINE	PAINT
2	LAV	ASPHALT TILE	—	CERAMIC TILE	—	SAND PLASTER	—	DO	DO
2A	LAV CL	DO	—	SAND PLASTER	—	DO	—	DO	DO
3									
4									

Figure 6. A room finish schedule.

ELECTRICAL SCHEDULE

LOCATION	SYMBOL	NO.	WATT	DESIGNATION	EXAMPLE
GARAGE	⊕ / O_A	2 / 2	100 / 100	DUPLEX OUTLET / CEILING MOUNT	PASS & SEYMOUR #41
LIVING ROOM	⊕ / O_B / O_C	6 / 1 / 12	100 / 100 / 60	DUPLEX OUTLET / WALL MOUNT / WALL VALANCE	GENERAL #1606 / PASS & SEYMOUR #41
KITCHEN	⊕ / O_D / O_E	4 / 1 / 1	100 / 100 / 100	DUPLEX OUTLET / FLUSH CEILING / DO	HOLOPHANE #RL-732 / DO #RL-796
BEDROOM					

Figure 7. An electrical schedule.

16

Stair Details

Stairways often require special planning by the architect and special construction by the builder. Consequently, nearly every set of working plans contains some stair details. Complete stair details include a section or elevation of each stairway together with partial or complete plan views. Details of tread construction and handrail construction may also be included.

Types of Stairways

Common types of stairs are illustrated in Figure 1. *Straight run stairs* take up the least amount of floor area and are the simplest to construct. However, some designs require a stair to turn or to be shorter in length than a straight run stair. In these cases, the designer specifies a *U-type* or *L-type* stair with a platform at the turn. The platform has the advantage of breaking up a long run of stairs and providing a place to pause and rest.

When space is restricted, diagonal steps called *winders* are used in place of the platform. Winders are designed so that the same tread depth is maintained at the normal path of travel: 18″ from the inside corner. Since the tread depth is reduced inside the normal path of travel, winders are dangerous and are used only as a last resort. *Spiral stairs* may be

obtained in packaged units and satisfy unique design requirements.

Moving stairs (*escalators*, Figure 4) are specified for heavy traffic in buildings such as department stores of two to six floors. Standard escalator widths are 32″ and 48″, and the standard angle of incline is 30°. The capacity of a 48″-wide moving stair is 8,000 persons/hr. at a speed of 1 mi./hr. Moving stairs are not acceptable as fire exits.

Moving passenger belts are also available for long horizontal distances such as found in airport terminals and arenas. The belt speed remains at 1 or 2 mi./hr., but belts with speeds up to 10 mi./hr. have been developed which operate with the aid of an accelerator at entrances and a decelerator at exits. The accelerator is composed of a number of linked platforms which slowly accelerate to the speed of the belt. Belts can be used for slight inclines, to 11° maximum.

Terms

Terms generally used in stairway construction are illustrated in Figure 5.

Step, or *riser*, is the vertical distance from one tread top to another.

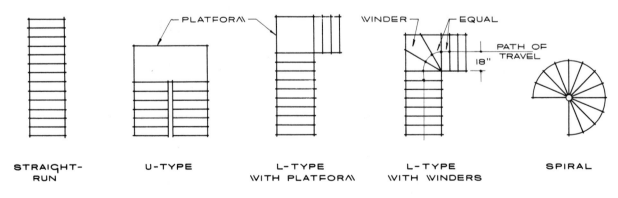

| STRAIGHT-RUN | U-TYPE | L-TYPE WITH PLATFORM | L-TYPE WITH WINDERS | SPIRAL |

Figure 1. Stair types.

Figure 2. Stair treads cantilevered from a central support.

Figure 3. A large-radius spiral stairway.

Tread, or *run*, is the horizontal distance from the face of one riser to the next. Notice that there will always be one fewer tread than riser.

Total rise is the vertical distance from one finished floor to the next.

Total run is the horizontal distance of the entire stairway.

Headroom is the vertical distance from the outside edge of the step to the ceiling above.

Stringer is the side of a flight of stairs; the supporting member cut to receive the treads and risers.

Nosing is the projection of the tread beyond the riser. It is about 1 1/8", as shown in Figures 6–8.

Figure 4. Moving stairs in the U.S. Steel Building, Pittsburgh.

Stairway Construction

Stairs are built with *closed risers* (Figure 6) or *open risers* (Figure 7). (Be careful not to confuse these terms with *closed stringers* and *open stringers*.) The closed risers of Figure 6 are shown joined to the treads with tongue-and-groove joints. Butt joints are used in more economical construction.

Closed stringers (Figure 9) are slightly different from open stringers in that no triangular pieces are cut from the closed stringer. Rather, 1/2" grooves are routed to receive the treads and risers which are wedged and glued in place. This completely conceals their ends. Open stringers are constructed of 2" × 12" members. Incidentally, the triangular pieces cut from this 2" × 12" are often nailed to a 2" × 4" serving as a middle stringer for extra support.

Prefabricated stairways are becoming increasingly popular. A stairway assembly entirely of metal is usually fabricated at the factory and then delivered as a completed unit to the construction site.

Handrails are an important safety requirement whenever stairs are built. Several modern handrails are shown in Figure 10, and a traditional handrail is shown in Figure 13. Stock

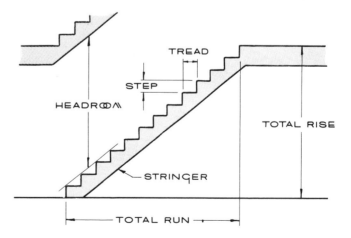

Figure 5. Stairway terminology.

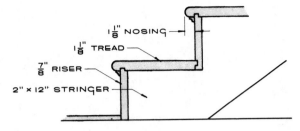

Figure 6. Closed-riser stair.

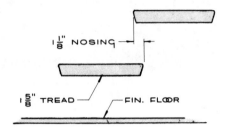

Figure 7. Open-riser stair.

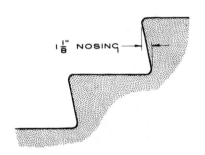

Figure 8. Concrete stair.

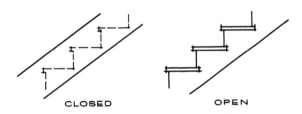

Figure 9. Stringer types.

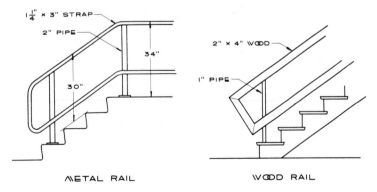

Figure 10. Handrails.

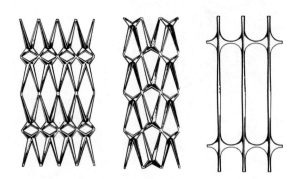

Figure 11. Use of treillage.

components are usually used for railings in commercial buildings.

Balcony railings and retaining walls require special attention to safety considerations. The national standard requires a minimum height of 3'-6" because that height is above the center of gravity of even a tall person. Railing bars should be less than 5" apart to prevent children from squeezing through. Most standards presently require that railings be strong enough to withstand at least 200 pounds of impact pressure, but much greater strength than that is advisable.

An architectural screen or lattice work is called treillage.[1] Treillage is used for building facing, partitions, room dividers, privacy fences, or for concealing unsightly elements. Stock components are available in many patterns (Figure 11).

---

1. Pronounced *trail-lige* in French, with the accent on the first syllable. The last syllable is pronounced like the last syllable in the word *pillage*.

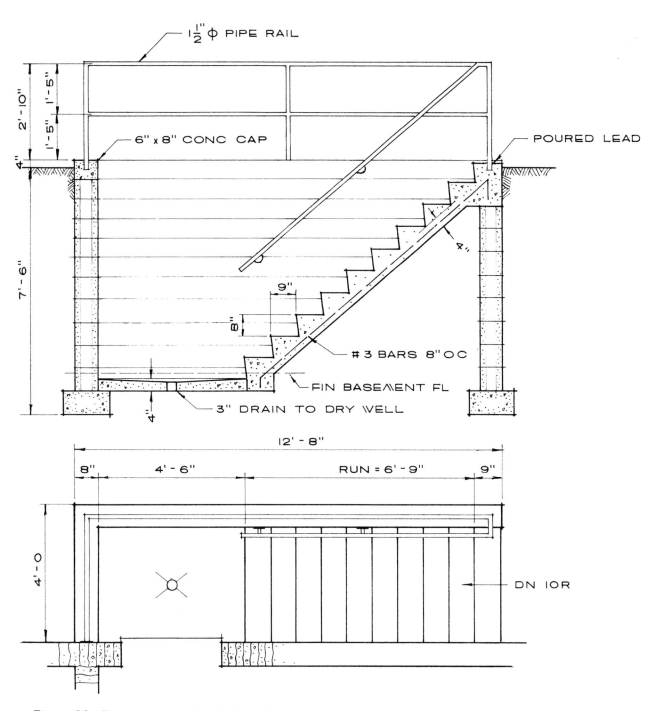

Figure 12. Exterior stairway detail of the Z residence.

Stair Details

A complete set of stair details includes a section or elevation together with a partial or complete plan view of each stairway. Details of tread construction and handrail construction are also included. Some of these drawings may be incorporated with other plans. The stair plan, for example, may be satisfactorily shown on the floor plan. Notice in Figure 13 that arrows with the notations "UP" and "DN" are used to show stair direction. The number of risers is also included. When reading a stair plan, be careful not to misread lowercase "up"

and "dn" notations, since when viewed upside down, a lowercase "up" looks like "dn" and a lower case "dn" looks like "up". When there are both "up" and "down" stairs, one over another, they are separated by a break line as shown in Figure 13 on page 112.

Figure 12 shows the details for the exterior masonry stairway of the Z residence. Figure 13 shows the details for the interior wood stairway of the A residence. Study both these stairways until you thoroughly understand their construction. Make a note of any detail you do not understand and check with your instructor at the first opportunity.

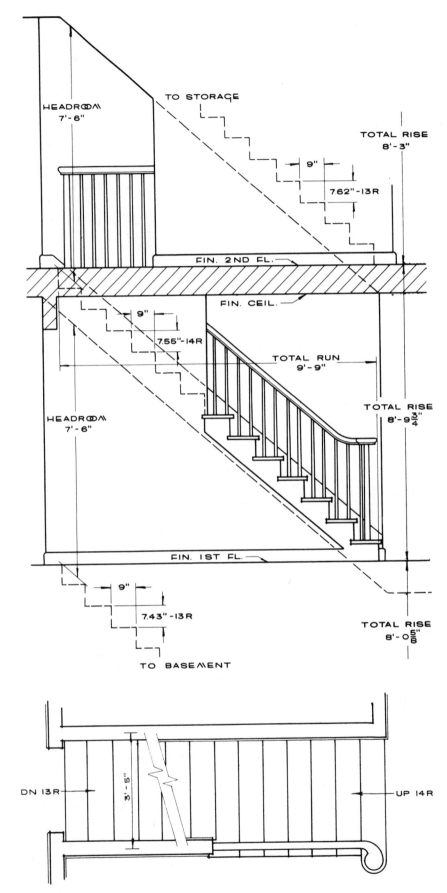

Figure 13. Interior stairway detail of the A residence.

17

Fireplace and Chimney Details

Although the fireplace is no longer a necessity as the major heat source in a home, it is considered by many to be a "must" luxury and consequently is often included in residential plans. The fireplace is usually the major element of interior design in a living room or family room. In addition, it is occasionally specified for a family-type kitchen or master bedroom.

Types of Fireplaces and Chimneys

Several types of fireplaces are illustrated in Figure 2. Fireplace openings may be *single-faced* (the basic type), *double-faced* (with faces on adjacent or opposite sides), *three-faced* (serving as a peninsula partition between two areas), or even *freestanding* (in the center of an area). Multifaced fireplaces are associated with modern designs, but corner fireplaces have been in use for many years. Double-faced (opposite sides) and three-faced fireplaces are often used as room dividers.

A fireplace may be located on an exterior wall, on an interior partition, in a corner, on a projecting corner, or may be freestanding. A frame structure is weakened by having a masonry fireplace and chimney on an exterior wall, whereas a masonry structure is stiffened. Split-level houses pose a special problem because the chimney should not emerge at a location close to higher-elevation roofs. The chimney will not draw properly unless it is extended at least 2' higher than any portion of the roof located within 10' (see Figure 1).

Hearths may be flush with the floor or raised to any desired height. The back hearth serves as the base for the fire; the front hearth protects a combustible floor from sparks. The front hearth and edges of the fireplace opening may be surfaced with an ornamental material such as a ceramic tile, which is highly heat resistant. Mantels may be of various designs or omitted entirely.

Brick, block, stone, tile, and metal are used for fireplace construction. When the fireplace is used as the primary element in the decorative scheme, log bins, shelves, or cabinets are often included.

Sizes

Figures 3 and 4 give the working dimensions for single-faced and multifaced fireplace designs. Some of these dimensions will vary according to the size category as shown in Table II. The size category will depend upon the room size and the emphasis to be placed upon the fireplace. Notice that the dimensions in Figure 3 are nearly all multiples of 4". To reduce the amount of brick trimming and waste, a modular system is established such as that shown in Figure 5. Here a 2 1/6" × 3 1/2" × 7 1/2" modular brick is laid up with 1/2" joints, resulting in a 4" module. Table III may be consulted

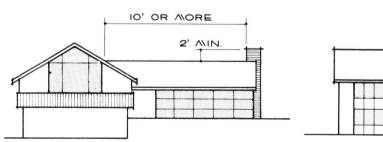
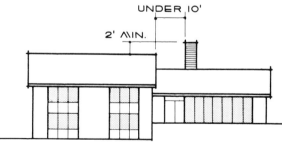

Figure 1. Minimum chimney height.

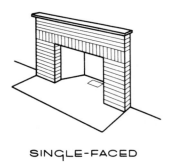

SINGLE-FACED

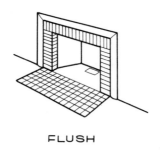

FLUSH

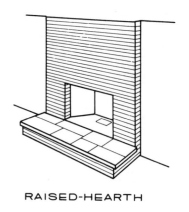

RAISED-HEARTH

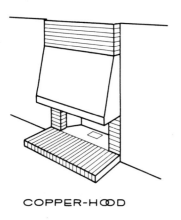

COPPER-HOOD

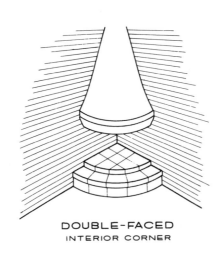

DOUBLE-FACED
INTERIOR CORNER

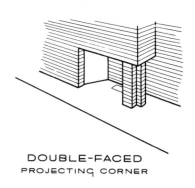

DOUBLE-FACED
PROJECTING CORNER

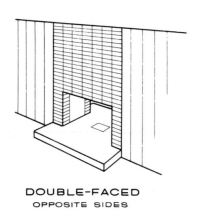

DOUBLE-FACED
OPPOSITE SIDES

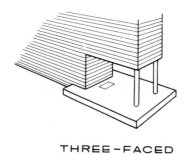

THREE-FACED

FREESTANDING

Figure 2. Fireplace types.

for a quick reference of modular sizes of brick, tile, and block. If common brick, Norman brick, Roman brick, or some other tile or block size is specified, a similar table would be helpful. The actual sizes of these masonry units are given in Table I.

Fireplace Construction

A chimney is a complete structure in its own right, unsupported by any wooden member of the house framing. Recall how often you have seen a house that has burned to the ground, yet the chimney remained standing. It is equally improper for the chimney to be used as a support for girders, joists, or rafters, since a wooden member framing into a chimney may eventually settle and crack it. Actually, no framing lumber is installed closer than 2″ from the chimney due to the fire hazard. The 2″ space is filled with noncombustible material to act as a fire stop. However, subflooring, flooring, and roof sheathing may come within 3/4″ of the chimney.

Figure 6 shows the type of overlapping flashing used at the

roof. This allows movement between the chimney and roof due to settling without damage to the flashing.

The construction of a fireplace and chimney is entrusted only to experienced workers, since improper construction can cause a fire hazard or a smoking fireplace. Due to its great weight, the chimney is built on a sizable footing. Each fireplace is usually fitted with an ash dump (5″ × 8″ is a common stock size) to the ash pit, which is fitted in turn with a clean-out door (12″ × 12″ is often used). The hearth may be supported by a 4″-thick concrete slab reinforced with 3/8″-diameter bars spaced 6″ oc both ways. The opening to the fireplace is spanned by a steel angle lintel, perhaps of 4″ × 3 1/2″ × 5/16″ stock.

The back and sides of the fireplace are fire brick laid up in fire-clay mortar, which is more heat resistant than ordinary brick and mortar. The sides are sloped to direct the heat toward the room and the smoke to the smoke chamber. A metal damper set below the smoke chamber is used to control the draft. The damper and the base of the smoke chamber form a smoke shelf which is important in preventing back-draft. The smoke chamber is corbeled into the flue itself, which conducts the smoke and waste gas safely outside.

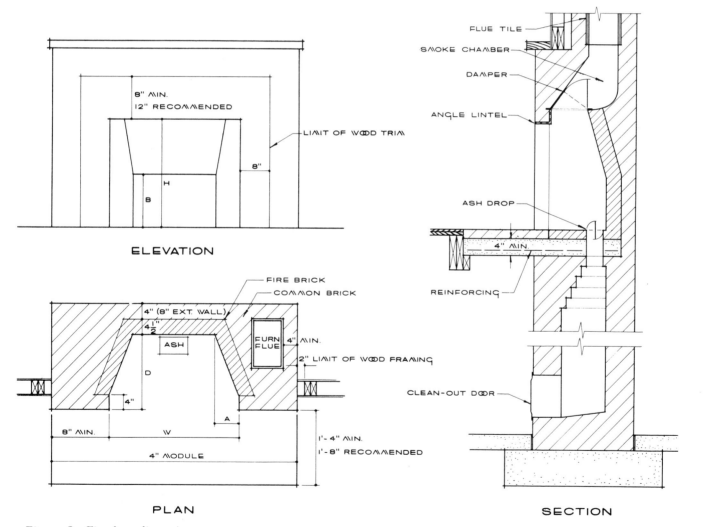

Figure 3. Fireplace dimensions.

The flue is often constructed of rectangular terra-cotta tiles surrounded by 4″ or 8″ masonry. For proper draft, the area of the flue should not be less than a tenth of the area of the fireplace opening. When computing the flue size of multifaced fireplaces, the areas of all faces are included. The flue tile sizes given in Table II meet this requirement. A sharp chimney capping, usually obtained by extending the flue tile 4″ above the masonry, also improves draft. The chimney must extend 2′ higher than any portion of a roof located within 10′. A tall chimney has a naturally better draft than a short chimney.

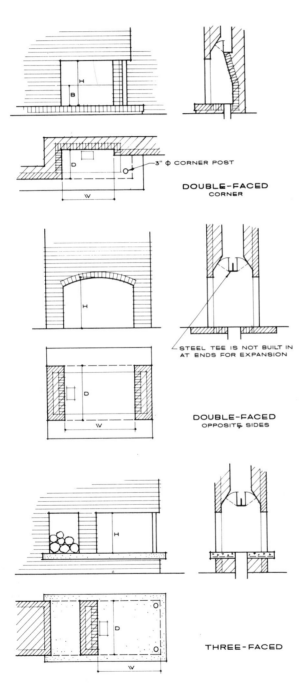

Figure 4. Multifaced fireplace designs.

Table I. Masonry sizes

Modular brick	2 1/6″ × 3 1/2″ × 7 1/2″
Common brick	2 1/4″ × 3 3/4″ × 8″
Norman brick	2 1/4″ × 3 3/4″ × 12″
Roman brick	1 5/8″ × 3 3/4″ × 12″
Fire brick	2 1/2″ × 4 1/2″ × 9″
Tile	4 5/6″ × 7 1/2″ × 11 1/2″
Block	7 5/8″ × 7 5/8″ × 15 5/8″

Each fireplace or furnace must have a separate flue to prevent the interference of drafts, although these flues may all be combined within a common chimney. This is usually stated, "a flue for every fire." For example, an average home may have two flues: one for the oil furnace and another for the living room fireplace. Both flues are set side by side in one chimney separated by 4″ of brick (called a *wythe*). Even a house with no fireplace must have a chimney if it is heated by an oil-, coal-, or gas-fired furnace. For the flue size, the manufacturer's specifications are consulted. The size 12″ × 12″ is often used.

Prefabricated Flue

The prefabricated nonmasonry flue and chimney shown in Figure 7 consist of insulated and fireproof flue sections and a metal housing placed above the roof to simulate a masonry chimney. This costs considerably less than a masonry chimney and is often used for oil and gas furnace flues. Figures 8 and 9 show some installation details.

Fireplace Liner

Since a skilled mason is needed for the proper construction of a masonry fireplace, metal fireplace liners are often used (Figure 10). These liners consist of the fireplace sides and back, damper, smoke shelf, and smoke chamber all in one prefabricated unit and provide a form for the mason to work to. They also contain a duct system that draws in the room air through inlet registers, warms it, and then discharges it back to the room through outlet registers. This increases the heating capacity of the fireplace.

Metal Fireplaces

Fireplaces constructed entirely of metal have been used for many years, and faithful simulations of these early models are still manufactured. Some modern types of sheet steel are shown in Figures 11 and 12. Since a metal fireplace is usually used with a metal chimney, the cost is quite low. In addition, a metal fireplace heats up faster and gives more heat than a masonry fireplace.

Metal fireplaces are sold in a variety of sizes, colors, and coatings. Some are made of porcelain enamel steel in a choice of colors. Others use sheet steel painted black. Others come with a factory prime coat over heavy-gauge sheet steel, leaving the final choice of color to the user. Steel fireplaces are hung from a wall or ceiling, stand on a platform on their own legs, or are recessed into the floor.

Table II. Sizes for fireplace layout

Size Category	Width of Opening, W	Height of Opening, H	Depth of Opening, D	A*	B*
Single-faced					
Small	2'- 8"	2'- 3"	1'- 8"	6 1/2"	1'- 2"
Medium	3'- 0	2'- 5"	1'- 8"	6 1/2"	1'- 2"
Large	4'- 0	2'- 8"	2'- 0	9"	1'- 4"
Double-faced, corner					
Small	2'- 8"	2'- 3"	1'- 8"		1'- 2"
Medium	3'- 0	2'- 5"	1'- 8"		1'- 2"
Large	4'- 0	2'- 5"	2'- 0		1'- 2"
Double-faced, opposite sides					
Small	2'- 8"	2'- 5"	3'- 0		
Medium	3'- 0	2'- 5"	3'- 0		
Large	4'- 0	2'- 8"	3'- 0		
Three-faced					
Small	3'- 4"	2'- 3"	3'- 0		
Medium	3'- 8"	2'- 3"	3'- 0		
Large	4'- 8"	2'- 3"	3'- 0		

*See Figure 3 or 4.

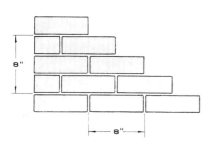

Figure 5. Common brick modular dimensions.

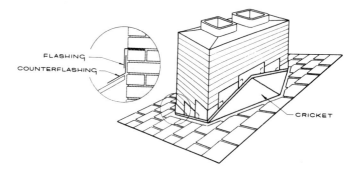

Figure 6. Chimney flashing.

Table III. Masonry sizes (3 brick + 3 joints = 8")

Modular Brick	Tile	Block	Size
			Number of Courses
1			2 2/3"
2	1		5 1/3"
3		1	8"
4	2		10 2/3"
5			1'- 1 1/3"
6	3	2	1'- 4"
7			1'- 6 2/3"
8	4		1'- 9 1/3"
9		3	2'- 0
10	5		2'- 2 2/3"
11			2'- 5 1/3"
12	6	4	2'- 8"
13			2'- 10 2/3"
14	7		3'- 1 1/3"
15		5	3'- 4"
16	8		3'- 6 2/3"
17			3'- 9 1/3"
18	9	6	4'- 0
19			4'- 2 2/3"
20	10		4'- 5 1/3"
21		7	4'- 8"
22	11		4'- 10 2/3"
23			5'- 1 1/3"
24	12	8	5'- 4"
25			5'- 6 2/3"

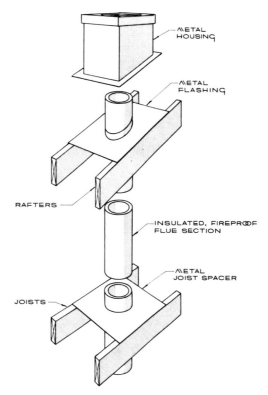

Figure 7. Prefabricated flue.

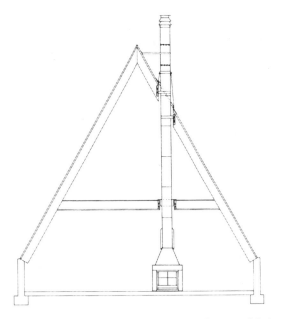

Figure 8. Installation of a metal fireplace prefabricated flue.

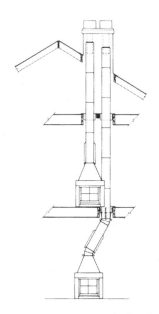

Figure 9. Installation of metal fireplaces on two
levels.

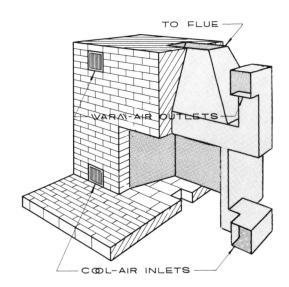

Figure 10. Metal fireplace liner.

Fireplace and Chimney Details

The architect shows the fireplace and chimney design by means of detail drawings and specifications. The detail drawings usually consist of a front elevation showing the design of the fireplace opening and trim, and sectional plans showing dimensions of the fireplace and chimney together with flue placement. A side vertical section may be included. A $1/2'' = 1' - 0$ scale is often used. Some dimensions, such as the height of the chimney above the roof, are shown in the house elevation views.

Figure 13 shows the detail drawings of the living room and recreation room fireplaces for the A residence. Modular brick is used. Notice that dimensions are based upon the 4″ module to reduce the amount of brick cutting. Study these details until you understand them completely. Make note of any questions, and check with your instructor at the first opportunity.

Figure 11. Wall-hung steel fireplace.

Figure 12. Metal fireplace in an office.

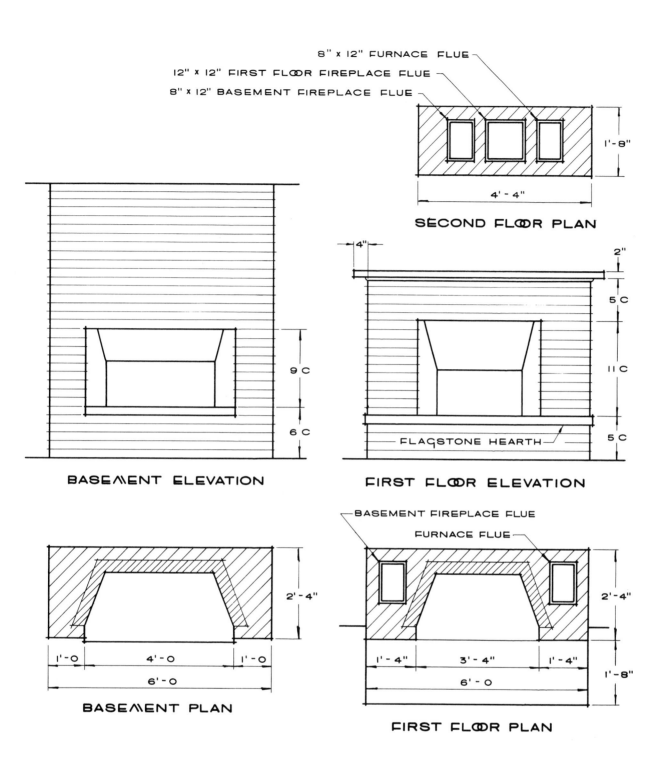

Figure 13. Fireplace details of the Z residence.

119

18

Electrical Plans

Electrical plans describe a building's electrical system which provides for lighting and operation of electrical appliances. Appliances are important to a building, for they contribute both to its usefulness and to its aesthetic effect. Nearly all the mecha. cal servants in the home, necessities and luxuries, are operated by electricity. The lighting system not only enables the building to be used at night, but it provides a major design feature in some rooms during daytime as well (Figure 1).

To understand electrical plans, you must be thoroughly familiar with fixtures, switches, and outlets, together with the symbols for them.

Fixtures

The symbol used for an electric fixture is either a 3/16"-diameter circle for an incandescent lamp or a 1/8"-wide rectangle for a fluorescent lamp on a 1/4" = 1'- 0 scale plan (Figure 3). These simple symbols, however, may represent a wide variety of fixture types and mountings, the exact design

Figure 1. This library's lighting is an important part of the building design during both night and day.

being further detailed to a larger scale and outlined in the specifications.

Fixture types may be either: (1) direct lighting, as provided by the more commonly used fixtures, recessed lights, and spotlights; or (2) indirect lighting, as provided by valance and cove lighting. Some fixtures provide a combination of direct and indirect lighting. A detailed classification of fixture types and mountings is given in Figure 2.

All of the fixture types shown in Figure 2 (except spot-lighting) may be obtained with either incandescent or fluorescent lamps. Fluorescent lamps are available in lengths between 6" and 24" at 3" intervals and in 3', 4', 5', and 8' lengths.

Switches

Wall switches are often used to control the fixtures in rooms and halls. In living rooms and bedrooms, the switch may also control one or two convenience outlets. As in the case of fixtures, the symbol for a switch (the letter *S*, Figure 3) may represent a wide variety of switch types. These include the simple on-off *toggle switch* (inexpensive), the *quiet switch* (very faint click), and the *mercury switch* (completely silent). There are also *push-button* types with button sizes ranging up to the *push plate* in which the entire plate acts as the button. For special requirements, the *dimmer switch* permits the light intensity to be varied, and the *delayed action switch* permits light for a minute after the switch has been turned off.

Switches are usually located 4' above the floor and a few inches away from the doorknob side of each entrance to a room. They are placed inside most rooms. Occasionally you will find the switch outside the room entrance (as in a walk-in closet). Three-way switches are specified when a room contains two entrances over 10' apart. Two sets of three-way switches are used at the head and foot of stairs: one set for the upstairs hall and another set for the downstairs hall. When it is desirable to control a fixture from three or more locations, three-way switches are used at two locations and four-way switches must be used for each additional location. Figure 4 shows the wiring of these switches. Pull-switch fixtures in each clothes closet are often specified.

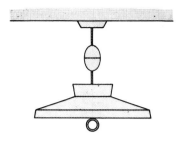

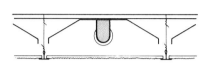

PENDANT
USED FOR GENERAL ILLUMINATION

REEL
PERMITS FIXTURE TO BE ADJUSTED
TO DESIRED HEIGHT

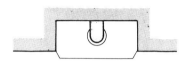

LUMINOUS CEILING
USED WITH A SUSPENDED CEILING

RECESSED
PERMITS BUILT-IN LIGHTING AT
SELECTED POSITIONS

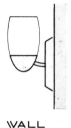

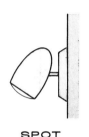

WALL
USED FOR GENERAL OR DECORATIVE
ILLUMINATION

SPOT
USED FOR ACCENT ILLUMINATION

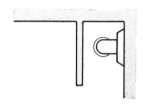

VALANCE
USED AT EDGE OF CEILING AND UNDER
KITCHEN CABINETS

COVE
REFLECTS UP AT CEILING FOR SOFT,
INDIRECT LIGHTING

Figure 2. Types of fixtures.

Outlets

Duplex room outlets are specified no further than 10′ apart. They are provided wherever needed so that no extension cord longer than 6′ need be used. Hall outlets are usually specified for every 15′ of hall length.

Outlets are located 18″ above the floor except in the kitchen and dining area, where higher positions are used to accommodate counter appliances. Symbols for convenience outlets are given in Figure 3. The circles are 1/8″ in diameter on a 1/4″ = 1′- 0 scale plan. The two-line symbol indicates a 120-V outlet, and the three-line symbol indicates a 240-V heavy-duty outlet such as would be required for a range, oven, or dryer. Outdoor outlets for Christmas decorations or patio are marked "WP" (weatherproof) on the plan.

In addition to individual outlets, *plug-in strips* are avail-

able containing outlets spaced 6″, 18″, 30″, or 60″ apart. These plug-in strips are often used behind kitchen counters when many outlets are required. They are also available as replacements for room baseboards as shown in Figure 5. Both individual outlets and plug-in strips may be wired to a set of dual outlets: one to obtain constant electrical service and the other having switch-controlled service.

Telephones

The symbol used for a telephone is an equilateral triangle, as shown in Figure 3. As a minimum, one telephone will normally be specified for each active floor level. Telephones may be desired in the kitchen planning center, master bedroom, den or study, living room, teenager's bedroom, guest room, recreation room, patio, and workshop. A home computer center may include dual telephone lines to permit linking the home computer with the office computer simultaneously with telephone conversation. Some occasionally used rooms may be equipped for portable plug-in telephones.

Reading Electrical Conventions

After you have become familiar with the symbols for fixtures, switches, and outlets, it is a simple matter to learn to read an electrical plan. A freehand hidden line is shown connecting each fixture with its controlling switches. Remember, this line does not represent an actual electric wire, but merely indicates that a particular switch controls a particular fixture or outlet. Examples of some typical plans are shown in Figure 7. Study them carefully.

Service

Electricity is normally supplied to the homes by means of an overhead three-wire service with a capacity for 150 A. The minimum wire size for this service is #2-gauge wire (see Figure 6). A large home (over 3,000 sq. ft.) or a home with electric heat would require a larger service of 200 A. At extra cost, unsightly overhead wires can be eliminated by underground conductors.

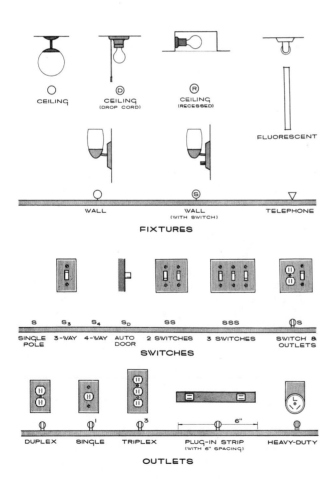

FIXTURES

SWITCHES

OUTLETS

Figure 3. Electrical symbols.

Circuits

To distribute electricity throughout the house, branch circuits of various capacities are installed. Several outlets or fixtures may be placed on one branch circuit for protection by a common circuit breaker in the entrance panel. Normally, house circuits are of three types:

1. *Light-duty* circuits (outlets, 2400 W maximum[1]):
   Amperage: 20
   Voltage: 120[2]
   Wire size: #12-gauge wire
   Description: ordinary lights
2. *Appliance* circuits (one circuit for kitchen, one circuit for laundry, and so forth):
   Amperage: 20
   Voltage: 120[2]
   Wire size: #12-gauge wire
   Description: refrigerator, freezer, toaster, iron, washer, TV
3. *Heavy-duty* circuits (one individual circuit for each appliance):
   Amperage: 30
   Voltage: 240[2]
   Wire size: #6-gauge wire
   Description: range, oven, water heater, dryer, air conditioner

For residential buildings, you will usually find information on branch circuits only in the specifications. For example, the maximum wattage per circuit or the maximum number of outlets or fixtures per circuit might be specified. However, for commercial buildings, this circuit information is located on the electrical plan by the use of branch circuit lines drawn to connect all outlets or fixtures on each circuit. Detailed information on each circuit is then given in electrical panel schedules. See "Reading Commercial Plans," Chapter 32, for examples. In either case, the electrical system would be designed to meet the requirements of the National Electric Code and existing state and municipal codes, as well as the requirements of the local utility company.

Reading the A Residence Electrical Plan

The electrical plan of the first floor of the A residence is shown in Figure 8. Study this plan until you are confident you understand all symbols and conventions. Take note of these special points:

1. All rooms except the living room contain either incandescent or fluorescent lighting fixtures controlled by a switch.
2. Two of the seven convenience outlets in the living room are controlled by a switch. Notice how you can tell which outlets are switch-controlled and which outlets are always "hot."
3. Three-way switches are specified to control a fixture from two locations.
4. All outdoor fixtures and outlets are marked "WP" (weatherproof).

1. 20 A × 120 V = 2400 W.
2. These voltages may be 120–240 V, 115–230 V, or 110–220 V, depending on the service supplied by the power company.

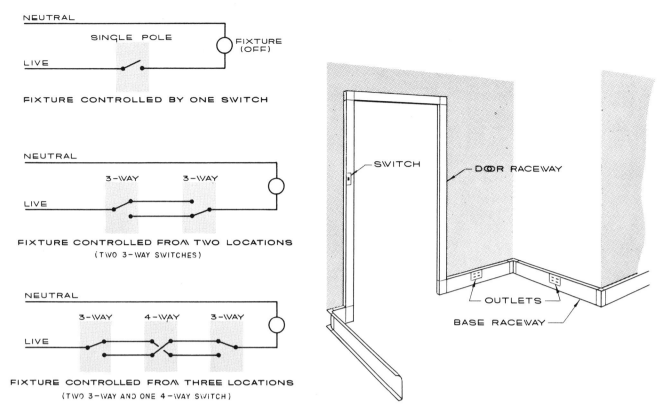

NEUTRAL

SINGLE POLE

LIVE

FIXTURE (OFF)

FIXTURE CONTROLLED BY ONE SWITCH

NEUTRAL

3-WAY   3-WAY

LIVE

FIXTURE CONTROLLED FROM TWO LOCATIONS
(TWO 3-WAY SWITCHES)

NEUTRAL

3-WAY   4-WAY   3-WAY

LIVE

FIXTURE CONTROLLED FROM THREE LOCATIONS
(TWO 3-WAY AND ONE 4-WAY SWITCH)

SWITCH

DOOR RACEWAY

OUTLETS

BASE RACEWAY

Figure 4. Theory of electric switches.   *Figure 5.* Plug-in strip.

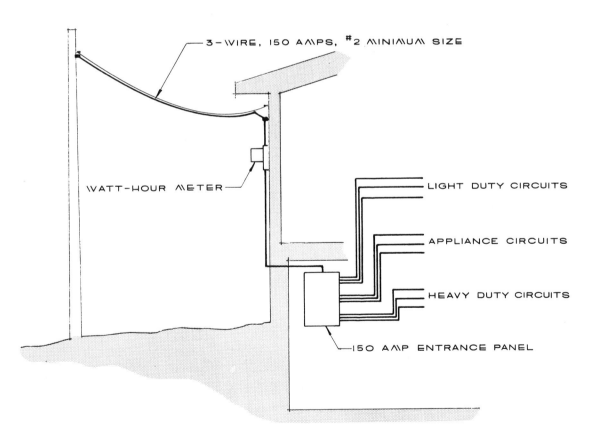

3-WIRE, 150 AMPS, #2 MINIMUM SIZE

WATT-HOUR METER

LIGHT DUTY CIRCUITS

APPLIANCE CIRCUITS

HEAVY DUTY CIRCUITS

150 AMP ENTRANCE PANEL

Figure 6. Typical electrical supply to the home.

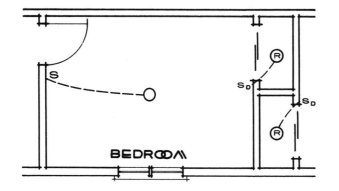

INTERPRETATION:

I CEILING FIXTURE CONTROLLED BY I SWITCH,
RECESSED CLOSET LIGHTS CONTROLLED BY AUTOMATIC DOOR SWITCHES.

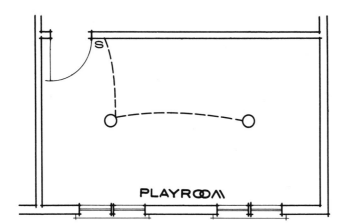

INTERPRETATION:

2 CEILING FIXTURES CONTROLLED BY I SWITCH

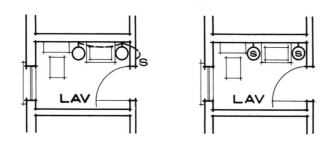

INTERPRETATION:

2 WALL FIXTURES CONTROLLED BY I SWITCH
OR
2 WALL FIXTURES WITH INTEGRAL SWITCH

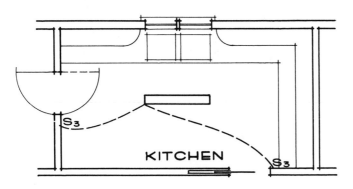

INTERPRETATION:

I FLUORESCENT CEILING FIXTURE CONTROLLED BY 2 SWITCHES

Figure 7. Typical electrical plans.

124

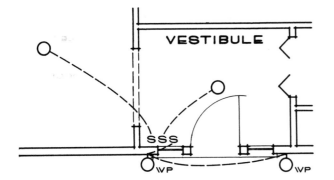

INTERPRETATION:

I VESTIBULE CEILING FIXTURE,
I FAMILY ROOM CEILING FIXTURE,
2 OUTDOOR WALL FIXTURES,
CONTROLLED BY 3 SWITCHES IN I PLATE

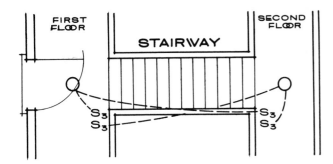

INTERPRETATION:

FIRST FLOOR HALL FIXTURE AND
SECOND FLOOR HALL FIXTURE
CONTROLLED BY SWITCHES ON
BOTH FLOORS

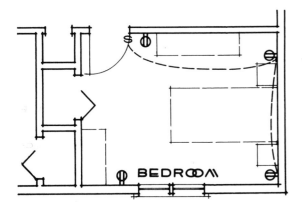

INTERPRETATION:

CONVENTIONAL NUMBER OF OUTLETS,
2 CONTROLLED BY SWITCH

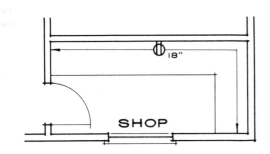

INTERPRETATION:

PLUG-IN STRIP WITH OUTLETS
SPACED 18" APART

Figure 7. continued.

125

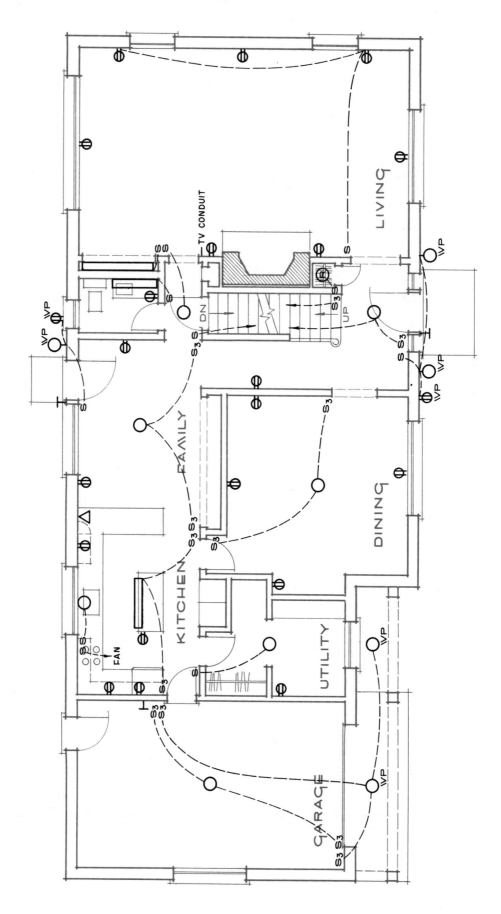

Figure 8. First-floor electrical plan of the A residence.

19

Piping and Plumbing Plans

Architectural working drawings include mechanical plans—piping, plumbing, heating, electrical, and structural—in addition to the architectural plans. Although piping and plumbing plans are occasionally omitted from the design of a small residence (leaving all decisions to the contractor), they are always included in the design of a larger building. To understand piping and plumbing plans, you must first understand a building's piping and plumbing systems. The piping system performs the function of water distribution; the plumbing system performs the function of sewage disposal.

The *water distribution* system consists of the supply pipes that conduct water from the water main or other source to lavatories, bathtubs, showers, and toilets. A portion of this must be routed through a water heater to provide hot water. Most of the water piped into a building must also be drained out together with water-carried wastes. The *sewage disposal* system is composed of the waste pipes that conduct this water to the public sewer or disposal field.

Water Distribution

Piping. A wide variety of water supply pipes are used.

Copper tubing with soldered joints is often used in residential work. The nominal diameter indicates the approximate inside diameter of the tubing. The designations "K," "L," and "M" indicate wall thickness from heavy to light. Compare the following inside and outside diameters (I.D. and O.D., respectively):

1″ cu. tubing type K: 0.995″ I.D. 1.125″ O.D.
1″ cu. tubing type L: 1.025″ I.D. 1.125″ O.D.
1″ cu. tubing type M: 1.055″ I.D. 1.125″ O.D.

The designation "DWV" (drainage, waste, and vent) indicates a still-lighter tubing intended for sewage disposal only.

Plastic pipe has become very popular in residential work, since plumbing codes now permit it to be used for water supply as well as waste disposal. Plastic pipe and fittings are joined by heat fusion. Available nominal diameters (which approximate the inside diameters) are 1/2″, 3/4″, 1″, 1 1/2″, 2″, 3″, 4″, and 6″

Brass pipe is more rigid than copper and plastic and is used with screwed fittings in large, expensive buildings.

Iron pipe is used for underground supply outside buildings, but is not used inside.

Steel pipe is inexpensive but not durable due to corrosion. Both iron and steel pipe must be galvanized or coated with hot pitch to reduce this corrosion.

Fittings. Pipe fittings and their symbols are shown in Figure 1. Pipe is joined by *couplings* to connect straight runs, or *elbows* to connect 45° or 90° bends. *Tees* are used for 45° and 90° branches. *Gate valves* are used to completely shut off the water supply for repair; *globe valves* to provide a range of water regulation from off to on (like a faucet). *Check valves*

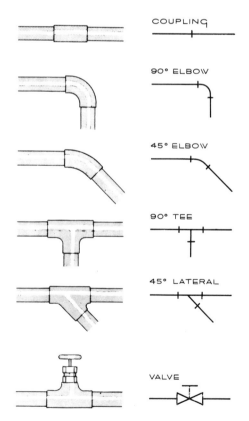

Figure 1. Pipe fittings.

127

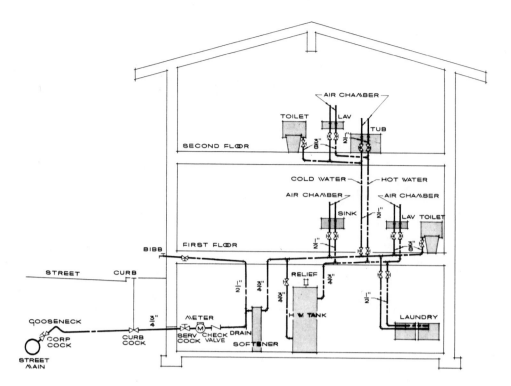

Figure 2. Water distribution.

permit flow in one direction only and are used when there is a possibility of back-pressure. Valves are also called *cocks*, *bibbs*, and *faucets*.

Cold-Water Supply. Let us trace the path of the water from the street main to the house faucets as shown in Figure 2. Upon request, the city water department excavates the street to the public water main and installs a *tap* (pipe) to the property line. A gooseneck is included to allow for future settling of the pipe. Two cocks are installed on the tap: one close to the main, called the *corporation cock*, and the other close to the property line, called the *curb cock*. The curb cock is attached to a long valve stem reaching up to the ground so that water can be disconnected without another excavation.

The contractor connects 3/4″ copper tubing to the curb cock and runs it in a trench below the frost line to the building. It enters the building through a caulked pipe sleeve, and immediately the service cock, water meter, check valve, and drain valve are installed. The *service cock* is a gate valve that allows the owner to shut off water throughout the building. The *water meter* registers the quantity of water used. The *check valve* protects against a back-flow of unpotable (undrinkable) water as a result of a break in the street main. It also protects the water meter from drainage as a result of a malfunctioning water heater. The *drain valve* is used when it is necessary to drain all water from the system. If a water softener is to be included, lines for hard-water hose bibbs are first connected.

A 3/4″ cold-water feeder line is then installed in the basement ceiling with 1/2″ risers running directly to each fixture. Each riser is extended 2′ higher than the fixture connection to provide an air chamber to reduce knocking (water hammer). Valves are installed at the bottom of each

riser so that repairs can be made without shutting off the water for the entire house.

Hot-Water Supply. A tee is installed on the 3/4″ cold-water supply line so that some water is routed through the water heater—entering at 70°F and leaving at 130°F. A 3/4″ feeder and 1/2″ risers are again installed leading to each fixture (the lavatory, tub, and shower require hot and cold water, but a toilet requires only cold). A gate valve is installed at the entrance to the water heater so that it can be shut off for repair. Water may be heated by the existing house heating system or independently by means of electric, gas, or solar heaters. A 66-gal. water heater is adequate for a family of three. A larger family should have an 80-gal. water heater. Electric water heaters are available as quick-recovery units and low-wattage units. To conserve energy, the low-wattage units are preferred.

Pipe Sizes. Pipe sizing will vary depending on a number of factors, such as the average water consumption, peak loads, available water pressure, and friction loss in long runs of pipe. For the average residence, however, the sizes are selected by the use of the minimum sizes recommended by the Federal Housing Administration. Hot- and cold-water lines are usually 3/8″ to 3/4″. Waste branches and vent stacks are usually 1 1/4″ to 3″.

Sewage Disposal

The water distribution system just described is roughed in a new house before the interior walls are finished. The sewage disposal system which conducts waste water from the home is

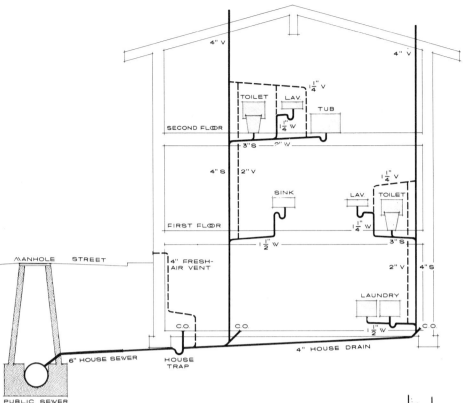

Figure 3. Sewage disposal.

installed at the same time. The fixtures themselves are added after the interior walls are finished. Let us trace the path of the waste water from the fixtures to the public sewer, as shown in Figure 3.

Fixture Branches. The fixture branches are nearly-horizontal pipes that conduct the waste water from the fixtures to the vertical waste stacks (vertical pipes are called *stacks*). They are pitched 1/8″ to 1/2″ per foot away from the fixtures, and they are as short as possible.

Traps. To prevent sewer gases in the fixture branches from entering the living quarters, a U-shaped fitting called a *trap* is connected close to each fixture. This trap catches and holds waste water at each discharge, thus providing a water seal. Lavatory and bathtub traps like those shown in Figure 4 are installed in the fixture branch lines; toilet traps are cast as part of the fixture.

Vent Stacks. A sudden discharge of waste causes a suction action that may empty the trap. To prevent this, vent pipes are connected beyond the trap and extended through the roof to open air. Vent stacks are installed not less than 6″ nor more than 5′ from the trap. Vent stack sizes are 1 1/4″ to 2″. The portion extending through the roof is increased to 4″ in diameter to prevent stoppage by snow or frost. The 4″ section begins at least 1′ below the roof, extends 1′ above the roof, and is no closer than 12′ to ventilators or higher windows.

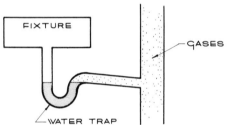

Figure 4. Fixture trap.

Waste and Soil Stacks. It would be very costly to carry each fixture branch separately to the sewer; therefore the fixture branches are connected at each floor level to a large vertical pipe. This pipe is called a *waste stack* if it receives discharge from any fixture except a toilet. It is called a *soil stack* if it receives discharge from a toilet, with or without other fixtures. Soil stacks are often 4″ in diameter, waste stacks 3″ in diameter. As with vent stacks, their upper ends are 4″ in diameter and extend 1′ above the roof to open air. This retards the decomposition of organic matter, since bacteria do not work in the presence of free oxygen. For maximum economy, fixtures are grouped so that all fixture branches drain into only one or two stacks.

House Drain and House Sewer. The soil and waste stacks discharge into the house drain—an extra-heavy cast-iron pipe with lead joints under the basement floor. It is a 4″-diameter pipe running under the footing and 5′ past the foundation wall. The house drain is then connected to the house sewer, which may also be of 4″ cast iron or of 6″ vitrified clay. Both the house drain and house sewer are sloped 1/4″/ft. to the public sewer.

Clean-Outs. Clean-outs are elbows projecting through the basement floor to permit cleaning the house drain and sewer. They are installed in the house drain beyond the last stack, just inside the basement wall, and in between at points not over 50' apart. It is best to include clean-outs at the foot of each waste or soil stack and at each change of direction of the horizontal run. Threaded plugs are used to close the clean-outs.

House Trap. The trap installed next to the building in the house drain is called a *house trap.* It furnishes a water seal against the entrance of gas from the public sewer to the building piping. Clean-outs are located at the top of one or both sides of the trap.

Fresh-Air Inlet. A 4"-diameter air vent installed next to the house trap admits fresh air to the house drain. The fresh-air inlet does not run through the roof, but rather to a convenient place 6" above the ground. It is finished with a gooseneck bend or grille.

Septic Tank. In sparsely populated areas without public sewers, private disposal fields are used. Usually the sewage is directed to a 750-gal. underground septic tank where solid waste is decomposed by the bacteria contained in the sewage itself. The remaining liquid is distributed to the ground through porous pipes in the disposal field.

Reading Piping and Plumbing Plans

The water distribution and sewage disposal systems may be shown in an elevation (as in Figures 2 and 3) or in an isometric drawing, but it is usually shown in plan (as in Figures 5 and 6). The water distribution system is shown in the *piping plan,* and the sewage disposal system is shown in the *plumbing plan.* Notice that since these plans are schematic drawings, it is not necessary to hold to scale.

Some typical instructions appearing on such plans follow.

1. All underground piping should be type K copper (soft temper) with screwed pressure-type joints.
2. All hot- and cold-water piping inside the building should be type L copper (hard temper) with soldered joints.
3. All soil and waste piping above ground should be type M copper with soldered joints.
4. All soil and waste piping under ground should be heavy cast iron with lead and oakum bell-and-spigot joints.
5. Furnish and install stop valves in all hot- and cold-water lines before fixtures; if visible, valves to have same finish as fixture trim.
6. All fixtures shown on drawings to be furnished and completely connected with approved chrome-plated brass trim, traps, and suitable supports. Furnish and install chrome-plated escutcheon plates where pipes pierce finish walls.

For more detailed information than is given in this chapter, obtain the *ASHRAE Guide* from the American Society of Heating, Refrigerating, and Air Conditioning Engineers, or the *National Plumbing Code* from the U.S. Government Printing Office in Washington, D.C.

Reading the M Residence Piping Plan

The piping plan of the M residence (described in Chapters 5 and 6) is shown in Figure 5 of this chapter. Notice that you can trace the path of the water supply from the main supply line to each fixture. Notice also that some cold water is diverted through the water heater to be heated before further distribution. All cold-water lines (designated "CW") can be identified by one short dash; all hot-water lines (designated "HW") can be identified by two short dashes. Vertical pipe lines are shown as small circles.

Reading the M Residence Plumbing Plan

The plumbing plan of the M residence is shown in Figure 6. Notice that you can trace the path of waste or soil water from each fixture to the house sewer pipe. Also notice that the locations of four vent stacks are shown. Study both the plumbing and piping plans of the M residence. Check any questions with your instructor.

Future Trends

Sovent Plumbing. A single-stack, self-venting sewage disposal system was developed recently and holds promise for multistory buildings. This system is called *sovent,* indicating a combination of soil stacks and vent stacks. The key to this system is an aerator fitting that is located at the connection of each fixture branch to the soil stack. This fitting limits the sewage flow velocity in the stack, thus reducing the suction which would siphon the traps. The sovent stack extends through the roof and acts both as a soil stack and a vent stack.

Solar Water Heating. Solar hot-water preheating has become quite common and is considered to be one of the most cost-effective means of using the sun's energy. This is because hot water is needed year-round, but space heating is needed only during cold weather. The principal elements of most solar hot-water systems are a flat plate collector used to directly heat water, a hot-water distribution system of piping, a hot-water storage unit, appropriate automatic controls, and some method of protecting the water from freezing. Several types of solar hot-water collectors are described in Chapter 20. A solar hot-water heating system does not require as much collector area as does a space heating system.

Solar heaters for swimming pools are also available in a wide variety of systems.

Solar Stills.[1] In some locations a supply of potable (drinkable) water has become a critical need. The solar still provides an effective solution. Small home stills to convert seawater to drinking water are being manufactured by the Sunwater Company of San Diego and have been installed along the coasts of California and Mexico. These stills consist of shallow pans covered by glass panels. Installed on a flat roof, an automatic feed pump provides a constant supply of seawater. The daily output of such an installation is about 1 1/2 gal. of potable water. This type of usage predictably will increase.

1. Courtesy Horace McCracken, Solar Equipment Consultant.

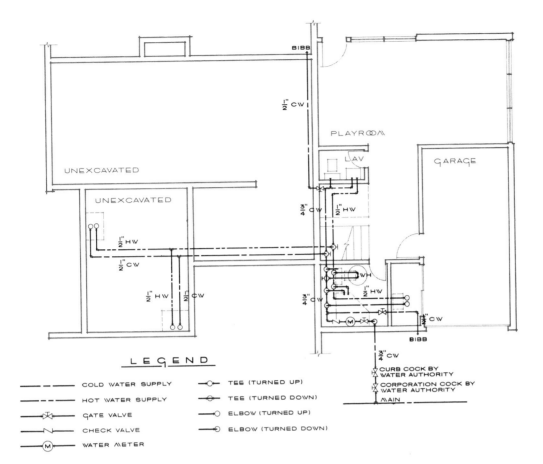

Figure 5. Piping plan of the M residence.

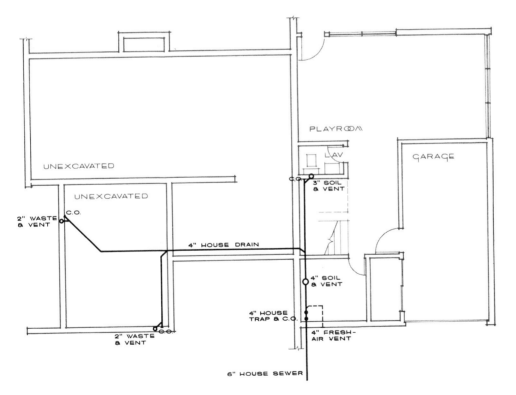

Figure 6. Plumbing plan of the M residence.

20

Heating and Air Conditioning Plans

In addition to the heating and cooling of a building, a complete environmental control system includes humidity control, ventilation, and filtering. Installation details of all these elements are found in the heating and air conditioning plans and specifications. Let's look at each.

Heating

The earliest known central heating systems were built by the Romans to heat their bath houses. Tile hot-air ducts were used to heat the buildings, and lead pipes were used to conduct hot water to the baths. Although such systems have been used in palaces for several thousand years, they were not used for small-home heating until about a hundred years ago. Today a multitude of systems are available which include cooling, humidity control, ventilation, and filtering, in addition to heating.

The most expensive appliance in a building is the heating system—its initial cost amounts to about 10 percent of the total house cost, and the fuel costs amount to several hundred dollars per year. A building's heating system is specified by an architectural engineer (specializing in heating) after consulting with the client. An architectural drafter prepares heating plans from the heating engineer's calculations and sketches. To read these plans, you should be familiar with all heating systems and how they are represented. We will consider heating systems of four general types:

1. Warm air
2. Hot water
3. Electric
4. Solar

Warm Air

In *forced warm air*, warm air is circulated through sheet-metal supply ducts to the rooms, and cold air is pulled through return ducts to the furnace for reheating (usually to about 150°F). Duct work may consist of a number of small individual ducts leading to each room (*individual duct system*,

Figure 1), or a master duct which reduces in size as it branches off to feed the rooms (*trunk duct system*, Figure 2). Circular ducts are 4″-diameter tubes that slip together like stovepipe, with flexible elbows to form any angle up to 90°. Rectangular ducts are custom-made to fit in spaces between joists and studs.

A fan, operating either continuously or intermittently, circulates the air. The thermostat controls the fan in the intermittent system. The fan may be similar to a common electric fan, but more probably it will be a centrifugal type called a *blower*.

A *thermostat* is an instrument sensitive to changes in temperature. One type contains two metal strips brazed together, each strip having a different temperature coefficient. One end of the strip is fixed, but the free end will move due to dissimilar expansion of the metals. This closes an electric contact to start a motor that controls the heating and cooling systems.

For even temperature throughout the house, the warm air should be delivered to the places that lose heat fastest—the exterior walls. The warm air is supplied through grilles with manually operated louvers located in the exterior walls or floor, preferably under windows. These grilles are called *registers* or *diffusers*. In place of registers, warm-air *baseboard units* (Figure 3) may be used to distribute the heat along a wider portion of the exterior wall.

Since the heating element, air, is actually blown into the room, warm-air heating has the inherent disadvantage of distributing dust throughout the house. This is somewhat checked by *filters*—pads of spun metal or glass coated with oil to catch dust. These must be replaced or cleaned often to be effective. Another method is attracting dust by a high-voltage screen.

Perimeter Heating. This forced warm-air system was developed for a special need: to heat the basementless house. As previously described, warm air is delivered to the exterior walls, or *perimeter*, of a building. Perimeter heating, however, has an additional function—to warm the floor itself, thus replacing the heat lost through the concrete slab floor or the wood floor over a crawl space.

The recommended perimeter heating system for a slab floor is the *perimeter loop* (Figure 4). This consists of a 6″-diameter tile duct embedded in the outer edge of the slab and supplied by warm air fed through radial ducts. The ducts warm the slab, and floor registers in the ducts supply heat to the rooms.

Another perimeter heating method is called the *perimeter radial* system (Figure 5). Radial ducts run directly to the floor registers with no outer loop. This system is often used in crawl spaces.

The *crawl space plenum* system (Figure 6) uses the entire crawl space as a plenum (warm-air reservoir). Short ducts (6′ minimum length) from the furnace heat the crawl space plenum, which then supplies heat to the rooms through perimeter floor registers. All perimeter heating requires careful insulation of the foundation to prevent excessive heat loss.

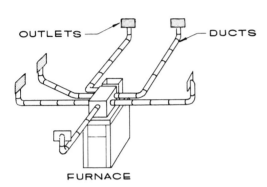

Figure 1. Individual duct system.

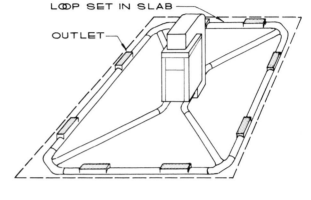

Figure 4. Perimeter loop system.

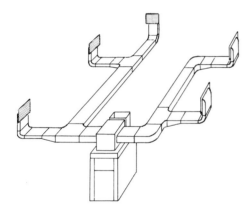

Figure 2. Trunk duct system.

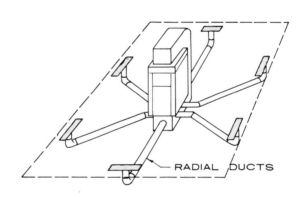

Figure 5. Perimeter radial system.

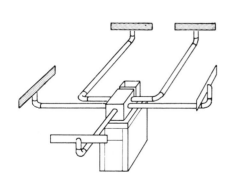

Figure 3. Warm-air baseboard units.

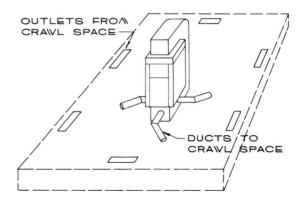

Figure 6. Crawl space plenum system.

In *forced circulation hot water*, a hot-water boiler heats the circulating water to between 200°F and 215°F. The entire system contains water under slight pressure to prevent the formation of steam at 212°F. An electric pump controlled by the thermostat circulates the heated water through narrow (1/2″ to 3/4″) flexible tubing to radiators or convectors giving up heat to the room. The temperature of the return water is about 20°F lower than the boiler delivery. The temperature of the delivery water can be automatically adjusted by a mixing valve that determines the amount of hot water required in the circulating system, or each radiator can be regulated by automatic or manual valves. Usually the boiler is fitted with additional heating coils to supply hot water, winter and summer, to the sinks, tubs, and laundry.

A hot-water system is also called *hydronic heating*. Three hot-water piping systems can be used:

1. Series loop
2. One-pipe
3. Two-pipe

Series Loop.   The series loop system (Figure 7) is, in effect, a single baseboard radiator extending around the entire house and dropping under doorways and window walls. Hot water enters the baseboard near the boiler and travels through each baseboard section and back to the boiler for reheating. It is often used in small homes because it is inexpensive to install, but there can be no individual control of the heating units. Either the entire house is heated or none of it. A compromise is the installation of *two* series loops in two zones which may be independently controlled.

One-Pipe.   The one-pipe system (Figure 8) is often specified for the average-size residence. Hot water is circulated through a main; special tee fittings divert a portion of the water to each radiator. Radiators can be individually controlled by valves and can be located either above the main (*upfeed* system) or below it (*downfeed* system). Downfeed is less effective because it is difficult to coax the water into the branches.

Since water expands when heated, a compression tank is connected to the supply main. A cushion of air in the tank adjusts for the varying volume of water in the system as the water temperature changes.

Two-Pipe.   The two-pipe system is used for large installations. The hot water is circulated by two main pipes, one for supply and one for return. The water is diverted from

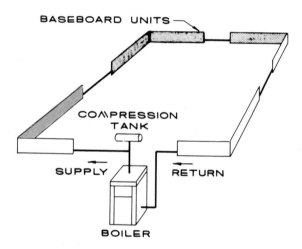

Figure 7. Series loop.

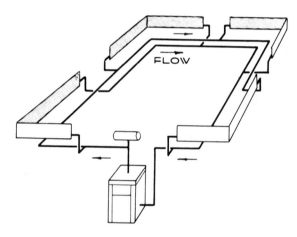

Figure 9. Two-pipe system, reversed return.

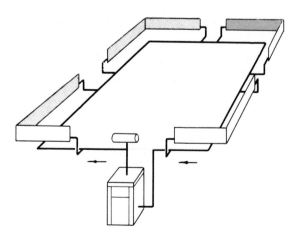

Figure 8. One-pipe system.

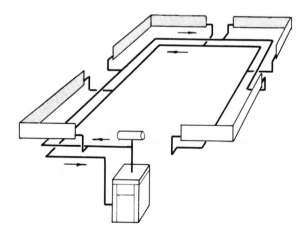

Figure 10. Two-pipe system, direct return.

the supply main to a radiator, and then flows from the radiator to the return main. In this manner, all radiators receive hot water at maximum temperature. The *reversed return* system of Figure 9 is preferred to the *direct return* system of Figure 10. Piping is saved in the direct return system, but the total length of supply and return piping is the same in the reversed return system, ensuring equal flow due to equal friction.

Piping in the one- and two-pipe systems needs no pitch except for drainage. All hot-water systems must be drained or kept operating to prevent freezing when the house is not occupied.

Heating Units. The heating units used in hot-water heating are either radiators, convectors, or combinations of radiator and convector. A *radiator* has large, exposed surfaces to allow heat to radiate to the room. Radiant heat does not depend upon air movement; it passes through the air directly to any object. A *convector*, however, draws in cool air from the room at the bottom, warms it by contact with closely spaced fins, and forces it out into the room again. Heat is therefore circulated by air movement. The major disadvantage of convection is that the heat rises to the ceiling, leaving the floor cold.

Radiators and convectors (Figure 11) may be recessed into the wall to increase floor space. Baseboard heating may be radiant or convector. The distribution system is identical for conventional and baseboard heating.

Radiant Panel Heating. In this system the entire floor, the ceiling, or the walls serve as radiators. The heating element may be hot water in tubing, hot air, or even electricity. In the hot-water system, prefabricated loops of tubing are embedded into a concrete floor (Figure 12) or attached to the ceiling or walls before plastering (Figure 13). In drywall construction, the tubing is installed behind the wall or ceiling panels. In the warm-air system, ducts may be laid in the floor or ceiling, or the entire space above the ceiling may be heated by blowing warm air into it.

Electric Heat

Electric heating systems offer many advantages: low installation cost, no exposed heating elements, individual room control, cleanliness, and silent operation. The main disadvantage is the high cost of operation in localities not offering low electric rates. Heavy insulation is required to keep operation costs to a minimum. The most popular electric heating systems for homes are:

1. Electric resistance cable
2. Electric panels
3. Electric baseboards
4. Heat pump

Electric Resistance Cable. Covered wire cables are heated by electricity and concealed in the ceiling or walls. The wires are manufactured to specific lengths to provide the rated wattage. They are stapled to gypsum lath in a gridlike pattern, only a few inches apart. Then they are covered by a 1/2″ brown coat and finish coat of plaster (Figure 14) or gypsum board (Figure 15). The temperature of each room can be individually controlled by thermostats.

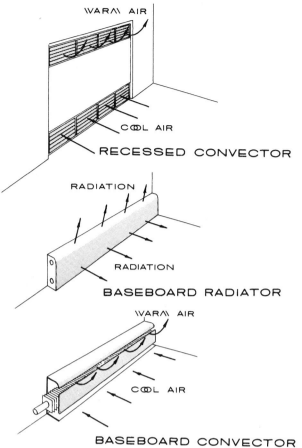

Figure 11. Types of heating units.

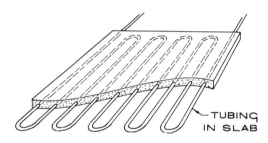

Figure 12. Radiant floor panel.

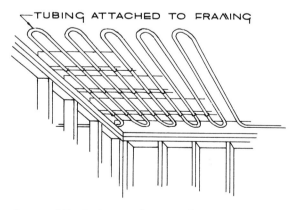

Figure 13. Radiant ceiling panel.

Electric Panels. Prefabricated ceiling panels (Figure 16) are only 1/4″ thick and constructed of a layer of rubber containing conductive material and backed with insulating material. They cover the entire ceiling, and can be painted, plastered, or papered. Smaller glass wall panels are backed with an aluminum grid for the resistance element and are available in radiant, convection, and fan-forced types. These panels are set into the outside walls under the windows and are best suited for supplemental or occasional heating.

Electric Baseboard. Most electric baseboards are convection heaters (Figure 18). This type of heater consists of a heating element enclosed in a metal baseboard molding. Slots at the bottom and top of the baseboard permit the circulation of warmed air.

Heat Pump. The heat pump works on the same principle as the refrigerator, which takes heat out of the inside compartments and discharges it into the room. The heat pump takes heat from the outdoors and brings it into the house. It does this by further "refrigeration" of the outside air. A *refrigerant* (which acts to absorb heat) circulates between two sets of coils: the evaporator and the condenser. During cold weather the outside air is blown over the evaporator coils. Although this air is cold, the refrigerant is much colder and thus absorbs heat as it changes from liquid to gas. The warmed refrigerant is then pumped to the condenser, where the room air is blown over the coils, and the air is heated by the refrigerant, as it changes back to a liquid. The still-colder outside air is blown back outdoors again. During warm weather the operation is reversed so that heat is removed from the room.

Heated or cooled air from a heat pump can be circulated through supply ducts (Figure 18) in the same manner as warm air.

Solar Heat

A solar heating system uses the sun's rays as the heating source. Although a comparatively new concept, many homes are now being built with solar space heating and cooling or solar hot-water heating systems. Due to the diffuse nature of solar energy, most solar heating systems supply only about half of the space heating requirements of a building, the other half being supplied by auxiliary conventional heating systems. Solar heating systems are usually described by the type of collector used. Some of the most common types are:

1. South-facing windows
2. Flat-plate collectors
   a. Air-type
   b. Liquid-type
   c. Trickle
3. Focusing collectors

South-facing Windows. The simplest of solar heating systems consists of large glass areas on the southern wall which permit the sun's rays to heat the house. As shown in Figure 19, the roof overhang is designed to permit the winter sun swinging low on the horizon to warm the house, but exclude the summer sun which is high in the sky. The exact angle of the sun by hour, date, and latitude is given in standard reference books. Some form of adjustable screen is needed to prevent heat from escaping through the same glass areas during the evening and on cloudy days.

A south-facing window system is designed to use available solar heat, but without overheating during midday. Some methods used are:

1. Interior designed to permit warm air to rise and heat additional rooms above.
2. Fans to circulate warm air to other parts of the building.
3. Windows facing east of true south to provide quick morning heat and less heat in the afternoon.
4. A heat storage system such as a masonry wall or concrete floor that absorbs the heat and will return it to the building for a few hours after the sun disappears. Windows facing west of due south are best for this system because they extend the heat return still later into the evening.
5. A separately zoned solar-heated room such as a greenhouse or sun room, which can be closed off from the other rooms when desired.

The preceding systems are called "passive" systems. The following systems are called "active" systems.

Flat-Plate Collectors. A flat-plate collector system consists of exterior solar collectors to heat air or liquids which are then piped to a heat storage container. A second piping loop is used to pipe the heat from the storage container to the building. An auxiliary conventional heating system is included as shown in Figure 20.

Air-Type Collectors (Figures 21 and 22). An air-type collector consists of "flat" panels, each about 4″ thick, 3′

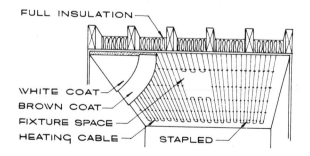

Figure 14. Electric cable in plaster ceiling.

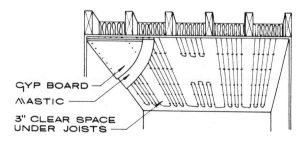

Figure 15. Electric cable in gypsum board ceiling.

wide, and 7′ long. A solar heat absorber is inside the panel. The absorber surface is made of a good heat conductor such as aluminum, copper, stainless steel, or galvanized steel. The panel is covered with a translucent sheet of tempered glass or plastic. This permits sunlight to enter, but prevents the radiation of longer wavelengths given off by the absorber from leaving. Thus heat is trapped inside the collector. There is, of course, insulation at the bottom of the panel. The panels can be mounted horizontally, vertically, or inclined. Cool air is drawn through the panel (under the absorber) by an automatic fan that operates only when the absorber temperature is sufficiently high. Usually the air enters at the bottom of an inclined or vertical panel and leaves at the top. The absorber surface is irregular in texture (such as corrugated) to cause the air to tumble. This increases the amount of heat transferred from the absorber to the air underneath. Also, the absorber metal usually has a special surface chemically or electrolytically applied to increase its absorption capacity. Viewed closely, it looks like the bluing on a gun barrel, but from a distance the collectors look like dark windows.

Air-type collector systems have lower installation costs than liquid-type collector systems. They have no water freezing problems, and they are, in general, less complicated. However, they are not as efficient for hot-water heating, and they require hot-air ducts which are many times larger than hot-water tubing. Also, rock storage containers (often used with air-type systems) require more space than hot-water storage (used with liquid-type systems).

Liquid-Type Collectors (Figures 23 and 24). A liquid-type collector is similar in operation to an air-type collector except that the heat transfer medium is water or antifreeze that is pumped through copper tubing soldered to a copper absorber plate. The water system is drained during cold nights to prevent freezing. Some antifreezes are toxic and special precautions must be taken to prevent leakage into the hot-water supply. The water or antifreeze may be either pumped from the eave up to the ridge or from the ridge down to the eave.

Another form of liquid collector, the *evacuated tube*, is shown in Figure 25. This collector consists of three concentric metal or glass tubes. Cool liquid is supplied through the smallest feeder tube to the end of the assembly. The liquid picks up solar heat as it returns through the midsized absorber tube. There is a partial vacuum (an *evacuation*) between the absorber tube and the largest cover tube. The vacuum helps to reduce condensation and heat loss.

Trickle Collectors (Figure 26). A trickle collector is a liquid-type collector which has cool liquid flowing from 1/32″ holes drilled in a header tube and trickling down open absorber channels rather than in closed absorber tubes. After the liquid is warmed, it is collected in an open gutter for distribution to storage. Compared to a closed system, the trickle collector is less costly to install and has fewer freezing problems, but lower efficiency due to evaporation and condensation on the cover sheet.

Focusing Collectors (Figure 27). Focusing collectors concentrate diffuse solar radiation onto a smaller absorber area and at a higher temperature. Figure 27 shows a parabolic

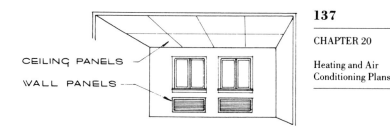

Figure 16. Electric panels.

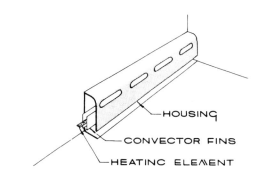

Figure 17. Electric baseboard.

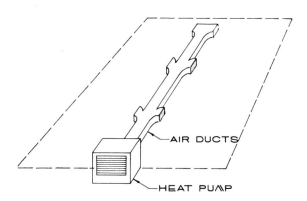

Figure 18. Heat pump.

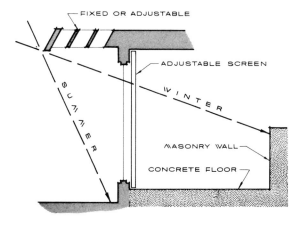

Figure 19. Design of roof overhang for solar windows.

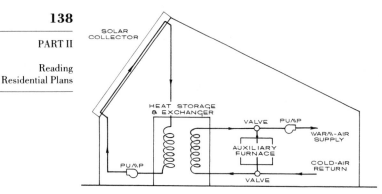

Figure 20. A flat-plate solar collector system.

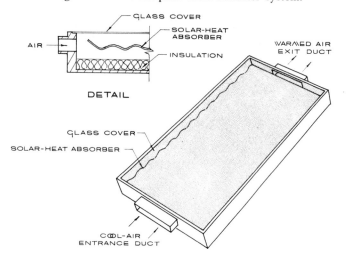

Figure 21. An air-type solar collector.

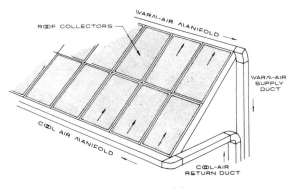

Figure 22. An air-type assembly.

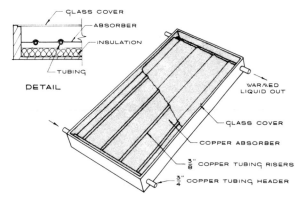

Figure 23. A water-type solar collector.

reflector which focuses on the absorber pipe. Other reflector shapes have been used. Some systems include automatic tracking control to enable the collector to follow the sun's direction. A focusing collector, connected to a heat pump, can provide both heating and cooling.

Photovoltaic Cells. Photovoltaic cells convert solar radiation directly into electricity rather than into heat. Semiconductor chips are used which develop an electric field in the presence of sunlight. The chips are connected in a grid to produce electric current. This is a costly system, however, and consequently it is not often installed.

Heat Storage. In all solar heating systems, heat must be stored for future use in evenings and on cloudy days. Some of the most common types of heat storage are:

1. Rock storage
2. Liquid storage
3. Heat of fusion

Rock Storage. Rock is usually used to store heat collected by air-type collectors. The heated air is drawn through an insulated container filled with pieces of rock or large-sized gravel. As the air flows through the spaces between the rock, the rock is heated and some of that heat will remain for use several days later. The container, however, must be quite large—about 1 cu. ft. for each 2 sq. ft. of collector surface.

Liquid Storage. Water is usually used to store heat collected by liquid-type collectors. This can be accomplished either by storing the heated liquid directly in an open-loop system or by circulating the heated liquid through a tank of water in a closed-loop system. The water tank will gain heat from the heated liquid, thus acting as a "heat exchanger." A liquid storage system requires only about one-third the volume of a rock storage system.

Heat of Fusion. The most promising system uses the *heat of fusion* to store heat. A great amount of heat is required to melt a solid into a liquid. When this melting, or *fusion*, occurs, the temperature does not change. For example, 1 Btu of heat is required to raise the temperature of 1 lb. of water 1°F, but 144 Btu are needed to melt 1 lb. of 32°F ice to 32°F water. In the heat of fusion system, heated air or heated liquid is circulated through tubing surrounded by a chemical compound having a melting point of about 90°F. As the chemical compound is melted from a solid to a liquid, it stores heat until the heat is released later by its changing back to a solid again.

Heat Distribution. There are two common systems used to distribute stored heat in the building:

1. Forced warm air
2. Forced-circulation hot water

They differ from standard distribution systems only in that heat must be delivered in larger volume because it is at a comparatively low temperature. Conventional furnaces deliver warm air at about 150°F and hot water at about 190°F. In comparison, solar storage units deliver heat at about 100°F. Usually, an auxiliary conventional heating system is provided that automatically cuts in as needed. If space cooling is desired in addition to space heating, in most cases a liquid system is better adapted than an air system.

Examples of Solar-Heated Buildings. The California residence shown in Figure 28 is a cluster of ten connected rooms. Solar heat enters through automatically adjusted skylights. Heat is stored in interior masonry walls. Auxiliary heat is provided by electric resistance panels.

The Oregon residence in Figure 29 has an air-type solar collector on a roof sloping 60°. The rock storage system contains 60 tons of 2″ stone in a 6′ × 12′ × 18′ insulated bin. Auxiliary heat is electric forced warm air.

The Oklahoma house in Figure 30 has a water-type solar collector on a roof sloping 50°. The open-loop water storage system is a 2,000-gal. concrete basement tank. Auxiliary heat is electric hot water. Earth banked on several sides provides additional insulation.

The Colorado building of Figure 31 has a trickle collector on a 45° roof. The heat storage system is a 1,800-gal. steel water tank sized 4′ × 5′ × 12′. Auxiliary heat is provided by natural gas.

Reading the M Residence Heating Plan

Obviously there are a great many different types of heating systems, and each is shown in the most appropriate way on heating plans and specifications. Some common symbols used on heating plans are shown in Figure 32. For one example, assume that a series loop baseboard hot-water system has been planned for the M residence (described in Chapters 5 and 6). A piping plan such as described in Chapter 19 would be used to show two loops on the main levels: a loop through the vestibule, kitchen-laundry, and dining-living areas; and a second loop through the bedrooms, bathroom, and study.

A heating plan such as shown in Figure 33 would be used to show the location and type of baseboard heating unit in each room. These units were selected by the heating engineer from available radiant and radiant convector baseboards as shown in Table I. Each unit was then sized (in length) to give a heat output slightly greater than the heat loss from each room. For example, the heating unit in the study is marked "12′ RH 365"; this specifies a 10″-high radiant baseboard (see Table 1) 12′ long with a rated output of 365 Btu/hr./ft. The heating unit in the bathroom is marked "4′ RCH 605"; this specifies a 10″-high radiant convector baseboard 4′ long with a rated output of 605 Btu/hr./ft.

Air Conditioning

Heat will transfer from a warm surface to a cooler surface. Air cooling may be accomplished by withdrawing heat from the air by transferring it to the cooler surface of evaporator coils in a refrigerating unit. As described in the section on heat pumps, a *compressor* circulates a *refrigerant* between two sets of coils: *evaporator coils* and *condenser coils*. The refrigerant is a volatile liquid with such a low boiling point that it is a gas (vapor) under normal pressure and temperature. Common

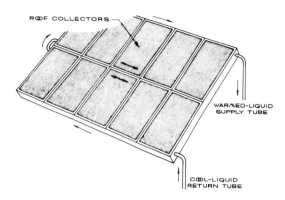

Figure 24. A water-type assembly.

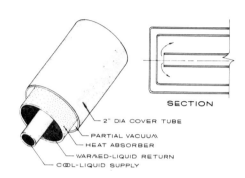

Figure 25. An evacuated-tube collector.

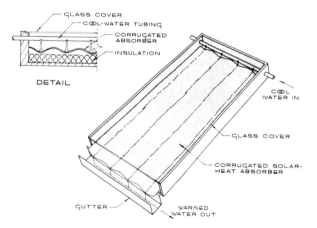

Figure 26. A trickle-type solar collector.

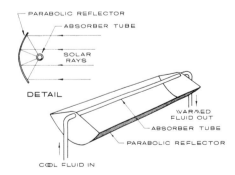

Figure 27. A parabolic focusing solar collector.

Figure 28. Clustered modules with solar skylights.
(Courtesy of Peter Hollander.)

Figure 30. A water-type solar collector.
(Courtesy of Peter Hollander.)

Figure 29. An air-type solar collector.
(Courtesy of Peter Hollander.)

Figure 31. A trickle-type solar collector.
(Courtesy of Peter Hollander.)

refrigerants are freon 11 (CCl_3F) and freon 12 (CCl_2F_2). As a vapor the freon is compressed in the compressor, increasing its temperature. At this high pressure and temperature, the vapor passes through the condenser coils to be cooled by the surrounding water and condensed into a liquid as shown in Figure 34. Still under pressure, the liquid refrigerant enters through the expansion valve into the evaporator where the pressure is lowered by the suction stroke of the compressor. The boiling point of the liquid refrigerant drops, and it changes into a gas (it *vaporizes*). For this vaporization, a great deal of heat is withdrawn from the air or water surrounding the evaporator coils. The vaporized refrigerant is drawn back into the compressor through the suction valve to be again compressed in a continuous cycle.

In large air conditioning systems, water is chilled in the evaporator and piped to the desired portion of the building. In smaller systems, such as unit air conditioners, the air to be cooled is allowed to enter the evaporator cabinet directly.

Humidity Control

As far as human comfort is concerned, temperature and humidity are inseparable. In dry air (low humidity), perspiration evaporates readily and cools the skin. Consequently, winter heating is enhanced by *humidification* of the air. In moist air (high humidity), perspiration will not evaporate, and the skin and clothing become wet and uncomfortable. Summer cooling, then, is aided by *dehumidification*.

It is generally agreed that a comfortable winter temperature is 74° with a relative humidity between 30 and 35 percent. Lower humidity will dry furniture and house members, causing them to crack and warp. Higher humidity

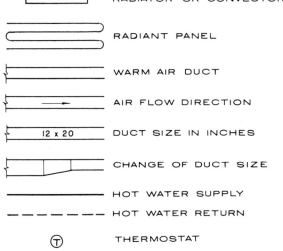

RADIATOR OR CONVECTOR

RADIANT PANEL

WARM AIR DUCT

AIR FLOW DIRECTION

12 x 20   DUCT SIZE IN INCHES

CHANGE OF DUCT SIZE

HOT WATER SUPPLY

HOT WATER RETURN

(T)   THERMOSTAT

Figure 32. Heating symbols.

Table I. Radiant and radiant convector baseboard units
(average water temperature = 200°F)

Type	Height	Rated Output (Btu/hr./ft. of baseboard)
R (Radiant)	L (Low: 7″)	255
R (Radiant)	H (High: 10″)	365
RC (Radiant convector)	L (Low: 8″)	430
RC (Radiant convector)	H (High: 10″)	605

causes condensation on windows and possibly on walls. A summer temperature of 76° at a relative humidity[1] under 60 percent is desirable. Indoor temperatures in the summer are not lowered more than 15° below the outdoor temperatures to prevent an unpleasant chill upon entering or the feeling of intense heat upon leaving the building.

In addition to thermostats for controlling temperature, air conditioners are provided with *hygrostats* (also called *humidistats*), which are sensitive to and control the humidity of the air. Separate humidifiers and dehumidifiers in portable units are also available.

1. *Relative humidity* is the ratio of the quantity of water vapor actually present to the greatest amount possible for the air to hold at a given temperature.

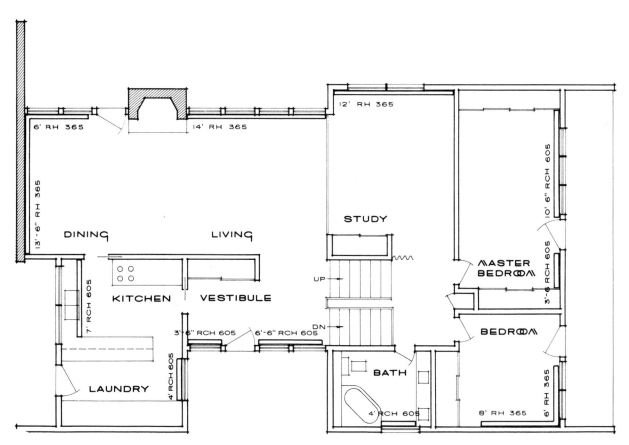

Figure 33. Heating plan of the M residence.

Temperature, humidity, and ventilation are all important to human comfort. A too-warm room having a gentle air motion may be more comfortable than a cooler room containing still, stale air. For air motion, a velocity of about 25 ft./min. is considered satisfactory. Much higher velocities cause uncomfortable drafts. Air conditioning systems in large buildings continuously introduce some fresh outdoor air and exhaust stale air containing excess carbon dioxide, reduced oxygen, and unpleasant odors. Air from toilets, kitchen, and smoking and meeting rooms is not recirculated but is exhausted directly. A complete air change every 15 minutes is recommended for most activities. In an uncrowded home, natural infiltration provides a satisfactory amount of fresh outdoor air.

Filtering

Air contaminated with dust, smoke, and fumes can be purified by filters and air washers of many designs. The most commonly used air filters are dry filters, viscous filters, and electric precipitators. *Dry filters* are pads of fibrous material, such as spun glass or porous paper or cloth, which must be cleaned or replaced to remain effective. *Viscous filters* are screens coated with sticky oil to trap dust. They may be cleaned by air or water and recharged by dipping in oil. *Electric precipitators* remove particles by passing the air through a high-voltage field. This charges the dust particles, which are then attracted to plates of opposite polarity.

Air Conditioning Systems

Air conditioning systems are designated central or unit systems. A *central system* may be designed as part of the heating system, using the same blower, filters, ducts or pipes, and registers. A *unit system* is separate from the heating system, having its own distribution method. In general, a single, combined, all-season system is more economical than two separate ones which must duplicate equipment.

For greater accuracy of control, it is often desirable to divide a building into zones for cooling as well as for heating. Frequently the sections of a house vary in the amount of heating and cooling required due to different exposures to prevailing winds and sun, varying construction materials, and different uses. A thermostat is placed in each zone. A zone may be a group of rooms or a single room.

Cooling systems may be combined with most heating systems. The warm-air system can supply cooled air as well. Chilled water can be circulated through the same pipes used in hot-water or steam heating systems. In this case, the room convectors are equipped with blowers to circulate the warm room air over the chilled coils. The operation of the heat pump can be reversed to either supply or withdraw heat as required.

Self-contained room-sized *unit systems* are particularly effective in buildings with naturally defined zones. The units may be controlled automatically or manually, as desired.

The air conditioning engineer selects, from manufacturers' catalogs, air conditioning units having appropriate cooling rates. The cooling rates are in British thermal units per hour or in tons of refrigeration. (A ton of refrigeration is the amount of refrigeration produced by melting a ton of ice in 24 hours.) A ton is equivalent to 12,000 Btu/hr. A small house will usually require a 2- or 3-ton unit, a large house a 5-ton (60,000 Btu/hr) unit.

Solar Air Conditioning

Research is now under way to perfect an air cooling system powered by some natural process rather than by a costly mechanical process. Recently an experimental solar air-conditioned home was built in Phoenix, Arizona. This building has a flat water-film roof in thermal contact with metal ceilings beneath; the roof is covered by horizontal plastic panels. During winter daylight, the panels are retracted to allow the sun to heat the water and the house. The panels are retracted during summer nights also, but for a different reason: this allows the water film to evaporate, which cools the water and the house.

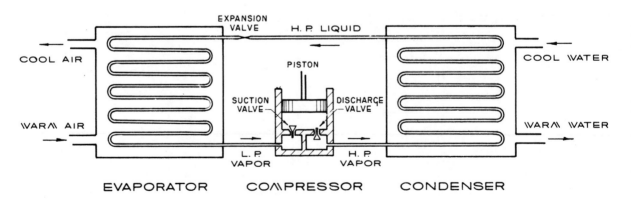

Figure 34. Mechanical air conditioner.

21

Energy Conservation

The necessity to conserve energy has become increasingly evident and is a worldwide goal. When reading a plan, you should develop the ability to determine if the proposed building is energy-efficient or energy-extravagant. Some of the principal areas of residential energy conservation are in the reduction of waste in home heating and cooling, hot-water heating, and electrical use.

Heat Conservation

Residential and commercial buildings require approximately one-third of the total energy we use. Most of this energy is needed to heat or cool buildings as shown in Figure 1, so the search for improvement has concentrated on improved insulation and other methods to save heat.

Insulation

Houses should be insulated to obtain the maximum efficiency from the heating and cooling systems, and to provide the comfort of a steady temperature. Properly installed insulation can reduce heating and cooling costs by as much as 40 percent while at the same time making the house warm in winter and cool in summer.

Insulation is available in many forms. For new house construction, batts or blankets (rolls) are often specified. They are sized to fit snugly between joists or rafters and between studs. Most frame houses in cold climates are now being built with $2'' \times 6''$ studs spaced $24''$ oc (rather than $2'' \times 4''$ studs at $16''$ oc) to permit $6''$ of wall insulation. Ceiling insulation is often $9''$ or $12''$ thick. However, it is important to understand that the insulating ability of different materials varies considerably. To provide a dependable system of comparison, insulating ability is specified by *R-values* (resistance values).

R-values. R-values are marked on all types of insulation and are the best indication of insulating effectiveness. A type or brand of insulation with a high R-value has a higher insulating value than insulation with a low R-value. Two different types or different brands of insulation with identical R-values will have the same insulating value, even if they have different thicknesses. Insulation in batts and blankets is commonly produced with R-values of 38, 30, 19, and 11 as shown in Table I. R-values are additive. That is, two R-19 batts equal one R-38 batt. Table II indicates the amount of insulation recommended for houses in cold climates.

Installation. Obviously, insulation will not be very effective if carelessly installed. For example, batts and blankets should fit tightly without "fishmouth" gaps between the insulation and the studs. Small spaces and cracks should be hand-packed with loose wool. As shown in Figure 2, as much insulation should be installed as the available stud and joist depths allow. However, foil-faced insulation must be

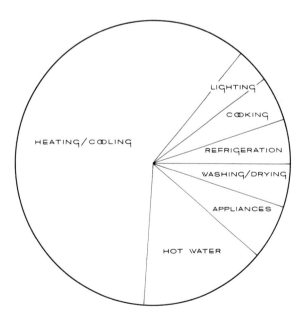

Figure 1. Home energy consumption.

143

Table I. Common R numbers for mineral fiber batts

R Number	Thickness
R-11	3 1/2″
R-19	6″
R-30	9 1/2″
R-38	12″

Table II. Recommended insulation in cold climates

Building Component	Recommended Insulation
Ceiling	R-30 or R-38
Walls	R-11 or R-19
Basement walls	R-11
Floors (over unheated space)	R-19
Slab-on-grade	R-7 (2″ rigid insulation)

installed with a 3/4″ air space as shown in Figure 3 to benefit from the reflective value of the foil.

Most insulation batts and blankets are made with a vapor barrier on one side, which is installed facing the inside (warm side) of the house to prevent condensation. Condensation occurs only when moisture reaches a cold surface through which it cannot readily pass, and the vapor barrier, when properly installed, does not become cold. If the insulation is improperly installed, with the vapor barrier toward the outside (cold side) of the house, moisture will condense upon contact with the cold vapor barrier, making the insulation ineffective. Also, any breaks in the vapor barrier will decrease its effectiveness. All such breaks should be repaired before the insulation is covered by the wall surface.

For fire safety, insulation must not be installed within 3″ of recessed lighting fixtures or other heat-producing equipment.

Superinsulation. Buildings insulated more heavily than recommended in Table II are termed *superinsulated*. Buildings have been built, for example, with R-30 wall insulation by staggering 2″ × 4″ studs within a 10″ wall, thus preventing any heat loss by direct passage through the studs.

Types of Insulation. Two forms of insulation are commonly available: mineral wool (fiber glass and rock wool) and cellulose.

Mineral wool is manufactured in batts, blankets (rolls), and loose-fill. The loose-fill is installed by pouring or blowing under pressure. Mineral wool is preferred over other types of insulation because it is not combustible (since it is made from glass or rock), and does not slump under pressure.

Cellulose, on the other hand, is a paper product and is chemically treated to make it fire-retardant. Unfortunately,

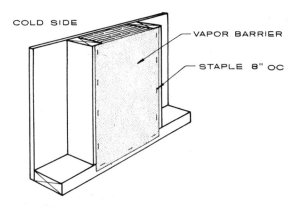

Figure 2. Nonfoil insulation should completely fill the available space.

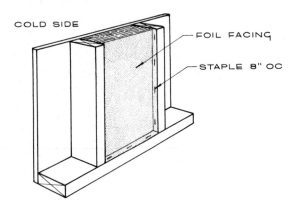

Figure 3. Foil-faced insulation requires a 3/4″ air gap.

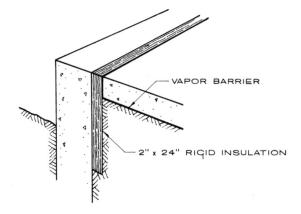

Figure 4. Perimeter insulation for slab construction.

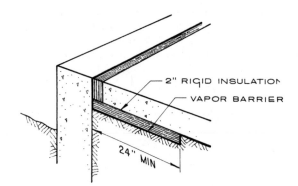

Figure 5. Alternate method of installing perimeter insulation.

the chemicals can be driven off by summer heat. Also, they leach out when the insulation becomes wet. Cellulose insulation slumps to about half its volume when wet.

Rigid insulation made of asphalt-impregnated fiberboard, and *foamed plastics*, such as Styrofoam and Urethane, are frequently used as insulation under built-up roofs. A common size for these materials is 24″ × 48″ in thicknesses of 1/2″ to 3″ in 1/2″ increments. Foamed plastics are popular as perimeter insulation, installed between the foundation and the floor slab. Perimeter insulation is often 2″ thick by 24″ wide as shown in Figures 4 and 5. Insulation can also be sprayed on the interior of a building in thicknesses up to 2″.

To insulate existing buildings, loose-fill insulation can be poured between studs and joists, or blowing wool can be blown in, filling the walls to the full depth of the studs and to the desired depth between joists.

Additional Measures

In addition to insulation, many additional actions can help conserve heat:

1. Double glazing (such as thermopanes or storm windows over single panes) reduces heat loss through the windows by about 60 percent. Double glazing of low-E glass (low-emissivity glass manufactured with a microthin transparent coating that reflects inside heat in the winter and outside heat in the summer) reduces heat loss by about 66 percent. Triple glazing (storm windows over thermopanes) is even more effective and reduces heat loss by about 75 percent. Double and triple glazing also has the advantages of reducing noise and condensation on the windows.

2. Appropriate glazing can also help cool the house in the summer. To reduce solar heat and glare, windows can be glazed with heat-absorbing glass. Such glass, combined with an ingenious design, reduced the solar heat load by 75 percent in the Norfolk City Hall shown in Figure 6. An outer window wall is fastened 3′ from the inner window wall with tubular steel trusses. This permits a cooling air flow between both layers of glass as illustrated in Figure 7. The upper grid serves as a solar screen and is also used as a walkway for window washers.

3. Storm doors reduce transmitted heat loss through doors by about 40 percent. Storm doors also reduce the amount of heat lost when the door is opened.

4. Weatherstripping reduces heat lost by infiltration around doors by about 50 percent. Windows also should be weatherstripped if they do not close tightly. Weatherstripping is available in foam rubber, felt strips, flexible vinyl, spring metals, and other materials.

5. For maximum energy conservation, some houses are built partially or completely underground. The earth, with a more uniform temperature than air, protects against both the heat of summer and the cold of winter. At 10′ below the surface, the temperature of the earth remains at about the average year-round temperature at that location. This is about 50°F in a temperate zone. *Underground* structures (also called *earth-sheltered* structures) are often built not entirely underground. Designs vary from side-hill exposures to atrium concepts which are open to the sky.

Figure 6. Norfolk City Hall glazed with heat-absorbing glass.

Figure 7. Typical window section of Norfolk City Hall.

22

Reading Residential Plans

The architectural and mechanical plans for two buildings, the A residence and the M residence, have been used for examples throughout the preceding chapters. The A residence, an English garrison traditional design, appears in Chapters 9, 10, 12, and 16–18. The M residence, a split-level design, appears in Chapters 5, 6, 10, 19, and 20. Metric plans for the M residence are given in Figures 1–6 of the appendix.

The plans of a third residence, the Z residence, are given in Figures 7–12 of the appendix to give you another example of a set of architectural plans. The Z residence is a contemporary residence designed for a narrow plot having the best view to the rear. Scale indications are deleted from these fold-out plans because they are reduced from their original size. You should study these plans until you feel you understand them completely. Photographs of the finished building are included in this chapter to help you understand the plans. Photos of the exterior elevations are in Figures 1–3, and interior views of the living area, dining area, and master bedroom are in Figures 4–6. After studying both the plans and photographs, make a list of any questions and check them with your instructor at the first opportunity. Then complete the exercises as assigned. Review your answers carefully before submitting them to your instructor.

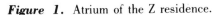

Figure 1. Atrium of the Z residence.

Figure 2. Front elevation of the Z residence.

Figure 3. Rear elevation of the Z residence.

Figure 4. Living room of the Z residence, looking toward the atrium.

Figure 5. Master bedroom of the Z residence.

Figure 6. Dining area of the Z residence, showing the breakfast bar and kitchen.

III

Reading Commercial Plans

23

Timber Construction

Timber construction was one of the earliest methods of building used by settlers in the New World. It has continued in popularity through the years, but not for the same reasons. Originally, timber was used because of the difficulty in hand-sawing logs into smaller lumber. Later, when lumber was readily available in all sizes, a type of timber construction called *mill construction* was used for factories and warehouses where the loads were heavy and the fire danger high. In mill construction, a few heavy posts and beams support a solid wood floor 3″ to 6″ thick—since a few large members will resist fire longer than many small members. In recent years, mill construction for industrial buildings has been replaced by steel and concrete construction methods. But timber construction still continues in popularity for structures such as residences, churches, schools, gymnasiums, and commercial buildings where the timber is left exposed to present a permanent, yet warm, effect. Some of the most outstanding examples of contemporary architecture (Figure 1) have used this method of framing.

Heavy Timber

Heavy timber construction is similar to the plank-and-beam framing described in Chapter 8, but heavier members are used. Heavy timber construction, as defined by many building codes, consists of solid or glue-laminated wood columns at least 6″ × 8″ for supporting roof and ceiling loads and at least 8″ × 8″ for supporting floor loads. Beams are at least 6″ wide × 10″ deep. Floors and roofs have no concealed spaces but are built of solid or glue-laminated, continuous-span planking, splined or tongue-and-grooved, at least 2″ thick for roof support and at least 3″ thick for floor support. Major advantages are:

1. A few large structural members replace many small members.
2. Fire hazard is reduced.
3. Timbers and planks are often left exposed, eliminating the need for additional interior finish.

Some disadvantages of this type of construction are:

1. Special furring must be used to conceal pipes and electrical conduits installed on the ceiling.
2. Additional roof insulation must be used due to the elimination of dead air spaces between the roof and ceiling.
3. It is more difficult to control condensation. Exhaust fans are used to reduce moisture in the building to a minimum.

It should be mentioned that combinations of heavy timber and conventional construction are possible using the advantageous features of each type.

Construction Details. Figures 2–7 illustrate some common construction details. The location of fasteners in these figures is indicated by center lines. Bolts are usually

Figure 1. Visitor Information Center of timber construction, Jamestown, Virginia.

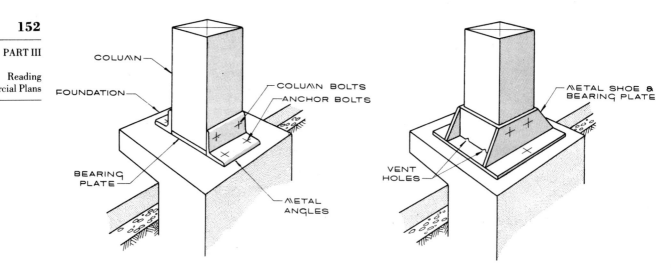

Figure 2. Column anchorages.

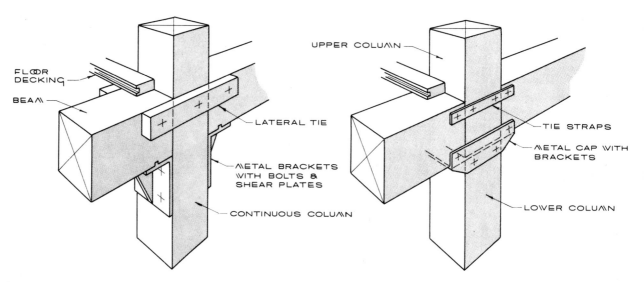

Figure 3. Floor beam and column framing.

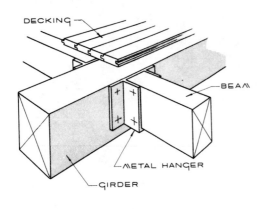

Figure 4. Beam and girder framing.

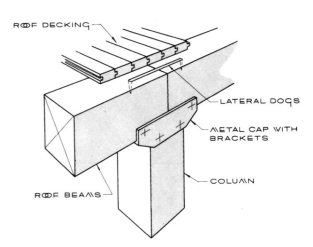

Figure 5. Roof beam framing.

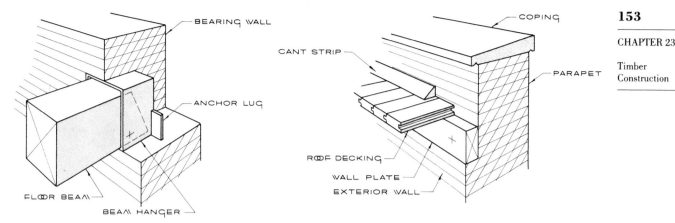

Figure 6. Beam framing at wall.

Figure 7. Plank framing at wall.

used with shear plates which distribute the load over a greater area. Shear plates are shown in Figure 8. They are completely embedded flush with the timber surface in precut *daps* (circular grooves). Shear plates are used for both timber-to-timber and timber-to-steel connections. Shear plates are 2 1/2″ to 4″ in diameter.

Laminated Timber

Laminated timber is fabricated in sizes and shapes that are difficult to obtain in solid timber. Also, seasoning and inspection of laminations can be better controlled, and select lumber can be used where good appearance and strength is desired, with less costly lumber used elsewhere.

Laminations are usually 2″ thick and glued together under pressure. This is best accomplished at a factory, since nails or other fasteners are not used to hold the laminations in contact while the glue sets. Water-resistive casein glue is used for interior uses, and waterproof resin glue is employed for exterior uses. This glue-laminated method of fabrication is sometimes called *gluelam construction*.

Laminated timber is usually fabricated of Douglas fir, southern yellow pine, or ponderosa pine. The laminations can be vertical, as in Figure 13, or horizontal, as in Figure 14. Vertically laminated timbers are often used for straight beams of moderate size; horizontally laminated timbers are used for curved or special shapes in large spans, such as arches, rigid frames, or tapered girders. Laminations 2″ thick can be bent to a radius of 24′. When the laminations must be spliced, scarfed end joints, beveled 1 in 8, are used. Laminated timber is typically spaced 6′ to 20′ oc.

Laminated timber is often finished at the factory. To protect the timber from moisture and the finish from scratches, it is wrapped in a waterproof membrane at the factory. The membrane is kept in place until the beam is in position and protected from moisture and construction damage.

Typical connection details are similar to those shown in Figures 9–11. Notice that metal connectors can be exposed or concealed when desired.

Laminated Decking. Laminated decking (Figure 12) is available in thicknesses from 2″ to 5″ and in widths from 6″ to 12″. Typically the core and back laminations will be Douglas fir or West Coast hemlock with the face lamination of red cedar. Routing for concealed wiring can be cut in the top of the decking parallel to the span. When perpendicular to the span, routing must be done only over support members. It is also possible to cover wiring with rigid insulation without routing.

Box Beams

Box beams are lightweight, economical, and easily fabricated into a variety of tapered, arched, or curved shapes (Figure 16). They may be used as an alternate to built-up girders and lintels in light frame construction and as an alternate to solid or laminated beams in post-and-beam construction. They are used for spans from 8′ to 120′.

Box beams are hollow, structural units composed of vertical plywood webs fastened to seasoned lumber flanges. Vertical spacers are also included to prevent web-buckling and to provide a backup at the joints of the plywood. See Figure 17.

Several typical box beam designs are detailed in Figures 19 and 20. Notice how the plywood web joints are staggered in both instances. Figure 18 illustrates the use of box beams in a rigid frame type of construction.

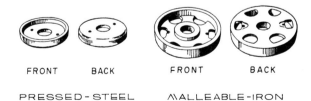

Figure 8. Shear plates.

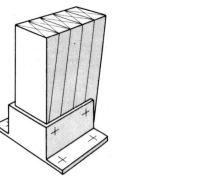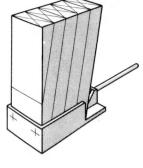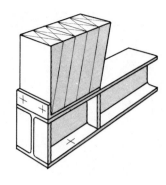

HORIZONTAL THRUST TO FLOOR SLAB   HORIZONTAL THRUST TO TIE ROD   HORIZONTAL THRUST TO STEEL BEAM

Figure 9. Arch anchorages.

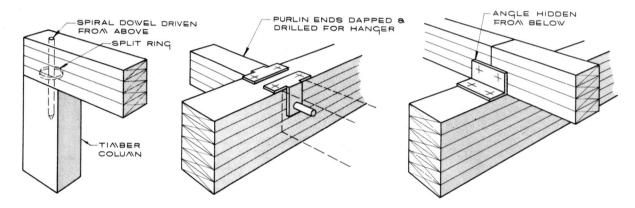

Figure 10. Concealed beam connections.

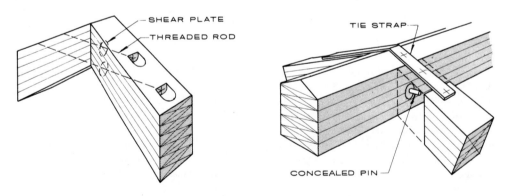

Figure 11. Concealed crown connections.

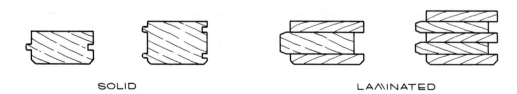

SOLID   LAMINATED

Figure 12. Types of tongue-and-grooved planking.

Figure 13. Vertically laminated beam with tongue-and-grooved planking.

Figure 14. Horizontally laminated arch—buttress connection detail.

Figure 15. A folded-plate roof of stressed-skin panels.

Stressed-Skin Panels

Stressed-skin panels are used for floors, roofs, and walls in all types of prefabricated building construction. Flat stressed-skin panels are made by glueing and nailing plywood sheets to lumber joists, as shown in Figure 23. Usually 4'-wide sheets are glued to four joists and two headers, thus replacing conventional joist and subflooring construction.

In conventional floor and roof framing, joists act as the sole structural support for dead and live loads,[1] including the dead load of the subflooring. In stressed-skin panel construction, plywood sheets are bonded to the joists to provide an

integral structural unit. The upper sheet of plywood aids in resisting compressive stresses, and the lower sheet aids in resisting tensile stresses in much the same manner that the upper and lower flanges of a steel beam resist compressive and tensile stresses. Figure 21 shows workers installing stressed-skin panels.

Folded-plate roofs are often constructed of stressed-skin panels. The inclined panels lean against one another and are stabilized by tie rods. The end of each valley is supported by columns (Figure 15). Folded-plate sections may be assembled at the factory and delivered to the job site.

Curved stressed-skin panels (Figure 24) are used for the construction of unique roof shapes. Construction is similar to the construction of flat panels, but curved, laminated ribs are used to replace straight joists. Figure 22 shows workers installing curved stressed-skin panels.

1. The *live load* is the weight supported by a building (contents, people, wind, and snow loads), and the *dead load* is the weight of the building itself.

Figure 16. Some box beam shapes.

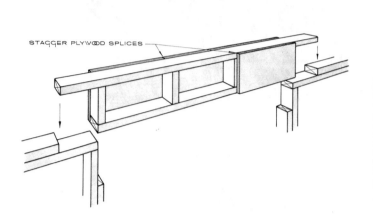

STAGGER PLYWOOD SPLICES

Figure 17. Installing a 12′ box beam lintel.

Figure 18. Box beams used for rigid frame construction.

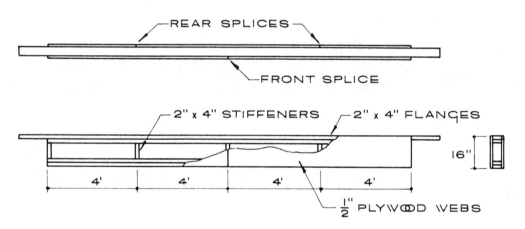

REAR SPLICES

FRONT SPLICE

2″ x 4″ STIFFENERS   2″ x 4″ FLANGES

16″

4′   4′   4′   4′

½″ PLYWOOD WEBS

Figure 19. Detail of a 16′ garage door header box beam.

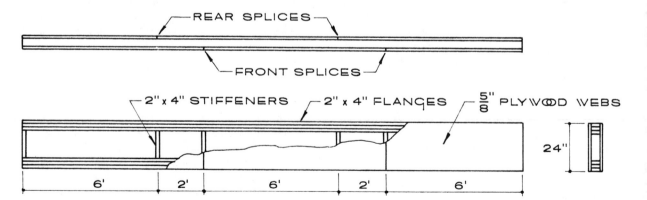

REAR SPLICES

FRONT SPLICES

2″ x 4″ STIFFENERS   2″ x 4″ FLANGES   ⅝″ PLYWOOD WEBS

24″

6′   2′   6′   2′   6′

Figure 20. Detail of a 22′ ridge box beam.

Figure 21. Installing flat stressed-skin panels.

Figure 22. Installing curved stressed-skin panels.

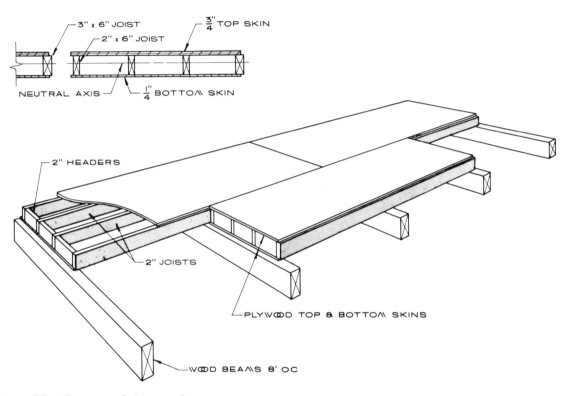

Figure 23. Flat stressed-skin panel.

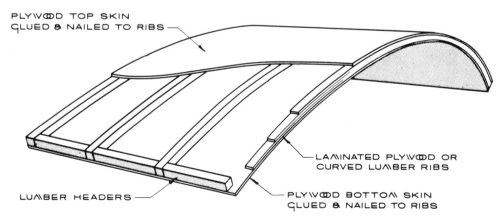

Figure 24. Curved stressed-skin panel.

24

Masonry Construction

Masonry construction refers to buildings made of stone, brick, concrete block, and structural clay tile—all materials used by masons. Stone and brick have been important building materials for thousands of years, stone being the oldest natural building material and brick the oldest manufactured material. Later, new materials such as concrete block, structural clay tile, and even glass block were developed.

Concrete Masonry

Concrete masonry units, usually called *concrete* block,[1] are commonly used as a construction material. Their use exceeds the combined use of all other types of masonry units. Concrete block are manufactured by molding under pressure a

1. The words *block*, *brick*, and *tile* are used to describe both singular and plural units.

stiff mixture of portland cement, aggregates, and water in steel molds. The "green" block holds its shape even though immediately removed from the mold. Curing (drying) is accomplished within a day by treating with steam in a drying kiln. Both heavyweight units (concrete block) and lightweight units (cinder block) are available. The stronger heavyweight unit is composed of crushed stone or gravel aggregate. The aggregate of the lightweight unit is crushed coal cinders, which is superior for insulation, nailability, and resistance to fire.

Sizes. Concrete block, like masonry units, are manufactured in modular sizes based on the 4″ module. The 8″ × 8″ × 16″ *stretcher* (Figure 1) is the unit most often used. The actual size of such a unit is 7 5/8″ × 7 5/8″ × 15 5/8″ to allow for 3/8″ mortar joints. Block in 10″ and 12″ nominal widths are manufactured for use in thicker walls. The *corner block* is used for squared corners and the *bullnose block* for

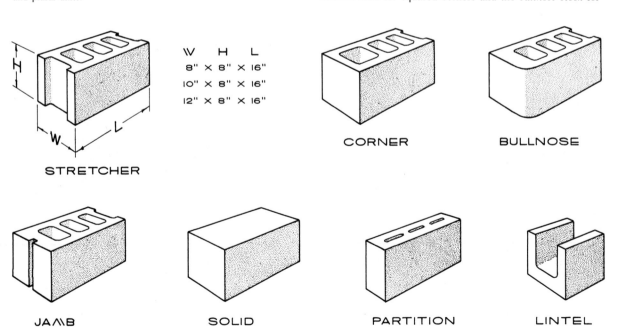

W	H	L
8″	8″	16″
10″	8″	16″
12″	8″	16″

STRETCHER   CORNER   BULLNOSE

JAMB   SOLID   PARTITION   LINTEL

Figure 1. Typical concrete block units.

rounded corners. *Jamb block* are laid around window and door openings. *Solid* (uncored) *block*, available in widths of 2″, 3″, 4″, 6″, 8″, 10″, and 12″, are used as bearing block. *Partition block* are available in 3″, 4″, and 6″ widths and are used to form interior partitions, exterior cavity walls, and composite walls. *Lintel block* are used as forms for reinforced concrete when constructing lintels over openings or bond beams around the entire structure. They have the added advantage of continuing the pattern formed by the stretcher block. Half-length units 8″ long are available for most of the block shown in Figure 1.

Variations. Block *glazed* on the exposed surfaces are available in all colors. Some types of units are shown in Figure 2. The glazed facing is 1/8″ thick and is quite resistant to abrasion, impact, and chemicals. Units glazed on opposite sides are used for interior partitions. Also available are units in a variety of patterned surfaces. Pierced grille block are used for solar screens and special effects.

Mortar and Joints. Mortar may be applied to the webs as well as to the edges of concrete block (called *full mortar bedding*) or to the edges only (called *face-shell bedding*). Full mortar bedding is used in laying the starting course of block on a footing or to support heavy loads. Face-shell bedding is used for all ordinary work.

The simplest masonry joint is the *flush joint* (Figure 3) which is made by trimming excess mortar with the trowel. A hairline crack may appear between mortar and block, so this is not always a watertight joint. The *concave joint* is produced by a circular tool, and the *vee joint* by a square tool. These are very weather-resistant joints and are recommended in areas of heavy rain and wind or freezing temperatures. The *weathered joint* and the *struck joint* are cut with a trowel. The weathered joint is somewhat compacted and sheds water. The struck joint is commonly used because it is easy to make when the mason is working from the inside of a wall. There is some compaction, but the small ledge tends to hold moisture longer. The *raked joint* is made with a square-edged tool. It is not a dependable weather-resistant joint but is often specified by architects to emphasize the mortar joints. A popular treatment is raked horizontal joints with flush vertical joints to create strong horizontal lines.

Concrete Masonry Construction

Concrete block are used for bearing and curtain (non-load-bearing) walls and partitions. Concrete block can also serve as a backing for brick, stone, and other facings, and as fireproofing for steel structural members. Properly reinforced, they are used as columns and lintels. *Concrete brick* units are also available.

Single-Wythe Walls. The starting course of block is laid to a chalk line snapped on the footing. A full bed of mortar is spread on the footing, and a corner block is laid to the line, level and plumb. Adjacent block are laid and are constantly checked for accurate positioning. When the starting course has been completed, the usual practice is to lay the corner block first, then stretch lines between them to serve as guides in laying the stretcher block (Figure 4).

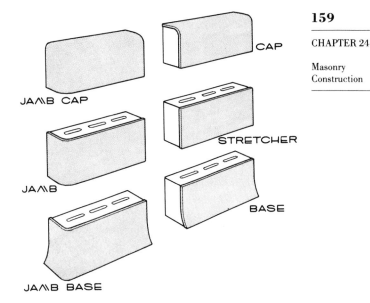

Figure 2. Glazed partition block.

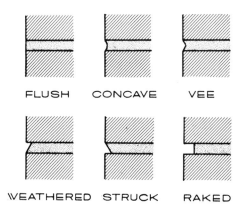

Figure 3. Types of mortar joints.

Figure 4. Laying a single-wythe block wall.

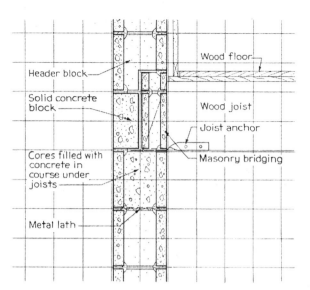

Figure 5. Wood joist floor framing into a single-wythe wall.

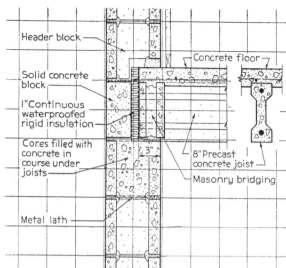

Figure 6. Concrete slab floor framing into a single-wythe wall.

When beams or floor slabs frame into a block wall, the supporting course should be of solid masonry. This serves to distribute the load on the wall and also deters termites. Either a course of solid block can be used, or the cores of hollow block can be filled with mortar, as shown in Figures 5 and 6. The mason places strips of metal lath in the joint below to support the mortar filling the cores.

It is common practice to strengthen concrete block walls by the use of a *bond beam* at each story height. Bond beams are constructed by placing two reinforcing bars in a continuous course of lintel block and filling the trough with concrete. Vertical reinforcing is also possible by pouring concrete around reinforcing rods set in the cores of block at corners, wall openings, and regular intervals between wall openings. The vertical reinforcing should be tied in with the horizontal bond beams, as shown in Figure 7.

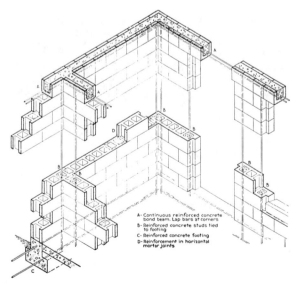

Figure 7. Reinforcing block walls.

Intersecting concrete block walls are not tied together by a masonry bond (except at corners). Rather, metal tie bars are used to tie bearing walls together, and metal lath (hardware cloth) to tie nonbearing walls to bearing walls.

Jamb block are used to form the sides of window and door openings. Precast concrete sills are available for use with both metal and wood sash. Reinforced concrete beams, used as window and door lintels, are commonly available in 4″ and 6″ nominal widths and an 8″ nominal height (Figure 8). Two lintels placed side by side (called *split lintels*) are used in walls thicker than 6″. If a floor load—in addition to the normal wall load—has to be supported by the lintel, a special beam designed by an architectural engineer is used.

When a block wall is to be covered by a wood-framed roof, wood top plates are fastened to the top of the wall by anchor bolts. The bolts are set in mortar poured in the cores of the top two courses of block.

Masonry walls may also be finished by *parapets*. A parapet acts as a safety wall for anyone walking on the roof. It also screens unsightly roof projections such as ventilators and stacks. To prevent moisture from entering the cores of the block, the parapet is topped with a *coping* as shown in Figure 9.

Expansion Joints and Control Joints. Building materials are in a state of relative motion at many times. This motion, although quite small, is sufficient to seriously damage a building not designed to accommodate this factor. There are three major causes for movement: temperature changes, moisture changes, and settlement. A 100′-long masonry wall, for example, expands nearly 1/2″ due to a 100° temperature increase from winter to summer. Unless vertical *expansion joints* (separations filled with a flexible material) are provided in such a wall, cracks will appear. Figure 10 illustrates some forms of expansion joints. The weather side of the joint is sealed with calking compound or the newer polymer sealing compound.

A form of expansion joint called a *control joint* may be

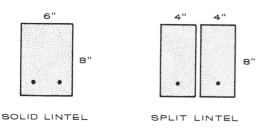

SOLID LINTEL   SPLIT LINTEL

Figure 8. Reinforced concrete lintels.

provided by raking the mortar from a continuous vertical joint to a depth of 3/4″. The recess is then filled with calking compound. Obviously, a control joint is not compressible, but it does reduce unsightly, random cracks.

Composite Walls. Concrete block can be used as a backing for a more costly facing such as brick (Figure 11). In this manner, the required wall thickness is efficiently obtained without sacrificing the desired architectural effect. Commonly used are 8″ and 12″ composite walls (also called *faced walls*). Bonding between the wythes of facing and backing may be accomplished through the use of 3/16″-diameter steel wall ties (Figure 11).

Bonding may also be achieved by pouring *grout* (mortar thinned to a pouring consistency) into the cavity between wythes. When reinforcing rods have been placed between the wythes, as shown in Figure 12, they are surrounded and bonded by the grout. This produces a reinforced masonry wall and is often specified in areas subject to earthquakes.

A composite wall is shown in Figure 14. Notice that the cores of the hollow block wythe provide a passage for the installation of plumbing and electrical conduits.

Cavity Walls. A cavity wall consists of two wythes of masonry separated by a 2″ air space (Figure 13). The air space provides greater protection against rain penetration than does a composite wall. The air space also provides insulation. The two wythes are tied together with metal ties. A cavity wall detail is shown in Figure 15.

Brick Masonry

Brick, structural clay tile, and architectural terra-cotta are produced from clay, the most plentiful raw material used to manufacture any building product. The clay is crushed, ground, screened, and mixed with water to a plastic consistency. The clay is molded to shape, dried in ovens, and then *burned* (fired) in kilns. Face, common, glazed, and fire brick are all produced by this process. *Face brick* are manufactured with special color and texture to exposed surfaces. Face brick may be backed with *common brick*, which are used for general construction. *Fire brick* are made from fire clays. Their resistance to heat permits them to be used in furnaces and chimneys. *Glazed brick* are also made from fire clay and are finished with glazes in many colors.

Sizes. The size of a standard brick is often 3 3/4″ × 2 1/4″ × 8″, but brick sizes vary widely with the locality and

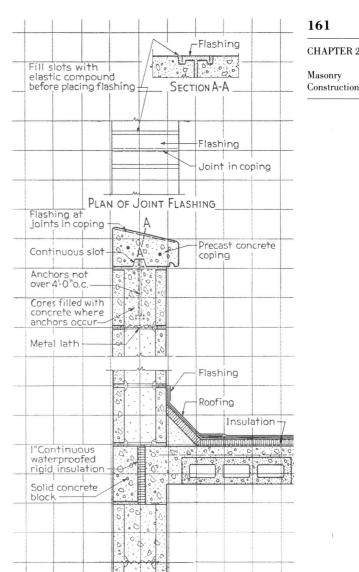

Figure 9. Coping and parapet construction on a single-wythe wall.

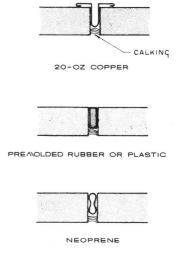

Figure 10. Expansion joints.

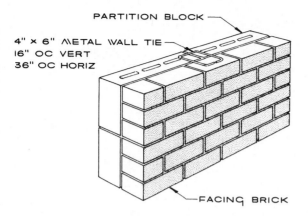

Figure 11. 8″ composite wall—wall tie bonded.

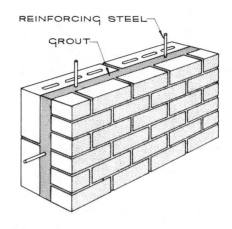

Figure 12. Reinforced masonry.

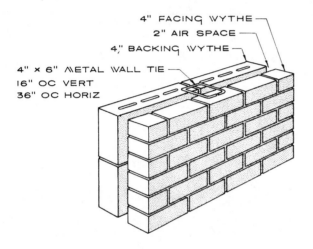

Figure 13. 10″ cavity wall.

Figure 14. Installation of plumbing and electrical conduits in block wall.

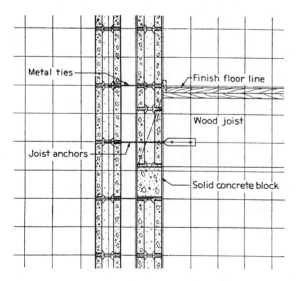

Figure 15. Wood joist floor framing into a cavity wall.

manufacturer. Four common types of modular brick (called modular, Roman, Norman, and SCR) are listed in Table I. Their modular dimensions will not vary, but their actual dimensions will vary depending upon the intended thickness of the mortar joint. The actual dimensions shown in this table are based on 1/2″ mortar joints. Notice that the joint thickness can be added to the actual dimensions to obtain the modular dimensions. In general, 1/2″ joints are used for general construction, 3/8″ joints for facing brick, and 1/4″ joints with glazed brick. Figure 16 shows how various brick types fit in a 4″ modular system. The Roman and Norman brick are shown in a one-third bond. This means that each brick is covered by a third of another brick in the course above, thus reducing the number of bricks that have to be cut. Brick may be manufactured with hollow cores to reduce their weight.

SCR brick was developed and named by the Structural Clay Products Research Foundation. It is formed with a 3/4″ × 3/4″ jamb slot at one end. The SCR brick is intended for use in 6″ solid, load-bearing masonry walls for single-story structures. Ordinarily, 2″ × 2″ furring is applied to

Table I. Brick sizes

	Actual Dimensions			Modular Dimensions			
	Width	*Height*	*Length*	*Width*	*Height*	*Length*	*Coursing*
Standard	3 3/4″	2 1/4″	8″				
Modular	3 1/2″	2 1/6″	7 1/2″	4″	2 2/3″	8″	3C = 8″
Roman	3 1/2″	1 1/2″	11 1/2″	4″	2″	12″	2C = 4″
Norman	3 1/2″	2 1/6″	11 1/2″	4″	2 2/3″	12″	3C = 8″
SCR	5 1/2″	2 1/6″	11 1/2″	6″	2 2/3″	12″	3C = 8″

STANDARD MODULAR ROMAN NORMAN SCR

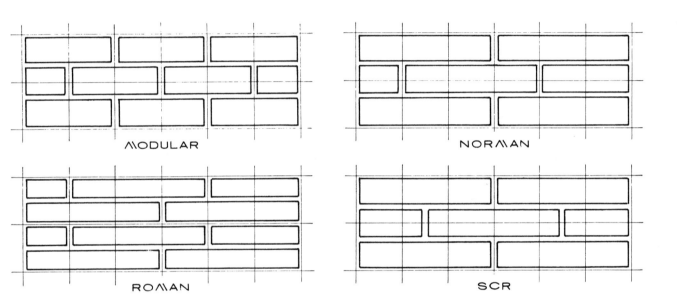

MODULAR NORMAN

ROMAN SCR

Figure 16. Modular coordination of brick types.

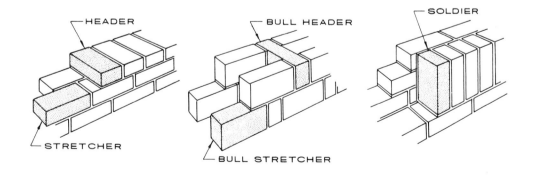

HEADER BULL HEADER SOLDIER

STRETCHER BULL STRETCHER

Figure 17. Brick terminology.

Figure 18. Bucks County Courthouse, Doylestown, Pennsylvania.

Figure 19. High School in Columbus, Indiana.

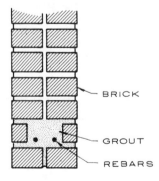

Figure 20. Reinforced brick lintel.

the interior face to provide a moisture barrier and to permit installation of blanket insulation, electrical fixtures, pipe, and ducts. Building codes do not permit pipe or duct chases to be built into masonry walls less than 8″ thick.

Brick are also available in a variety of special shapes for use as sills, caps, lintels, and corners.

Brick wall patterns are most interesting when headers or bull headers (Figure 17) are used in structural bonding. Of course all the pattern bonds shown can be formed using half-brick headers, called *snap headers*, in a veneer wall.

Brick Masonry Construction

Although brick walls tend to look alike, there are a number of different ways in which brick can be used in those walls. The brick can be merely a facing—a 4″ non-load-bearing veneer covering a wood, steel, or concrete skeleton. Or the brick may be used to construct a load-bearing wall—a solid brick wall of 6″ single-wythe or 8″ (or more) multiple-wythe, a reinforced brick masonry wall, or a cavity wall. Often, the face brick you see is only on the outside of a building and is backed up by less costly materials, such as concrete block or structural clay tile.

Brick Masonry Arches. The arch shape has appealed to many ancient civilizations and is still used today. One of the principal advantages of the arch is its ability to bridge a space using materials, such as brick, that have a greater resistance to compression than to tension. Arches may be used as minor design elements such as window and door lintels, as shown in Figure 18, or as major design elements, as shown in Figure 19.

Arches are built over temporary forms that carry the dead load of the masonry until the mortar has hardened. These forms can be removed seven days after the masonry work is finished. Usually mortar joints are tapered to provide the required curvature of the arch, but specially tapered brick may also be obtained. As shown in Figure 21, both soldier and header bonds are types commonly used in brick arch work. The *flat arch* is often supported by a steel lintel. When this occurs, it is not considered a true arch. A *segmental arch* is in the form of a circular arc but is less than a *semicircular arch*.

Reinforced Brick Lintels. Reinforced brick lintels have the aesthetic advantage of using the same material for both the wall surface and the lintel surface. Reinforced brick lintels are usually built in place using temporary shoring. The lintel thickness is equal to the wall thickness. After the soffit brick are laid, reinforcing steel is placed and surrounded by grout. An example of a reinforced brick lintel is shown in Figure 20.

Stone Masonry

Stone has been the favorite building material for large structures for thousands of years. Although it is now seldom used for structural purposes, stone is still a popular finish material, as a result of a combination of desirable characteristics. Stone represents strength, permanence, and quality. It also looks more natural than the manufactured appearance of most other building materials. *Stone* refers to quarried pieces of *rock*, but these terms are also used synonymously.

Rock is quarried by removing the overburden by machine or explosives. The exposed rock may be stratified in horizontal *beds*, such as sandstone, or may be structured in masses such as granite. In either instance the rock may be separated by *seams* which can run in any direction. When the rock is already broken up by beds and seams, it is removed by wedges and crowbars. But when it is unbroken, vertical cuts are made by channeling machines or by drilling a line of closely spaced holes. Steel wedges are then hammered into the holes until the rock splits. Horizontal separations are made by wedges between the bedding planes or by another line of drilled holes.

Stone may be used as it comes from the quarry without additional dressing. The faces of such stone are called *seam-faced* when caused by a natural seam, *split-faced* when split along beds, and *quarry-faced* when caused by the quarrying operations. Additional forming and finishing may be done at a stone mill where power gang saws are used to cut stone into 4″ building stone for facing, 2″ flagstones, or 1″ veneers.

Stone Masonry Construction

Three general classifications of stone masonry are *rubble*, *ashlar*, and *cut stone*. Rubble masonry consists of stones that have not been cut to any special shape. When the stones are stratified, the bed faces are laid horizontally, resulting in *coursed rubble*. Uncoursed rubble is called *random rubble*. Ashlar consists of stones whose edge surfaces have been cut into plane surfaces. The stones are laid with horizontal bed joints and either vertical or inclined head joints. When the bed joints are continuous, the masonry is termed *coursed ashlar*; when not continuous, it is called *random ashlar*. Figure 22 shows these classifications.

The term *cut stone* (Figure 23) designates stone that has been individually cut to the architect's specifications. Each stone is then numbered in accordance with the shop drawings to facilitate identification and installation.

Stone work is set in full mortar joints 1/4″ to 1/2″ thick. Ashlar stone facing can be backed with rubble stone, concrete, concrete block, or brick. The facing and backing wythes are bonded together by metal anchors, bond stones, or bond courses. When both wythes act as a single structural unit, the wall is called a *faced* wall. When the facing wythe is merely attached to backing that carries the load, the wall is called a *veneered* wall. The veneer can also be hung from a steel frame backing using noncorrosive metal anchors.

Openings in a stone wall may be spanned by stone arches or lintels. Stone lintels no longer than 6′ are usually supported by a steel angle. An I beam or a channel section is used for longer lintels.

Stone windowsills and doorsills are called *slip sills* when they are the same length as the opening, and *lug sills* when they are long enough to be built into the wall on either side. Slip sills are less likely to crack on settlement of the wall, but the mortar may wash out of their end joints.

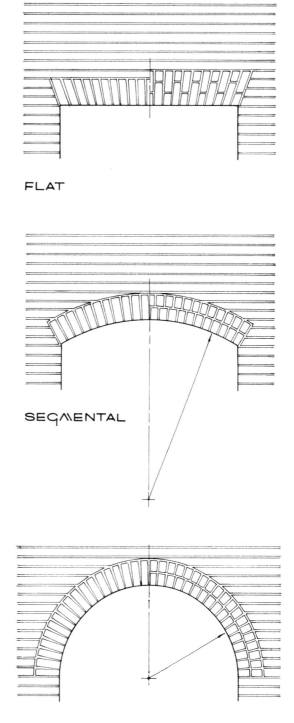

FLAT

SEGMENTAL

SEMICIRCULAR

Figure 21. Masonry arch forms.

Cast Stone. Cast stone is an imitation stone of cast concrete. Most stone shapes and textures can be obtained in cast concrete, in addition to original finishes that do not imitate any structural stone. Installation is similar to laying stone or brick facing.

Coursed Rubble

Random Rubble

Coursed Ashlar

Random Ashlar

Figure 22. Types of stone masonry.

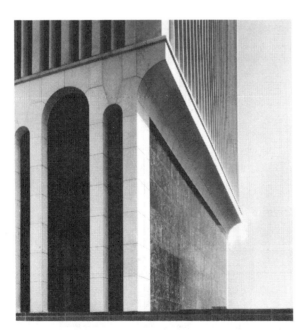

Figure 23. Cut stone used on the Manufacturers & Traders Trust Company Building, Buffalo, New York.

Glass Masonry

Building units of glass, commonly called *glass block*, are often specified for their decorative effect, but they also provide controlled light transmission, insulation, condensation protection, and sound reduction. Glass block are available in transparent, translucent, and opaque units (translucent means that light will be transmitted but without a clear image showing through).

A glass block is formed of two cast glass shells that are hermetically fused together to form a hollow unit containing a partial vacuum (Figure 24). This partial vacuum decreases heat transmission and surface condensation. The faces of the block can be smooth to provide vision through the block, textured to provide only light transmission, or fired with a ceramic finish to provide an opaque surface. Textured patterns are often cast on the interior surfaces, allowing the exposed surfaces to be smooth as an aid in cleaning. Some of these units are shown in Figure 25. Light-directing units, also illustrated in Figure 25, direct light up to the ceiling; from there, it reflects down on work surfaces some distance from the wall.

Sizes. The common modular size of glass block is 8″ square × 4″ thick. Also available are 6″ square, 12″ square, and 4″ × 8″ and 4″ × 12″ rectangular units—all 4″ thick. Actual sizes are 1/4″ smaller to allow for 1/4″ mortar joints.

Glass Masonry Construction

Glass block are used to construct both interior and exterior panels, but they are not structural building units and can support only their own weight. When large areas are desired, vertical mullions or horizontal shelf angles are introduced to support smaller areas. Glass block are laid using a stack bond.

A glass block panel is illustrated in Figure 26. Notice that chases were provided in the masonry jamb and head to hold expansion strips. These strips are 3/8″ thick and allow the glass block panel to expand without cracking. Mortar is applied only at the sill and between units. Glass block are manufactured with coarse edges to aid in bonding with the mortar. Oakum is tightly packed at the jamb and head. Sill, jamb, and head are then all calked.

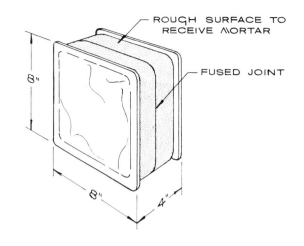

Figure 24. Glass block.

Transparent

Translucent Parallel Flutes

Translucent Perpendicular Flutes

Sculptured Interior

Sculptured Exterior

Light-directing

Figure 25. Forms of glass block.

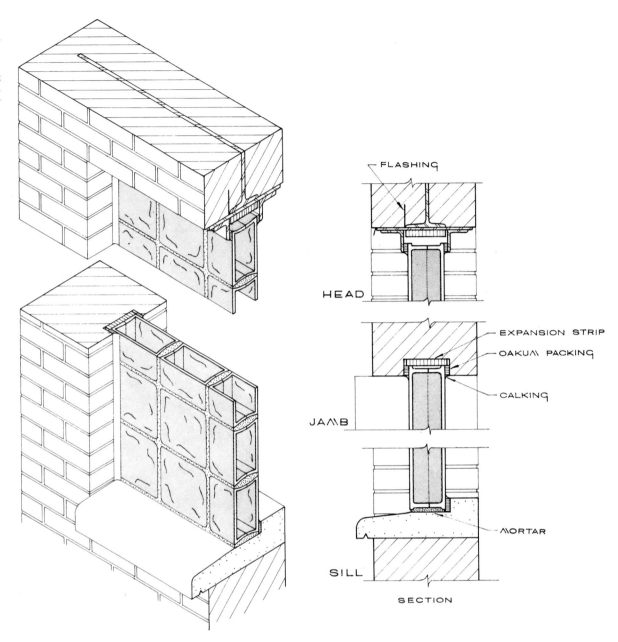

Figure 26. A glass block panel in a masonry wall.

25

Reinforced Concrete Construction

Concrete is one of the most widely used and important building materials used today. Concrete made of natural cement was initially developed by the ancient Romans and, to their credit, some of their concrete structures still exist—nearly 2,000 years later.

Amazingly, the art of making concrete was nearly lost after the decline of the Roman Empire until the invention of *portland cement* by Joseph Aspdin, a British bricklayer, in 1824. He named it "portland cement" because its color resembled the gray limestone mined in Portland, England. Rather than a mix of volcanic ash and lime mixed with water as used by the Romans, portland cement is a mix of finely crushed, burned limestone and clay. Jack Monier, a French gardener, is credited with inventing *reinforced concrete* as early as 1850 by reinforcing garden pots with embedded wire. The first factory to produce portland cement in quantity was built near Allentown, Pennsylvania, in 1871. Each successive manufacturer used a different formula until 1917, when the U.S. Bureau of Standards and the American Society for Testing and Materials (ASTM) approved standards for portland cement. The United States now manufactures and uses more than twice as much portland cement as any other country. *Prestressed concrete* was developed in 1927 by Eugene Freyssinet, a French engineer.

Portland Cement

Cement manufacture begins by crushing man-sized pieces of quarried limestone into smaller fist-sized pieces using *hammer mills*. After other raw materials are added, further grinding is accomplished in rotating *ball mills* containing steel balls. The finely ground mixture is fed into the higher end of a huge, 15° sloping, rotating kiln. These kilns are among the largest moving machinery used in any industry. They may be 15′ in diameter and over 500′ long. The raw materials emerge from the lower end four hours later as a new, marble-sized substance called *clinker*. After this substance has been cooled, gypsum is added, and it is again ground into cement powder and packaged in sacks of 1 cu. ft. (weighing 94 lb. each) or shipped in bulk by rail, truck, or barge.

The standards of ASTM include eight types of portland cement.

Type I General Purpose Use. Type I is the cement stocked by all suppliers and is delivered unless another type of cement is specified.

Type II Moderate Heat. All concrete gives off considerable heat during the curing process. Type II is used where less heat is desired, such as in large abutments, since too much heat speeds the curing and weakens the concrete. Type II is also moderately resistant to sulfate erosion.

Type III High Early Strength. Freezing temperatures also weaken the concrete. Type III cures rapidly and is used when pouring must be done in cold weather or when freezing weather is expected.

Type IV Low Heat. Type IV is used in very large masses, such as dams, to reduce the amount of heat generated.

Type V Sulfate Resistant. Type V is used where exposure to sulfate action is expected, such as in Western states having water and soil of high alkali content.

Types IA, IIA, IIIA Air Entrained. These types are similar to types I, II, and III, but include *air entrainment* (minute air bubbles) to reduce damage from salt and frost. Air-entrained concrete is often used for highway pavements.

Concrete

Concrete is produced by mixing a batter of cement and water with a *fine aggregate* such as sand. Usually a coarse aggregate such as *crushed stone* or gravel is also included. When mixed in proper proportions, the cement unites chemically with the water and can be poured into *forms*. After several hours, the concrete *sets* and binds the aggregates into a dense mass similar to stone. Freshly placed concrete is protected from rapid evaporation of water for seven days. During this *curing* period, the concrete continues to gain strength. The ultimate strength is reached after twenty-eight days.

Proportioning. Proportioning the ingredients greatly affects the strength and durability of concrete. For ordinary work, concrete is specified by its dry proportions of cement,

Figure 1. Mixing trucks deliver concrete to the footing forms for the U.S. Steel Building in Pittsburgh.

Figure 2. Conveyor belt used for concrete placement on the U.S. Steel Building.

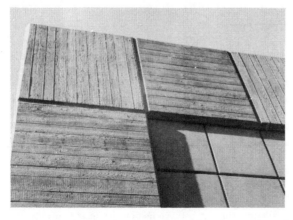

Figure 3. Textured concrete created by forms of wood planks.

fine aggregate, and coarse aggregate, all by volume. For example, a 1:2:4 mix consists of 1 part by volume of cement, 2 parts sand, and 4 parts crushed stone. This will produce concrete with a compressive strength of at least 2,000 pounds per square inch (psi). For more critical work, the *water-cement ratio* is used, because the proportion of water to cement is the most important ratio in controlling the strength of concrete. This ratio is expressed in terms of gallons of water per sack (1 cu. ft.) of cement. For example, a water-cement ratio of 6 indicates 6 gal. of water per cubic foot of cement. With a 1:2:3 dry mix, this would produce a compressive strength of 3,000 psi. In general, concrete is weakened by adding more water than is necessary for workability. Another adverse effect of excess water is that a watery layer forms puddles on the upper surface of the curing concrete. This is called *laitance*[1] and is very weak and undesirable.

Mixing. Concrete is mixed by machine either on the site or at a central plant. After water is added, an *agitator* can keep the concrete in a workable condition for about an hour before placing. Often the concrete is dry-mixed centrally, and then water is added automatically by *transit mixers* while on the way to the job site (Figure 1).

Placing. If connected chutes from the truck cannot reach the form, wheelbarrows, powered buggies, or conveyor belts are used (Figure 2). Also, it is possible to pump concrete from the truck to its final position using hoses or pipes. Pumped concrete is called *pumpcrete*.

Concrete can be sprayed into place through use of a pneumatic spray gun at high velocity to cover shell surfaces such as domes and pools. This is called *shotcrete* when wet mix is shot and *gunite* when dry mix and water are pumped to the gun through separate hoses and then shot into place by force of the compressed air.

Curing. For concrete to obtain its maximum strength, the chemical reaction between cement and water must continue for about twenty-eight days. During this period, the concrete is sprinkled and covered to retard the loss of moisture.

Protection from freezing or excess heat is also important for the first seven days of curing. During freezing weather the water or aggregates may be heated before mixing and kept above 50°F for the seven days after placing. Often this is done by building a temporary framework covered by tarpaulins over the concrete and heating with *salamanders* (oil-burning stoves). *High early strength cement* (Type III) can be used when freezing weather is expected, since it cures rapidly and gains "seven-day strength" in only three days. The heat produced during this rapid curing also helps protect the concrete from low temperatures.

Excess heat is a problem when large masses of concrete are placed, since the heat causes rapid curing which lowers the strength of the concrete and causes cracking due to early surface contraction. Type II or Type IV cement is used under these conditions, or the heat is removed by cooling water pipes embedded in the concrete.

1. Pronounced *le-tarns*. This is a French word with the accent on the last syllable, which is pronounced like *barns*.

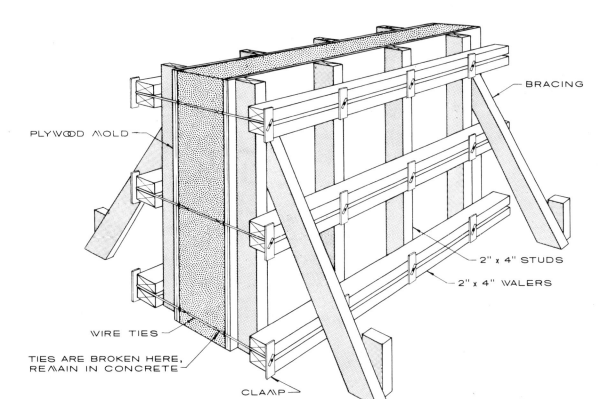

Figure 4. Typical wall form.

Forms. Forms are nearly always required to mold fresh concrete into the desired shape. Forms must be accurate and sturdy, yet economical, since they often cost more than both the concrete and the reinforcing steel.

It is easy to underrate the strength needed to support wet concrete, and construction accidents caused by collapsed formwork are all too common. Concrete is more than twice as heavy as water. Also, the pressure of fresh concrete increases in proportion to its depth just as the pressure water exerts on a dam increases. Thus the lower portion of a form for a concrete column must be able to resist tremendous bursting forces. As with water, the horizontal area does not affect this pressure.

Wood forms are framed of well-braced beams covered with waterproof plywood. Wood planks are used in place of plywood to achieve special textured effects, as shown in Figure 3. Before concrete is placed, wood forms are moistened or covered with form oil or plastic liners so that moisture will not be absorbed from the concrete. All forms are designed to facilitate later *stripping* (removal of the forms). Plywood forms are factory- or field-coated with commercial compounds to prevent adhesion to the concrete. Some common methods of building wood forms are illustrated in Figures 4–6.

Reusable steel forms are also used. Sometimes they are rented from companies specializing in formwork. Steel forms are commonly used to shape ribbed or waffled floors. Steel floor forms are supported by wood *centering*, which is in turn supported by *shoring*. See Figures 7–9.

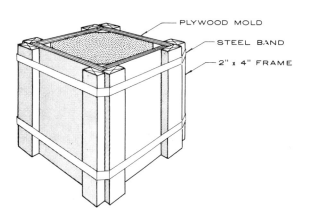

Figure 5. Typical column form.

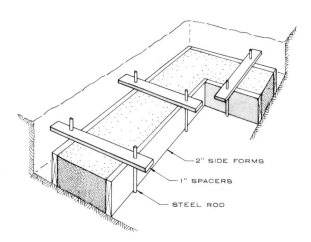

Figure 6. Typical footing form.

Figure 7. Installing steel forms on plywood centering for a waffled concrete floor.

Figure 8. Forms omitted to permit additional reinforcing about column.

Figure 9. Forms are stripped using air guns applied to nozzle at center of each form.

Plastic-surfaced cardboard tubes are used for cylindrical posts. Stripping is accomplished by making a vertical cut with a circular saw, the blade set to the thickness of the tube.

As discussed in Chapter 24 on masonry construction, *expansion joints* must be provided to control cracking in large areas due to temperature changes, moisture changes, and settlement.

Reinforced Concrete

Concrete can be mixed to develop a compressive strength after twenty-eight days curing of 7,000 psi, but the tensile strength of concrete is only about one-tenth the compressive strength. Actually it is standard design practice to assume that concrete has no ability to withstand tension. Rather, steel rods called *reinforcing bar* (abbreviated *rebar*) are embedded in the concrete to resist any tensile forces. This is called *reinforced concrete*. Concrete without reinforcing is called *plain concrete*.

Reinforcing bars are available in sizes from #2 (1/4"-diameter) to #18 (2 1/4"-diameter). The rebar designations indicate the diameter in eighths of an inch. For example, a #4 bar is 4/8" (= 1/2") in diameter.

For maximum bond strength, the reinforcing bars must be completely surrounded by concrete. The wet concrete is rodded or vibrated mechanically, as it is placed, to remove any possible air pockets. To ensure a strong bond between the reinforcing steel and concrete, reinforcing bars are rolled with ridged surfaces. These bars are called *deformed bars* (see Figure 10). The only bars not available with these deformations are #2 bars. The ends of reinforcing bars are often bent into hooks to obtain greater holding strength.

Bar Placement. A structural engineer calculates the number, size, shape, and placement of reinforcing steel necessary to meet all design requirements. The reinforcing steel is ordered to these specifications, placed in the form, and wired in position. Steel *saddles* and *chairs* are used to help hold the reinforcing bars in place.

A typical reinforced concrete beam contains several horizontal reinforcing bars located near the *bottom* of the beam to resist tension at the middle of the span. But when the beam passes over a support, the *top* of the beam is in tension, and consequently the bars are bent to be located near the top of the beam over supports. Also the beam must resist shear near its supports. This is accomplished by the use of reinforcing steel *stirrups*. These are usually U-shaped bars placed vertically.

A typical reinforced concrete slab would also contain reinforcing bars located near the bottom of the slab. In a one-way slab, these bars would all be parallel to one another. To prevent cracking between these bars due to moisture and

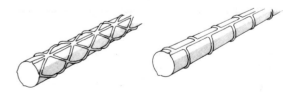

Figure 10. Deformed reinforcing bars.

Table I. Common welded wire mesh sizes

Square	Rectangular
6×6-10/10	6 × 12-4/4
6×6-8/8	6 × 12-2/2
6×6-6/6	6 × 12-1/1
6×6-4/4	
	4 × 12-8/12
4×4-10/10	4 × 12-6/10
4×4-8/8	
4×4-6/6	4 × 16-8/12
4×4-4/4	4 × 16-6/10

temperature changes,[2] additional horizontal reinforcing bars called *temperature steel* are placed at right angles to the tension bars.

Bars must often be spliced by *clamping, lapping,* or *welding.* A rule of thumb for lapped splices is that the bars should be overlapped and wired together for a distance at least equal to thirty bar diameters. For example, spliced #4 bars should overlap 30 × 1/2″ = 15″. Splices are not made in critical areas, of course.

Wire Mesh. For slabs, *welded wire mesh* is often used to prevent cracking. Wire mesh (also called *welded wire fabric*) is produced from cold-drawn steel wire welded together in a square or rectangular pattern. A popular wire mesh is 6×6 - 10/10, which indicates a 6″ square pattern of #10-gauge wire in each direction. A heavier wire mesh with a tighter pattern is 4×4 - 8/8. A 4×16 - 8/12 wire mesh indicates #8-gauge wire spaced 4″ apart with #12-gauge wire spaced 16″ apart. Table I shows some common sizes.

Figures 11–13 show the use of rebars and wire mesh in the construction of a folded-plate roof.

Reinforced Concrete Structures

A typical reinforced concrete structure consists of round or square reinforced columns supporting one-way or two-way floor slabs. The term *one-way* refers to tension rebars all placed parallel to each other, or "one-way." For example, the structure shown in Figure 14 has a slab containing parallel rebars that stretch from beam to beam. Of course the concrete beams also contain rebars, as do their supporting girders and columns.

The intermediate beams of Figure 14 can be replaced by two sets of rebars installed in each direction as shown in Figure 15. This is called a *two-way slab.* Two-way slabs are commonly used for square or nearly-square floor panels.

When the column-to-column girders are also omitted under a two-way slab, a *flat slab* floor system results, as shown in Figure 16. The upper portion of the columns in flat slab floors are strengthened by flaired capitals and drop panels.

Ribbed (Figure 17) and *waffle* (Figure 18) floor systems are efficient refinements of the one-way and two-way systems. These floors are cast with the aid of reusable steel forms (previously shown in Figures 7–9).

2. A 100′ concrete slab will change approximately 1/2″ in length due to moisture changes and an additional 1/2″ during a 100° change in temperature.

Figure 11. Installing forms over open centering for a folded-plate roof on the Treasure Island Shopping Center near Milwaukee.

Figure 12. Folded-plate roof reinforcing steel in place.

Figure 13. Completed folded-plate roof for Treasure Island Shopping Center.

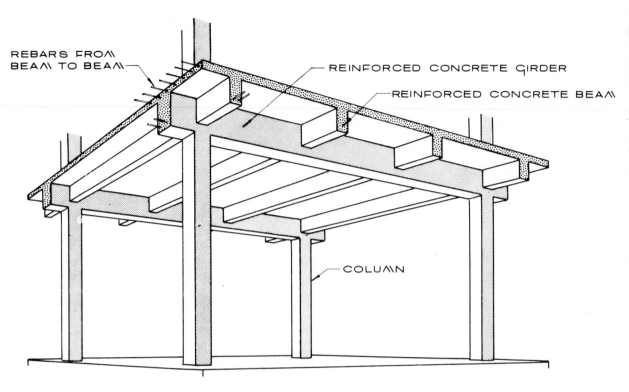

Figure 14. A one-way slab-and-beam floor.

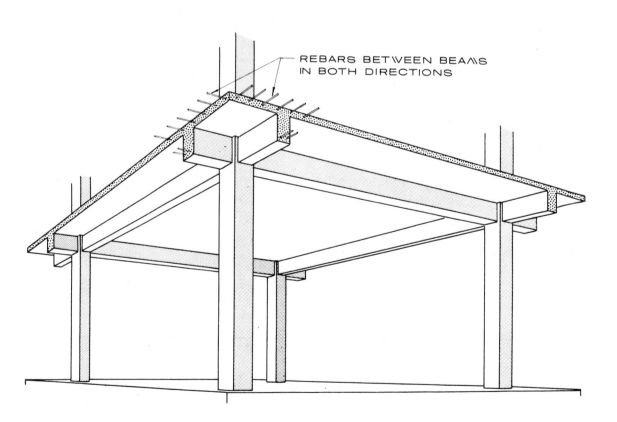

Figure 15. A two-way slab floor.

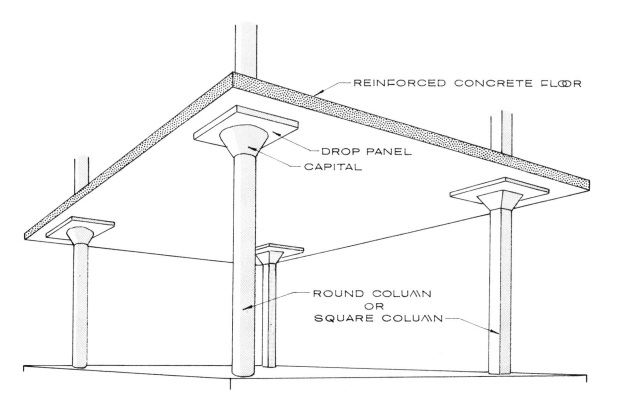

Figure 16. A flat slab floor.

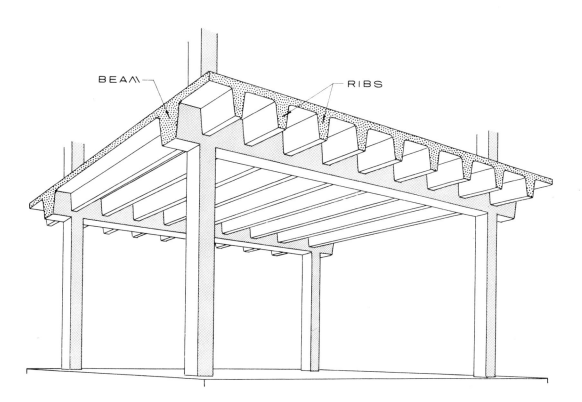

Figure 17. A ribbed concrete floor.

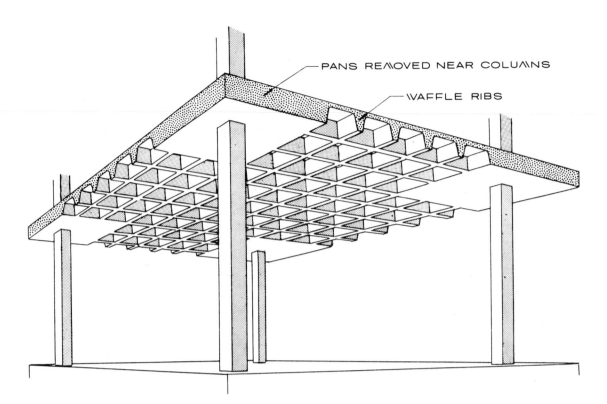

Figure 18. A waffled concrete floor.

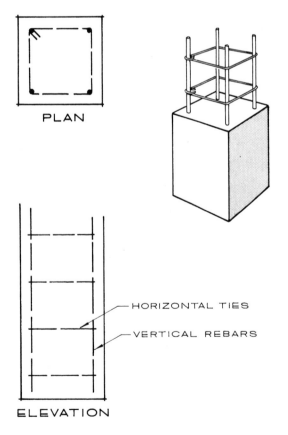

Figure 19. Typical reinforced concrete column.

Reading Reinforced Concrete Drawings

Examples of some elevations and plans showing footings, walls, slabs, and columns of reinforced concrete are shown in Figures 19–21. Notice that the end view of a rebar (reinforcing bar) is shown as a small, solid circle; the side view is shown as a dashed line. Study these drawings together with their accompanying pictorials until you are confident that you are able to read them.

Precasting Concrete

Precasting refers to the casting of a reinforced concrete member in a mold not located at its final position in the structure. The principle of precasting is not new, but precasting in quantity began only in about 1955 with the establishment of specialized manufacturing plants. Precast concrete is manufactured by placing reinforcing steel and concrete in forms which may be made of wood, plastic, concrete, or steel. Waterproof plywood forms are most common. Fiberglass-reinforced plastic molds are used for fabrication into intricate shapes. These molds are usually stripped within twenty-four hours after casting and can be reused about seventy-five times.

Members such as face panels can be precast with exposed aggregate facings. A thin layer of facing concrete containing the aggregate to be exposed is cast first and backed up with reinforced concrete. After initial curing, the facing concrete

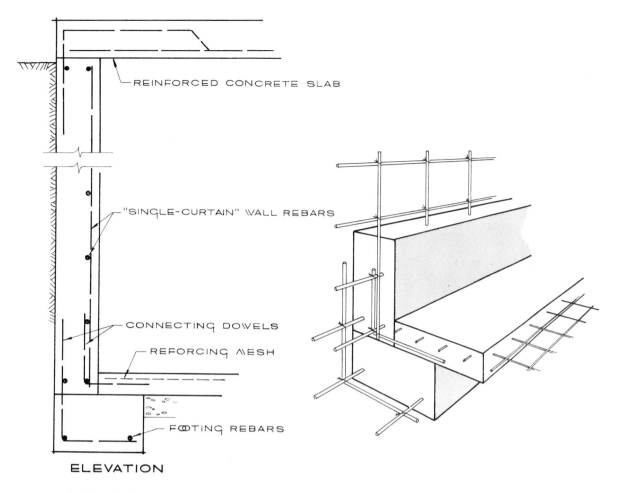

—— REINFORCED CONCRETE SLAB

—— "SINGLE-CURTAIN" WALL REBARS

—— CONNECTING DOWELS

—— REFORCING MESH

—— FOOTING REBARS

ELEVATION

Figure 20. Typical concrete footing and single-curtain wall.

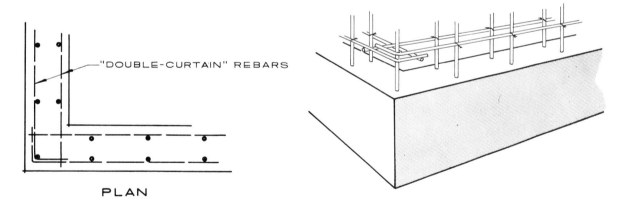

—— "DOUBLE-CURTAIN" REBARS

PLAN

Figure 21. Typical double-curtain concrete wall.

is partially removed by brushing, sandblasting, or chemical treatment to expose the desired amount of aggregate.

Precast members are trucked to the construction site and hoisted into position by attaching to hooks cast into the beams or panels. These hooks may serve double-duty to anchor the member to the structure. Field connections between the precast member and structure may be in the form of welding, bolting, or cast concrete connections. Joints are sealed by calking over a flexible joint filler. Some typical precast members are illustrated in Figure 22. These members are also often *prestressed*.

A *double tee* is a basic shape used for floor and roof

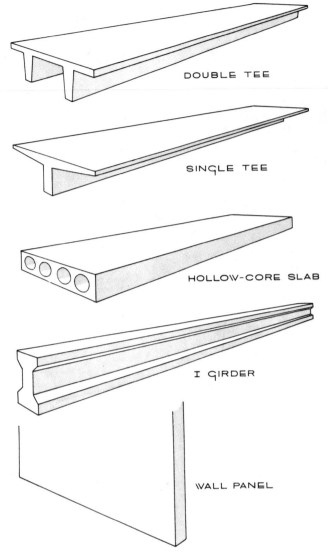

Figure 22. Typical precast concrete members.

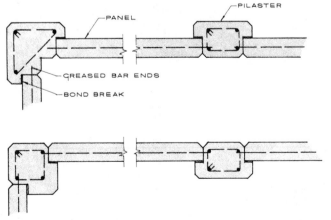

Figure 23. Joint details for tilt-up construction.

construction as a combined deck and joists. Spans to 60' are common. Double tee shapes may be cantilevered or used vertically as a wall.

Single tees are used for floor and roof decks with larger spans to 125'.

Hollow-core slabs are commonly used for decks to 40' span where flat ceilings are required. The cores are used as raceways for electrical and mechanical systems.

I girders are used for long spans and heavy loads. They often serve as the principal girder in a beam-and-deck system.

Wall panels are used for bearing and curtain walls, often with special textured finishes. They are sometimes called *cast stone*, as discussed in Chapter 24 on masonry. These panels may be combined with insulating material, such as a 6"-thick panel that is comprised of 2" outer shells of concrete surrounding a 2" inner layer of rigid insulation.

Tilt-Up Construction

Precast concrete generally refers to members precast at a factory. Tilt-up construction refers to walls and other members that have been custom-precast on the site and then lifted by crane (tilted up) into their final vertical position. Tilt-up construction reduces formwork, simplifies the placing of reinforcement and concrete, and permits ground-level installation of components such as window frames. Some typical joint details for tilt-up construction are shown in Figure 23. Columns may be placed either before or after the tilt-up panels are in position. Usually the columns and panels are not bonded so that slight movement is permitted for temperature and moisture expansion.

Lift-Slab Construction

Another method of site precasting is called lift-slab construction. The sequence of operations is shown in Figure 25. After columns are erected, each floor slab is cast on the ground, one on top of the other, using a membrane to prevent adhesion. The slabs are cast directly below their final position surrounding the columns with sliding steel collars cast in each slab about each column (Figure 24). Special hydraulic jacks are located at the top of each column and connected first to the cured roof slab. The roof slab is hoisted slowly (about 1 in./min.) to its final position and fastened to each column by welding or by some other method. The procedure is repeated for each additional floor slab.

Prestressing

A concrete beam or slab will deflect downward under live and dead loading as shown in Figure 26A. The upper side will be compressed, but the lower side will be stretched (in tension) and may weaken and crack. Prestressing refers to a method of compressing concrete members so that they do not deflect when in position, and both upper and lower sides remain in compression. Steel rods or strands inserted through the member near the lower side are tensioned to produce a slight upward arch, or camber, as shown in Figure 26B. When

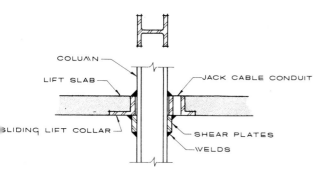

Figure 24. Detail of lift-slab column connection.

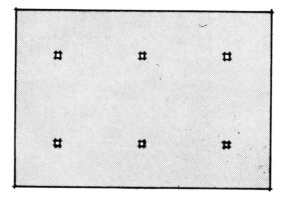

PLAN

in position and loaded, the member flattens but remains in compression throughout.

Most precast concrete construction is also prestressed. Prestressing can be accomplished by *pretensioning* or *post-tensioning*. In pretensioning, steel tendons are placed in empty concrete forms and stretched (tensioned) using hydraulic jacks. The tendons are usually high-strength, spiraled wire strands 1/4″ to 1/2″ in diameter and are often *draped* as shown in Figure 27. Draping increases the effectiveness of the pretensioning. Concrete is placed about the tendons and cured. Tendons are *bonded* to the concrete, and when the jacks are removed, part of the tension in the tendons is transferred to the concrete as compression. Of course, some of the tension is lost due to concrete shrinkage upon curing, shortening under compression, and *creep* (further shortening under continued pressure over a long time).

In post-tensioning, unbonded tendons are stressed *after* the concrete has cured. The tendons are either surrounded with tubing or are greased to prevent adhesion to the concrete. The tension is applied by hydraulic jacks, and anchors at the end of each tendon are installed. To protect tendons from corrosion, they may be bonded *after* post-tensioning by forcing cement grout around them. Post-tensioning is not as commonly used as pretensioning, but it may have advantages when used for members too large or too heavy to permit moving from factory to site.

A large reinforced concrete building is shown in Figure 28.

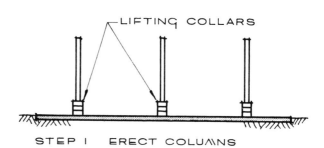

STEP 1   ERECT COLUMNS

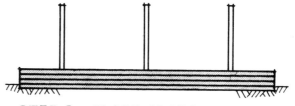

STEP 2   PLACE SLABS

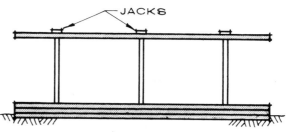

STEP 3   LIFT ROOF SLAB

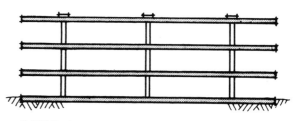

STEP 4   LIFT FLOOR SLABS

Figure 25. Sequence of operations for lift-slab construction.

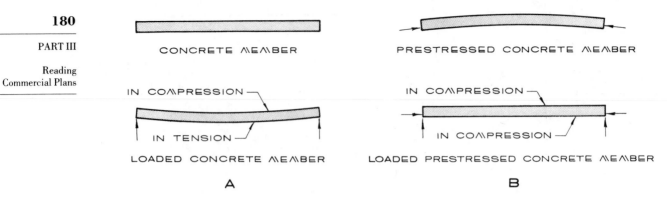

Figure 26. The principle of prestressed concrete.

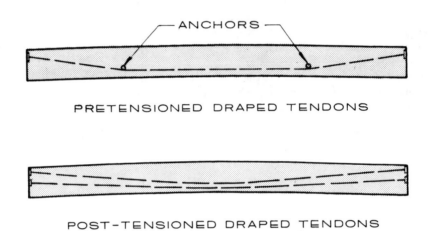

Figure 27. Draped tendons for prestressing concrete.

Figure 28. Cadet dormitory at the U.S. Air Force Academy constructed of reinforced concrete.

26

Structural Steel Construction

The nature of architecture is greatly affected by the kind of building materials available. At first, humans depended only upon natural materials such as wood and stone for the construction of shelter. The baking of clay into brick was an early attempt to alter and improve a natural material. But only recently, with the production of steel in large quantities, has an artificial material been available with such desirable properties of strength and workability.

Steel is manufactured from iron, and iron is made from iron ore, found in nearly every country of the world. Iron ore is simply rock containing some proportion of iron. Most iron ore is mined in open pits by stripping away the surface to uncover the ore, which is then loaded by power shovel to railroad hopper cars. The ore is combined with coke[1] for fuel, limestone for flux, and heated air in a blast furnace to produce pig iron.[2] Pig iron is not used as a finished product but rather as the major ingredient in the manufacture of cast iron, wrought iron, steel, and alloy steels.

Cast iron is manufactured by melting a mixture of pig iron and scrap iron in a coke-burning furnace called a *cupola*. The molten iron is then cast in molds to its final shape. Cast iron is quite brittle and is seldom used in buildings.

Wrought iron is manufactured by pouring refined pig iron in a molten state over silicate slag (melted sand) to form puddle balls which are then squeezed and rolled to shape. Wrought iron (*wrought* means "worked") is easily worked and welded. It is used for pipe and ornamental iron work.

Steel

Most steel is manufactured in basic oxygen furnaces by pouring molten pig iron over scrap iron and then blowing pure oxygen at high pressure onto the surface of the charge to increase the temperature and oxidize impurities. Alloys are carefully added when making steel to obtain desired charac-

teristics. For example, when chromium is added, corrosion resistance is greatly increased. This product is called *stainless steel*.

Most *structural steel* is made by reheating the steel ingots produced by the basic oxygen furnaces in *soaking pits* until white-hot. Steel ingots cannot be sent directly to the rolling mill from the furnace due to the temperature difference between the interior and exterior of the ingots: either the interior is too soft or the exterior is too cold and hard for working. The soft ingots are then squeezed between the rollers of *rolling mills*. As the ingots are passed back and forth between rollers, they are flattened and stretched. The rolling improves strength and workability. Finished shapes are rolled in *finishing mills* where rollers gradually change the ingots to their desired shape. As shown in Figure 1, a rectangular ingot is shaped into an I section by passing through each roller in the numbered order. In addition to structural steel shapes, the finishing mill rolls bars, plates, sheets, and strips.

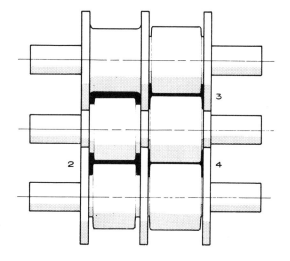

Figure 1. Rolling a structural steel shape.

---

1. *Coke* is manufactured by heating coal without the presence of air in coking ovens. As a fuel, coke produces intense heat.
2. This was called *pig iron* because formerly it was cast into bars called *pigs*. Today, molten pig iron runs directly to the steel-making furnaces.

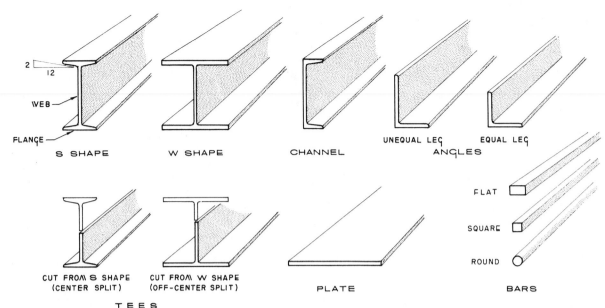

Figure 2. Structural steel shapes.

Structural Steel Shapes

Structural steel members are extruded in the finishing mill to various cross-sectional shapes (Figure 2). The shape most commonly used for beams and columns is in the form of an I or H. As a beam, this shape is economical because a large proportion of the material is located at the extremity of the shape where the bending stresses are greatest. It is also more useful as a column than a channel or angle, due to its symmetry in both directions. There are two standard shapes in this form. They are called the *S shape* (formerly *American Standard I-beam*) and the *W shape* (formerly *wide-flange shape*).

S shapes are available in several weights for each nominal size. The inner faces of the flanges are sloped 2 to 12 as shown in Figure 2. S shapes are available in sizes from 3″ deep to 24″ deep. S shapes are not as popular as W shapes, but they do have the advantage of narrower flanges, which may be desirable for some designs.

W shapes have wider flanges and thinner webs than the S shapes. Thus they have even more material located at the extremity and are more efficient in resisting bending. W shapes vary from a square proportion to a rectangular proportion. The shapes with square proportions are often used as columns; the shapes with rectangular proportions are often used as beams. The inner faces of the flanges remain parallel to the outer faces. W shapes are available in sizes from 4″ deep to 36″ deep.

Channel shapes are rolled in sizes from 3″ to 15″ deep. The inner faces of channel flanges are sloped 2 to 12 like S shape flanges. Channels are used in pairs for the top and bottom chords of heavy steel trusses. Because of the flat face on one side, channels are often used to frame floor openings such as stairwells and elevator shafts. They are also used for stairway supports, roof purlins, and lintels.

Lighter-weight sections are available in both beam and channel shapes. The beams are called *M shapes* and the channels are called *miscellaneous channels*. They are used in the same manner as regular shapes but for lighter loads or shorter spans.

Angles are rolled with legs of equal and unequal length. Equal-leg angles range in size from 1″ × 1″ × 1/8″ to 8″ × 8″ × 1 1/8″. Unequal-leg angles range from 1 3/4″ × 1 1/4″ × 1/8″ to 9″ × 4″ × 1″. Angles are often used for built-up trusses, beams, and columns, for connectors, and for lintels of short span to support masonry.

Structural tees are manufactured by shearing or flamecutting the webs of either I-beams or wide-flange shapes. Orders may be placed for center or off-center splitting. Tees can also be rolled by special order. Tees are used for the top and bottom chords of welded steel trusses. Inverted tees are used to support roof slabs of gypsum or concrete.

Plates and *bars* are usually specified by size rather than weight. In general, bars are 8″ or less in width; plates are over 8″ wide. Rectangular bars (called *flat bars*) are rolled in increments of 1/8″ thickness and 1/4″ width. *Square and round bars* are rolled in 1/16″ increments. Plates are rolled at most mills in width increments of even inches to 60″. Plates are used for the webs of built-up columns and girders and for reinforcement of the web or flange of steel shapes. Plates are called *bearing plates* when used to provide bearing areas under columns and beams resting upon concrete. Bars are used for bracing, hangers, and special structural applications.

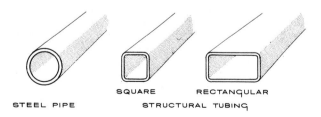

Figure 3. Steel pipe and structural tubing.

Table I. Designation of rolled steel shapes

"New" Designation	Interpretation	"Old" Designation
S 8 × 18.4	S shape, 8″ depth, 18.4 #/ft.	8 I 18.4
W 8 × 31	W shape, 8″ nominal depth, 31 #/ft.	8 WF 31
C 8 × 11.5	American Standard Channel, 8″ depth, 11.5 #/ft.	8 [11.5
M 8 × 6.5	M shape (formerly junior beam)	8 JR 6.5
MC 10 × 6.5	Miscellaneous channel (formerly junior channel)	10 JR [6.5
L 4 × 4 × 1/4	Equal-leg angle, 4″ leg × 4″ leg × 1/4″ thickness	∠ 4 × 4 × 1/4
L 6 × 4 × 1/4	Unequal leg angle, 6″ leg × 4″ leg × 1/4″ thickness	∠ 6 × 4 × 1/4
ST 4 × 9.2	Structural tee cut from an S 8 × 18.4	ST 4 I 9.2
WT 4 × 15.5	Structural tee cut from a W 8 × 31	ST 4 WF 15.5
PL 1/2 × 12	Plate, 1/2″ thick × 12″ wide	PL 12 × 1/2
Bar 1 3/4 × 1	1 3/4″ × 1″ flat bar	Bar 1 3/4 × 1
Bar 1 ▱	1″ square bar	Bar 1 ▱
Bar 1 ⊘	1″-diameter round bar	Bar 1 ⊘

Steel Pipe and Structural Tubing

Steel pipe (round) and *structural tubing* (square and rectangular) are manufactured in several sizes and wall thicknesses (Figure 3). Normal pipe diameters range from 1/2″ to 12″ in three weights: *Standard, Extra Strong,* and *Double-Extra Strong.* Square tubing ranges from 2″ × 2″ to 10″ × 10″ outside dimensions. Rectangular tubing ranges from 3″ × 2″ to 12″ × 8″ outside dimensions. As columns, these sections have aesthetic and structural advantages over W shapes, but at the sacrifice of fastening convenience.

Reading Steel Shapes

Rolled steel shapes are specified by the shape symbol, the nominal depth in inches, and the weight in pounds per foot of length. Inch marks and pound symbols are omitted. Some examples are shown in Table I. The "new" designations were established by the American Institute of Steel Construction in 1970. However, the "old" designations appear on plans that were prepared before that time.

The quantity of rolled steel shapes of a given length is indicated in Table II.

Fabrication

Structural steel shapes are cut to size and fastened together to form structural units of convenient size at the *fabricating plant.* These structural units are then shipped to the building site and are eventually placed in position, or *erected* (Figure 4). Connections made at the fabricating plant are called *shop connections* and are usually welded. Connections made at the building site are called *field connections* and are usually bolted. For example, in the steel framework of Figure 5, the angle seats would be shop-welded to the columns, and the angle connections would be shop-welded to the girders. Erection is then completed by simply resting the

girder on its seat and bolting the connection through predrilled holes.

Bolting

Bolts are classified as *unfinished* bolts and *high-strength* bolts as listed in Table III. ASTM A307 unfinished bolts are made of low-carbon steel and are quite inexpensive. ASTM A325 high-strength bolts are made of heat-treated medium-carbon steel and are about twice as strong as A307 bolts. ASTM A490 high-strength bolts are made of heat-treated alloy steel and are about 50 percent stronger than A325 bolts.

Figure 4. Steel erection by "crawler" cranes (which operate from ground level) and "creeper" cranes (which move up every third floor as construction progresses).

Table II. Designation of multiple steel units

Designation	Interpretation
10-W 8 × 31 × 12′- 8″	10 units of W 8 × 31, each unit 12′- 8″ long

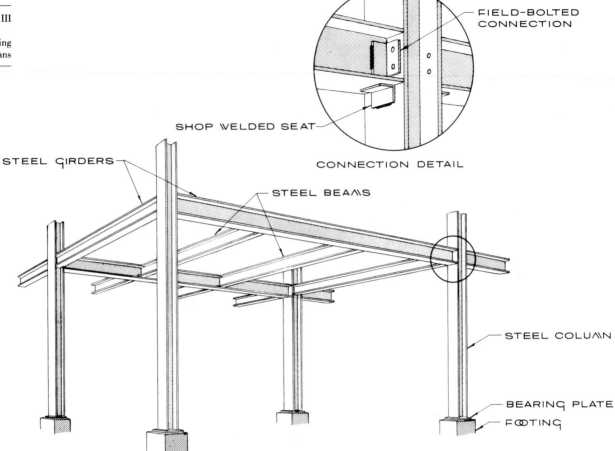

Figure 5. Typical building framework fabricated of steel.

A325 and A490 bolts are identified by the mark "A325" or "A490" on the top of the bolt head, as shown in Figure 6. High-strength bolts are often used for connecting beams and girders to columns, column splices, and connections subjected to loads that produce impact or reversal of stress (such as large cranes or running machinery). This is to prevent loosening of joints by continued vibration. Unfinished bolts are used for most other connections. Unfinished bolts are also used temporarily in all structures to hold members in alignment during high-strength bolting or welding operations.

Installation. Holes for bolts are drilled 1/16″ larger than the nominal bolt diameter.

High-strength bolts are tightened to their required tension by the *turn-of-nut* method using hand or powered impact wrenches (Figure 8). The nut is drawn up to a snug position and then tightened an additional half turn. Washers are not needed with A325 bolts, but the harder A490 bolts and nuts do require hardened washers to prevent galling of the softer steel members. When the steel members are sloped, bevel washers are used to compensate for the slope. Clipped washers are used where clearances are too small for regular washers.

A325 *interference-body bolts* (Figure 7) combine the best features of high-strength bolts and rivets. They have raised ribs on the shank and are driven into smaller-diameter holes with a maul. This interference fit provides a firm bearing between the bolt and the sides of the hole.

Welding

Welding (Figure 9) is a popular method of connecting structural steel members and has some advantages over bolting. For example, fabrication is simplified by reducing the number of individual parts to be cut, punched with holes, handled, and installed. Also, a welded joint is stronger than the joined members.

There are a number of different methods of welding, but the *electric arc process* (Figure 10) is almost exclusively used for structural welding. In this process, a generator is used to supply high voltage to the structural metal and to a coated welding rod that serves as an electrode. When the rod is close to the metal, an electric arc is formed which creates enough

Table III. Types of structural steel bolts

ASTM Designation	Bolt
A307	Unfinished bolt
A325*	High-strength bolt*
A490	High-strength bolt

*Also available as interference-body bolts.

heat to melt and fuse both members being welded. In addition, the tip of the core of the welding rod melts and is transferred through the arc to the weld seam.

Semiautomatic welding is provided by feeding the electrode and flux automatically to the welding head. This increases the rate of weld metal deposit by a factor of three: from the hand rate of 10 lb. of weld metal per hour to 30 lb. per hour. Also the welder's helper is no longer needed. Before welding, the beam is first bolted to an erection angle. This angle also serves as a backing bar for the weld. The angle and bolts are left in place after welding.

Automatic welding is seldom used in the field but is often used for shop fabrication. There are many types of automatic welding equipment. The most advanced processes can deposit 200 lb. of weld metal per hour.

Types of Welded Joints. The most commonly used weld for structural steel is the *fillet weld*. As shown in Figure 11, the size of a fillet weld refers to the length of a leg of its triangular cross section.

Butt welds can be made in several ways. The ends of the members to be joined can be squared, mitered, or grooved. The butt weld is called a *bevel weld* when only one member is mitered, and it is called a *vee weld* when both members are mitered. These miters must be cut before assembling the member. When a fabricator is equipped to gouge rather than miter, *J-groove* and *U-groove welds* have some advantages. Gouging can be done either before or after assembly. Also, J-groove and U-groove welds usually require less weld metal than bevel and vee welds. The members to be joined can be adjacent or slightly separated by a distance called the *root opening*. Members can be welded on one or both sides.

Figure 6. High-strength bolts.

Figure 7. Interference-body bolt.

Figure 8. Madison Square Garden's compression ring sections being bolted with A490 high-strength bolts.

Figure 9. Welders working in pairs to make column splices.

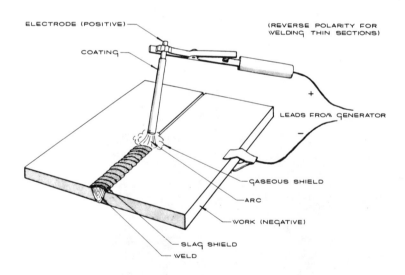

Figure 10. Electric arc welding.

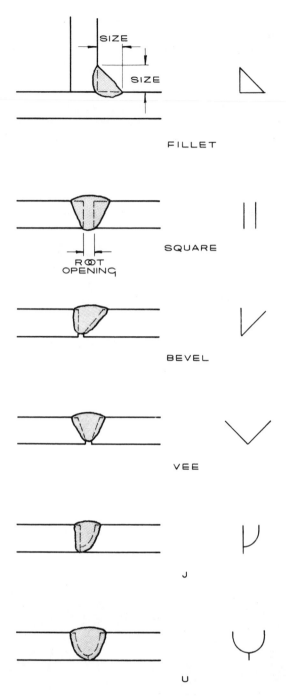

Figure 11. Basic welds and their symbols.

Welding Symbols. Welds are specified by a standardized "bent arrow" as shown in Figure 12. The arrow points to the joint to be welded, and the appropriate weld symbol from Figure 11 is attached to the horizontal shank. This weld symbol is placed *below* the shank when only the *near* side (arrow side) of the joint is to be welded, *above* the shank when the opposite side of the joint is to be welded, and on *both* sides of the shank when both sides of the joint are to be welded (see Figure 13). The vertical (perpendicular) leg of

the weld symbol is always drawn on the left side, and the other specifications are always arranged from left to right regardless of the direction of the arrow. Although a number of specifications are shown in Figure 12, some may not apply on occasion and are omitted. The weld symbol and weld size are always shown, and the field weld symbol and all-around symbol are often shown. Study Figures 34 and 35 in the appendix to understand how welding symbols are used in actual drafting room practice.

186

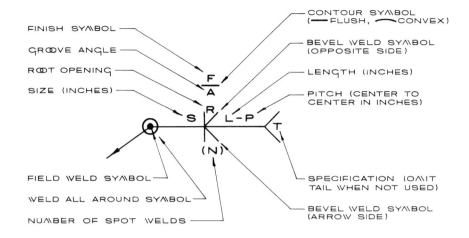

NOTES:

1) WHEN ARROW & TAIL ARE INTERCHANGED, OTHER SPECIFICATIONS STILL READ FROM LEFT TO RIGHT.

2) PERPENDICULAR LEG OF WELD SYMBOLS ALWAYS DRAWN ON LEFT.

Figure 12. The welding symbol.

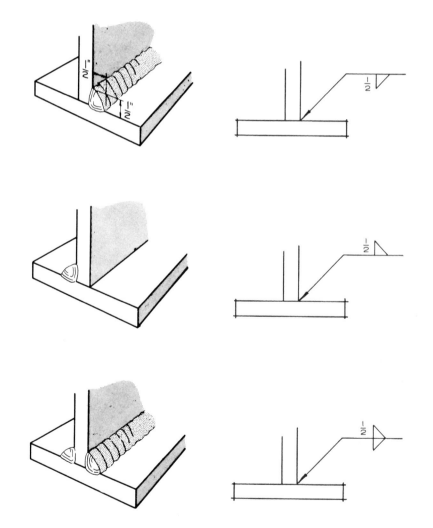

Figure 13. Use of welding symbols.

27

Fire Protection

When reading the architectural plans for any structure, you will find numerous features that have been included by the architect to improve building safety. Many of these features are required by building codes to ensure acceptable standards of health and safety with special emphasis on protection from fire. The architect, owner, and builder have both moral and legal obligations to follow the building code requirements of the city in which a building is constructed. Actually, everyone should understand the need for building codes and should support safety measures.

Building Codes

The basic concept of a building code or a zoning ordinance is that individual actions should be regulated in favor of the welfare of the general public. It has been shown many times that such protection is necessary, and courts have supported the inherent power of the government to protect citizens from unsafe building practices. Building codes specify acceptable building materials and construction methods, allowable loads and stresses, mechanical and electrical requirements, and other specifications for health and safety.

The earliest record of an attempt to improve building safety is the Code of Hammurabi, a Babylonian king and lawmaker in 2100 B.C.: "In the case of collapse of a defective building the architect is to be put to death if the owner is killed, and the architect's son if the owner's son is killed."

Laws governing building construction and land use were first introduced by the ancient Romans. During the reign of Julius Caesar, Rome grew rapidly, and tall, speculative apartments were built which often collapsed. Roman law first limited heights to 70′ and later reduced them to only 60′. In the fourteenth century the city of London adopted a law that prohibited the building of wooden chimneys. Building codes governing building construction methods and zoning ordinances governing land use were adopted in English, French, and Prussian cities by the nineteenth century and were accepted by all U.S. cities and most towns in the early twentieth century.

Fire Protection Codes

Among the most important portions of any building code are the sections on fire protection. One need not experience the terror of fire to realize how necessary it is to require that buildings not be a hazard to their occupants. In the United States, over 10,000 persons are killed each year in fires. Many of these deaths occur in buildings that are in violation of fire protection codes.

Fire Ratings. Fire protection sections of building codes are based on studies made by fire protection engineers who have tested various building methods to determine the fire resistance of each. The *standard fire test* (E119-58) of the American Society for Testing and Materials (ASTM) is the accepted standard for such tests. The degree of fire resistance of each building method is measured in terms of its ability to withstand fire for a time from one to four hours. For example, a two-hour fire rating would indicate that a structural member could withstand the heat of fire (or the cooling of a fire hose) for two hours before serious weakening, or that a wall, floor, or roof would not allow passage of flame and hot gases for two hours.

Masonry and concrete walls have fire ratings from one to four hours based on their thickness, as shown in Tables I and II. However, steel columns and beams must be screened by additional fire protection to achieve a fire rating. As shown in Figures 1–7 associated with Tables III and IV, this is usually accomplished by plastering, sprayed mineral fibers, or concrete encasement. Consequently, when reading structural steel plans, you must always look for the detail drawings of columns and beams that show the method of fireproofing. Steel floor and roof systems (Figures 8–11 and Table V) also may require fire protection. As with columns and beams, detail drawings will show specific information.

Extinguishing Systems

Building codes often require automatic water sprinkler systems, for they give excellent fire protection in all types of buildings. Records show that when fires occurred in sprin-

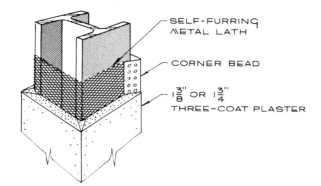

Figure 1. Plaster-on-metal-lath fire protection of columns.

SELF-FURRING METAL LATH

CORNER BEAD

$1\frac{3}{8}$" OR $1\frac{3}{4}$" THREE-COAT PLASTER

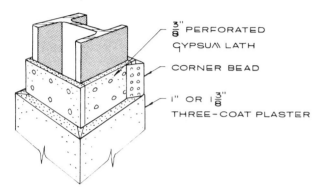

Figure 2. Plaster-on-gypsum-lath fire protection of columns.

$\frac{3}{8}$" PERFORATED GYPSUM LATH

CORNER BEAD

1" OR $1\frac{3}{8}$" THREE-COAT PLASTER

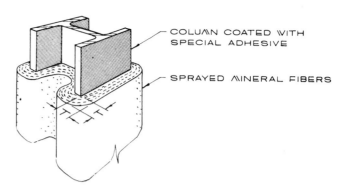

Figure 3. Sprayed fibrous fire protection of columns.

COLUMN COATED WITH SPECIAL ADHESIVE

SPRAYED MINERAL FIBERS

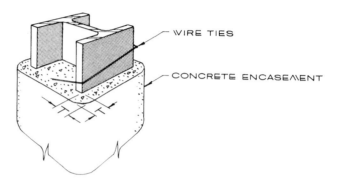

Figure 4. Concrete fire protection of columns.

WIRE TIES

CONCRETE ENCASEMENT

kler-protected buildings, 80 percent of those fires were extinguished by the sprinklers, and another 18 percent were held in check.

A sprinkler system consists of a network of piping placed under the ceiling and provided with a number of nozzles called *sprinklers* (Figure 12). When activated, the sprinklers spray water downward in a circular pattern. The sprinkler systems are *fixed-temperature* and *rate-of-rise*.

Fixed-Temperature Sprinkler Systems. Fixed-temperature sprinkler heads are usually designed so that temperatures of 135°F to 170°F will cause them to open automatically. Fixed-temperature sprinkler heads are color-coded to show their temperature ratings. Fixed-temperature sprinkler systems are *wet-pipe*, with water stored in the piping, and *dry-pipe*, with no water in the piping.

The *wet-pipe system* is commonly used for most indoor conditions where temperatures will not fall below freezing. The water in the piping is kept under pressure behind each sprinkler. Sprinklers contain fusible links that melt when hot and automatically open the sprinkler. Only sprinklers exposed to heat will open, thus preventing unnecessary water damage. A fire alarm sounds when the first sprinkler is opened. An antifreeze solution may be used in the piping for limited protection from freezing.

Buildings likely to have temperatures below freezing, such as unheated warehouses, can be protected by the *dry-pipe system*. The piping contains air under pressure rather

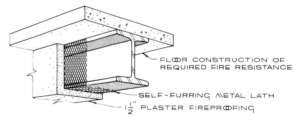

Figure 5. Plaster fire protection of beams.

FLOOR CONSTRUCTION OF REQUIRED FIRE RESISTANCE

SELF-FURRING METAL LATH

$1\frac{1}{2}$" PLASTER FIREPROOFING

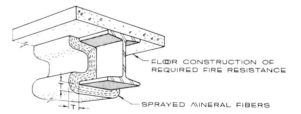

Figure 6. Sprayed fibrous fire protection of beams.

FLOOR CONSTRUCTION OF REQUIRED FIRE RESISTANCE

SPRAYED MINERAL FIBERS

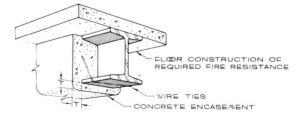

Figure 7. Concrete fire protection of beams.

FLOOR CONSTRUCTION OF REQUIRED FIRE RESISTANCE

WIRE TIES

CONCRETE ENCASEMENT

189

Table I. Fire resistance ratings for masonry walls

Type of Masonry Wall	Minimum Thickness for Ratings of			
	4 hr.	3 hr.	2 hr.	1 hr.
Heavyweight concrete masonry units* (coarse aggregate, siliceous gravel)	6.7"	6.7"	4.5"	3"
Lightweight concrete masonry units* (coarse aggregate, unexpanded slag)	5.9"	5"	4"	2.7"
Lightweight concrete masonry units* (coarse aggregate, expanded slag)	4.7"	4"	3.2"	2.1"
Solid brick masonry†	8"	8"	8"	4" (nonbearing)
Clay tile masonry†	16"	12"	12"	8"
Solid stone masonry*	12"	12"	12"	8"

*Abstracted from National Building Code (1955).
†Abstracted from Uniform Building Code (1958).

Table II. Fire resistance ratings for concrete walls

Type of Concrete Wall	Minimum Thickness for Ratings of			
	4 hr.	3 hr.	2 hr.	1 hr.
Plain concrete	7 1/2"	6 1/2"	5 1/2"	4" (nonbearing)
Reinforced concrete (unplastered)	7 1/2"	6 1/2"	5 1/2"	4" (nonbearing)
Reinforced concrete (3/4" portland cement or gypsum plaster, each side)	6"	5"	4"	3"

Abstracted from National Building Code (1955).

Table III. Fire resistance ratings for steel columns (Figures 1–4)

Type of Column Protection	Minimum Thickness for Ratings of			
	4 hr.	3 hr.	2 hr.	1 hr.
Vermiculite or perlite-gypsum plaster on self-furring metal lath (see Figure 1)	1 3/4"	1 3/8"		
Perlite-gypsum plaster on 3/8" perforated gypsum lath (see Figure 2)		1 3/8"	1"	
Sprayed mineral fiber (see Figure 3)	2 1/2"	2"	1 1/2"	
Concrete encasement (see Figure 4)	3"	2 1/2"	2"	1 1/2"

Abstracted from *Fire-Resistant Construction in Modern Steel-Framed Buildings*, AISC (1959).

Table IV. Fire resistance ratings for steel beams, girders, and trusses (Figures 5–7)

Type of Beam Protection	Minimum Thickness for Ratings of			
	4 hr.	3 hr.	2 hr.	1 hr.
Vermiculite or perlite-gypsum plaster on self-furring metal lath (see Figure 5)	1 1/2"			
Sprayed mineral fiber (see Figure 6)	1 7/8"	1 7/16"	1 1/8"	
Concrete encasement (see Figure 7)	3"	2 1/2"	2"	1 1/2"

Abstracted from *Fire-Resistant Construction in Modern Steel-Framed Buildings*, AISC (1959).

than water. When heat from a fire opens one of the sprinklers, the air is released and water flows into the piping network and through any opened sprinklers. A fire alarm also sounds.

Rate-of-Rise Sprinkler Systems. Detectors in a rate-of-rise system open valves to the sprinkler piping rather than to the sprinkler heads. Rate-of-rise detectors open valves upon any abnormal increase of temperature. They are very sensitive and consequently give quicker warning of a fire hazard. Rate-of-rise sprinkler systems may be *deluge* or *preaction.*

The *deluge system* is used for extra-hazard conditions. All sprinkler heads are open, but the piping is dry. When a rate-of-rise detector opens the water supply valve, water

Table V. Fire resistance ratings for floor and roof systems (Figures 8–11)

Type of Floor and Roof Protection	Minimum Thickness for Ratings of			
	4 hr.	3 hr.	2 hr.	1 hr.
Light-gauge steel, not fireproofed (see Figure 8); sand-limestone concrete slab of thickness equal to:			5 1/4″	4 1/2″
Light-gauge steel, contact fireproofing (see Figure 9); 2 1/2″ sand-gravel slab with sprayed mineral fiber of thickness equal to:		3/4″	1/2″	
Light-gauge steel, membrane fireproofing (see Figure 10); 2″ sand-gravel slab and 1″ vermiculite-gypsum fireproofing on metal lath installed at a distance of:	2″	15″		
Precast cellular system, not fireproofed (see Figure 11); 1 1/2″ sand-gravel concrete topping over a limestone concrete precast unit of thickness equal to:		6″		

Abstracted from *Fire-Resistance Construction in Modern Steel-Framed Buildings*, AISC (1959).

rushes into the piping and out through all heads simultaneously, giving better protection for difficult conditions such as flammable liquid fires. An alarm also sounds.

The *preaction system* is used when it is important to reduce the possibility of accidental water damage. The principal difference between a preaction and a standard dry-pipe system is that the water supply valve operates independently of the sprinkler heads; that is, a rate-of-rise detector first opens the valve and sounds an alarm. The fixed-temperature sprinkler heads do not open until their temperature ratings are reached. This gives time for small fires to be extinguished manually before the heads open.

Standpipes. Standpipes are vertical water pipes with fire hose outlets at each floor. They can be equipped with small (1 1/2″) hose to be used by the building occupants in the event of fire, or large (2 1/2″) hose to be used by fire departments, or both. Standpipes are usually wet-pipe rather than dry-pipe. At ground level, branches extend outside the building and are finished with "Siamese connections." Should there be insufficient pressure in the public water system, the fire department can pump water into the standpipe through these connections to increase the pressure. Check valves relieve the pumps from back-pressure.

Standpipes are located so that any fire can be reached by a stream of water from not more than 75′ of small hose or 100′ of large hose.

The *National Fire Codes* and local codes contain more detailed requirements than can be given here.

Some other extinguishing systems are foam, carbon dioxide, halons, and dry chemical. Foam is an aggregate of tiny gas-filled or air-filled bubbles used to smother fire by excluding air. Because foam contains water, it also has cooling properties. The principal use for foam is in fighting fires involving flammable liquids. Carbon dioxide, the halons, and dry chemical are nonconductive and therefore can be used on electrical fires as well as on flammable liquid fires.

High-Rise Buildings. Research is constantly being conducted to find better ways to prevent or control building fires. Special attention is being given to the problem of fire safety in high-rise buildings, because their construction is increasing—some to heights of 1,000 ft. and more. These buildings may contain more than 25,000 persons—equivalent to the population of a small city. Special precaution for fire protection must be taken in such buildings, for prompt evacuation is usually not possible. In addition, the building height may contribute a stack effect that spreads the fire quickly upward, and many floors may be beyond the reach of fire department aerial equipment. Therefore, fire in a high-rise must be controlled and fought internally. A combination of three methods is usually used:

1. All building materials and furnishings selected to provide no potential fuel for a fire, including none that might emit smoke or toxic gases
2. Compartmented structures capable of resisting and containing a fire within a relatively small portion of the building
3. Automatic fire-extinguishing systems capable of prompt and effective operation

Reading Sprinkler Plans

A sprinkler plan consists of a layout of the pattern and spacing of the sprinkler heads, showing how they are connected to the piping network. The size of piping and other details are also included. The layout of a sprinkler system is performed by a professional engineer using established standards as a guide. Sprinkler layout depends upon the building classifications. For example, the *National Fire Codes* specify the following under a smooth ceiling construction:

1. *Light Hazard.* The protection area per sprinkler must not exceed 200 sq. ft. The maximum distance between lines and between sprinklers on lines is 15 ft. Sprinklers need not be staggered. See Figure 13.
2. *Ordinary Hazard.* The protection area per sprinkler must not exceed 130 sq. ft. The maximum distance between lines or between sprinklers on lines is 15 ft. Sprinklers on alternate lines must be staggered if the distance between sprinklers on lines exceeds 12 ft.
3. *Extra Hazard.* The protection area per sprinkler must not exceed 90 sq. ft. The maximum distance between lines and between sprinklers on lines is 12 ft. The sprinklers on alternate lines must be staggered.

The *National Fire Codes* and local codes contain more detailed requirements.

Reading the Sprinkler Plan of an Office-Warehouse

The sprinkler plan of a combined office and warehouse is shown in Figure 14. A wet-pipe system is specified for the heated portions (the office, drafting room, and packing area),

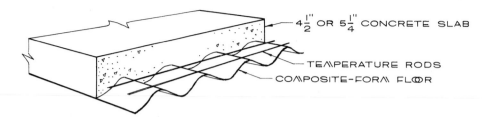

Figure 8. Unprotected floors and roofs.

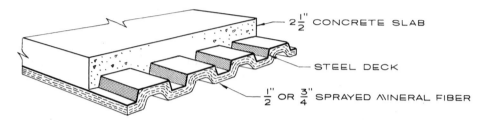

Figure 9. Sprayed fibrous fire protection of floors and roofs.

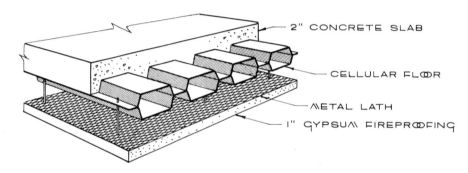

Figure 10. Membrane fire protection of floors and roofs.

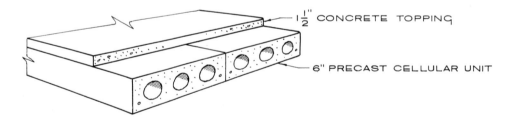

Figure 11. Unprotected cellular floors and roofs.

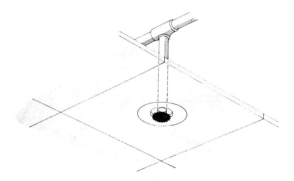

Figure 12. A flush-type ceiling sprinkler.

but a dry-pipe system is specified for the unheated warehouse. Notice in the warehouse that the sprinkler water enters the sprinkler heads through *overhead branch lines*. The branch lines are fed by an overhead *cross main* which in turn is fed by a 5″ overhead *feed main* connected to a 6″ underground tap from the public water main. A 2 1/2″ *riser* is used to feed the second floor. The piping sizes (all in inches) on the plan show that the diameter of the piping must increase as more sprinkler heads are fed. Diagonal marks show where the overhead pipes are hung from the roof joists. The circular symbol enclosing "18/WET/165" indicates 18 wet-pipe sprinkler heads having a fusible link temperature rating of 165°F.

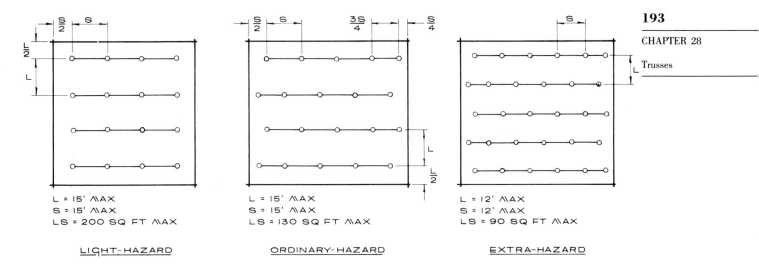

Figure 13. Sprinkler layouts for a smooth ceiling.

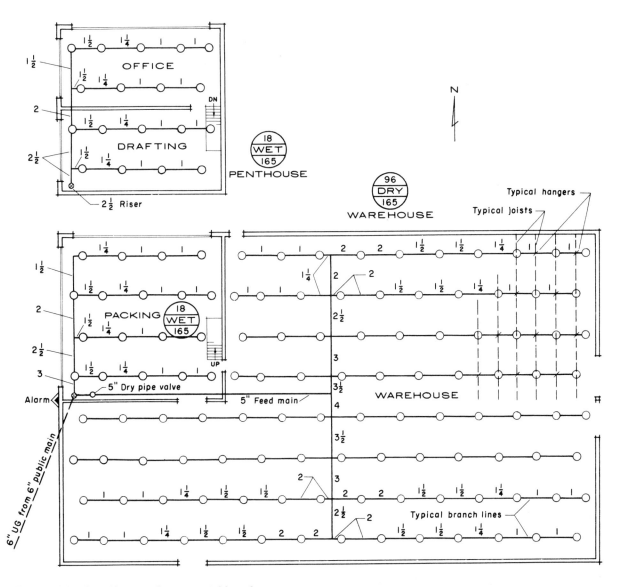

Figure 14. An office-warehouse sprinkler plan.

28

Trusses

Trusses are commonly used to support long roof spans, and you will often see them specified on the plans for commercial buildings. Wooden trusses were developed in the Middle Ages as a natural outgrowth of the gable roof. Builders used horizontal joists to tie together opposite walls in order to resist the outward thrust of sloping rafters. The resulting triangular structure was rigid, and it was discovered that a combination of triangular forms would also be rigid. Thus large spaces could be spanned by a number of pinned beams each lighter and shorter than required for a single lintel. Truss members can be smaller than lintels, because truss members are subjected only to tension or compression, but lintels are subjected to bending stress. Most materials resist tension and compression better than bending. For example, it is difficult to break a pencil in two by pulling the ends apart (tension) or pushing them together (compression), but it is easy to break a pencil by bending it. Trusses may be of wood, steel, or a combination of wood and steel. Steel rods are efficient tension members of a truss; timber or steel angle are better for the compression members.

Terminology

Trusses consist of principal members called *top chords* and *bottom chords* which are joined together by vertical or diagonal members called *webs*. The webs divide the truss into a number of segments called *panels*, usually of equal width. The top chords may be horizontal (or nearly horizontal) for flat roofs or inclined for pitched roofs. The depth of flat trusses is usually one-eighth to one-tenth of the span. For normal slopes, the depth of pitched trusses is one-fourth to one-fifth of the span. Depending upon the number of panels and strength of members, most trusses are economical for 20' to 80' spans.

Adjacent trusses are usually spaced about 15' or 16' apart (but also 8' to 20') and are joined by horizontal *purlins* on the top chords. When adjacent trusses are spaced closely enough that purlins or similar framing are unnecessary, the trusses are called *trussed rafters*.

Types

Some common types of trusses are shown in Figure 1. Heavy lines indicate members that are usually in compression for vertical loading, and light lines indicate members that are usually in tension. The number of panels depends on the material and span.

King Post Truss. The king post truss is often used for relatively short spans (20' to 30'). The top and bottom chords are often of wood and the vertical web of steel rod.

Inverted King Post Truss. This is also called a *trussed beam*. The tension rods greatly increase the load-bearing capacity of the horizontal beam.

Pratt and Howe Truss. *Pratt* and *Howe* trusses are somewhat similar. They both contain vertical webs that can be extended up through the roof for framing *monitors*. A monitor is a clerestory that permits light or ventilation at the middle of the trussed roof. The Pratt truss contains diagonal webs in tension; the Howe truss contains vertical webs in tension.

The Pratt flat truss is preferred when it is built integral with columns, since the direction of the diagonal webs permits columns to extend to the crown, giving better wind bracing. The Howe truss, however, is usually more economical for similar loading conditions. When two trusses frame to each side of a common column, a Pratt may be used on one side and a Howe on the other, since both webs do not then frame to the same place.

Belgium Truss. The compression web members of the Belgium truss are perpendicular to the top chords, permitting easy framing of the purlins at these panel points.

Warren Truss. Warren trusses are not often used for built-up roof trusses, but the Warren principle is the basis for all open-web joists.

Fink Truss. Fink trusses are used with steep roofs to reduce the length of the compression members. In Belgium

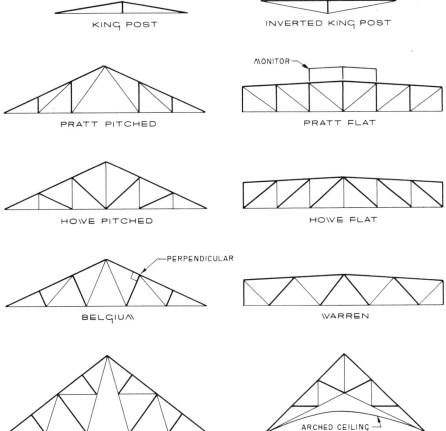

Figure 1. Common truss types.

trusses, for example, the compression members may be too long for reasonably sized members.

Scissors Truss. Scissors trusses are used in buildings such as churches where an arched ceiling is to be hung from the bottom chords.

Bowstring Truss. For spans from 80′ to 250′, the bowstring truss is particularly economical in comparison to other types of trusses. Wood bowstring trusses have been made with laminated curved top chords. Segmental bowstring trusses have straight top chords.

Wood Trusses

Wooden trussed rafters (Figure 26 of Chapter 8) are commonly used for small spans of 20′ to 50′, and wooden trusses are often used for spans to 80′. Wooden bowstring trusses are the most economical form of wooden truss for large spans over 100′ and have been used for spans of 250′.

Figure 2. Split ring.

Figure 3. Shear plate.

Wood trusses can be factory- or shop-fabricated. Connections are made by machine bolts with washers and split rings (Figure 2) or shear plates (Figure 3). Split rings transmit

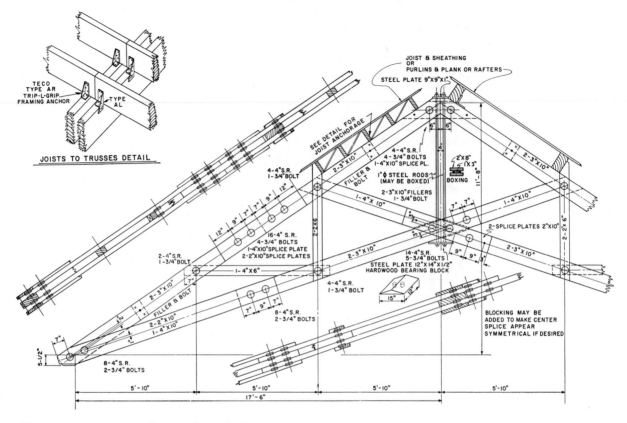

Figure 4. Construction drawing of a wood scissors truss.

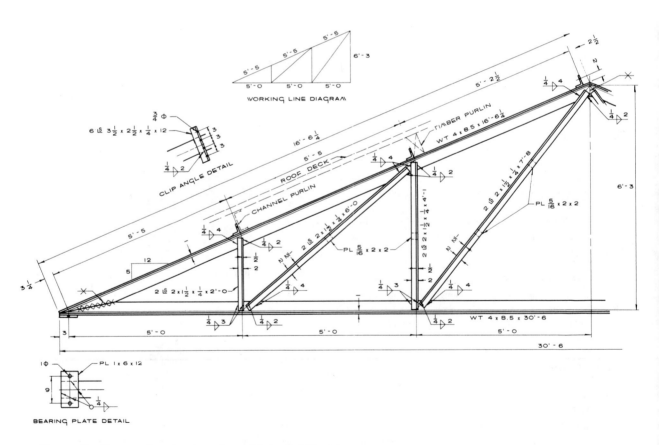

Figure 5. Construction drawing of a welded steel Pratt truss.

196

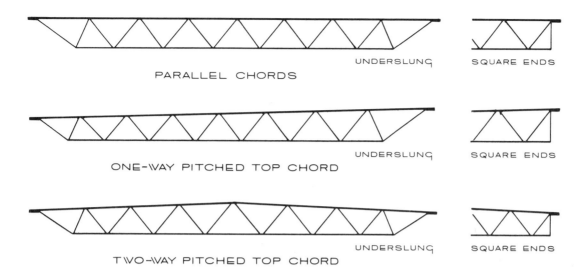

PARALLEL CHORDS

UNDERSLUNG   SQUARE ENDS

ONE-WAY PITCHED TOP CHORD

UNDERSLUNG   SQUARE ENDS

TWO-WAY PITCHED TOP CHORD

UNDERSLUNG   SQUARE ENDS

Figure 6. Types of open-web joists.

forces from one wooden member to another, the only function of the bolt being to hold the members together. Shear plates transmit the forces to the bolt which then resist the entire shearing stress. Split rings are used for wood-to-wood connections. Shear plates are used for wood-to-wood or wood-to-steel connections. Both split rings and shear plates are embedded in precut circular grooves, called *daps*, routed in the wooden members. They serve the function of distributing the forces over a greater area of each member. Thus larger forces can be transmitted than is possible with a bolt alone.

The construction drawing of a wood scissors truss of 35' span is shown in Figure 4. Notice the central steel tension rods, the chord splices, and the detail of fastening joists to the truss. Study this layout and make note of any questions you have. Check such questions with your instructor at the first opportunity.

Steel Trusses

Fabricated two-dimensional trusses of steel are commonly used in bridge design, and three-dimensional trusses (called *space frames*) are commonly used in contemporary building design. One of the earliest large steel-trussed structures, the 986' high Eiffel Tower, was built for the 1889 World's Fair in Paris. The steel cantilever truss of the Quebec Bridge, built in 1917, contains one span of 1,800'. The tallest man-made structure is a steel-trussed radio mast 2,120' high built in 1974 near Warsaw, Poland.

For buildings with spans less than 144', open-web joists are usually preferred for light loading. For heavy loading or large spans, fabricated steel trusses may be specified. The Pratt and Warren trusses are commonly used for flat roofs, and the Fink for steeply sloping roofs. The bowstring truss is often specified for buildings such as field houses having very long spans. Welding and high-strength bolting are the usual methods of fabrication.

The construction drawing of a welded steel Pratt truss is illustrated in Figure 5. The top and bottom chords of this truss are 4" structural tees cut from **W** shapes. The web members are doubled 2" × 1 1/2" unequal-leg angles. The

2" square plates tend to keep each pair of angles in alignment. The chord members are joined by vee welds, and the web members are fastened to the chords by 1/4" fillet welds.

On truss plans, you may see a *working line diagram*. This diagram is used to establish the theoretical principal dimensions. Then the designer attempts to lay out the truss members so that the center-of-gravity axes of each member coincide with the working lines. In this instance, the flange faces of the structural tees are 1" from the working lines, and the angle faces are 1/2" from the working lines. If you have questions after studying this construction drawing, check with your instructor at the first opportunity.

Open-Web Joists

Small prefabricated steel Warren trusses, called *open-web joists*, are commonly used to support floors and roofs (Figures 6 and 7). Available in sizes to span distances from 8' to 144',

Figure 7. Open-web steel joists for floor and roof support.

Figure 8. Open-web joist with cold-formed chords.

Figure 9. Open-web joist with angle and bar chords.

Figure 10. Long-span joist with tee-section chords.

Table I. Open-web joist designations

	Based on Available Stress of	
	22,000 psi	*30,000 psi*
Open-web steel joists	J	H
Long-span steel joists	LJ	LH
Deep long-span steel joists	DLJ	DLH

Table II. Comparison of open-web joist series

Joist Series	Joist Depth	Span
J and H	8″–24″	8′–48′
LJ and LH	18″–48″	25′–96′
DLJ and DLH	52″–72″	89′–144′

open-web joists are economical, strong, lightweight, and easily erected. The open webs permit installation of electric conduits, heating pipes, and air ducts. When used with an incombustible top slab and metal lath plaster ceiling, open-web joists can carry fire protection ratings of four hours. As shown in Figure 6, open-web joists can be obtained with underslung or square ends. Ceilings can be better hung from joists with square ends. Open-web joists can also be obtained either with the top chord parallel to the bottom chord (for floors) or pitched in one or both directions (for roofs). The standard pitch is 1/8″/ft., which permits roof drainage. An upward camber of 3/8″ to 8 5/8″ (depending on the span) is also provided to prevent sagging when fully loaded.

Steel joists are manufactured in three series, as shown in Table I: open-web steel joists, long-span steel joists, and deep long-span steel joists.

Open-Web Steel Joists. Open-web steel joists, called the *J series*, are available in lengths from 8′ to 48′ and in depths from 8″ to 24″. (The *joist depth* refers to the nominal depth at the middle of the span.) J-series joists are manufactured with cold-formed chords shaped like a hat (Figure 8) or angle and bar chords (Figure 9). The hat-shaped and angle chords provide a flat backing for deck and ceiling support, but the bar chords are preferred when the ceiling is to be hung by tie wires.

The J series is based on a tensile working stress of 22,000 psi. A heavier H series based on a tensile working stress of 30,000 psi will support heavier loads.

Long-Span Steel Joists. Long-span steel joists, called the *LJ series*, are available in lengths from 25′ to 96′ and in depths from 18″ to 48″. Tee sections are used for the top and bottom chords (Figure 10). The LJ series is also based on a tensile working stress of 22,000 psi. A heavier LH series based on a tensile working stress of 30,000 psi will support heavier loads.

Deep Long-Span Steel Joists. Deep long-span steel joists, called the *DLJ series*, are available in lengths from 89′ to 144′ and in depths from 52″ to 72″, as shown in Table II. The DLJ series is based on a tensile working stress of 22,000 psi, and the heavier DLH series is based on 30,000 psi.

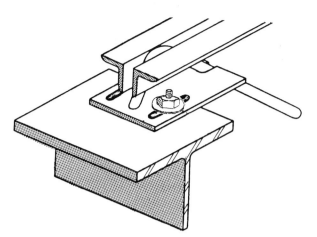

Figure 11. Bolted connection.

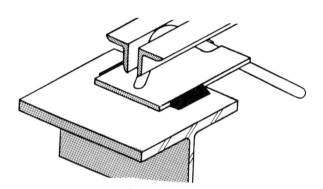

Figure 12. Welded connection.

Figure 13. Column connection.

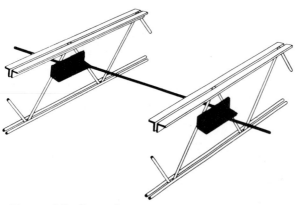

Figure 15. Sag rods.

Figure 16. Joist extensions.

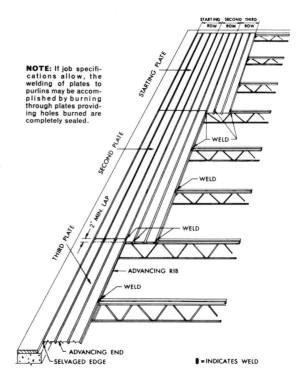

NOTE: If job specifications allow, the welding of plates to purlins may be accomplished by burning through plates providing holes burned are completely sealed.

■ = INDICATES WELD

Figure 17. Installing centering on open-web joists.

Roof Decking. Floor and decks are installed on the top chords of open-web joists, and ceilings may be hung from the bottom chords. The floor and roof decks may be precast concrete planks, concrete poured on formed steel decking, wood fiber panels, or wood planking. The ceiling is often of metal lath and plaster to serve as fire protection for the joists.

Poured floor and roof slabs are constructed by attaching formwork of ribbed, corrugated, or cellular steel sheets, ribbed metal lath, or paper-backed welded wire fabric to the top chords of the joists. This formwork is called *centering* (Figure 17). Steel centering sheets are available in lengths to 24′ and in widths to 32″. They are laid with nesting side laps and 2″ minimum end laps. The centering sheets are securely fastened to the top chords by welding or by metal clips. These attachments also serve to stay the top chords laterally.

Concrete is poured on the centering to a minimum thickness of 2″. The centering acts as positive reinforcement, in addition to being a form. Often reinforcing steel near the top

of the slab is included for negative reinforcement. (*Positive reinforcement* resists U-shaped bending; *negative reinforcement* resists inverted U-shaped bending.) Utilities may also be embedded in the poured slab. Lightweight poured concrete, although not as structural, gives fire protection for the joists. When lightweight concrete is used, vent clips are installed along the side laps between supports to permit escape of moisture.

Space Frames

A truss is a two-dimensional structural member. A three-dimensional trussed system is called a *space frame*. The three-dimensional trussed system shown in Figure 19, for example, is composed of two-dimensional trusses perpendicular to each other. Figure 20 shows a folded-plate roof constructed of inclined trusses. Truly integrated three-

Table III. Some available sizes of J-series open-web joists

Designation	Depth (in.)	Top Chord Angles (in.)	Bottom Chord Bars (in.)	Approximate Weight (lb./ft.)
8J2	8	1 × 1 × 1/8	15/32	4.2
10J2	10	1 × 1 × 1/8	15/32	4.2
10J3	10	1 1/4 × 1 1/4 × 1/8	17/32	4.8
10J4	10	1 1/2 × 1 1/2 × 1/8	19/32	6.0
12J2	12	1 × 1 × 1/8	15/32	4.5
12J3	12	1 1/4 × 1 1/4 × 1/8	17/32	5.1
12J4	12	1 1/2 × 1 1/2 × 1/8	19/32	6.0
12J5	12	1 1/2 × 1 1/2 × 5/32	21/32	7.0
12J6	12	1 1/2 × 1 1/2 × 3/16	23/32	8.1

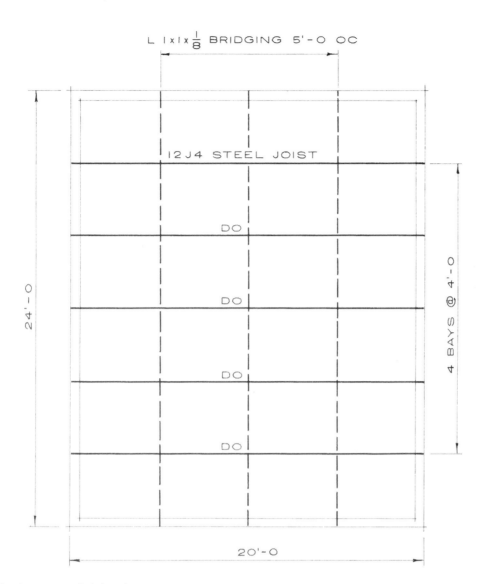

Figure 18. An open-web joist plan.

dimensional truss systems, however, are shown in Figures 21–24.

True space frames may take many forms but are often based upon a tetrahedron (a pyramid with a triangular base) rather than a triangle. Just as the triangle is a rigid structure, so is the tetrahedron a rigid structure. Figure 21 shows a popular form of space frame based upon the tetrahedron.

Any regular polyhedron can be made rigid by making all its faces rigid. This is often accomplished by triangulation. The upper horizontal plane in Figure 21, though, need not be triangulated since an attached floor or roof system will achieve rigidity in this plane. The example in Figure 22 shows a space frame based upon a rectangular form. As shown in Figure 23, the space frame concept can be expanded for use as columns or towers. A complete roof and column design is illustrated in Figure 24.

Space frames are usually constructed of steel or aluminum tubing. For modular purposes, all tubular members have the same outside diameter, but thicker walls are specified when increased strength is needed.

The major feature in any space frame system is the manner of connecting the truss members. Welding is probably the most common method; some alternate methods are shown in Figure 25. The *Mannesmann system* of clamping was first developed for scaffolding. The clamps can be used to fasten tubing at any desired angle. The *Unistrut system* uses specially formed plates to which channel members are bolted. This system produces square panels 49″ center to center permitting the use of 48″ panel materials with 1″ joints. The *Mero system* consists of spherical connectors having threaded holes. Up to eighteen members can be fastened to each connector.

Example

The entire structure of the Frank C. Bishop Library (Figures 26 and 27) is a space frame that permits a column-free interior. The truss members are 2 1/2″ steel angles and tees, which were shop-welded to a large extent. Roofing is wood shakes.

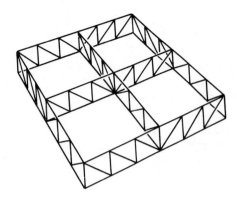

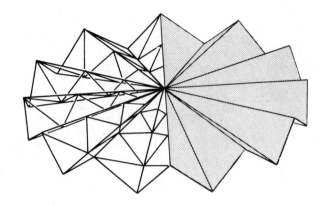

Figure 19. A three-dimensional truss system.　　　*Figure 20.* A folded-plate trussed roof.

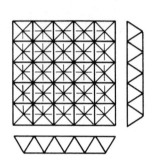 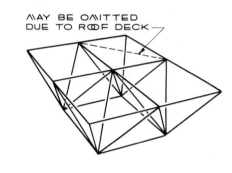 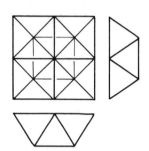

MAY BE OMITTED
DUE TO ROOF DECK

Figure 21. A space frame based on a tetrahedron.

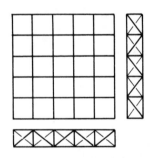 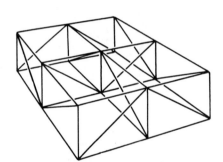 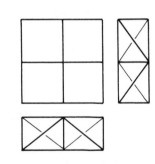

Figure 22. A space frame based on rectangular forms.

 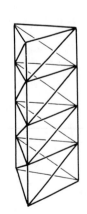 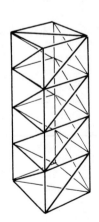 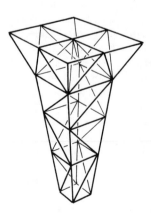

Figure 23. Space frame columns.

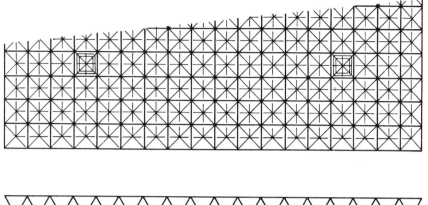

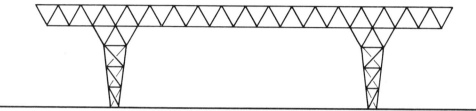

Figure 24. A space-framed structure.

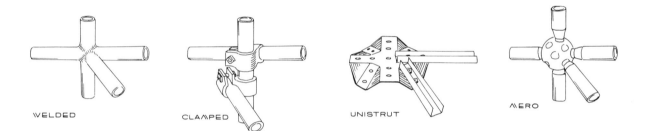

WELDED   CLAMPED   UNISTRUT   AERO

Figure 25. Fastening space frames.

Figure 26. Interior of the Frank C. Bishop Library, York School, Monterey, California.

Figure 27. Exterior of the Bishop Library.

29

Glossary

This is a glossary of approximately 400 architectural terms that often appear on plans and specifications of residential and commercial buildings. You should make a strong effort to add these terms to your technical vocabulary. For most people, the best way to accomplish this is as follows.

First, read through the entire glossary to determine which terms are familiar to you. Cross out all familiar terms.

Second, divide the unfamiliar terms into workable study groups of no more than fifty each. Study each group of terms on successive days by covering the definitions and then trying to recall them and write them out. Compare your descriptions with the definitions given here. The *exact wording* of each definition is not important. Repeat until you are confident that you *understand* each term. About five reviews are usually required. Cross out terms as you learn them so you can concentrate on the difficult ones.

Finally, spot check the entire glossary by having someone randomly select twenty terms for you to define as a last review.

Active solar system   A solar heating system in which the heat flow is forced by some mechanical means.

A-frame   Any frame in the shape of an inverted V.

Aggregate   Material such as broken stone, gravel, cinders, or slag used as one of the constituents of concrete, the other constituents being sand, cement, and water.

Alcove   A recessed space connected with or at the side of a larger room.

Anchor   A metal piece used to attach building members to masonry.

Anchor bolt   A threaded rod used to fasten the sill plate to the foundation.

Angle iron   A metal bar, L-shaped in section.

Apron   The finish board immediately below a windowsill.

Arcade   A series of arches supported by a row of columns.

Arch   A curved structure that carries the weight over an opening.

Architect   A person who plans buildings and oversees their construction.

Architectural terra-cotta   Terra-cotta building blocks having a ceramic finish.

Areawall   The wall of an areaway.

Areaway   A subsurface enclosure to admit light and air to a basement.

Ashlar masonry   Masonry composed of squared units laid with horizontal bed joints.

Asphalt   An insoluble material used in waterproofing.

Backfill   Earth replaced around a foundation.

Balcony   A platform projecting from the wall of a building, above the ground.

Balloon frame   A type of building frame in which the studs extend from sill to eaves without interruption.

Balusters   The small, vertical members of a railing between the bottom and top rails.

Banister   A handrail.

Baseboard   The finishing board covering a wall where it meets the floor.

Basement   The lowest story of a building, partially or entirely below ground.

Batten   A strip of board for use in fastening other boards together.

Batter   Sloping a masonry or concrete wall.

Batter board   A horizontal board nailed to posts and used to lay out the excavation and foundation.

Bay   Any division or compartment of an arcade, roof, building, space between floor joists, or other area.

Beam   A horizontal structural member that carries a load.

Bearing partition   A partition supporting any vertical load in addition to its own weight.

Bearing plate   A support member used to distribute weight over a larger area.

Bench mark   A reference point used by surveyors to establish lines and grades.

Bent   A rigid, transverse framework.

Bevel weld   A butt weld with one mitered member.

Bibb   A threaded faucet.

Blocking   Small, wood framing members.

Bluestone   A hard, blue sandstone.

Board foot   The amount of wood contained in a piece of rough green lumber 1″ thick × 12″ wide × 1′ long.

Bond   Mortar bond between mortar and masonry units; structural bond between wythes; pattern bond for decorative effect.

Bond beam A reinforced concrete beam used to strengthen masonry walls.

Box beam A hollow, built-up structural unit.

Brick veneer A brick facing laid in front of frame construction.

Bridging Cross-bracing between floor joists to add stiffness to the floors.

Brownstone A brown sandstone used as an exterior facing.

Btu (British thermal unit). A unit used to measure heat.

Building board Boards made from repulped paper, shredded wood, or similar material (also wallboard).

Building line An imaginary line on a plot beyond which the building may not extend.

Building paper A heavy, waterproof paper used over sheathing and subfloors to prevent passage of air and water.

Built-up beam A beam constructed of smaller members fastened together with the grains parallel.

Built-up roof A roofing composed of several layers of felt and asphalt, pitch, or coal tar.

Butt *See* Door butt.

Butt weld A weld of members butting against each other.

Calking A waterproof material used to seal cracks.

Canopy A sheltering roof.

Cant strip A form of triangular molding.

Cantilever A beam or girder fixed at one extremity and free at the other. "To cantilever" is to employ the principle of the lever to carry a load.

Carport A garage not fully enclosed.

Casement A window whose frame is hinged at the side.

Casing The framing around a door or window.

Catch basin An underground structure for surface drainage in which sediment may settle.

Cavity wall A masonry wall having an air space of about 2″.

Cement A masonry material purchased in the form of a highly pulverized powder usually medium gray in color.

Centering Formwork for poured concrete floor and roof slabs; temporary formwork for the support of masonry arches or lintels during construction.

Center-to-center Measurement from the center of one member to the center of another (noted "oc").

Ceramic veneer Architectural terra-cotta having large face dimensions and thin sections.

Channel A standard form of structural rolled steel, consisting of three sides at right angles in channel form.

Chord A principal member of a truss.

Circuit The path for an electric current.

Clapboard A narrow board, thicker at one edge, for weather boarding frame buildings; siding.

Clerestory A window between roof planes.

Client A person who employs an architect.

Collar beam A horizontal member tying two opposite rafters together at more or less a center point on the rafters.

Column A vertical supporting member.

Common brick 3 3/4″ × 2 1/2″ × 8″ brick used for general construction.

Composite wall A masonry wall of at least two adjacent wythes of different materials.

Concrete A masonry mixture of portland cement, sand, aggregate, and water in proper proportions.

Condensation Water formed by warm, moist air contacting a cold surface.

Conductor A vertical drainpipe or material permitting passage of electric current.

Conduit A pipe or trough that carries water, electrical wiring, cables, and so forth.

Conifer *See* Softwood.

Contractor A builder.

Control joint A joint to divert cracking in a masonry wall. Formed by raking mortar from a continuous vertical joint.

Convector A heat transfer surface that uses convection currents to transmit heat.

Coping A masonry cap on top of a wall to protect it from water penetration.

Corbel A bracket formed in a wall by building out successive courses of masonry.

Corner bead A metal molding, built into the plaster corners to prevent the accidental breaking off of the plaster.

Cornice That part of a roof which extends or projects beyond the wall; the architectural treatment thereof, as a "box cornice."

Counterflashing A flashing used under the regular flashing.

Course A horizontal row of bricks, tile, stone, building blocks, or similar material.

Court An open space surrounded partly or entirely by a building.

Crawl space The space between the floor joists and the surface below when there is no basement. This is used in making repairs on plumbing and other utilities.

Cricket A roof device used at intersections to divert water.

Cupola A small structure built on top of a roof.

Curtain wall An exterior wall that provides no structural support.

Cut stone Stone cut to given sizes or shapes.

Damper A movable plate to regulate the draft in a chimney.

Dap A circular groove (for split rings and shear plates).

Decay Disintegration of wood through the action of fungi.

Deciduous *See* Hardwood.

Door buck A door frame (usually metal).

Door butt A hinge.

Door check A device to slow a door when closing.

Doorstop A device to prevent a door from hitting the wall when opening.

Dormer A structure projecting from, or cut into, a sloping roof, usually to accommodate a window or windows.

Double-faced fireplace A fireplace having two fireplace openings.

Double-hung window A window having top and bottom sashes each capable of movement up and down in its own grooves.

Downspout A vertical drainpipe for carrying rainwater from the gutters.

Drafter A man or woman who prepares plans using drafting instruments or computer equipment.

Drain A pipe for carrying waste water.

Dressed size *See* Finished size.

Drip A molding designed to prevent rainwater from running down the face of a wall, or to protect the bottom of a door or window from leakage.

Dry rot A dry, crumbly wood rot.

Dry wall A wall finished with wallboard in place of plaster; stone wall built without mortar.

Dry well A shallow well used for the disposal of rainwater.

Duct Sheet-metal conductor for air distribution.

Eave The lower portion of a roof that extends beyond the wall.

Efflorescence An undesirable white crystallization that may form on masonry walls.

Elbow An L-shaped pipe fitting.

Electric arc process A welding process that uses an electric arc to fuse both members.

Elevation An orthographic projection of the vertical side of a building.

Escalator A moving stairway.

Excavation A hole formed by removing earth.

Expansion joint A separation in a masonry or concrete surface to permit expansion due to temperature and moisture changes.

Facade The front or face of a building.

Face brick A special brick used for facing a wall. Face bricks are more uniform in size than common bricks and are made in a variety of colors and textures.

Faced wall *See* Composite wall.

Facing Any material, forming a part of a wall, used as a finished surface.

Fascia (Facia), Fascia board A flat, banded projection on the face of the cornice; the flat vertical member of the cornice; the flat surface running above a shop window on which the name of the shop may be displayed.

Fenestration The arrangement of windows in a wall.

Fiber glass A material composed of thin glass threads used for insulation or with resin for a finished surface.

Fiberboard Sheet material of refined wood fibers.

Fieldstone Building stone found loose on the ground (field), regardless of its exact variety. Don't confuse with *flag*stone.

Filigree Fine, decorative openwork.

Fillet weld A butt weld with the weld metal filling an inside corner.

Finish lumber Dressed wood used for building trim.

Finished size The dimensions of lumber after planing; usually 1/2″ less than nominal (rough) size. For example, a 2″ × 4″ stud actually measures 1 1/2″ × 3 1/2″.

Fire brick A brick made of a refractory material (fire clay) that withstands great heat; used to line furnaces, fireplaces, and so on.

Fire cut An angular cut at the end of a joist framing into a masonry wall.

Fire stopping Obstructions across air passages in buildings to prevent the spread of hot gases and flames; horizontal blocking between wall studs.

Fire wall A wall extending from foundation through the roof to subdivide a building in order to restrict the spread of fire.

Fireproofing Any material protecting structural members to increase their fire resistance.

First-angle projection A type of multiview projection that results in the plan appearing below the elevations.

Fixture A piece of electric or plumbing equipment.

Flagstone Flat stone used for floors, steps, and walks.

Flashing The sheet-metal work used to prevent leakage over windows and doors, around chimneys, and at the intersections of different wall surfaces and roof planes.

Floor plan An orthographic projection of the floor of a building.

Flue A passage in the chimney to convey smoke to the outer air.

Flue lining Terra-cotta pipe used for the inner lining of chimneys.

Footing The bases upon which the foundation and posts rest.

Formica A plastic veneer trade name.

Foundation The supporting wall of a building below the first-floor level.

Framing Lumber used for a building's structural members.

Frost line The depth of frost penetration in soil.

Furring Wood strips fastened to a wall or ceiling for the purpose of attaching wallboards or ceiling tile.

Gable The triangular portion of an end wall formed by a sloping roof.

Gambrel A gable roof, each slope of which is broken into two planes.

Geodesic dome A double-faced dome formed of members of nearly equal length.

Girder A large horizontal structural member, usually heavier than a beam, used to support the ends of joists and beams or to carry walls over openings.

Glazed brick Brick finished with ceramic, clay-coated, or salt glaze.

Grade or grade line The level of the ground around a building.

Granite A durable and hard igneous rock.

Green efflorescence An undesirable green stain that may form on masonry walls.

Ground cover Usually, roll roofing laid on the ground in crawl spaces to reduce moisture.

Grounds Wood strips attached to the walls before plastering, serving as a plaster stop and nailing base for trim.

Grout Mortar of pouring consistency.

Gunite Sprayed concrete using a dry mix and water.

Gutter A trough or depression for carrying off water.

Gypsum board Board made of plaster with a covering of paper (also plasterboard).

Half-timbering A frame construction where the spaces are filled in with masonry.

Hanger An iron strap used to support a joist or beam.

Hardboard Sheet material of compressed wood fibers.

Hardwood Wood from trees having broad leaves in contrast to needles. The term does not necessarily refer to the hardness of the wood.

Header A beam perpendicular to joists, into which they are framed; a masonry unit laid horizontally with the end exposed.

Headroom The vertical clearance in a room or on a stairway.

Hearth The masonry portion of a floor in front of a fireplace.

High-strength bolt A medium-carbon or heat-treated alloy steel bolt.

Hip roof   A roof with four sloping sides.

House drain   Horizontal sewer piping within a building which receives waste from the soil stacks.

House sewer   Horizontal sewer piping 5′ outside the foundation wall to the public sewer.

Humidifier   A device to increase relative humidity.

I-beam   A steel beam with an I-shaped cross section.

Insulation   Material for obstructing the passage of sound, heat, or cold from one surface to another.

Interference-body bolt   A high-strength bolt with raised ribs on the shank.

Jack rafter   A short rafter placed between the ridge and the hip rafter or valley rafter.

Jacuzzi   Trademark for whirlpools made by Jacuzzi Inc.

Jalousie   A type of window consisting of a number of long, thin, hinged panels.

Jamb   The inside vertical face of a door or window frame.

J-groove weld   A butt weld with one gouged member.

Joist   A member directly supporting floor and ceiling loads and in turn supported by bearing walls, beams, or girders.

Kalamein door   A fireproofed door covered with metal.

Keystone   The last, wedge-shaped stone placed in the crown of an arch.

King post truss   A simple truss consisting of one vertical web (the king post).

Knot   A lumber defect caused by an embedded limb.

Kraft paper   A strong, brown paper made from sulphate pulp.

Laitance   An undesirable watery layer found in the upper surface of curing concrete.

Lally column   A steel column.

Laminate   To bond together several layers of material.

Lanai   A roofed living area or passage with open sides.

Landing   A stair platform.

Lath (metal)   Sheet-metal screening used as a base for plastering.

Lath (wood)   Thin wood used to level a surface in preparation for plastering or composition tiles (also called furring).

Lattice   Openwork made by crossed or interlaced strips of material.

Lavatory   A washbasin or room with a washbasin.

Ledger   A wood strip nailed to the lower side of a girder to provide a bearing surface for joists.

Lift-slab   A precast concrete construction method of casting all slabs on the ground and lifting them into final position.

Limestone   A sedimentary rock of calcium carbonate.

Lintel   The horizontal member supporting the wall over an opening.

Lobby   An entrance hall or reception room; vestibule.

Lookout   A short timber supporting a projecting cornice.

Lot line   The limit of a lot.

Louver   A ventilating window covered by sloping slats to exclude rain.

Low-E glass   Low-emissivity glass manufactured with a microthin transparent coating that reflects heat.

Lumber   Wood that has been sawed, resawed, planed, crosscut, or matched.

M shape   A lightweight structural steel I-beam.

Manhole   A sewer opening to allow access for a worker.

Mansard   A hip roof, each slope of which is broken into two planes.

Mantel   The shelf over a fireplace.

Marble   A metamorphic rock used for building.

Masonite   A hardboard trade name.

Masonry   Material such as stone, brick, and block used by a mason.

Mastic   A waterproof material used to seal cracks.

Meeting rail   The horizontal rails of double-hung sash that fit together when the window is closed.

Member   A part of a building unit.

Millwork   Woodwork that has been finished (milled) in a milling plant.

Miter   A beveled cut.

Modular brick   4″ × 2 2/3″ × 8″ brick.

Module   A standardized unit of measurement.

Molding   Strips used for ornamentation.

Mortar   A mixture of cement, sand, and water used as a bonding agent by masons.

Mullion   The large vertical or horizontal division of a window opening.

Muntin   The small members that divide the glass in a window frame.

Newel or newel post   The post where the handrail of a stair starts or changes direction.

Niche   A small recess in a wall.

Nominal size   The "name" size by which lumber is identified and sold.

Norman brick   4″ × 2 2/3″ × 12″ brick.

Nosing   The rounded edge of a stair tread.

On center   Measurement from the center of one member to the center of another (noted "oc").

One-point perspective   A type of perspective having one vanishing point for normal lines.

Open-web joist   A prefabricated steel Warren truss.

Outlet   An electric socket.

Overhang   The horizontal distance that a roof projects beyond a wall.

Panel   A flat surface framed by thicker material.

Panelboard   The center for controlling electrical circuits.

Parapet   The portion of a wall extended above the roof.

Parging   Cement mortar applied to a masonry wall (also pargeting).

Parquetry   An inlaid floor.

Particle board   Wood fiberboard.

Partition   An interior wall. (*Wall:* an exterior wall.)

Passive solar system   A solar heating system in which heat flows naturally rather than being forced by some mechanical means.

Penny   A term for the length of a nail, abbreviated "d." Originally, it meant the price per hundred nails (i.e., 8-penny = 8¢ per hundred nails).

Penthouse   A housing above the roof for elevator machinery.

Pier   A rectangular masonry support either freestanding or built into a wall.

Pilaster   Specifically, an attached pier used to strengthen a wall.

Pitch   A term applied to the amount of roof slope. It is found by dividing the height by the span. Also a liquid material used in roofing. Also the center-to-center distance between bolts.

Plank   Lumber 2″ or more in thickness.

Plate   A horizontal member in a wall framework that rafters, joists, studs, and so forth, rest on or are secured to, as in *sole plate, sill plate, top plate*.

Plumb   Vertical.

Ply   The number of layers of roofing felt, plywood veneer, or other materials.

Plywood   Wood made up of three or more layers of veneer bonded with glue.

Pointing   Filling of joints in a masonry wall.

Post-and-beam construction   A type of building frame in which cross-beams rest directly on vertical posts.

Precasting   A casting in a mold that is not located at its final position in the structure.

Prestressing   A method of compressing concrete members so that they will not deflect when in position.

Priming   The first coat of paint, filling the pores of the surface preparatory to receiving subsequent coats.

Pumpcrete   Pumped concrete.

Purlin   A horizontal roof framing member, laid perpendicular to main trusses and supporting the roof.

R value   A classification number that indicates the effectiveness of insulation.

Radiant heating   Heating by radiating rays without air movement.

Rafter   A member in a roof framework running from the eave to the ridge. There are hip rafters, jack rafters, and valley rafters.

Rebar   Reinforcing bar.

Reflective insulation   Sheet material with a surface of low heat emissivity used to reduce heat loss.

Reinforced concrete   Concrete containing more than 0.2 percent of reinforcing steel.

Resistance number   *See* R value.

Retaining wall   A wall designed to resist lateral pressure of earth.

Retemper   To replace water evaporated from wet mortar.

Return   A molding turned back to the wall on which it is located.

Reveal   The depth of masonry between its outer face and a window or door set in an opening.

Ribbon   A wood strip let into the studding to provide a bearing surface for joists.

Ridge   The top edge of the roof where two slopes meet.

Ridge cap   A wood or metal cap used over roofing at the ridge.

Ridgepole   The highest horizontal member in a roof. It supports the heads of the jack rafters.

Riprap   Stone placed on a slope to prevent erosion.

Riser   The vertical board of a step. It forms the front of the stair step.

Rocklath   A flat sheet of gypsum used as a plaster base.

Roll roofing   Roofing material of fiber and asphalt.

Roman brick   4″ × 2″ × 12″ brick.

Roof boards   The rough boarding over the roof framework on which is laid the roof covering (also, roofers).

Rubble   Irregularly shaped building stone, partly trimmed.

S shape   A structural steel I beam.

Saddle   A small, double-sloping roof to carry the water away from the back of chimneys. Sometimes called *cricket*.

Salvaged brick   Used brick.

Sandstone   A sedimentary rock of cemented quartz.

Sandwich wall   A wall of at least two adjacent and connected panels, usually reinforced concrete panels protecting an insulating panel.

Sash   A framing for windowpanes. A sash window is generally understood to be a double-hung, vertically sliding window.

Scab   A small member used to join other members, fastened on the outside face.

Scarf joint   A joint made by tapering the ends of each piece.

Schedule   A list of parts (such as a *window schedule*).

SCR brick   A 6″ × 2 1/2″ × 12″ brick developed by Structural Steel Products Research for use in 6″ solid, load-bearing walls.

Scratch coat   The first coat of plaster. It is scratched to provide a good bond for the next coat.

Seasoning   Removing moisture from green wood.

Section   An orthographic projection that has been cut apart to show interior features.

Septic tank   A sewage-settling tank.

Setback   The distance between a building and its front or side property lines.

Shake   A hand-split shingle.

Shear plate   A metal connector for timber-to-timber and timber-to-steel construction that distributes the load over a greater area.

Sheathing   The rough boarding on the outside of a wall or roof over which is laid the finished siding or the shingles.

Shim   A piece of material used to true up or fill in the space between two surfaces.

Shingles   Roof covering made of wood cut to stock lengths and thicknesses and to random widths. There are also fiber glass, asphalt, slate, and tile shingles.

Shotcrete   Sprayed concrete using a wet mix.

Sidelight   A narrow window adjacent to a door.

Siding   The outside layer of boards on a frame wall.

Sill   The stone or wood member across the bottom of a door or window opening. Also the bottom member on which a building frame rests (sill plate).

Slate   A metamorphic rock used for roofing and flagstone.

Sleeper   A wood member placed over a concrete slab to provide a nailing base for a wood floor.

Slump block   A concrete block resembling stone.

Smoke chamber   The portion of a chimney flue located directly over the fireplace.

Snap header   A half-brick header.

Soffit   The undersurface of a cornice, molding, or beam.

Softwood   Wood from trees having needles rather than broad leaves. The term does not necessarily refer to the softness of the wood.

Soil stack   A vertical pipe in a plumbing system that carries the discharge from a toilet.

Soldier   A masonry unit laid vertically with the narrow side exposed.

Sole   The horizontal framing member directly under the studs.

Sovent A single-stack, self-venting sewage disposal system.

Space frame A spatial truss system.

Spackle To cover wallboard joints with plaster.

Span The distance between structural supports (i.e., the length of a joist, rafter, or other member).

Spandrel The area between the top of a window and sill of the above window.

Spandrel wall An exterior wall that provides no structural support.

Specifications The written description accompanying the working drawings.

Split block A fractured solid concrete block laid with the split face exposed.

Split lintels Two lintels placed side by side in a wall.

Square 100 sq. ft. of roofing.

Stack A vertical pipe.

Stile A vertical member of a door, window, or panel.

Stirrup A metal U-shaped strap used to support framing members; a U-shaped rebar to provide shear strength in concrete beams.

Stool The wood shelf across the bottom and inside of a window. Also a water closet.

Stop *See* Doorstop.

Story (Storey) The space between two floors or between a floor and the ceiling above.

Stressed-skin panel A hollow, built-up panel used for floors, roofs, and walls.

Stretcher A masonry unit laid horizontally with the long face exposed.

Stringer The sides of a flight of stairs; the supporting member cut to receive the treads and risers.

Stucco A face plaster or cement applied to walls or partitions.

Stud The vertical member that forms the framework of a partition or wall.

Stud welding An electric arc-welding process used to weld threaded studs to structural steel.

Subfloor The rough flooring under the finish floor.

Tail beam A framing member supported by a header or trimmer.

Tee A structural steel member in a shape of a T.

Tempered hardboard Water-resistant hardboard.

Termite shield Sheet metal used to block the passage of termites.

Terra-cotta Hard-baked clay and sand often used for chimney flues.

Terrace A raised flat space outdoors.

Terrazzo Floor covering of marble chips and cement ground to a smooth finish. Metal strips are used to separate different colors and create designs.

Thermostat An instrument automatically controlling the heating plant.

Threshold The stone, wood, or metal piece directly under a door.

Tie bar A tie rod.

Tie beam A framing member between rafters.

Tie rod A steel rod used to keep a member from spreading.

Tilt-up construction A method of precasting members horizontally on the site and lifting into their final vertical position.

Toenail To drive nails at an angle.

Tongue A projection on the edge of a board that fits into a groove on an adjacent board (tongue-and-grooved).

Track A horizontal member in metal framing as in *top track* or *bottom track*.

Translucent Having the ability to transmit light but not a clear image.

Transom A small window over a door.

Transparent Having the ability to transmit clear images.

Trap A device providing a liquid seal to prevent passage of air and odor.

Tread The horizontal part of a step.

Treillage An ornamental screen.

Trim The finish frame around an opening.

Trimmer A joist or rafter around a floor or roof opening.

Truss A braced framework capable of spanning greater distances than the individual components.

Trussed rafter A truss spaced close enough to adjacent trusses that purlins are unnecessary.

U-groove weld A weld with one gouged member.

Unfinished bolt A low-carbon-steel bolt.

Valley The trough formed by the intersection of two roof slopes.

Valve A device that regulates the flow in a pipe.

Vapor barrier A thin sheet used to prevent the passage of water vapor.

Vault A curved surface supporting a roof.

Vee weld A butt weld with both members mitered.

Veneer A facing material not load-bearing.

Vent pipe Small ventilating pipe extending from each fixture of a plumbing system to the vent stack.

Vent stack A vertical pipe in a plumbing system for ventilation and pressure relief.

Vestibule A small lobby or entrance room.

W shape A structural steel, wide-flanged beam.

Wainscot (wainscott) An ornamental covering of walls often consisting of wood panels, usually running only part way up the wall.

Wall An exterior wall. (*Partition:* an interior wall.)

Wall tie A metal piece connecting wythes of masonry to each other or to other materials.

Wallboard A large, flat sheet of gypsum or wood pulp used for interior walls.

Waste stack A vertical pipe in a plumbing system that carries the discharge from any fixture.

Waterproof Material or construction that prevents the passage of water.

Weathering steel A high-strength steel that is protected from further corrosion by its own corrosion.

Weatherstrip A strip of metal or fabric fastened along the edges of windows and doors to reduce drafts and heat loss.

Weep hole An opening at the bottom of a wall to allow the drainage of moisture.

Well opening A floor opening for a stairway.

Whirlpool A jetted tub.

Wind bracing Bracing designed to resist horizontal and inclined forces.

Winder A tapering step in a stairway.

Working drawing A drawing containing information for the workers.

Wythe (Withe) A masonry partition, such as separating flues.

30

Abbreviations

Abbreviations must often be used by architectural drafters to fit notes into the available space. Usually, a legend of the abbreviations used is included on each set of drawings so that the meanings are perfectly clear to all reading the drawings. If such a legend is missing, a list of common abbreviations can be found in standard reference works such as *Time-Saver Standards* by Callendar.[1] The abbreviations shown in this section have been approved by architectural and engineering societies. They are based upon the following rules:

1. Capitals are used almost universally.
2. Periods are used only when necessary to avoid a misunderstanding (like the use of "IN." in place of "IN").
3. Spaces between letters are used only when necessary to clarify the abbreviation (such as "CU FT" in place of "CUFT").
4. The same abbreviation may be used for the singular and plural.

A	Area
@	At
AB	Anchor bolt
ABBREV	Abbreviation
AC	Alternating current
ACST	Acoustic
ACST PLAS	Acoustical plaster
ACT.	Actual
ADD.	Addition
ADH	Adhesive
AGGR	Aggregate
AIA	American Institute of Architects
AIR COND	Air conditioning
AISC	American Institute of Steel Construction
AL	Aluminum
ALUM	Aluminum
AMP	Ampere
AMT	Amount
APP	Approved
APPROX	Approximate

1. John H. Callendar, *Time-Saver Standards for Architectural Design Data*, rev. 6th ed. (New York: McGraw-Hill, 1982).

APT	Apartment
ARCH	Architect, architectural
ASA	American Standards Association
ASB	Asbestos
ASHRAE	American Society of Heating, Refrigerating, and Air Conditioning Engineers
ASPH	Asphalt
ASSEM	Assemble
ASSOC	Associate, association
ASSY	Assembly
ASTM	American Society for Testing and Materials
ATC	Architectural terra-cotta
ATM PRESS	Atmospheric pressure
AUTO	Automatic
AVE	Avenue
AVG	Average
AWG	American wire gauge
B	Bathroom
B1S	Beaded one side
B&S GA	Brown & Sharpe Gauge
BALC	Balcony
BASMT	Basement
BB	Bulletin board
BBL	Barrel, barrels
BC	Broom closet
BD	Board
BD FT	Board feet
BET.	Between
BEV	Beveled
BK SH	Bookshelves
BLDG	Building
BLKG	Blocking
BLO	Blower
BLT-IN	Built-in
BLVD	Boulevard
BM	Beam, benchmark, board measure
BOT	Bottom
BR	Brass, bedroom
BRKT	Bracket

BRZ	Bronze
BTU	British thermal unit
BUT.	Button
BUZ	Buzzer
C	Celsius, channel, closet, courses, hundred
CAB.	Cabinet
CARP.	Carpenter
CB	Catch basin
CC	Center to center (same meaning as oc)
CEM	Cement
CEM FL	Cement floor
CER	Ceramic
CFM	Cubic feet per minute
CHAM	Chamfer
CHG	Change
CHK	Check
CI	Cast iron
CIN BL	Cinder block
CIR	Circle
CIR BKR	Circuit breaker
CKT	Circuit
CL	Center line, class, closet
CLG	Ceiling
CLKG	Calk, calking
CLO	Closet
CLR	Clear
cm	Centimeter, centimeters
CM	Center matched
CMU	Concrete masonry unit
CO	Clean-out, company
COEF	Coefficient
COL	Column
COM	Common
COMB.	Combination
CONC	Concrete
CONC B	Concrete block
CONC FL	Concrete floor
CONST	Construction
CONTR	Contractor
CONV	Convenience
COP	Copper
COV	Cover
CP	Candlepower, cesspool
CSG	Casing
CSK	Countersink
CTR	Center, counter
CU	Copper, cubic
CU FT	Cubic foot, cubic feet
CU IN	Cubic inch, cubic inches
CU YD	Cubic yard, cubic yards
CW	Cold water
CYL	Cylinder
d	Penny (nail)
D	Drain, dryer
D&M	Dressed and matched
DB	Decibel
DC	Direct current
DEG	Degree
DET	Detail

DF	Drinking fountain
DH	Double-hung
DIA	Diameter
DIAG	Diagram
DIM	Dimension
DIST	Distance
DIV	Division
DMPR	Damper
DN	Down
DO	Ditto
DOZ	Dozen
DP	Deep, depth
DR	Dining room, door, drain, drawn
DS	Downspout
DUP	Duplicate
DW	Dishwasher, dry wall
DWG	Drawing
DWL	Dowel
E	East
EA	Each
EDR	Equivalent direct radiation
EG	Edge grain
EL	Elevation
ELEC	Electric
ELEV	Elevation, elevator
ELL	Elbow
EMER	Emergency
ENCL	Enclosure
ENGR	Engineer
ENT	Entrance
EQUIP	Equipment
EST	Estimate
EXC	Excavate
EXT	Extension, exterior
F	Fahrenheit
F to F	Face to face
FAB	Fabricate
FAM R	Family room
FAO	Finish all over
FBM	Board feet (feet board measure)
FBRK	Fire brick
FD	Floor drain
FDN	Foundation
F EXT	Fire extinguisher
FH	Fire hose
FIG.	Figure
FIN	Finish
FIN FL	Finished floor
FIN GR	Finished grade
FIX.	Fixture
FL	Flashing, floor
FLG	Flange, flooring
FLUOR	Fluorescent
FO	Fuel oil
FOB	Free-on-board (shipping designation)
FP	Fireproof
FPM	Feet per minute
FPS	Feet per second
FPSC	Fireproof self-closing
FR	Front

FS	Full size
FT	Foot, feet
FTG	Fitting, footing
FURN	Furnace
GA	Gauge
GAL	Gallon, gallons
GALV	Galvanized
GAR	Garage
GI	Galvanized iron
GL	Glass
GL BL	Glass block
GLUELAM	Glue-laminated
GOVT	Government
GR	Grade
GRTG	Grating
GYP	Gypsum
H	Hall
HB	Hose bibb
HD	Head
HDW	Hardware
HDWD	Hardwood
HEX	Hexagonal
HGT	Height
HM	Hollow metal
HOR	Horizon, horizontal
HORIZ	Horizon, horizontal
HP	Horsepower, HP-shape beam
HR	Hour
HSE	House
HT	Height
HTR	Heater
HW	Hot water
I	I beam ("old" designation)
ID	Inside diameter
IN.	Inch, inches
INFO	Information
INSUL	Insulation
INT	Interior
IP	Iron pin
ISO	International Organization for Standardization
JT	Joint
K	Kitchen
KAL	Kalamein
KC	Kitchen cabinet
KS	Kitchen sink
KW	Kilowatt
L	Left, angle
LAB	Laboratory
LAD.	Ladder
LAT	Latitude
LAU	Laundry
LAV	Lavatory
LB	Pound, pounds
LBR	Lumber
LC	Laundry chute
L CL	Linen closet

LD	Leader drain
LDG	Landing
LDR	Leader
LEV	Level
LG	Long
LGTH	Length
LH	Left-hand
LIB	Library
LIN FT	Linear feet
LINO	Linoleum
LNG	Lining
LR	Living room
LS	Limestone
LT	Light (pane of glass)
M	M-shape beam, thousand
MACH	Machine
MATL	Material
MAX	Maximum
MBM	Thousand board feet
MC	Medicine cabinet, miscellaneous channel beam
MECH	Mechanical
MED	Medium
MET.	Metal
MFD	Manufactured
MFG	Manufacturing
MFR	Manufacture, manufacturer
MIN	Minimum
MISC	Miscellaneous
MK	Mark
MLDG	Molding
mm	Millimeter, millimeters
MO	Masonry opening
MOD	Model
MT	Structural tee (cut from M-shape beam)
MW	Moderate weather (a common brick grade)
N	North
NATL	National
NEC	National Electrical Code
NIC	Not in contract
NLMA	National Lumber Manufacturers Association
NO.	Number
NOM	Nominal
NW	No weather (a common brick grade)
O	Oak
OC	On center (same meaning as CC)
OCT	Octagon
OD	Outside diameter
OFF.	Office
OPG	Opening
OPP	Opposite
ORN	Ornament
OVHD	Overhead
OZ	Ounce, ounces
P	Page
PAR	Paragraph, parallel

PASS.	Passage
PB	Push button
PC	Piece
P/C	Poured concrete
PED	Pedestal
PERF	Perforate
PERP	Perpendicular
PL	Plate
PLAS	Plaster
PLAT	Platform
PL GL	Plate glass
PLMB	Plumbing
PNL	Panel
POL	Polish
POS	Position
PR	Pair
PREFAB	Prefabricated
PROP.	Property
PSI	Pounds per square inch
PT	Point
PTD	Painted
PTN	Partition
QT	Quart, quarts
QTY	Quantity
R	Range, right, riser, room
RA	Radius
RAD	Radiator
RAD ENCL	Radiator enclosure
RD	Road, roof drain, round
RDWD	Redwood
REBAR	Reinforcing bar
RECP	Receptacle
RECT	Rectangle
REF	Reference, refrigerator
REG	Register
REINF	Reinforce, reinforcing
REQD	Required
RET	Return
REV	Revision
RF	Roof
RFG	Roofing
RGH	Rough
RH	Right-hand
RL&W	Random length and width
RM	Room
RPM	Revolutions per minute
S	S shape beam, sink, south, switch
S&M	Surfaced and matched
S1E	Surface one edge
S1S	Surface one side
S1S1E	Surface one side and one edge
S2E	Surface two edges
S2S	Surface two sides
S4S	Surface all sides
SC	Self-closing, sill cock
SCH	Schedule
SCR	Screw, structural clay research
SDG	Siding
SECT	Section

SERV	Service
SEW.	Sewer
SH	Shower
SHTHG	Sheathing
SK	Sink
SOC	Socket
SP	Soil pipe, station point
SPEC	Specifications
SQ	Square
SQ FT	Square foot, square feet
SS	Slop sink
ST	Stairs, street, structural tee (cut from S shape beam)
STA	Station
STD	Standard
STIR.	Stirrup
STK	Stock
STL	Steel
ST P	Standpipe
STR	Structural
SUB	Substitute
SUP	Supply
SUPP	Supplement
SUPSD	Supersede
SUR	Surface
SUSP CLG	Suspended ceiling
SW	Switch, severe weather (a common brick grade)
SYM	Symbol
SYS	System
T	Thick, thickness
T&G	Tongue-and-groove
TC	Terra-cotta
THD	Thread
THERMO	Thermostat
THK	Thick, thickness
TR	Tread
TS	Structural tubing
TYP	Typical
ULT	Ultimate
UNFIN	Unfinished
USASI	U.S.A. Standards Institute
USG	U.S. standard gauge
W	W shape beam, washer, water, watts, west
W/	With
WC	Water closet
W CAB	Wall cabinet
WD	Wood
WDW	Window
WF	Wide flange ("old" designation)
W GL	Wire glass
WH	Weep hole
WI	Wrought iron
W/O	Without
WP	Waterproof, weatherproof, white pine
WT	Weight, structural tee (cut from W shape)
WTH	Width
WV	Wall vent

✕	By (as in 2′ ✕ 4′)	@	At
XH	Extra heavy	₵	Center line
XHVY	Extra heavy	&	And
X-SECT	Cross section	′	Feet, foot
		″	Ditto, inch, inches
YD	Yard, yards	/	Per
YP	Yellow pine	‖	Parallel
YR	Year	∟	Angle
		⊥	Perpendicular
Z	Zinc	[	Channel ("old" designation)
ZN	Zinc	✕	By (as in 2′ ✕ 4′)
		#	Number, pound, pounds
		☐	Square
		π	Pi (ratio of circumference to diameter of a circle)
Symbols		⊢P	Horsepower
		℞	Plate
°	Degree	WF	Wide-flange beam ("old" designation)
%	Percent	WP	Waterproof, weatherproof
φ	Diameter, round		

31

Construction Documents

In addition to the working drawings, any large project also requires a number of written documents to advertise for and to obtain bids, to award a contract, and to ensure that the project will be satisfactorily completed. The index of a typical set of construction documents will give an idea of the many different documents required.

Types of Documents

I Index

Document	Title	
I	Index	
II	Invitation to Bid	
III	Instructions to Bidders	Bidding requirements
IV	Bid Form	
V	Agreement	
VI	Performance Bond	
VII	Labor and Material Bond	
VIII	Estimate of Payment Due	Contract forms
IX	General Conditions	
X	Supplementary Conditions	
XI	Specifications	
XII	Working Drawings	

Some of the sections listed are comparatively short, simple documents; others (like the specifications) may contain many hundreds of pages. Specifications are prepared by a "specs" writer who is specially trained to do this work. To give a better idea of the makeup of the various sections of the construction documents, let us look at each in more detail.

II Invitation to Bid

In public work, bid invitations are mailed to all contractors who might be interested in the proposed project. Also, newspaper advertisements for bids are placed. (Occasionally in private work only selected contractors are invited to bid.)

The advertisement is placed three times in three weeks and includes a brief description of the work and location, together with the requirements (time and place) of bid delivery. A sample *Invitation to Bid* is shown in Figure 1. A sample *advertisement for bids* is shown in Figure 2.

III Instructions to Bidders

This section gives more detailed instructions on the bidding procedure: information that a bidder needs to intelligently prepare and submit a bid. The information includes:

A. Availability of construction documents
B. Examination of construction documents and site
C. Resolution of questions
D. Approval for substitution of materials
E. Basis of bids
F. Preparation of bids
G. Bid security information
H. Requirements for the Performance Bond and the Labor and Material Bond
I. Requirements for listing any subcontractors
J. Identification and submission of bid
K. Modification or withdrawal of bid
L. Disqualification of bidders
M. Governing laws and regulations
N. Opening bids
O. Award of contract
P. Execution of contract

A sample *Instructions to Bidders* section is shown in Figure 3.

IV Bid Form

The *Bid Form* is a sample bidding letter from the bidder to the prospective owner. It contains blank spaces to be filled in by the bidder and a place for the bidder's signature (and for the seal of corporations) to indicate that the bidder agrees to all provisions. The Bid Form includes:

A. Acknowledgment that all construction documents were received by bidder.

215

Jones and Brown, Architects
5555 Main Street
Smithville, Ohio
Phone: 888 777-6666

INVITATION TO BID
STATE UNIVERSITY SCIENCE BUILDING
Project 3813
October__,19__

You are invited to bid on a General Contract, including mechanical
and electrical work, for a two-story, thin-shell concrete, circular
Science Building, approximately four hundred feet in diameter. All
Bids must be on a lump sum basis; segregated Bids will not be
accepted.

The State University Board of Governors will receive Bids until 3:00
p.m. Central Standard Time on Tuesday, November 8, 19_, at 233
Uptown Street, Room 313, Smithville, Ohio. Bids received after this
time will not be accepted. All interested parties are invited to
attend; Bids will be opened publicly and read aloud.

Drawings and Specifications may be examined at the Architect's office
and at:

    The Plan Center   Associated Plan Bureau
    382 West Third Street   1177 South Barnes
    Smithville, Ohio   Smithville, Ohio

Copies of the above documents may be obtained at the office of the
Architect in accord with the Instructions to Bidders upon depositing
the sum of $100.00 for each set of documents.

Any bona-fide bidder, upon returning the documents in good condition
immediately following the public opening of said bids, shall be
returned his deposit in full. Any non-bidder returning the documents
in good condition will be returned the sum of $75.00.

Bid Security in the amount of _____ percent of the Bid must accompany
each Bid in accord with the Instructions to Bidders.

The Board of Governors reserves the right to waive irregularities and
to reject Bids.

By order of the Board of Governors

State University
Smithville, Ohio

Hirmats J. Downe, Secretary

Figure 1. Sample Invitation to Bid (courtesy The Construction Specifications Institute).

B. Agreement statements that bidder will hold the bid open until a stated time and will abide by the Instructions to Bidders.

C. Price of project, including price of any alternatives. Alternate bids should be included in addition to the base bid as a means of keeping the project cost within the budget and as a "keep honest" feature; that is, the bid may be higher if there are no allowable substitutes for materials for competitive bidding. Some alternate bids for a large project might be:

   1. Asphalt tile as an alternative to rubber tile in corridors
   2. Quarry tile as an alternative to terrazzo on interior floor slabs
   3. Asphalt and slag roof as an alternative to a pitch-and-slag roof
   4. Cold-mixed bituminous surfacing as an alternative to hot-mixed asphaltic concrete surfacing course on driveways and service areas

D. Attachment statement that required information (such as a subcontractor listing or evidence of bidder's qualifications) is enclosed.

A sample Bid Form is shown in Figure 4.

V Agreement

The *Agreement* is one of several contract forms that are preprinted to simplify preparation of the contract. The contract forms supplied by the American Institute of Architects (AIA) are commonly used, but many governmental agencies have developed standard contract forms for their own uses.

The owner-architect agreement includes a statement of the architectural services ordinarily considered necessary and the owner's usual obligations. Many different forms of agreements are used, but they differ mainly in the method by which the architect's compensation is determined. The fee can be based on:

1. A percentage of the construction cost (usually from 5 to 15 percent)
2. A professional fee plus expenses
3. A multiple of personnel expense

VI Performance Bond

The *Performance Bond* is a guarantee to the client that the contractor will perform all the terms and conditions of the contract, and, if the contract is defaulted, it will protect the client up to the bond penalty. The Performance Bond should be distinguished from the Labor and Material Bond, which protects the laborers and material persons.

VII Labor and Material Bond

The *Labor and Material Bond* guarantees that the bills of the materials suppliers and subcontractors will be paid.

Bids: November 8, 19 _
STATE UNIVERSITY
SCIENCE BUILDING
SMITHVILLE, OHIO
Project 3813
October___, 19 _
Jones and Brown, Architects
5555 Main Street
Smithville, Ohio
Phone 888 777-6666

The Board of Governors, State University, Smithville, Ohio will receive sealed bids on a General Contract, including mechanical and electrical work, for a two-story thin-shell concrete circular Science Building, approximately four hundred feet in diameter.

All Bids must be on a lump sum basis; segregated Bids will not be accepted.

The State University Board of Governors will receive Bids until 3:00 p.m. Central Standard Time on Tuesday, November 8, 19 _ at 233 Upton Street, Room 313, Smithville, Ohio. Bids received after this time will not be accepted. All interested parties are invited to attend. Bids will be opened and publicly read aloud.

Drawings and Specifications may be examined at the Architect's office and at:

     The Plan Center
     382 West Third Street
     Smithville, Ohio
     Associated Plan Bureau
     117 South Barnes
     Smithville, Ohio

Copies of the above documents may be obtained at the office of the Architect in accord with the Instructions to Bidders upon depositing the sum of $100.00 for each set of documents.

Any bona-fide bidder, upon returning the documents in good condition immediately following the public opening of said bids, shall be returned his deposit in full. Any non-bidder returning the documents in good condition will be returned the sum of $75.00.

Contracts for work under this bid will obligate the Contractor and subcontractors not to discriminate in employment practices. Bidders must submit a compliance report in conformity with the President's Executive Order No. 11246.

This contract is Federally assisted. The Contractor must comply with the Davis-Bacon Act, the Anti-Kickback Act, and the Contract Work Hours Standards.

Bid Security in the amount of _____ percent of the Bid must accompany each Bid in accord with the Instructions to Bidders.

The Board of Governors reserves the right to waive irregularities and to reject Bids.

By order of the Board of Governors
     STATE UNIVERSITY
     SMITHVILLE, OHIO
     October___, 19_

Figure 2. Sample advertisement for bids (courtesy The Construction Specifications Institute).

Jones and Brown, Architects   INSTRUCTIONS TO BIDDERS
5555 Main Street   STATE UNIVERSITY SCIENCE BUILDING
Smithville, Ohio
Phone: 888 777-6666

To be considered, Bids must be made in accord with these instructions
to Bidders.

DOCUMENTS. Bonafide prime bidders may obtain _____ sets of
Drawings and Specifications from the Architect upon deposit of $_____
per set. Those who submit prime bids may obtain refund of deposits by
returning sets in good condition no more than _____ days after Bids
have been opened. Those who do not submit prime bids will forfeit
deposits unless sets are returned in good condition at least _____
days before Bids are opened. No partial sets will be issued; no sets
will be issued to sub-bidders by the Architect. Prime bidders may
obtain additional copies upon deposit of $_____ per set.

EXAMINATION. Bidders shall carefully examine the documents and the
construction site to obtain first-hand knowledge of existing
conditions. Contractors will not be given extra payments for
conditions which can be determined by examining the site and
documents.

QUESTIONS. Submit all questions about the Drawings and
Specifications to the Architect, in writing. Replies will be issued
to all prime bidders of record as Addenda to the Drawings and
Specifications and will become part of the Contract. The Architect
and Owner will not be responsible for oral clarification. Questions
received less than _____ hours before the bid opening cannot be
answered.

SUBSTITUTIONS. To obtain approval to use unspecified products,
bidders shall submit written requests at least ten days before the
bid date and hour. Requests received after this time will not be
considered. Requests shall clearly describe the product for which
approval is asked, including all data necessary to demonstrate
acceptability. If the product is acceptable, the Architect will
approve it in an Addendum issued to all prime bidders on record.

BASIS OF BID. The bidder must include all unit cost items and all
alternatives shown on the Bid Forms; failure to comply may be cause
for rejection. No segregated Bids or assignments will be considered.

PREPARATION OF BIDS. Bids shall be made on unaltered Bid Forms
furnished by the Architect. Fill in all blank spaces and submit two
copies. Bids shall be signed with name typed below signature. Where
bidder is a corporation, Bids must be signed with the legal name of
the corporation followed by the name of the State of incorporation
and legal signatures of an officer authorized to bind the corporation
to a contract.

BID SECURITY. Bid Security shall be made payable to the Board of
Governors, State University, in the amount of _____ percent of the
Bid sum. Security shall be either certified check or bid bond issued
by surety licensed to conduct business in the State of Ohio. The
successful bidder's security will be retained until he has signed the
Contract and furnished the required payment and performance bonds.
The Owner reserves the right to retain the security of the next _____
bidders until the lowest bidder enters into contract or until _____
days after bid opening, whichever is the shorter. All other bid
security will be returned as soon as practicable. If any bidder
refuses to enter into a Contract, the Owner will retain his Bid
Security as liquidated damages, but not as a penalty. The Bid
Security is to be submitted _____ day(s) prior to the Submission of
Bids.

Figure 3. Sample Instructions to Bidders (courtesy The Construction Specifications Institute).

PERFORMANCE BOND AND LABOR AND MATERIAL PAYMENT BOND. Furnish and
pay for bonds covering faithful performance of the Contract and
payment of all obligations arising thereunder. Furnish bonds in such
form as the Owner may prescribe and with a surety company acceptable
to the Owner. The bidder shall deliver said bonds to the Owner not
later than the date of execution of the Contract. Failure or
neglecting to deliver said bonds, as specified, shall be considered
as having abandoned the Contract and the Bid Security will be
retained as liquidated damages.

SUBCONTRACTORS. Names of principal subcontractors must be listed
and attached to the Bid. There shall be only one subcontractor named
for each classification listed.

SUBMITTAL. Submit Bid and Subcontractor Listing in an opaque,
sealed envelope. Identify the envelope with: (1) project name, (2)
name of bidder. Submit Bids in accord with the Invitation to Bid.

MODIFICATION AND WITHDRAWAL. Bids may not be modified after
submittal. Bidders may withdraw Bids at any time before bid opening,
but may not resubmit them. No Bid may be withdrawn or modified after
the bid opening except where the award of Contract has been delayed
for _____ days.

DISQUALIFICATION. The Owner reserves the right to disqualify Bids,
before or after opening, upon evidence of collusion with intent to
defraud or other illegal practices upon the part of the bidder.

GOVERNING LAWS AND REGULATIONS
NON DISCRIMINATORY PRACTICES. Contracts for work under the bid
will obligate the contractor and subcontractors not to discriminate
in employment practices. Bidders must submit a compliance report in
conformity with the President's Executive Order No. 11246.

U.S. GOVERNMENT REQUIREMENTS. This contract is Federally assisted.
The Contractor must comply with the Davis-Bacon Act, the Anti-
Kickback Act, and the Contract Work Hours Standards.

OHIO EXCISE TAX. Bidders should be aware of the Ohio Law (_____)
as it relates to tax assessments on construction equipment.

OPENING. Bids will be opened as announced in the Invitation to
Bid.

AWARD. The Contract will be awarded on the basis of low bid,
including full consideration of unit prices and alternatives.

EXECUTION OF CONTRACT. The Owner reserves the right to accept any
Bid, and to reject any and all Bids, or to negotiate Contract Terms
with the various Bidders, when such is deemed by the Owner to be in
his best interest.

Each Bidder shall be prepared, if so requested by the Owner, to
present evidence of his experience, qualifications, and financial
ability to carry out the terms of the Contract.

Notwithstanding any delay in the preparation and execution of the
formal Contract Agreement, each Bidder shall be prepared, upon
written notice of bid acceptance, to commence work within _____ days
following receipt of official written order of the Owner to proceed,
or on date stipulated in such order.

The accepted bidder shall assist and cooperate with the Owner in
preparing the formal Contract Agreement, and within _____ days
following its presentation shall execute same and return it to the
Owner.

Figure 3. *continued*

TO:
STATE UNIVERSITY SCIENCE BUILDING
The Board of Governors
Project 3813
State University
233 Uptown Street, Room 313
Smithville, Ohio

I have received the documents titled "Specifications for State
University Science Building" and Drawings A-1 through A-27, S-1
through S-10, and M-1 through M-15. I have also received Addenda Nos.
_____, and have included their provisions in my Bid. I have
examined both the documents and the site and submit the following
Bid:

In submitting this Bid, I agree:

   1. To hold my bid open until December 8, 19__.

   2. To accept the provisions of the Instructions to Bidders
regarding disposition of Bid Security.

   3. To enter into and execute a Contract, if awarded on the basis of
this bid, and to furnish Guarantee Bonds in accord with Article 30 of
the General Conditions of this Contract.

   4. To accomplish the work in accord with the Contract Documents.

   5. To complete the work by the time stipulated in the Supplementary
Conditions.

I will construct this project for the lump-sum price of _____
_____ dollars ($_____).

I will include the following alternatives as specified substitutes
for the additional costs listed:

   1. Elevators Nos. 5 and 6   +$_____

   2. Steam pipe system   +$_____

If the following items, which are based on unit prices, vary more
than 10 percent from the estimates furnished by the Architect, I will
adjust the Contract Sum in accord with the following rates:

Concrete piling   +$_____   -$_____

Interior gypsum partitions,
including plaster and paint,
per square foot   +$_____   -$_____

I have attached the required Bid Security and Subcontractor Listing
to this Bid.

                 Date:_____   Signed:_____

Figure 4. Sample Bid Form (courtesy The Construction Specifications Institute).

VIII Estimate of Payment Due

A first payment of 10 percent of the architect's fee is paid upon execution of the Agreement. Additional payments of the fee are made monthly in proportion to the services performed. The total payments are increased to the following percentage at the completion of each phase:

1. Schematic design   15%
2. Design development   35%
3. Construction documents   75%
4. Receipt of bids   80%
5. Construction   100%

IX General Conditions

This section is among the most important in the construction documents. The *General Conditions* contain additional contractual-legal requirements not covered by other contract forms. Although some architects use A.I.A. Document A-201 without change, others write the General Conditions to satisfy their own particular requirements. It is also possible to note only those modifications of the A.I.A. Document that apply to each job. Typical subsections are:

A. Definitions
B. Architect's supervision
C. Architect's decision
D. Notice
E. Separate contracts
F. Intent of plans and specifications
G. Errors and discrepancies
H. Drawings and specifications furnished to contractors
I. Approved drawings
J. Patents
K. Permits, licenses, and certificates
L. Supervision and labor
M. Public safety and security persons
N. Order of completion
O. Substitution of materials for those called for by specifications
P. Materials, equipment, and labor
Q. Inspection
R. Defective work and materials
S. Failure to comply with orders of architect
T. Use of completed parts
U. Rights of various interests
V. Suspension of work due to unfavorable conditions
W. Suspension of work due to fault of contractor
X. Suspension of work due to unforeseen causes
Y. Request for extension
Z. Stoppage of work by architect
AA. Default on part of contractor
BB. Removal of equipment
CC. Monthly estimates and payments
DD. Acceptance and final payment
EE. Deviations from contract requirements
FF. Estoppel and waiver of legal rights
GG. Approval of subcontractors and sources of material
HH. Approval of material samples requiring laboratory tests
II. Arbitration
JJ. Bonds
KK. Additional or substitute bonds
LL. Public liability and property damage insurance
MM. Workmen's Compensation Act
NN. Fire insurance and damage due to other hazards
OO. Explosives and blasting
PP. Damages to property
QQ. Mutual responsibility of contractors.
RR. Contractor's liability
SS. Familiarity with contract documents
TT. Shop drawings
UU. Guarantee of work
VV. Cleanup
WW. Competent workers (state law)
XX. Prevailing wage act (state law)
YY. Residence of employees
ZZ. Nondiscrimination in hiring employees (state law)
AAA. Preference to employment of war veterans (state law)
BBB. Hiring and conditions of employment (state law)

X Supplementary Conditions

The *Supplementary Conditions* contain special modifications to the basic articles of the General Conditions plus any additional articles of a contractual nature that might be needed for a particular project.

XI Specifications

The *Specifications* give detailed instructions on the required materials, finishes and workmanship. Instructions are grouped by building trades. Each trade is included in the order of actual construction. Nearly all offices use the standardized specification system as recommended by the Construction Specifications Institute (CSI). This system is called the *CSI Format* and consists of sixteen *Divisions* (grouped by building trades) and a number of related *Broadscope Sections* (grouped by units of work). The *Divisions* are shown in Table I, and the *Broadscope Sections* of the first ten divisions are shown in Figure 5. The Broadscope Sections (printed in

Table I. The Divisions of the CSI Format

DIVISION 1	GENERAL REQUIREMENTS
DIVISION 2	SITEWORK
DIVISION 3	CONCRETE
DIVISION 4	MASONRY
DIVISION 5	METALS
DIVISION 6	WOOD AND PLASTICS
DIVISION 7	THERMAL AND MOISTURE PROTECTION
DIVISION 8	DOORS AND WINDOWS
DIVISION 9	FINISHES
DIVISION 10	SPECIALTIES
DIVISION 11	EQUIPMENT
DIVISION 12	FURNISHINGS
DIVISION 13	SPECIAL CONSTRUCTION
DIVISION 14	CONVEYING SYSTEMS
DIVISION 15	MECHANICAL
DIVISION 16	ELECTRICAL

SPECIFICATIONS

DIVISION 1—GENERAL REQUIREMENTS

01010	SUMMARY OF WORK
01020	ALLOWANCES
01025	MEASUREMENT AND PAYMENT
01030	ALTERNATES/ALTERNATIVES
01040	COORDINATION
01050	FIELD ENGINEERING
01060	REGULATORY REQUIREMENTS
01070	ABBREVIATIONS AND SYMBOLS
01080	IDENTIFICATION SYSTEMS
01090	REFERENCE STANDARDS
01100	SPECIAL PROJECT PROCEDURES
01200	PROJECT MEETINGS
01300	SUBMITTALS
01400	QUALITY CONTROL
01500	CONSTRUCTION FACILITIES AND TEMPORARY CONTROLS
01600	MATERIAL AND EQUIPMENT
01650	STARTING OF SYSTEMS/COMMISSIONING
01700	CONTRACT CLOSEOUT
01800	MAINTENANCE

DIVISION 2—SITEWORK

02010	SUBSURFACE INVESTIGATION
02050	DEMOLITION
02100	SITE PREPARATION
02140	DEWATERING
02150	SHORING AND UNDERPINNING
02160	EXCAVATION SUPPORT SYSTEMS
02170	COFFERDAMS
02200	EARTHWORK
02300	TUNNELING
02350	PILES AND CAISSONS
02450	RAILROAD WORK
02480	MARINE WORK
02500	PAVING AND SURFACING
02600	PIPED UTILITY MATERIALS
02660	WATER DISTRIBUTION
02680	FUEL DISTRIBUTION
02700	SEWERAGE AND DRAINAGE
02760	RESTORATION OF UNDERGROUND PIPELINES
02770	PONDS AND RESERVOIRS
02780	POWER AND COMMUNICATIONS
02800	SITE IMPROVEMENTS
02900	LANDSCAPING

DIVISION 3—CONCRETE

03100	CONCRETE FORMWORK
03200	CONCRETE REINFORCEMENT
03250	CONCRETE ACCESSORIES
03300	CAST-IN-PLACE CONCRETE
03370	CONCRETE CURING
03400	PRECAST CONCRETE
03500	CEMENTITIOUS DECKS
03600	GROUT
03700	CONCRETE RESTORATION AND CLEANING
03800	MASS CONCRETE

DIVISION 4—MASONRY

04100	MORTAR
04150	MASONRY ACCESSORIES
04200	UNIT MASONRY
04400	STONE
04500	MASONRY RESTORATION AND CLEANING
04550	REFRACTORIES
04600	CORROSION RESISTANT MASONRY

DIVISION 5—METALS

05010	METAL MATERIALS
05030	METAL FINISHES
05050	METAL FASTENING
05100	STRUCTURAL METAL FRAMING
05200	METAL JOISTS
05300	METAL DECKING
05400	COLD-FORMED METAL FRAMING
05500	METAL FABRICATIONS
05580	SHEET METAL FABRICATIONS
05700	ORNAMENTAL METAL
05800	EXPANSION CONTROL
05900	HYDRAULIC STRUCTURES

DIVISION 6—WOOD AND PLASTICS

06050	FASTENERS AND ADHESIVES
06100	ROUGH CARPENTRY
06130	HEAVY TIMBER CONSTRUCTION
06150	WOOD-METAL SYSTEMS
06170	PREFABRICATED STRUCTURAL WOOD
06200	FINISH CARPENTRY
06300	WOOD TREATMENT
06400	ARCHITECTURAL WOODWORK
06500	PREFABRICATED STRUCTURAL PLASTICS
06600	PLASTIC FABRICATIONS

DIVISION 7—THERMAL AND MOISTURE PROTECTION

07100	WATERPROOFING
07150	DAMPPROOFING
07190	VAPOR AND AIR RETARDERS
07200	INSULATION
07250	FIREPROOFING
07300	SHINGLES AND ROOFING TILES
07400	PREFORMED ROOFING AND CLADDING/SIDING
07500	MEMBRANE ROOFING
07570	TRAFFIC TOPPING
07600	FLASHING AND SHEET METAL
07700	ROOF SPECIALTIES AND ACCESSORIES
07800	SKYLIGHTS
07900	JOINT SEALERS

DIVISION 8—DOORS AND WINDOWS

08100	METAL DOORS AND FRAMES
08200	WOOD AND PLASTIC DOORS
08250	DOOR OPENING ASSEMBLIES
08300	SPECIAL DOORS
08400	ENTRANCES AND STOREFRONTS
08500	METAL WINDOWS
08600	WOOD AND PLASTIC WINDOWS
08650	SPECIAL WINDOWS
08700	HARDWARE
08800	GLAZING
08900	GLAZED CURTAIN WALLS

DIVISION 9—FINISHES

09100	METAL SUPPORT SYSTEMS
09200	LATH AND PLASTER
09230	AGGREGATE COATINGS
09250	GYPSUM BOARD
09300	TILE
09400	TERRAZZO
09500	ACOUSTICAL TREATMENT
09540	SPECIAL SURFACES
09550	WOOD FLOORING
09600	STONE FLOORING
09630	UNIT MASONRY FLOORING
09650	RESILIENT FLOORING
09680	CARPET
09700	SPECIAL FLOORING
09780	FLOOR TREATMENT
09800	SPECIAL COATINGS
09900	PAINTING
09950	WALL COVERINGS

DIVISION 10—SPECIALTIES

10100	CHALKBOARDS AND TACKBOARDS
10150	COMPARTMENTS AND CUBICLES
10200	LOUVERS AND VENTS
10240	GRILLES AND SCREENS
10250	SERVICE WALL SYSTEMS
10260	WALL AND CORNER GUARDS
10270	ACCESS FLOORING
10280	SPECIALTY MODULES
10290	PEST CONTROL
10300	FIREPLACES AND STOVES
10340	PREFABRICATED EXTERIOR SPECIALTIES
10350	FLAGPOLES
10400	IDENTIFYING DEVICES
10450	PEDESTRIAN CONTROL DEVICES
10500	LOCKERS
10520	FIRE PROTECTION SPECIALTIES
10530	PROTECTIVE COVERS
10550	POSTAL SPECIALTIES
10600	PARTITIONS
10650	OPERABLE PARTITIONS
10670	STORAGE SHELVING
10700	EXTERIOR SUN CONTROL DEVICES
10750	TELEPHONE SPECIALTIES
10800	TOILET AND BATH ACCESSORIES
10880	SCALES
10900	WARDROBE AND CLOSET SPECIALTIES

Figure 5. Some Broadscope Sections of the CSI Format (courtesy The Construction Specifications Institute).

DIVISION 8—DOORS AND WINDOWS

Section Number	Title		Section Number	Title
08100	**METAL DOORS AND FRAMES**		08500	**METAL WINDOWS**
-110	Steel Doors and Frames		-510	Steel Windows
	Standard Steel Doors and Frames		-520	Aluminum Windows
	Standard Steel Doors		-530	Stainless Steel Windows
	Standard Steel Frames		-540	Bronze Windows
	Custom Steel Doors and Frames		-550	Metal Jalousie Windows
	Custom Steel Doors		-560	Metal Storm Windows
	Custom Steel Frames			
-115	Packaged Steel Doors and Frames		08600	**WOOD AND PLASTIC WINDOWS**
120	Aluminum Doors and Frames		-610	Wood Windows
-130	Stainless Steel Doors and Frames			*Metal Clad Wood Windows*
140	Bronze Doors and Frames			*Plastic Clad Wood Windows*
				Wood Storm Windows
08200	**WOOD AND PLASTIC DOORS**		-630	Plastic Windows
210	Wood Doors			*Reinforced Plastic Windows*
	Flush Wood Doors			*Plastic Storm Windows*
	Plastic Faced Flush Wood Doors			
	Metal Faced Wood Doors		08650	**SPECIAL WINDOWS**
	Panel Wood Doors		-655	Roof Windows
-220	Plastic Doors		660	Security Windows
			-665	Pass Windows
08250	**DOOR OPENING ASSEMBLIES**			
			08700	**HARDWARE**
08300	**SPECIAL DOORS**		-710	Finish Hardware
305	Access Doors		-720	Operators
-310	Sliding Doors			*Automatic Door Operators*
	Sliding Glass Doors			*Window Operators*
	Sliding Metal Fire Doors		-730	Weatherstripping and Seals
	Sliding Grilles			*Thresholds*
-315	Blast-Resistant Doors		740	Electrical Locking Systems
-318	Security Doors		-750	Door and Window Accessories
320	Metal-Clad Doors			*Flood Barriers*
-325	Cold Storage Doors			
-330	Coiling Doors		08800	**GLAZING**
	Coiling Counter Doors		-810	Glass
	Overhead Coiling Doors			*Mirror Glass*
	Side Coiling Doors		840	Plastic Glazing
340	Coiling Grilles		850	Glazing Accessories
	Overhead Coiling Grilles			
	Side Coiling Grilles		08900	**GLAZED CURTAIN WALLS**
350	Folding Doors and Grilles		-910	Glazed Steel Curtain Walls
	Accordian Folding Doors		-920	Glazed Aluminum Curtain Walls
	Panel Folding Doors		-930	Glazed Stainless Steel Curtain Walls
	Accordian Folding Grilles		-940	Glazed Bronze Curtain Walls
355	Flexible Doors		950	Translucent Wall and Skylight Systems
360	Sectional Overhead Doors		960	Sloped Glazing Systems
365	Multi-leaf Vertical Lift Overhead Doors		-970	Structural Glass Curtain Walls
	Vertical Lift Telescoping Doors			
370	Hangar Doors			
380	Sound Retardant Doors			
385	Safety Glass Doors			
-390	Screen and Storm Doors			
395	Flood Barrier Doors			
398	Chain Closures			
08400	**ENTRANCES AND STOREFRONTS**			
-410	Aluminum Entrances and Storefronts			
-420	Steel Entrances and Storefronts			
-430	Stainless Steel Entrances and Storefronts			
-440	Bronze Entrances and Storefronts			
-450	All-Glass Entrances			
-460	Automatic Entrance Doors			
-470	Revolving Entrance Doors			

Figure 6. Some Narrowscope Sections of the CSI Format (courtesy The Construction Specifications Institute).

capital letters) are further refined into *Narrowscope Sections* (printed in lowercase letters). The Narrowscope Sections of Division 8 are shown in Figure 6. A specifications writer will select only those sections that apply to a particular job. Notice that a five-digit numbering system is used for the designation of each Broadscope or Narrowscope Section. This helps offices that use automated printing and data retrieval systems.

The Construction Specifications Institute also recommends a uniform three-part approach for writing each section:

Part 1—General
  Description
  Quality assurance
  Submittals
  Product delivery, storage, and handling
  Job conditions
  Alternatives
  Guarantee

Part 2—Products
  Materials
  Mixes
  Fabrication and manufacture

Part 3—Execution
  Inspection
  Preparation
  Installation/application/performance
  Field quality control
  Adjust and clean
  Schedules

Although architects still refer to "writing" specifications, actually the majority of sections are assembled from a data book of carefully worded and approved paragraphs.

Three basic sentence structures are commonly used in specifications to convey the architect's intent clearly and concisely: the indicative mood, the imperative mood, and streamlining.

The indicative mood, requiring the use of *shall* in nearly every sentence, is the traditional language of specs writing: "*Two coats of paint shall be applied to each exposed surface.*"

The imperative mood is more concise. A verb is the first word of a sentence and immediately defines the required action: "*Apply two coats of paint to each exposed surface.*"

Streamlining is used to itemize products, materials, and reference standards:

Materials shall meet the following requirements:

    Portland cement: ASTM C 150, Type I.
    Aggregate: ASTM C 33.

Some additional rules of thumb for specifications writing are:

1. Use short sentences and simple, declarative statements.
2. Avoid complicated sentences whose meanings are so dependent on punctuation that inadvertent omission or insertion of punctuation changes the meaning or creates ambiguity.
3. Choose words and terms that are plain and well under-

stood to convey the information. Avoid any pompous or highly embellished language. For example, use "shall" rather than "it is incumbent upon" or "it is the duty." Use "the contractor may" rather than "if the contractor so elects, he may" or "the contractor is hereby authorized to." Use "means" rather than "shall be interpreted to mean." Use "by" rather than "by means of." Use "to" rather than "in order to." Never use "herein," "hereinbefore," "hereinafter," or "wherein." Avoid using "and/or," "etc.," and "as per."

4. Use the word "shall" for the work of the contractor. Use the word "will" for acts of the owner or architect. Do not use "must."
5. Numbers over twelve should usually be given as numerals (figures) rather than as words. For example: one, six, twelve, 13, 18, 100. But use numerals for all sums of money, for example, $1.00. Give numbers preceding a numeral as words, for example, fifteen 8-hour days.

To get a better idea of the specifications, let us look at one of the sections in more detail. We have chosen Division 8 (Doors and Windows), Broadscope Section 08800 (Glazing) for this detailed study.

Section 08800 Glazing

08801 Stipulation. Applicable requirements of the "General Conditions" apply to this entire Specification, and shall have the same force and effect as if printed here in full.

08802 Scope of Work. The work covered by this Section consists of furnishing all labor, materials, equipment, and services necessary to complete all glass and glazing required for the project, in strict accordance with this Section of the Specifications and the Drawings; including, but not limited, to the following:

a. Glazing of exterior doors, sidelights, transoms, and fixed metal window frames;
b. Glazing of interior doors, sidelights, and frames;
c. Mirrors.

08803 Work Excluded. The following items are included in other sections of the General Contract Specifications:

a. All bank equipment shall be factory glazed.

08810 Glass. All glass shall comply with Federal specification DD-G-45a for glass, flat, for glazing purposes.

08813 Tempered Glass. (Exterior doors and sidelights at doors) Tempered glass for the above locations shall be "Solarbronze Twindow" with 1/4″ polished plate Solarbronze exterior sheet and 1/4″ clear tempered plate interior sheet.

Section 08800 courtesy of Jack W. Risheberger & Associates, Registered Architects and Engineers.

Glass in doors shall be 13/16″ thick with 1/4″ air space. Other glass shall be 1-1/16″ thick with 1/2″ air space. Set in metal glazing beads.

08823 Insulating Glass. (Fixed exterior windows and transoms in aluminum frames) Insulating glass shall be 1-1/16″ thick "Solarbronze Twindow" set in metal glazing beads. Glass shall have a 1/4″ polished plate. Solarbronze exterior sheet, 1/2″ air space, and 1/4″ clear polished plate interior sheet.

08830 Mirrors. Over lavatories in toilet rooms, provide and install mirrors. Each mirror shall be of size indicated on the Drawings, equal to No. 53020, as manufactured by the Charles Parker Company, 50 Hanover Street, Meriden, Connecticut, complete with 1/4″ polished plate glass, moistureproof backing, removable back, narrow channel type plated brass or stainless steel frame, with concealed vandalproof mirror hangers. Mirrors shall be centered over lavatories, and set at height shown on Drawings or as directed by the Architect.

08840 Glazing Compound. Glazing compound for bedding glazing, Federal Specification TT-P-791a, Type I, elastic glazing compound. Glazing compound shall be specially prepared for the purpose, tinted to match frames, and shall remain plastic under a strong surface film similar to the product manufactured by "Tremco," "Pecora," or "Kuhls." *No putty will be accepted* (glass in doors and windows shall be set in glazing compound secured by glazing beads).

08841 Samples. Samples of each type of glass and glazing compound shall be submitted for approval of the Architect.

08842 Setting. All glass shall be properly bedded in glazing compound previously specified. Glazing compound shall not be applied in temperatures below 40°F, or during damp or rainy weather. Surfaces shall be dry and free of dust, dirt, or rust.

Glazing compound shall be used as it comes from the container without adulteration, and only after thorough mixing. If thinning is required, use only such type of thinner as recommended by the manufacturer.

08843 Replacement and Cleaning. Upon completion of the glazing, all glass shall be thoroughly cleaned, any paint spots and labels and other defacements removed, and all cracked, broken and imperfect glass, or glass which cannot be properly cleaned, shall be replaced by perfect glass.

At the time of acceptance of the building, all glass shall be clean, whole and in perfect condition, including glazing compound. Glazing compound applied after completion of painting shall be painted not less than two (2) coats.

08844 Labels. Each light shall bear the manufacturer's label indicating the name of the manufacturer and the strength and quality of the glass. Labels shall remain in place until after final acceptance of the building, at which time the labels shail be removed and glass shall be given its final cleaning.

XII Working Drawings

The *Working Drawings*, together with the Specifications, are the most important parts of the documents constituting the contract. In general, information on the design, location, and dimensions of the elements of a building is found on Working Drawings, and information on the quality of materials and workmanship is found in the Specifications. A good Working Drawing gives the contractor exactly the information needed, is clear and simple, is arranged in an orderly manner, and is accurately drawn so that scaled measurements will agree with dimensions (see Chapter 9 for more information).

Addenda and Change Orders

Addenda and change orders are used to correct or change the original construction documents. The main difference between an addendum and a change order is the timing. An addendum revises the original construction documents *before* the contract is awarded, but a change order is a revision *after* award of the contract. A sample addendum is shown in Figure 7, and a sample change order is shown in Figure 8.

JONES AND SMITH, Architects: John Doe Bldg.
Washington, D. C.
First National Bank of Brownsville: Project No. 11863

ADDENDUM NO. 2: August 15, 19

To: All prime contract bidders of record.

This addendum forms a part of the Contract Documents and modifies the
original specifications and drawings, dated July 1, 19 , and
Addendum 1, dated August 1, 19 , as noted below. Acknowledge receipt
of this Addendum in the space provided on the Bid Form. Failure to do
so may subject bidder to disqualification.

This Addendum consists of _____. (Indicate the
number of pages and any attachments or drawings forming a part of the
addendum.)

ADDENDUM NO. 1

1. Drawings, page AD 1-1. In line 3, number of the referenced Drawing
is changed from "G-1" to "G-7."

INSTRUCTIONS TO BIDDERS
2. Proposals. The first sentence is changed to read: "Proposed
substitutions must be submitted in writing at least 15 days before
the date for opening of bids."

GENERAL CONDITIONS
3. Article 13, Access to Work. The following sentence is added: "Upon
completion of work, the Contractor shall deliver to the Architect all
required Certificates of Inspection."

SUPPLEMENTARY CONDITIONS
4. Article 19, Correction of Work Before Substantial Completion. This
Article is deleted and the following is inserted in its place: "If
proceeds of sale do not cover expenses that the Contractor should
have borne, the Contractor shall pay the difference to the Owner."

SPECIFICATIONS
5. Division 7
Waterproofing: Page 4, following Paragraph <u>7C-02</u> <u>Materials,</u> add the
following: <u>"(d)</u> <u>Option.</u> Factory mixed waterproofing containing
metallic waterproofing, sand and cement, all meeting the above
requirements, may be used in lieu of job-mixed waterproofing."

6. Division 15
Refrigeration: Page 10, Paragraph 4--<u>Chillers</u> item "e" Line 4: Change
total square feet of surface from 298 to 316.

Liquid Heat Transfer: Page 17, Paragraph 10--<u>Convectors</u> item "b" Line
3: Delete "as selected--or owner."
<u>Page 23,</u> Paragraph 13--<u>Wall</u> <u>Fin</u>: Omit entirely.

DRAWINGS
7. S-9, Beam Schedule. For B-15 the following is added: "Size, 12 x
26; Straight, 3 - #6; Bent, 2 - #8, Top Over Columns: 3 - #7."

8. M-1: At room 602 change 12 x 6 exhaust duct to 12 x 18; at room
602 add a roof ventilator. See print H-1R attached and page 16,
paragraph 13 <u>Roof</u> <u>Ventilators</u> addenda above.

Figure 7. Sample addendum (courtesy The Construction Specifications Institute).

```
JONES AND SMITH, Architects/Engineers John Doe Bldg.,
                    Washington, D.C.
CHANGE ORDER NO. 5: September 9, 19
JOB NO. 11863: First National Bank of Brownsville
OWNER: ABC Corp., Brownsville, Virginia
CONTRACTOR: Bildum Construction Co., Washington, D.C.
CONTRACT DATE: July 4, 19---



TO THE CONTRACTOR: You are hereby authorized, subject to Contract
provisions, to make the following changes:
Bulletin No. 1                                       ADD $ 73.24
Bulletin No. 2                                       ADD   138.07
Bulletin No. 3 No Charge,/No Credit
Bulletin No. 4                    DEDUCT $ 75.32
Bulletin No. 5                    DEDUCT    36.99    _____

TOTAL                             DEDUCT $112.31     ADD $211.31
NET ADD $99.00



ORIGINAL CONTRACT AMOUNT:         $1,234,567.89
PRIOR CHANGE ORDERS (+, -):           +2,000.00
THIS CHANGE ORDER (+, -):              ___+99.00

REVISED CONTRACT AMOUNT:          $1,236,666.89



TIME EXTENSION/REDUCTION: None



OTHER CONTRACTS AFFECTED: None



SUBMITTED BY:_____DATE:_____
                (arch/engr's signature)


APPROVED BY:_____DATE:_____
               (owner's signature)


ACCEPTED BY:_____DATE:_____
               (contractor's signature)


DISTRIBUTION: Owner, Contractor, Architect/Engineer,
              Field Representative, Other _____.
```

Figure 8. Sample change order (courtesy The Construction Specifications Institute).

32

Reading Commercial Plans

There are important differences between the plans of a residence and the plans of a commercial building:

1. More plans are required for a commercial building due to its sheer size.
2. The plans for a commercial building are often more complex. A light wood frame construction as described in Chapter 8 is adequate for a residence, but a commercial building is usually framed in steel or reinforced concrete and finished with masonry or prefabricated composition panels.
3. In addition, the plans must be more completely detailed to permit all interested builders to bid on a competitive basis.

The working drawings of a small commercial structure, the South Hills Office Building recently designed and built in State College, Pennsylvania, will be used in this chapter to give you practice in plan reading. An exterior view of this completed building is shown in Figure 1, and interior views of three of its offices are shown in Figures 2–4. Much thought and planning were required before the working drawings were prepared. Perhaps you will be interested in the steps leading to the birth of this building.

Planning

Three businessmen—the owners of a law office, a real estate firm, and an advertising agency—joined together to solve a common problem: finding suitable space for their offices. They formed a partnership, purchased a half-acre site, and asked a local architect to design a building to satisfy their needs. As is customary with most architects, his design procedure consisted of four major stages:

1. The program
2. Presentation drawings of several schemes
3. Preliminary drawing of the chosen scheme
4. Working drawings and specifications

Program. At one of the early meetings, a program was prepared that indicated the owners' requirement of 4,000 sq. ft. of office space plus an additional 12,000 sq. ft. of rentable space for other companies. An attractive, contemporary exterior appearance was considered to be an important requirement. A preliminary study of the zoning and building code requirements showed that building height would be limited to 55′ (not including mechanical features occupying less than one-tenth of the roof area). It was also determined that one off-street parking stall would have to be provided for each office, for a total of twenty-four stalls.

Presentation Drawings. The architect proceeded to develop *sketch plans* and presentation drawings of three alternate solutions: a two-, three-, or five-story building. The solution preferred by the owners was a five-story basementless building with the first (plaza) level open to provide adequate parking. This solution included glass window walls and a central elevator shaft.

Preliminary Drawings Preliminary drawings consisting of 4′ modular plans and elevations were then prepared for this chosen solution. The framing was visualized as consisting of steel beams supported by ten steel columns. Each pair of columns would form a bent spanning 40′, and adjacent bents would be 24′ oc. Welded connections would be used where necessary to obtain a rigid frame. To provide uninterrupted glass window walls, the outer wall was cantilevered 4′ beyond the columns, resulting in a rectangular floor plan of 48′ × 104′. Stairwells were placed at both ends of the floor plan and were connected by a longitudinal corridor. The elevator shaft, restrooms, and maintenance room were placed in a central location. The remaining area was then available as clear floor space for maximum flexibility. A hydraulic piston elevator was chosen in preference to a hoist elevator to eliminate the unsightly elevator penthouse needed for the hoisting machinery. The piston elevator, however, requires that a piston shaft be drilled into the ground equal to the distance of the total lift. Piston elevators generally are not specified for lifts exceeding 60′ in height. Heating and cooling were provided by electric air conditioning space units installed in wall panels.

The preliminary drawings were approved by the owners with only one major change: the glass window walls were rejected due to the additional air conditioning capacity required. The architect replaced the window walls with vertically aligned windows and air conditioning units set in exterior brick walls. Vertical lines were emphasized by mullions framing each stack of windows.

Working Drawings. Working drawings of the final solution were prepared and are shown in Figures 13–36 in the Appendix. These drawings are nearly identical[1] to the set of working drawings used to construct the South Hills Office Building except they were redrawn in ink to ensure good reproduction in this book. Study these plans until you are confident that you understand how they are used to describe this project. The following remarks may help.

Drawing No. 1. Index (Figure 13 in the appendix). This is the cover sheet for the entire set of working drawings. In addition to the index of drawings, it includes a legend of all abbreviations and symbols used on the drawings. Some architectural offices also include a sketch of the building on the cover sheet.

Drawing No. 2. Plot plan (Figure 14 in the appendix). This plot plan positions the building on the site, shows the existing and proposed land contour, landscaping, parking, walls, gas lines, water lines, and sanitary waste lines. The note "Swale to CB" indicates a downward slope to a catch basin. "BC 100.5" fixes the bottom of the curb (road level) at an elevation of 100.5', and "TC 101.5" fixes the top of the curb (ground level) at an elevation of 101.5'.

Notice that two indications for north are given at the lower right corner. The large arrow enclosed in a circle is the direction of north, whereas "building north" shows the side of the building that is designated the "north elevation." This is particularly important when a building is positioned so that two sides might both be considered north elevations.

Drawing No. 3. Foundation plan (Figure 15 in the appendix). A 4' modular grid system is used with coordinate identification letters and numbers. This identification system helps to locate details on the plans, in the written specifications, and in the field. Notice that this system was adapted to use arrowheads to indicate both on-grid and off-grid dimensions. The callouts "0" and "6" refer to masonry courses, each 8" high. Thus the CMU (concrete masonry unit) wall marked "6" can be started 6 courses (48") above the walls marked "0." Refer to Drawing No. 11 (Figure 23 in the appendix) for a better understanding of these masonry course identification numbers.

A test boring was taken at each column location. Firm rock was only 6' to 8' deep at the three "A" locations, but was 16' to 18' deep at the seven "B" locations. Therefore, two types of footings were designed. Notice on Drawing No. 4 (Figure 16 in the appendix) that the contractor was given the

option of using the reinforced footing A at all ten locations. The contractor chose that alternative in preference to driving piles as required for footing B. To support walls, either 8"- or 12"-thick CMU foundations were used, depending on the weight of the wall to be supported. This and all similar plans were originally drawn to a scale of 1/4" = 1'-0.

Drawing No. 4. Footing details (Figure 16 in the appendix). Four details are included on this sheet to show the reinforced concrete construction of footing A, steel pile footing B, the column waterproofing, and the reinforced concrete footing for the CMU walls. The note "HP 10 × 42" refers to a 10" × 10" bearing pile weighing 42 lb. per foot of length. Note "5-#11 bars" means 5 reinforcing steel bars, each 11/8" in diameter. See Drawing No. 1 (Figure 13 in the appendix) for the meaning of all abbreviations. These and similar details were originally drawn to a scale of 1/2" = 1'-0.

Drawing No. 5. Plaza floor plan (Figure 17 in the appendix). Dashed lines are used to indicate overhead features, such as the building line or overhead simulated beams. Each room, stairway, or corridor has an identification number (such as "P2"). Doors also have an identification number which is coded to the proper room (such as "P2/1" and "P2/2"). See the legend on Drawing No. 1 (Figure 13 in the appendix) for the meaning of all such identification numbers.

Drawing No. 6. First-floor plan (Figure 18 in the appendix). Six air conditioning units are located on the south wall, but only four units are required for the north wall. This is because south wall cooling requirements are greater than north wall heating requirements.

Drawings No. 7–9. Elevations (Figures 19–21 in the appendix). Although 4' horizontal modules are used on the plans, 8" vertical modules are used on elevations to indicate courses of masonry 8" apart (a CMU course of 8" or 3 brick courses of 2 2/3"). For example, the balloon "39" means that the section floor is 39 courses, or 26' (39 × 8" = 26'), above the top of the footing marked with a balloon "0." Control joints are formed by raking and calking masonry joints. This directs any cracking along these joints rather than allowing it to occur at random. These elevations were originally drawn to a scale of 1/4" = 1'-0.

Drawing No. 10. Interior elevations (Figure 22 in the appendix). Interior elevations of all specially equipped rooms would be included in addition to these restroom elevations. The elevation identification "10/1" indicates Elevation No. 1 on Drawing No. 10.

Drawing No. 11. Longitudinal section (Figure 23 in the appendix). This section is needed to explain the structural system and ensure proper clearances and room heights. Only the more useful coordinate identification numbers are included. Note "AC CLG BD" is an abbreviation for acoustical ceiling boards.

Drawing No. 12. Typical sections (Figure 24 in the appendix). Section 12/1 is a vertical section cut through a

---

1. Some details, such as stair and elevation sections, are omitted.

Figure 1. Exterior view of the completed South Hills Office Building.

Figure 2. The law office in the South Hills Office Building.

Figure 3. The real estate office in the South Hills Office Building.

Figure 4. The advertising agency's conference room in the South Hills Office Building.

window [see Drawings Nos. 6 and 7 (Figures A-18 and A-19)]. Section 12/2 is a vertical section through a simulated plaza roof beam [see Drawing No. 7 (Figure A-19)]. Section 12/3 is a horizontal section through a column [see Drawing No. 7 (Figure A-19)]. Multiple balloons, such as "B" and "L" on Section 12/3, show that this section is typical of columns centered on both grid B and grid L.

Drawing No. 13. Typical details (Figure 25 in the appendix). Plan Detail 13/1 is a horizontal section cut through the window mullions [see Drawing No. 6 (Figure A-18)]. The two alternate details show the installation of panels and louvers. The callout "362 DS 16 PUN @ 16″ oc" refers to 3 5/8″ prefabricated metal studs as manufactured by the Keene Company: model no. 362, double-stud, 16-gauge, punched, 16″ on center.

Drawing No. 14 and 15. Schedules (Figures 26 and 27 in the appendix). Room finish information is contained in schedules such as shown in these two figures. Complete schedules for all floors require many more pages. The written specifications contain even more detailed information.

Drawing No. E1. Electrical plan (Figure 28 in the appendix). The dark rectangles represent the fluorescent ceiling fixtures, and dark circles represent incandescent fixtures. The letter within each fixture symbol identifies the type of fixture [see the lighting fixture schedule on Drawing No. 14 (Figure 26 in the appendix)]. The alphanumeric designation at the end of each home run identifies the floor level and circuit number [see the legend on Drawing No. 1 (Figure 13 in the appendix)]. An emergency lighting circuit is indicated by the letter *E* (see the legend for exit light information).

Drawing No. H1. Heating-cooling plan (Figure 29 in the appendix). The dark rectangles with diagonal lines represent Remington electric heating-cooling units, and the dark hexagons indicate Electromode electric baseboard heaters. See Drawing No. 14 (Figure A-26) for more detailed information. The two "hash marks" on each home run indicate 208-V circuits.

Drawings No. P1 and P2. Water supply and sanitary plan (Figures 30 and 31 in the appendix). Drawing No. P1 shows the hot- and cold-water supply piping and the dry-fire piping both in plan and pictorial projection. The plan also includes an air circulation system for the restrooms. Drawing P2 shows the waste and soil disposal systems.

Drawing No. S1. First-floor structural plan (Figure 32 in the appendix). Each heavy line indicates the location of a steel member. The designation "W 16 × 36 (− 4)" refers to a 16″-wide flange beam weighing 36 lb./ft., with its upper flange 4″ below the concrete slab surface. This and all similar plans were originally drawn to a scale of 1/8″ = 1′-0.

Drawing No. S2. Roof structural plan (Figure 33 in the appendix). The note "12 H5 EXT END (− 2 1/2)" refers to a 12″-deep, H5 series, open-web joist with an extended end and located 2 1/2″ below the roof surface. "DO" means "ditto." The dashed lines show the location of cross-bridging.

Type of Shape	"Old" Designation	"New" Designation
W shape (formerly wide flange)	8 WF 31	W 8 × 31
W shape (formerly light beam)	8 B 20	W 8 × 20
S shape (formerly American Standard I beam)	8 I 18.4	S 8 × 18.4
American Standard channel	8 [11.5	C 8 × 11.5
Angle	∠ 4 × 4 × 1/4	L 4 × 4 × 1/4
HP shape (formerly bearing pile)	8 BP 36	HP 8 × 36

Note: The notes "8 WF 31" and "W 8 × 31" refer to a wide-flange beam 8″ high weighing 31 lb. per foot of length.

The note "ship lone" means that elevator beam 6 B 16 should be shipped without any shop connections, because this beam is to be installed by the elevator technicians rather than by the structural fabricators.

Structural steel designations were revised by the American Institute of Steel Construction in 1970. The new designations were used on the plans of the South Hills Office Building and throughout this book; the old designations are shown on Drawing No. S2. It would be well to become familiar with these earlier designations since they will be seen on plans for many years.

Drawing No. S3. Column schedule (Figure 34 in the appendix). Refer to Drawing No. S1 (Figure A-32) for an explanation of the double designations "S3/1" and "S3/2." The column schedule shows a typical bent. Notice that the column sections are spliced between floors where the bending moment is smaller.

Drawing No. S4. Structural details (Figure 35 in the appendix). The location of Sections S4/1 and S4/2 is indicated on Drawings Nos. S1 and S2 (Figures A-32 and A-33). The welding symbols used on this sheet include a closed triangle for a fillet weld, an open triangle for a vee weld, a closed circle for a field weld, and an open circle for an all-around weld.

Drawing No. S5. Concrete slab plan (Figure 36 in the appendix). The note "#4 @ 9 TOP" refers to 4/8″-diameter steel reinforcing rods placed 9″ apart and near the top surface of the concrete slab. "Granco" is the trade name for a decking manufacturer.

Construction

Photographs of actual construction of the South Hills Office Building are shown in Figures 5–14. Review these photographs after you have studied the working drawings in the appendix to help you determine if you have read the plans correctly. Also, try to visit nearby construction sites at least once a week to become familiar with the latest construction techniques.

The main steel members (Figure 13) were erected and held in place by temporary bolting until the weldments were made. Secondary members were fastened by high-strength bolts or unfinished bolts as specified. Notice that steel angles were welded to the exterior I beams to form a masonry shelf at each floor level. Also notice that intermediate floor beams are required to support the concrete floor at each level except the roof. At the roof, steel open-web joists are sufficient to support the roof deck (Figure 5). All structural steel was fireproofed as specified by the architect (Figure 6).

Six-inch batt insulation was installed with special attention to the plaza roof (Figure 7). The plaza roof beams and tapered columns were simulated by light channels wired to shape and covered with a metal lath base used under the final coating of cement plaster.

A specialty metal company supplied the anodized aluminum components for window mullions which are so important to the exterior design. Figure 9 shows the entire four-floor section being field-fabricated before final erection. After erection, the electric heating-cooling units and window frames were placed in the mullions (Figure 10).

Interior partitions were framed in lightweight metal, as shown in Figure 11, using the system marketed by the Keene

Company. The partition members were shop-welded into convenient wall sections, then field-welded into final position. The vertical metal studs are supplied with a nailing groove to facilitate fastening the finished dry wall. This groove is formed by two channels fastened together in such a way that a nail can be driven between them. The nail is held not only by friction, but is also deformed when driven to provide greater holding power. The stairwells and elevator shaft were built of concrete masonry units. Wood strapping was nailed to the masonry units to provide a base for a dry wall of 1/2″ vinyl-covered gypsum board. A suspended system of steel channels was used to support the finished ceiling panels (Figure 12), and vinyl-asbestos tile flooring was laid directly over the concrete floor. The electrical and plumbing work was completed in appropriate steps during the various stages of construction.

Study all the plans in the Appendix and associated photographs in this chapter until you are confident that you have a general knowledge of this building. Then study each drawing in more detail as you complete the exercises assigned.

Figure 5. Corrugated decking over open-web roof joists.

Figure 7. Installing forms for simulated beams over the plaza level.

Figure 6. Detail of fireproofing sprayed on steel beams.

Figure 8. Outside wall detail before mullion installation.

Figure 9. Assembling aluminum window mullions before erection.

Figure 11. Steel interior partition framing.

Figure 10. Outside wall detail after mullion installation.

Figure 12. Hung metal channels will support ceiling panels.

Figure 13. Steel framing of the South Hills Office Building.

Figure 14. Completion of masonry.

Index

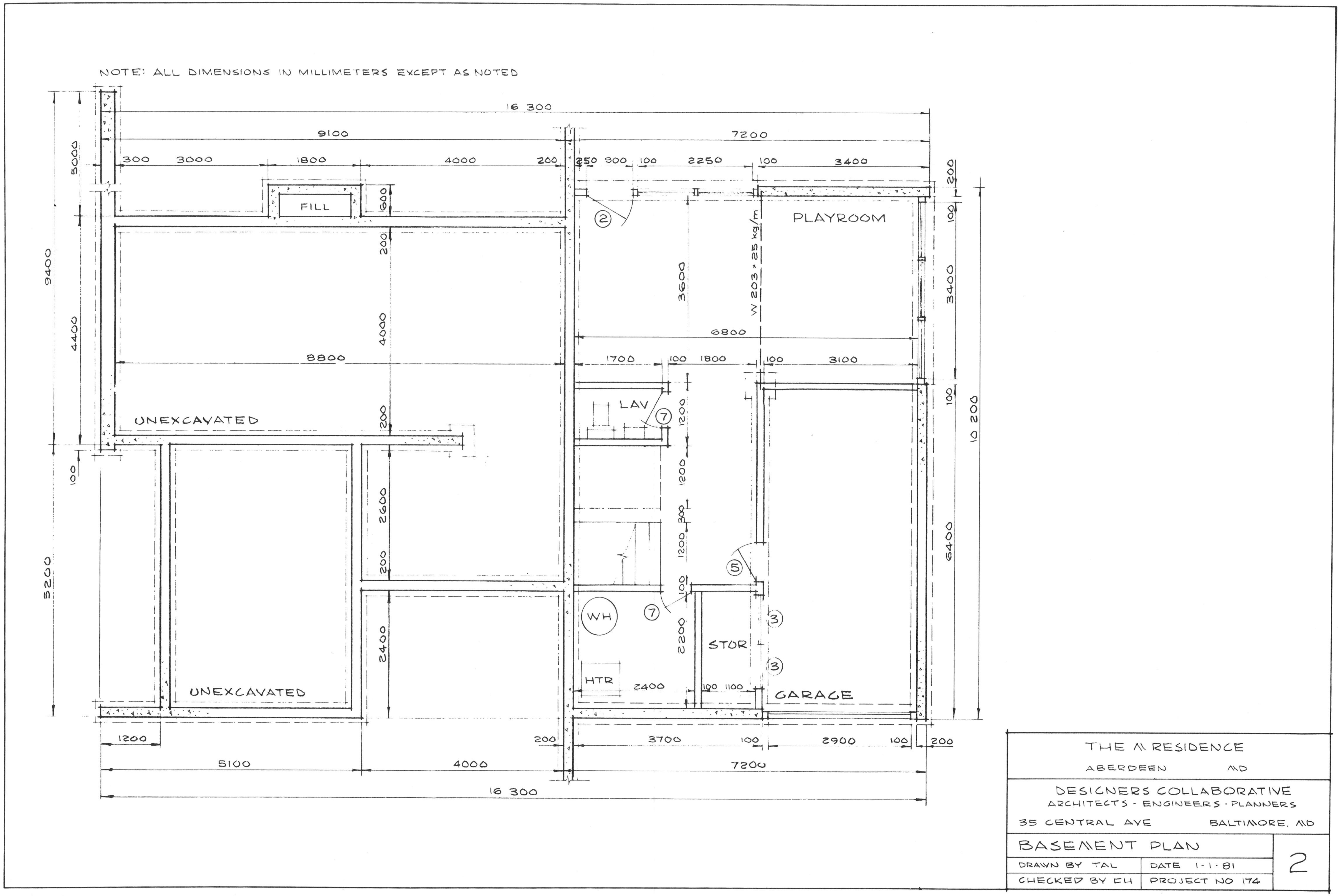
NOTE: ALL DIMENSIONS IN MILLIMETERS EXCEPT AS NOTED
16 300
9100
7200
300
3000
1800
4000
200
250
900
100
2250
100
3400
200
5000
9400
4400
FILL
600
200
PLAYROOM
100
3600
W 203 × 25 kg/m
3400
4000
6800
8800
1700
100
1800
100
3100
LAV
7
1200
100
10 200
UNEXCAVATED
200
100
1200
2600
300
1200
6400
5
200
100
5200
WH
7
3
2200
STOR
2400
3
HTR
2400
100
1100
GARAGE
UNEXCAVATED
1200
200
3700
100
2900
100
200
5100
4000
7200
16 300
THE M RESIDENCE
ABERDEEN MD
DESIGNERS COLLABORATIVE
ARCHITECTS - ENGINEERS - PLANNERS
35 CENTRAL AVE
BALTIMORE, MD
BASEMENT PLAN
2
DRAWN BY TAL
DATE 1-1-81
CHECKED BY FH
PROJECT NO 174

Figure 2. Metric basement plan of the M residence.

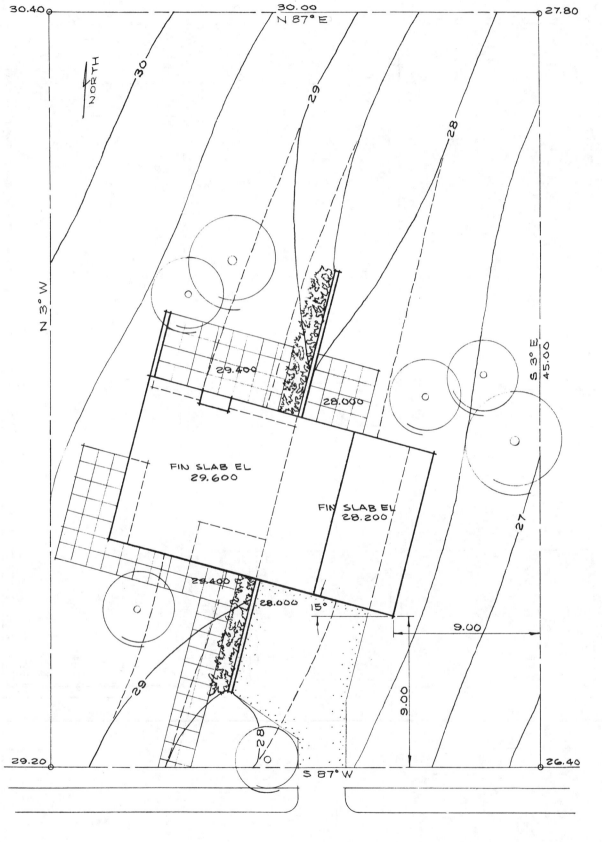

NOTE : ALL DIMENSIONS IN METERS

FIN SLAB EL
29.600

FIN SLAB EL
28.200

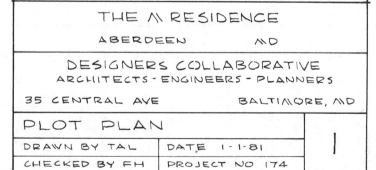

THE M RESIDENCE

ABERDEEN   MD

DESIGNERS COLLABORATIVE
ARCHITECTS · ENGINEERS · PLANNERS

35 CENTRAL AVE   BALTIMORE, MD

PLOT PLAN

| DRAWN BY TAL | DATE 1·1·81 | 1 |
| CHECKED BY FH | PROJECT NO 174 | |

Figure 1. Metric plot plan of the M residence.

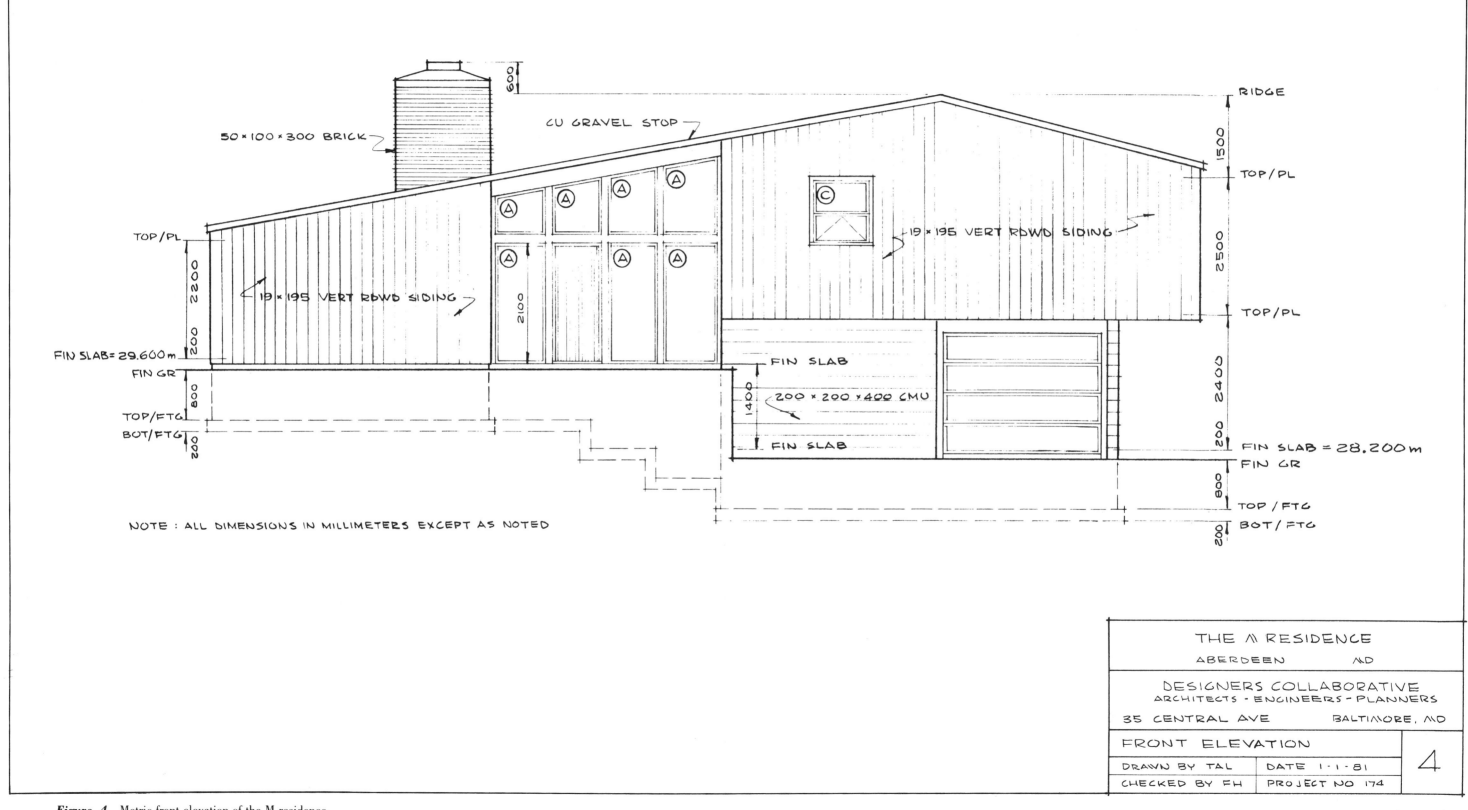

Figure 4. Metric front elevation of the M residence.

The following text appears within the drawing:

600

RIDGE

50×100×300 BRICK

CU GRAVEL STOP

1500

TOP/PL

TOP/PL

A A A A

C

A A A

19×195 VERT RDWD SIDING

2500

19×195 VERT RDWD SIDING

2200

200

2100

TOP/PL

FIN SLAB = 29.600 m

FIN GR

FIN SLAB

200×200×400 CMU

2400

800

1400

TOP/FTG

BOT/FTG

200

FIN SLAB

FIN SLAB = 28.200 m

FIN GR

200

800

TOP/FTG

BOT/FTG

200

NOTE : ALL DIMENSIONS IN MILLIMETERS EXCEPT AS NOTED

THE M RESIDENCE

ABERDEEN   MD

DESIGNERS COLLABORATIVE
ARCHITECTS · ENGINEERS · PLANNERS

35 CENTRAL AVE   BALTIMORE, MD

FRONT ELEVATION

DRAWN BY TAL | DATE 1·1·81

CHECKED BY FH | PROJECT NO 174

4

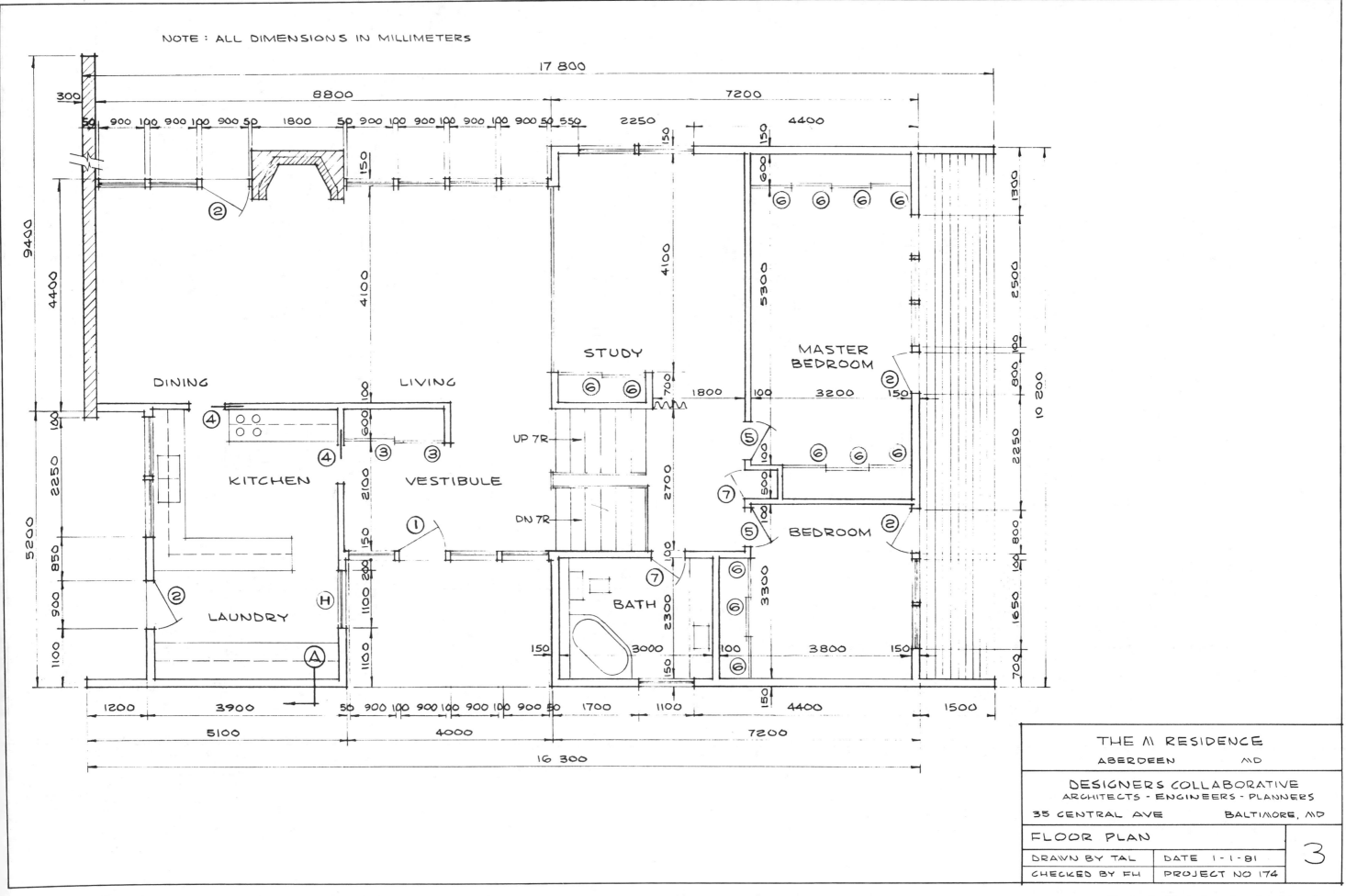

NOTE: ALL DIMENSIONS IN MILLIMETERS

DINING

KITCHEN

LAUNDRY

LIVING

VESTIBULE

STUDY

MASTER BEDROOM

BATH

BEDROOM

UP 7R

DN 7R

Figure 3. Metric floor plan of the M residence.

THE M RESIDENCE
ABERDEEN   MD

DESIGNERS COLLABORATIVE
ARCHITECTS - ENGINEERS - PLANNERS
35 CENTRAL AVE   BALTIMORE, MD

FLOOR PLAN

DRAWN BY TAL | DATE 1-1-81
CHECKED BY FH | PROJECT NO 174

3

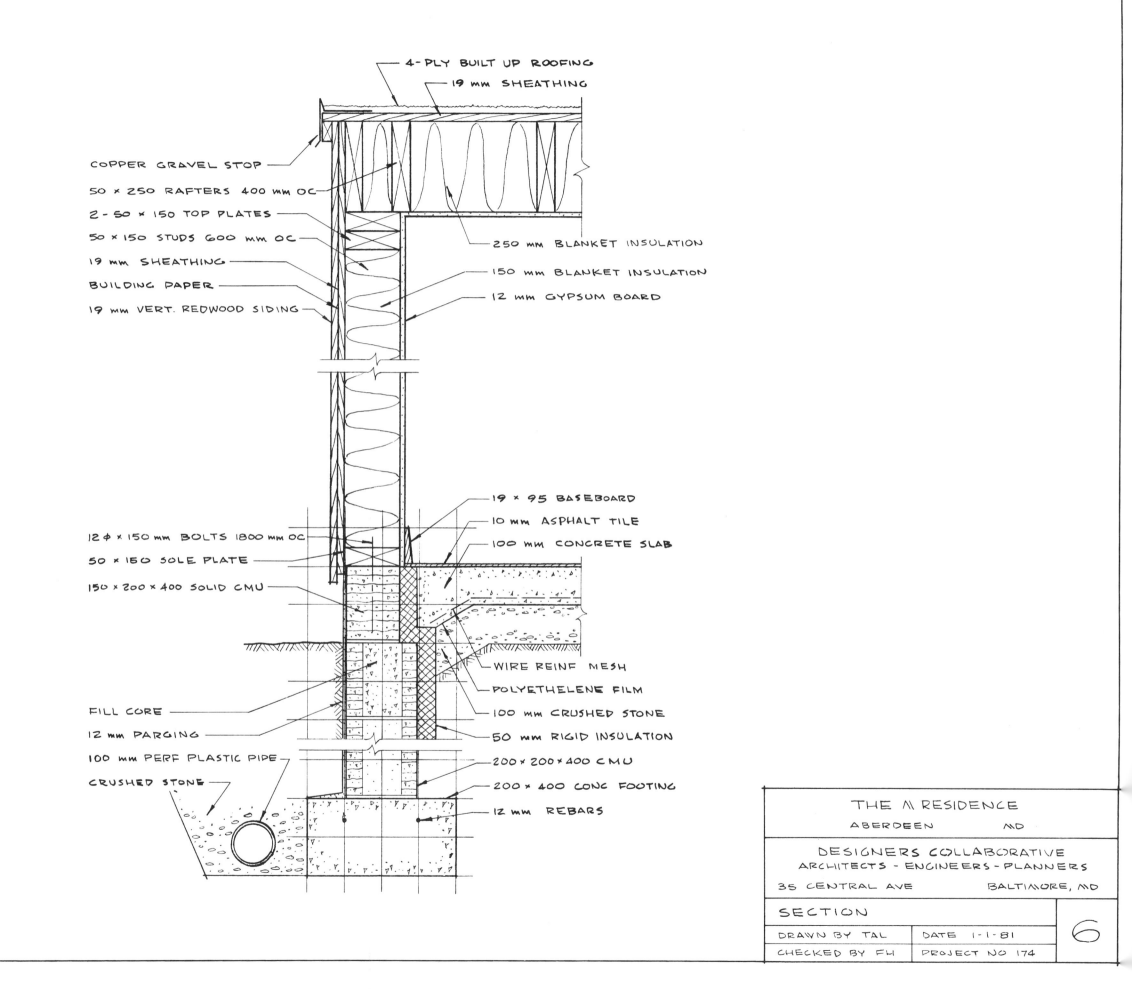

- 4-PLY BUILT UP ROOFING
- 19 mm SHEATHING
- COPPER GRAVEL STOP
- 50 × 250 RAFTERS 400 mm OC
- 2 - 50 × 150 TOP PLATES
- 50 × 150 STUDS 600 mm OC
- 19 mm SHEATHING
- BUILDING PAPER
- 19 mm VERT. REDWOOD SIDING
- 250 mm BLANKET INSULATION
- 150 mm BLANKET INSULATION
- 12 mm GYPSUM BOARD
- 19 × 95 BASEBOARD
- 10 mm ASPHALT TILE
- 100 mm CONCRETE SLAB
- 12 Ø × 150 mm BOLTS 1800 mm OC
- 50 × 150 SOLE PLATE
- 150 × 200 × 400 SOLID CMU
- WIRE REINF MESH
- POLYETHELENE FILM
- FILL CORE
- 12 mm PARGING
- 100 mm CRUSHED STONE
- 50 mm RIGID INSULATION
- 100 mm PERF PLASTIC PIPE
- CRUSHED STONE
- 200 × 200 × 400 CMU
- 200 × 400 CONC FOOTING
- 12 mm REBARS

THE M RESIDENCE
ABERDEEN   MD

DESIGNERS COLLABORATIVE
ARCHITECTS - ENGINEERS - PLANNERS
35 CENTRAL AVE   BALTIMORE, MD

SECTION

DRAWN BY TAL   DATE 1-1-81
CHECKED BY FH   PROJECT NO 174

6

Figure 6. Metric section A of the M residence.

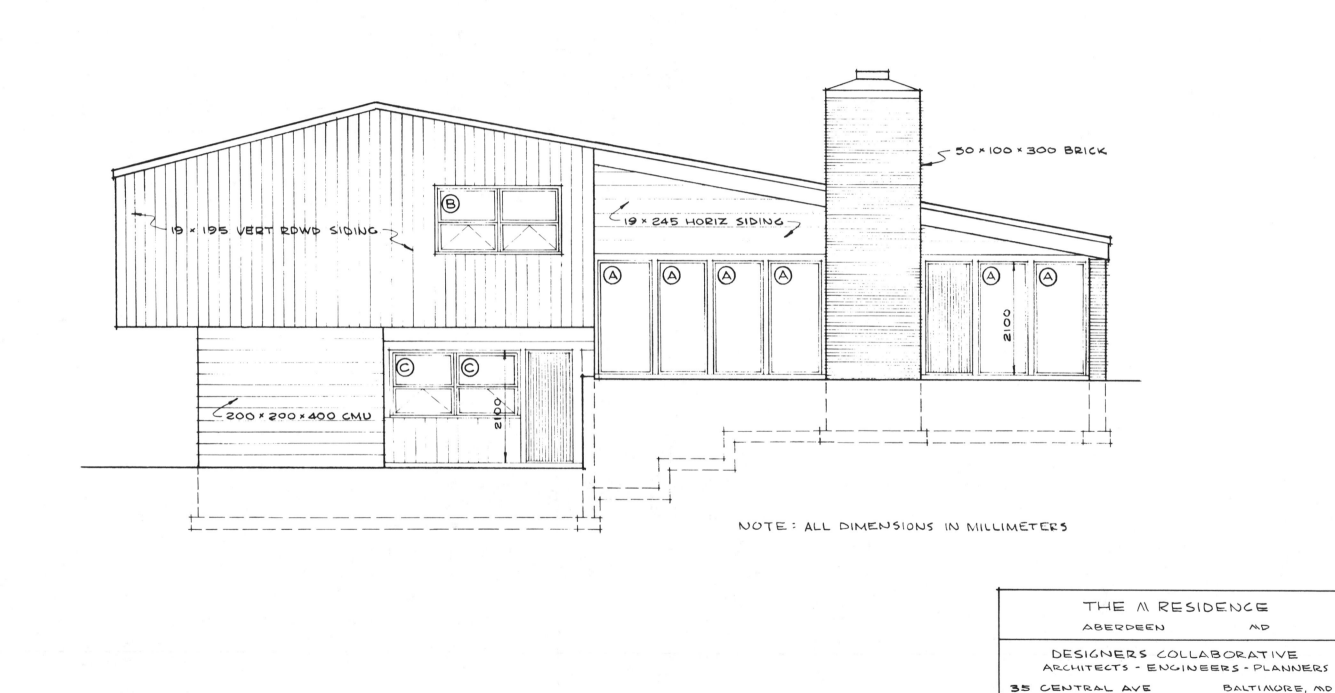

19 × 195 VERT ROWD SIDING

50 × 100 × 300 BRICK

19 × 245 HORIZ SIDING

Ⓑ

Ⓐ Ⓐ Ⓐ Ⓐ

Ⓐ Ⓐ

2100

Ⓒ Ⓒ

2100

200 × 200 × 400 CMU

NOTE: ALL DIMENSIONS IN MILLIMETERS

THE M RESIDENCE		
ABERDEEN	MD	
DESIGNERS COLLABORATIVE ARCHITECTS - ENGINEERS - PLANNERS		
35 CENTRAL AVE	BALTIMORE, MD	
REAR ELEVATION		5
DRAWN BY TAL	DATE 1-1-81	
CHECKED BY FH	PROJECT NO 174	

Figure 5. Metric rear elevation of the M residence.

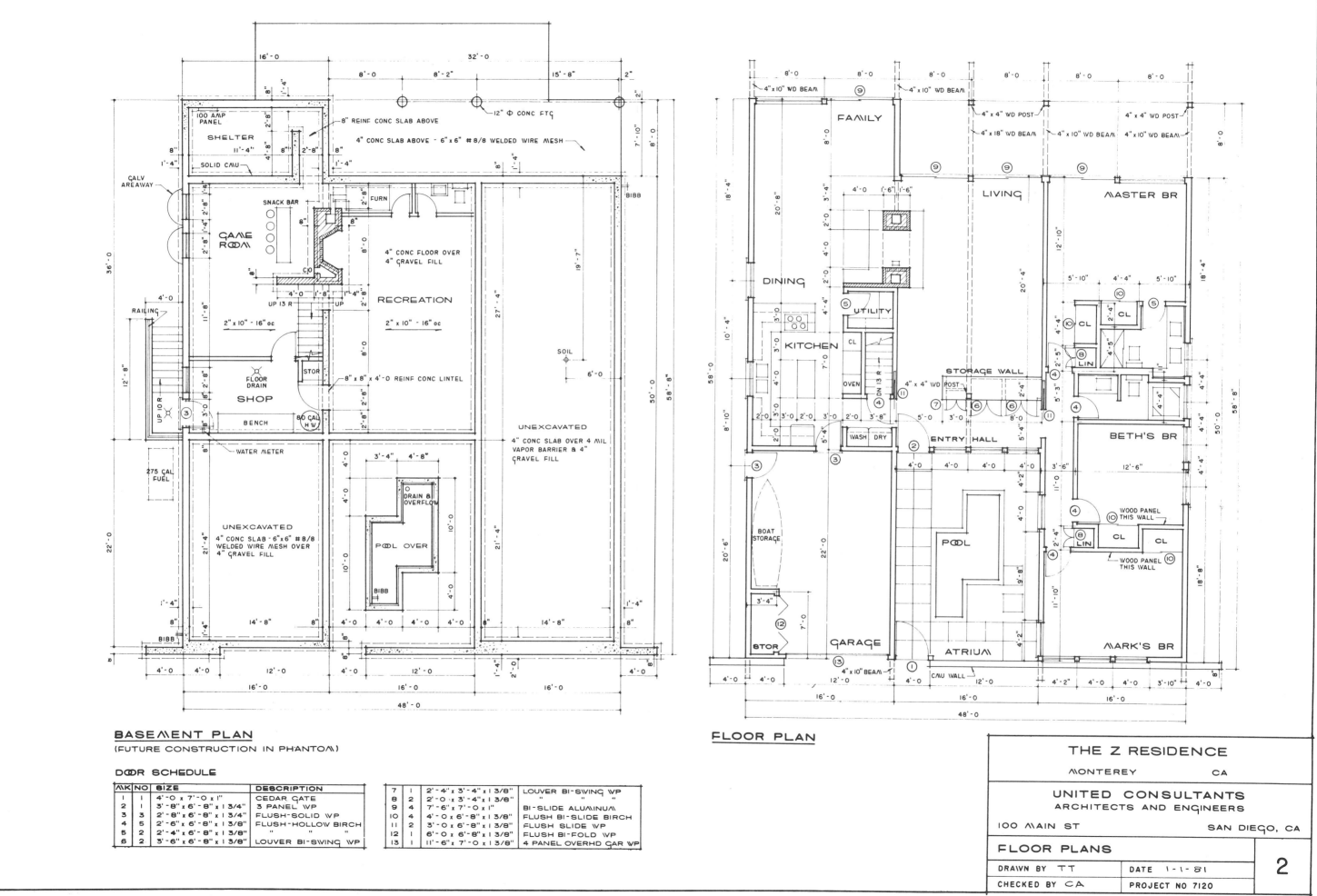

BASEMENT PLAN

(FUTURE CONSTRUCTION IN PHANTOM)

DOOR SCHEDULE

MK	NO	SIZE	DESCRIPTION
1	1	4'-0 x 7'-0 x 1"	CEDAR GATE
2	1	3'-8" x 6'-8" x 1 3/4"	3 PANEL WP
3	3	2'-8" x 6'-8" x 1 3/4"	FLUSH-SOLID WP
4	5	2'-6" x 6'-8" x 1 3/8"	FLUSH-HOLLOW BIRCH
5	2	2'-4" x 6'-8" x 1 3/8"	" " "
6	2	3'-6" x 6'-8" x 1 3/8"	LOUVER BI-SWING WP

7	1	2'-4" x 3'-4" x 1 3/8"	LOUVER BI-SWING WP
8	2	2'-0" x 3'-4" x 1 3/8"	" " "
9	4	7'-6" x 6'-8" x 1"	BI-SLIDE ALUMINUM
10	4	4'-0 x 6'-8" x 1 3/8"	FLUSH BI-SLIDE BIRCH
11	2	3'-0 x 6'-8" x 1 3/8"	FLUSH SLIDE WP
12	1	6'-0 x 6'-8" x 1 3/8"	FLUSH BI-FOLD WP
13	1	11'-6" x 7'-0 x 1 3/8"	4 PANEL OVERHD CAR WP

FLOOR PLAN

THE Z RESIDENCE

MONTEREY   CA

UNITED CONSULTANTS
ARCHITECTS AND ENGINEERS

100 MAIN ST   SAN DIEGO, CA

FLOOR PLANS

DRAWN BY TT	DATE 1-1-81
CHECKED BY CA	PROJECT NO 7120

2

Figure 8. Floor plans of the Z residence.

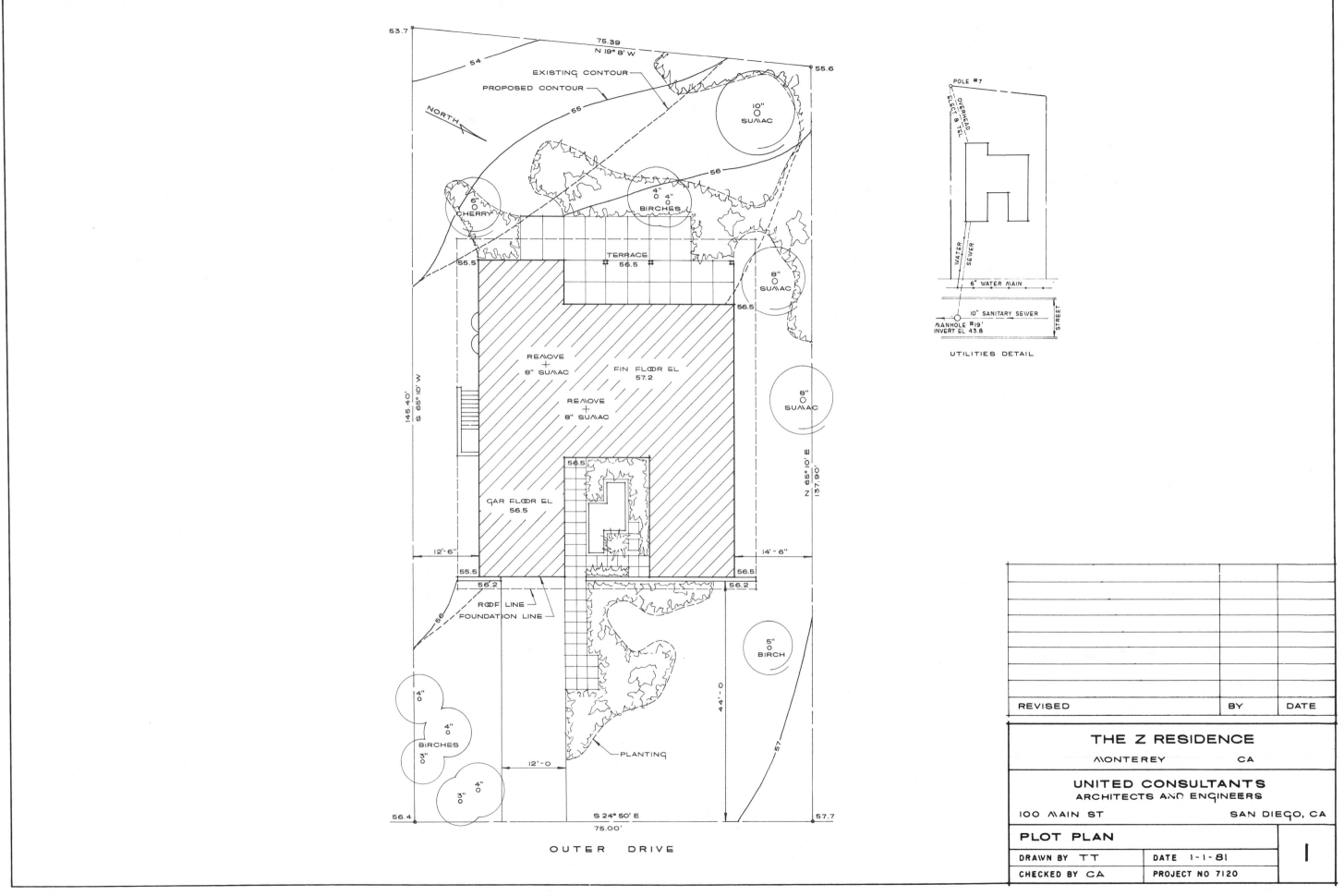

Figure 7. Plot plan of the Z residence.

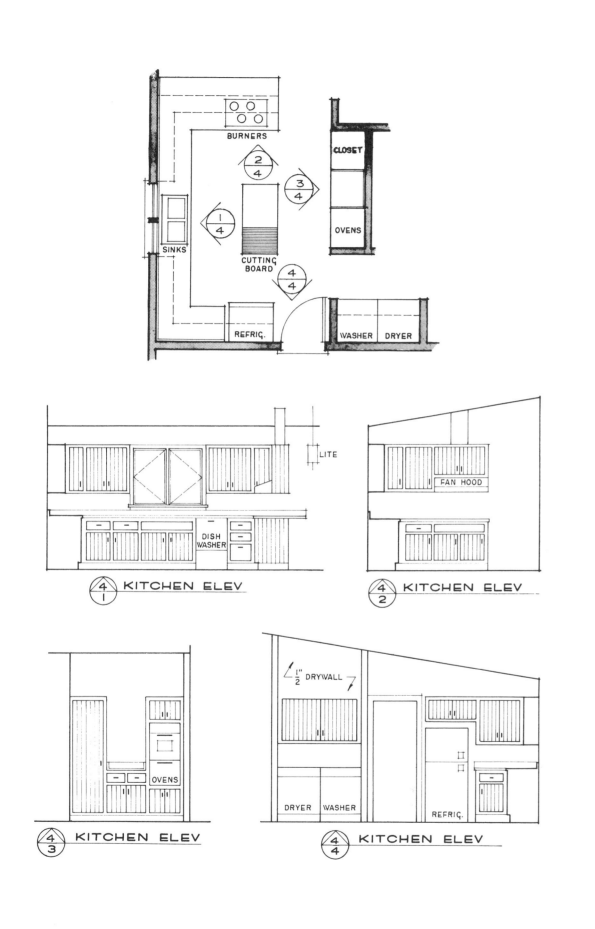

BURNERS

CLOSET

OVENS

SINKS

CUTTING BOARD

REFRIG.

WASHER | DRYER

LITE

④/① KITCHEN ELEV

DISH WASHER

④/② KITCHEN ELEV

FAN HOOD

OVENS

④/③ KITCHEN ELEV

½" DRYWALL

DRYER | WASHER

REFRIG.

④/④ KITCHEN ELEV

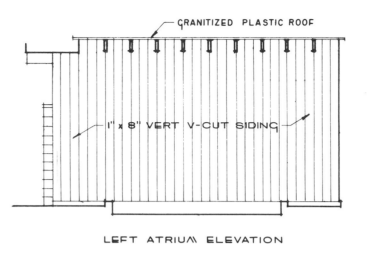

GRANITIZED PLASTIC ROOF

1" x 8" VERT V-CUT SIDING

LEFT ATRIUM ELEVATION

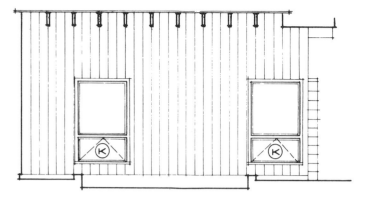

RIGHT ATRIUM ELEVATION

ATRIUM ELEVATIONS

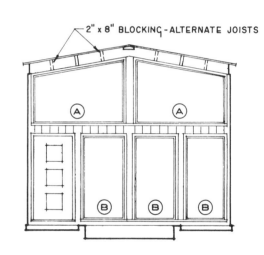

2" x 8" BLOCKING - ALTERNATE JOISTS

FRONT ATRIUM ELEVATION

WINDOW SCHEDULE

MK	NO	SIZE	DESCRIPTION
A	2	90"x 42" x 57"	1/4" FIXED PLATE GLASS
B	3	44"x 80"	" " " "
C	2	44" x 34" x 41"	" " " "
D	2	44"x 26" x 33"	" " " "
E	2	44"x18" x 25"	" " " "
F	2	90"x 38" x 53"	" " " "
G	2	90"x 22" x 37"	" " " "
H	2	90"x 6"x 21"	" " " "
J	2	90"x84"	" " " "
K	2	AP421	ANDERSEN AWNING-FIXED
L	2	W2N3	" CASEMENT
M	4	A41	" AWNING
N	3	2820	" BASEMENT

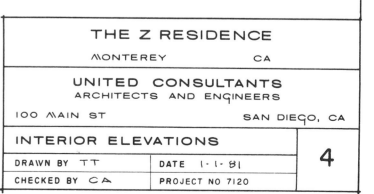

THE Z RESIDENCE

MONTEREY   CA

UNITED CONSULTANTS
ARCHITECTS AND ENGINEERS

100 MAIN ST   SAN DIEGO, CA

INTERIOR ELEVATIONS

4

DRAWN BY TT	DATE 1-1-81
CHECKED BY CA	PROJECT NO 7120

Figure 10. Interior elevations of the Z residence.

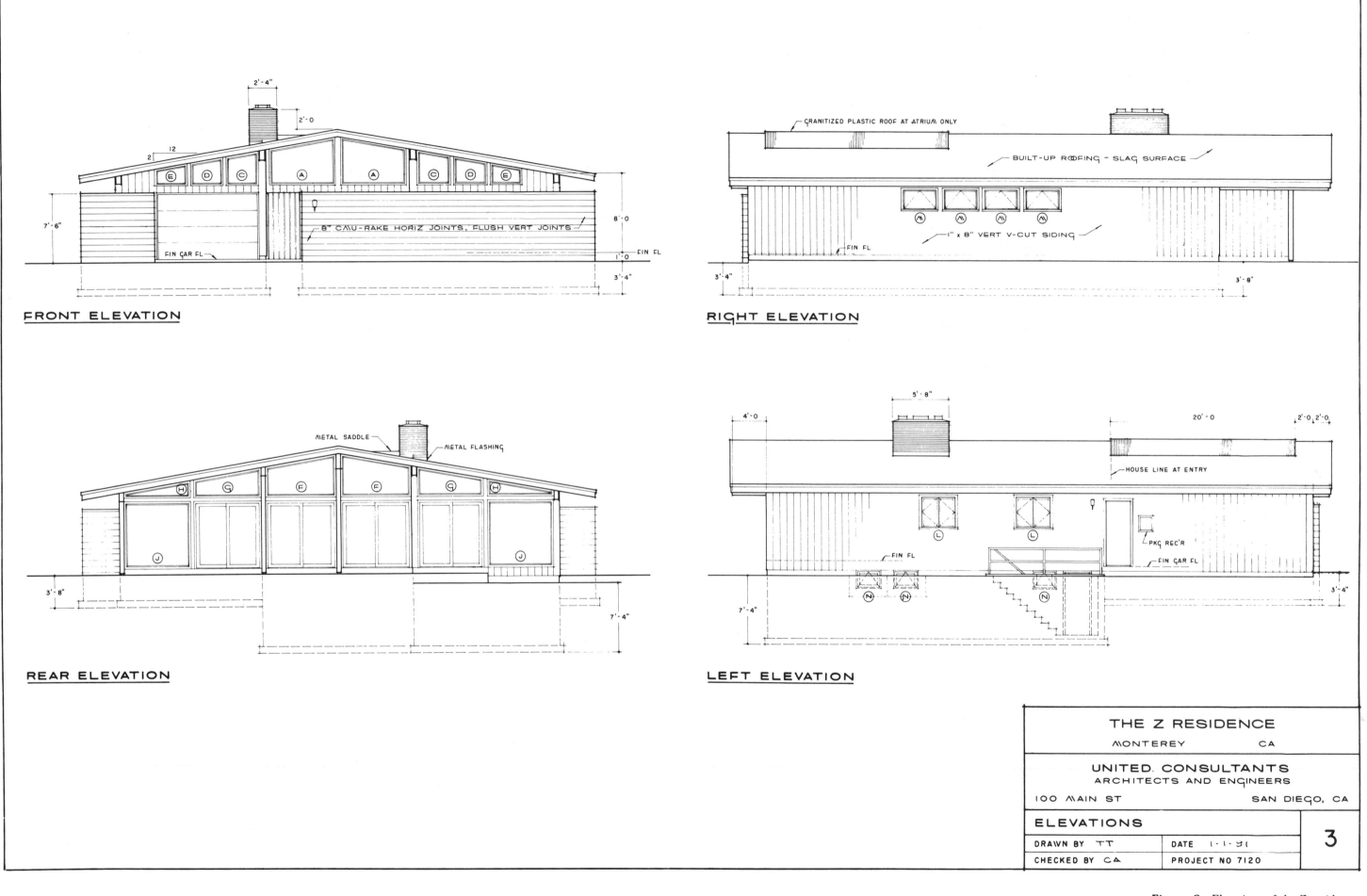

FRONT ELEVATION

2'-4"
2'-0
12
2
E D C A A C D E
7'-6"
8'-0
8" CMU-RAKE HORIZ JOINTS, FLUSH VERT JOINTS
FIN CAR FL
FIN FL
1'-0
3'-4"

RIGHT ELEVATION

GRANITIZED PLASTIC ROOF AT ATRIUM ONLY
BUILT-UP ROOFING - SLAG SURFACE
M M M M
FIN FL
1" x 8" VERT V-CUT SIDING
3'-4"
3'-8"

REAR ELEVATION

METAL SADDLE
METAL FLASHING
H G F F G H
J J
3'-8"
7'-4"

LEFT ELEVATION

5'-8"
4'-0
20'-0
2'-0 2'-0
HOUSE LINE AT ENTRY
L L
PKG REC'R
PKG REC'R
FIN FL
FIN CAR FL
N N N
7'-4"
3'-4"

THE Z RESIDENCE
MONTEREY   CA

UNITED CONSULTANTS
ARCHITECTS AND ENGINEERS

100 MAIN ST   SAN DIEGO, CA

ELEVATIONS

DRAWN BY TT   DATE 1-1-91

CHECKED BY CA   PROJECT NO 7120

3

Figure 9. Elevations of the Z residence.

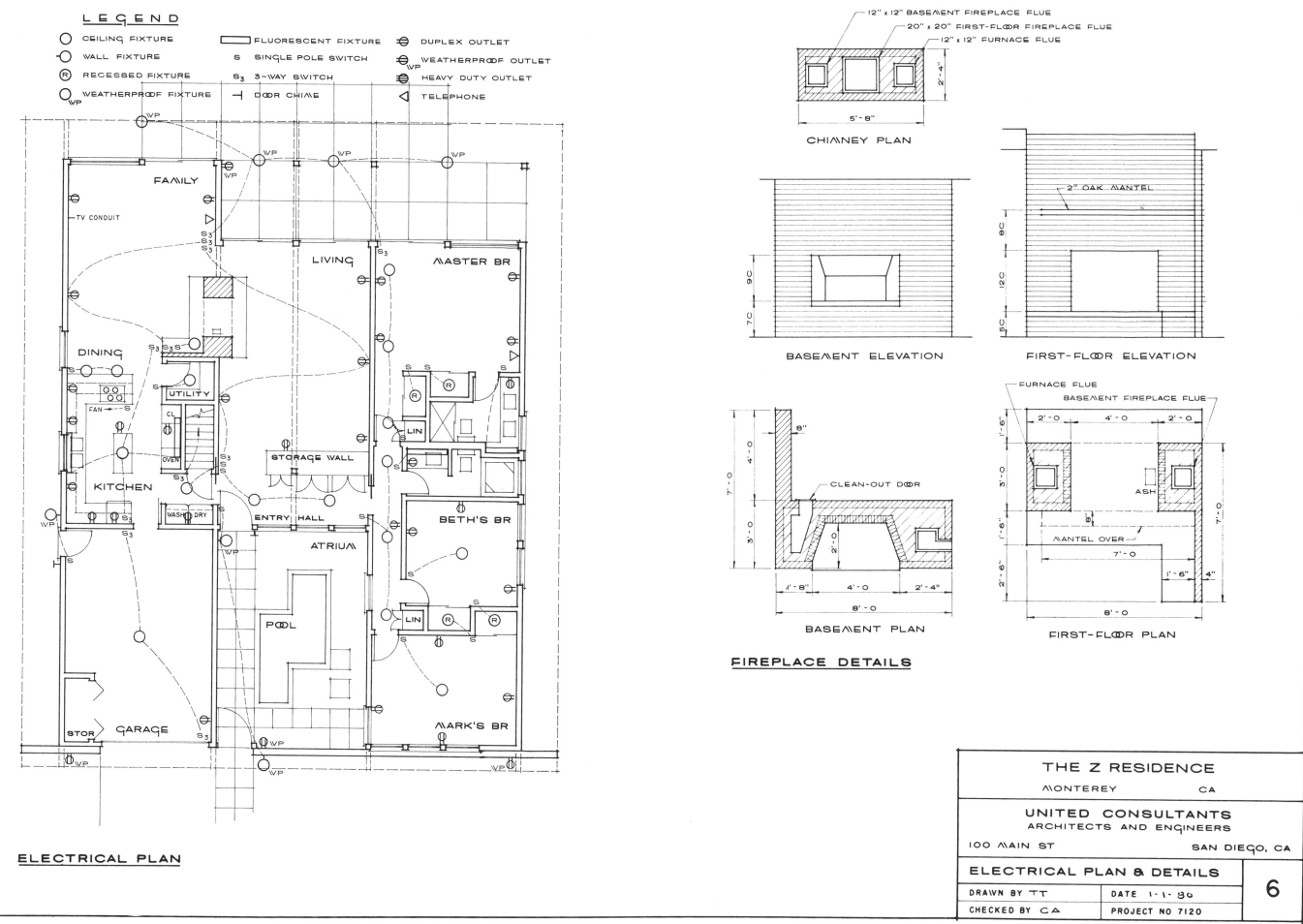

Figure 12. Electrical plan and details of the Z residence.

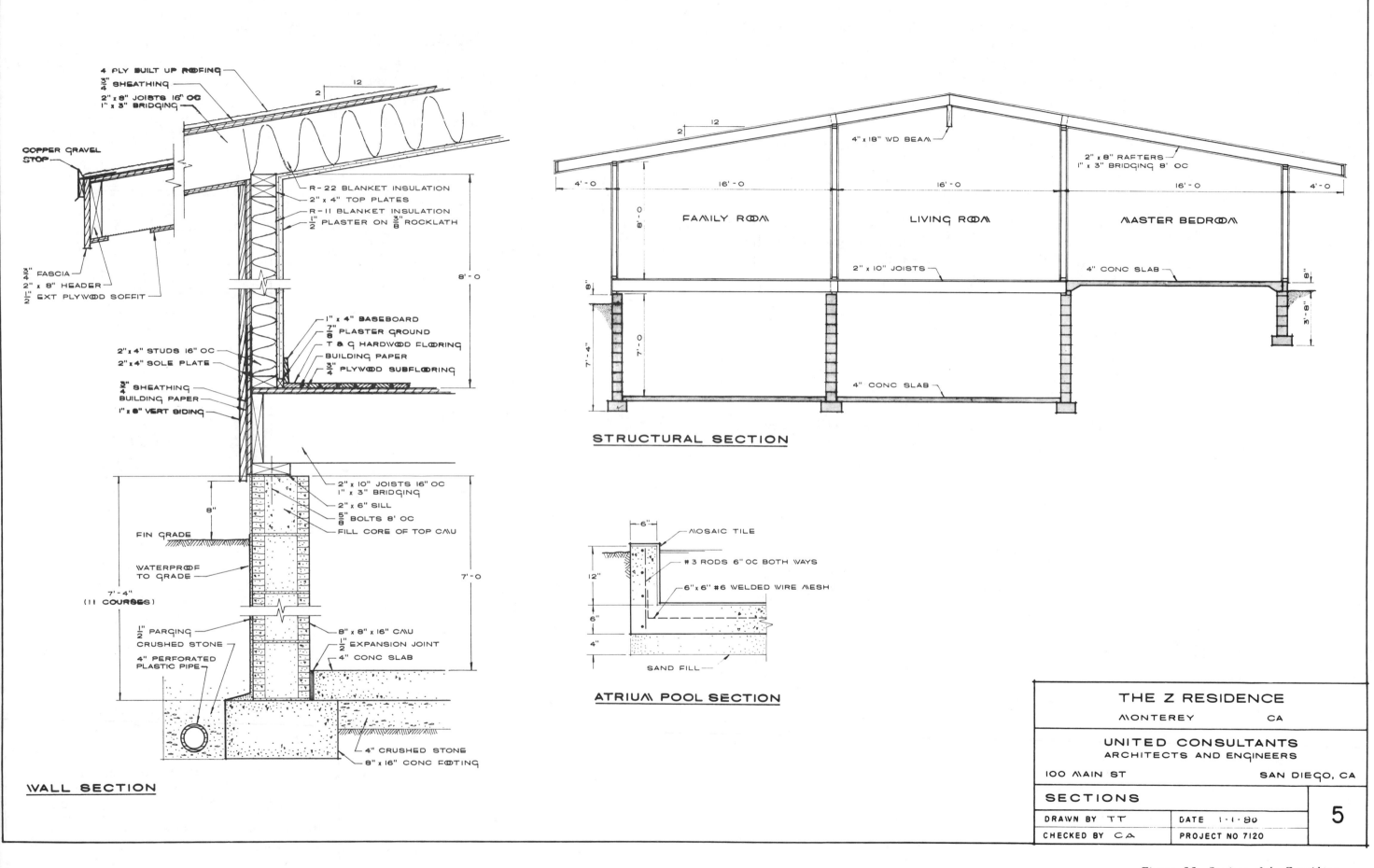

WALL SECTION

4 PLY BUILT UP ROOFING
¾" SHEATHING
2" x 8" JOISTS 16" OC
1" x 3" BRIDGING

COPPER GRAVEL STOP

R-22 BLANKET INSULATION
2" x 4" TOP PLATES
R-11 BLANKET INSULATION
½" PLASTER ON ⅜" ROCKLATH

¾" FASCIA
2" x 8" HEADER
½" EXT PLYWOOD SOFFIT

1" x 4" BASEBOARD
⅞" PLASTER GROUND
T & G HARDWOOD FLOORING
BUILDING PAPER
¾" PLYWOOD SUBFLOORING

2" x 4" STUDS 16" OC
2" x 4" SOLE PLATE

¾" SHEATHING
BUILDING PAPER
1" x 8" VERT SIDING

2" x 10" JOISTS 16" OC
1" x 3" BRIDGING
2" x 6" SILL
⅝" BOLTS 8' OC
FILL CORE OF TOP CMU

FIN GRADE

WATERPROOF TO GRADE

8"

7'-4"
(11 COURSES)

½" PARGING
CRUSHED STONE
4" PERFORATED PLASTIC PIPE

8" x 8" x 16" CMU
½" EXPANSION JOINT
4" CONC SLAB

7'-0

4" CRUSHED STONE
8" x 16" CONC FOOTING

8'-0

STRUCTURAL SECTION

2   12

4"x18" WD BEAM

2" x 8" RAFTERS
1" x 3" BRIDGING 8' OC

4'-0   16'-0   16'-0   16'-0   4'-0

FAMILY ROOM   LIVING ROOM   MASTER BEDROOM

8'-0

2" x 10" JOISTS

4" CONC SLAB

8"

8"   7'-4"   7'-0   3'-8"

4" CONC SLAB

ATRIUM POOL SECTION

6"

MOSAIC TILE

#3 RODS 6" OC BOTH WAYS

6"x6" #6 WELDED WIRE MESH

12"

6"

4"

SAND FILL

THE Z RESIDENCE
MONTEREY   CA

UNITED CONSULTANTS
ARCHITECTS AND ENGINEERS

100 MAIN ST   SAN DIEGO, CA

SECTIONS

| DRAWN BY TT | DATE 1-1-80 | 5 |
| CHECKED BY CA | PROJECT NO 7120 | |

Figure 11. Sections of the Z residence.

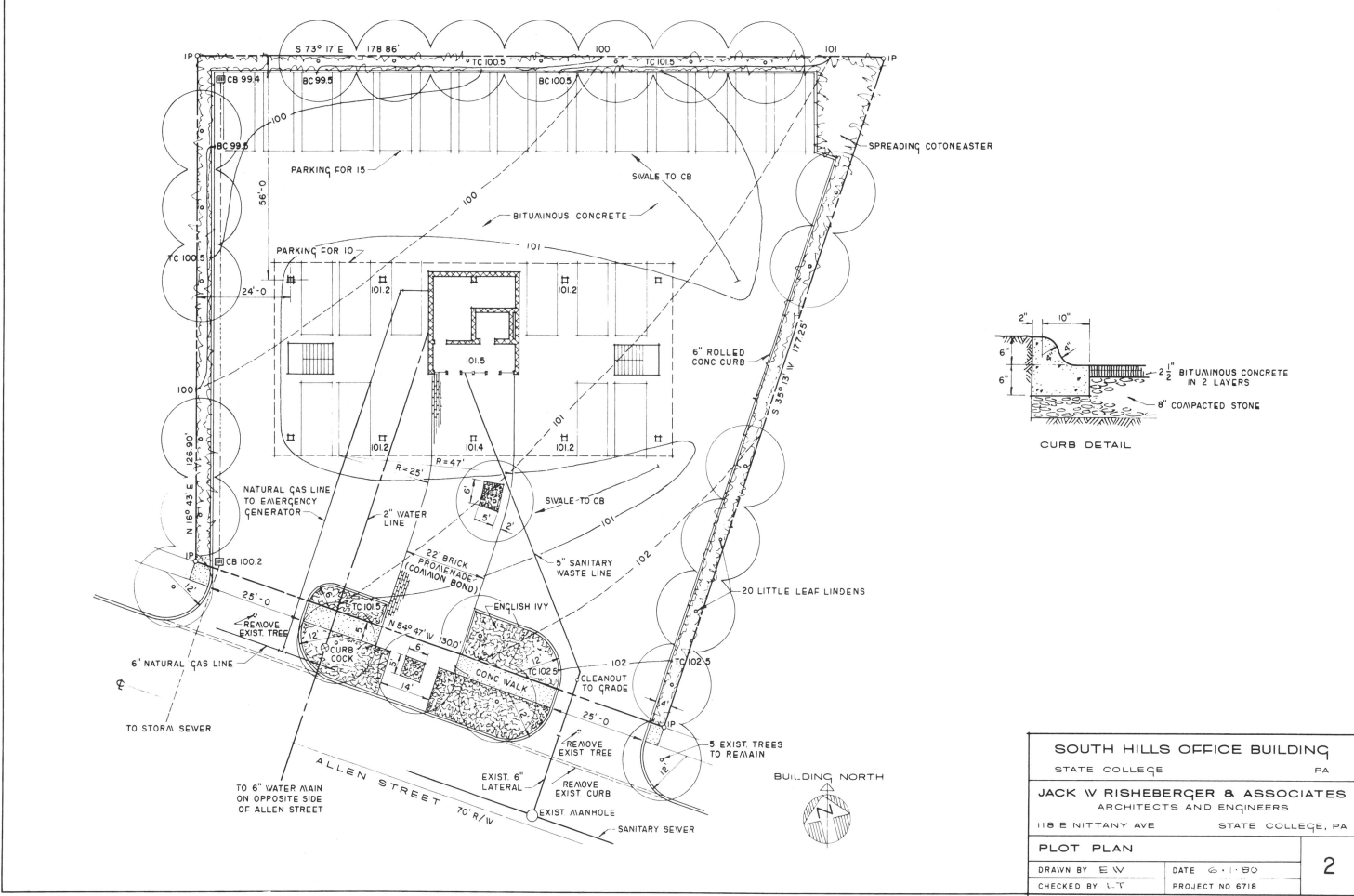

Figure 14. Drawing No. 2. Plot plan of the South Hills Office Building.

ABBREVIATIONS

ACOUSTIC	AC	HOLLOW METAL	HM
ALUMINUM	ALUM	HOT	H
AMPHERES	A	BEARING PILE	HP
ANGLE	L		
AT	@	INSULATION	INSUL
		IRON PIPE	IP
BEAM	B		
BEARING PILE	HP	JUNCTION BOX	JB
BITUMINOUS	BIT		
BOARD	BD	LAVATORY	L or LAV
BOTTOM OF CURB	BC	LIGHTING	LTG
BRITISH THERMAL UNIT	BTU		
BUILDING	BLDG	MANUFACTURER	MANUF
		MATERIAL	MAT'L
CABINET	CAB	MAXIMUM	MAX
CATCH BASIN	CB	METAL	MET
CEILING	CLG	MINIMUM	MIN
CEMENT	CEM		
CENTER LINE	₵	NORTH	N
CENTER TO CENTER	CC	NUMBER	NO or #
CERAMIC TILE	CER T		
CHANNEL	[or C	ON CENTER	OC
CLEAN OUT	CO		
CLEAR	CLR	PARTITION	PART
COLD	C	PHASE	φ
COLUMN	COL	PLASTER	PLAST
CONCRETE	CONC	PLATE	℞
CONCRETE MASONRY UNIT CMU		PORCELAIN	PORC
CONSTRUCTION	CONST	POUNDS PER SQUARE INCH	PSI
CUBIC FEET PER MINUTE	CFM	PUNCHED	PUN
DIAMETER	φ	RAIN WATER CONDUIT	RWC
DITTO	DO or "	RECEPTACLE	REC
DOUBLE STUDS	DS	RIGHT OF WAY	R/W
DOWN	DN	RISER, RADIUS	R
EACH	EA	SHOCK ABSORBER	SA
EAST, EMERGENCY	E	SLOP SINK	SS
ELEVATION, ELEVATOR	ELEV	SOUTH	S
EQUAL	EQ	SPECIFICATIONS	SPECS
EXHAUST	EXH	STEEL	STL
EXISTING	EXIST	SYSTEM	SYS
EXPANSION JOINT	EXP JT		
EXTENDED	EXT	THRESHOLD	THRESH
		TOP OF CURB	TC
FINISH	FIN		
FLASHING	FLASH	UNPUNCHED	UNP
FLOOR	FL	URINAL	U
FOOTING	FTG		
FRESH AIR	FA	VINYL ASBESTOS TILE	VAT
FURRING	FUR	VOLTS	V
GYPSUM	GYP	WASTE, WATTS, WEST	W
GLASS	GL	WATER CLOSET	WC
		WATER HEATER	WTR HTR
HEATING	HTG	WIDE FLANGE	W
HEXAGONAL	HEX	WITH	w/

CONSTRUCTION DRAWINGS
FOR THE
SOUTH HILLS OFFICE BUILDING
STATE COLLEGE, PENNSYLVANIA

JACK W RISHEBERGER & ASSOCIATES
ARCHITECTS AND ENGINEERS

LEGEND

---100---	EXIST CONTOUR	- - - - - -	SWITCH LEG
—100—	REVISED CONTOUR	— — — —	SWITCHED CIRCUIT
— — —	PROPERTY LINE	— — —	BRANCH CIRCUIT
	BRICK	D-I	HOME RUN w/ CIRCUIT NO
	CMU		208V HOME RUN
	CRUSHED STONE	○	INCANDESCENT FIXTURE, CLG
	EARTH	⊖	" " WALL
	STEEL		FLUORESCENT "
	CONCRETE SECTION	⊖	CONVENIENCE OUTLET
	" IN PLAN	S	SWITCH
	BITUMINOUS	S₃	THREE WAY SWITCH
	RIGID INSULATION	S₄	FOUR " "
	BATT "	—E—	EMERGENCY CIRCUIT
	ROUGH WOOD	○ₑ	" LIGHTING
	GYPSUM BOARD	⊗	EXIT LIGHT, GUTH B1412
	PLASTER	⊗	" " B1414
	CERAMIC TILE		HEATING-COOLING UNIT
	SHEET NO SECTION NO	(A)	BASEBOARD HEATING "
	SHEET NO ELEVATION NO	— — —	COLD WATER
	ROOM NO DOOR NO	— — —	HOT WATER
(A)	WINDOW SYMBOL	— — —	SANITARY WASTE
101	ROOM SYMBOL	- - - -	VENT

INDEX OF DRAWINGS

1	INDEX
2	PLOT PLAN
3	FOUNDATION PLAN
4	FOOTING DETAILS
5	PLAZA FLOOR PLAN
6	FIRST FLOOR PLAN
7	SOUTH ELEVATION
8	NORTH ELEVATION
9	EAST & WEST ELEVATIONS
10	INTERIOR ELEVATIONS
11	LONGITUDINAL SECTION
12	TYPICAL SECTIONS
13	TYPICAL DETAILS
14	ROOM SCHEDULES
15	DOOR & WINDOW SCHEDULES
E1	ELECTRICAL PLAN
H1	HEATING-COOLING PLAN
P1	WATER SUPPLY PLAN
P2	SANITARY PLAN
S1	FIRST FLOOR STRUCTURAL PLAN
S2	ROOF STRUCTURAL PLAN
S3	COLUMN SCHEDULE
S4	STRUCTURAL DETAILS
S5	CONCRETE SLAB PLAN

Figure 13. Drawing No. 1. Index of the South Hills Office Building.

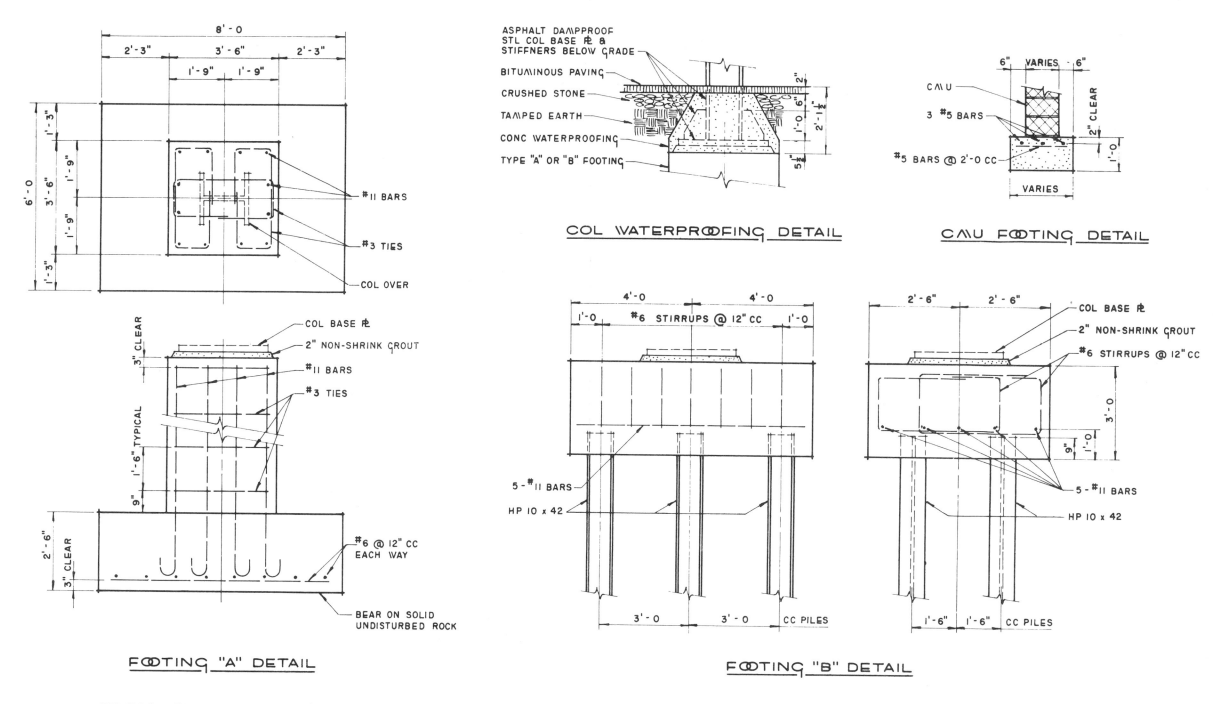

COL WATERPROOFING DETAIL

CMU FOOTING DETAIL

FOOTING "A" DETAIL

FOOTING "B" DETAIL

GENERAL FOUNDATION NOTES

1. FOOTING "A" MAY BE SUBSTITUTED FOR FOOTING "B" AT CONTRACTOR'S OPTION.

2. ALL CONCRETE SHALL HAVE AN ULTIMATE 28 DAY COMPRESSIVE STRENGTH OF 3000 PSI.

3. ALL REINFORCING STEEL SHALL BE ASTM A15 INTERMEDIATE GRADE.

4. STEEL BEARING PILES FOR FOOTING "B" SHALL BE ASTM A36. PILES SHALL BE DRIVEN TO REFUSAL ON SOLID ROCK. SEE TEST BORING RESULTS FOR APPROXIMATE DEPTH OF ROCK.

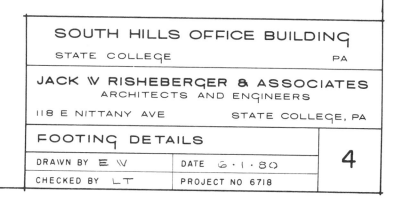

SOUTH HILLS OFFICE BUILDING
STATE COLLEGE   PA

JACK W RISHEBERGER & ASSOCIATES
ARCHITECTS AND ENGINEERS

118 E NITTANY AVE   STATE COLLEGE, PA

FOOTING DETAILS

| DRAWN BY E W | DATE 6·1·80 | 4 |
| CHECKED BY LT | PROJECT NO 6718 | |

Figure 16. Drawing No. 4. Footing details of the South Hills Office Building.

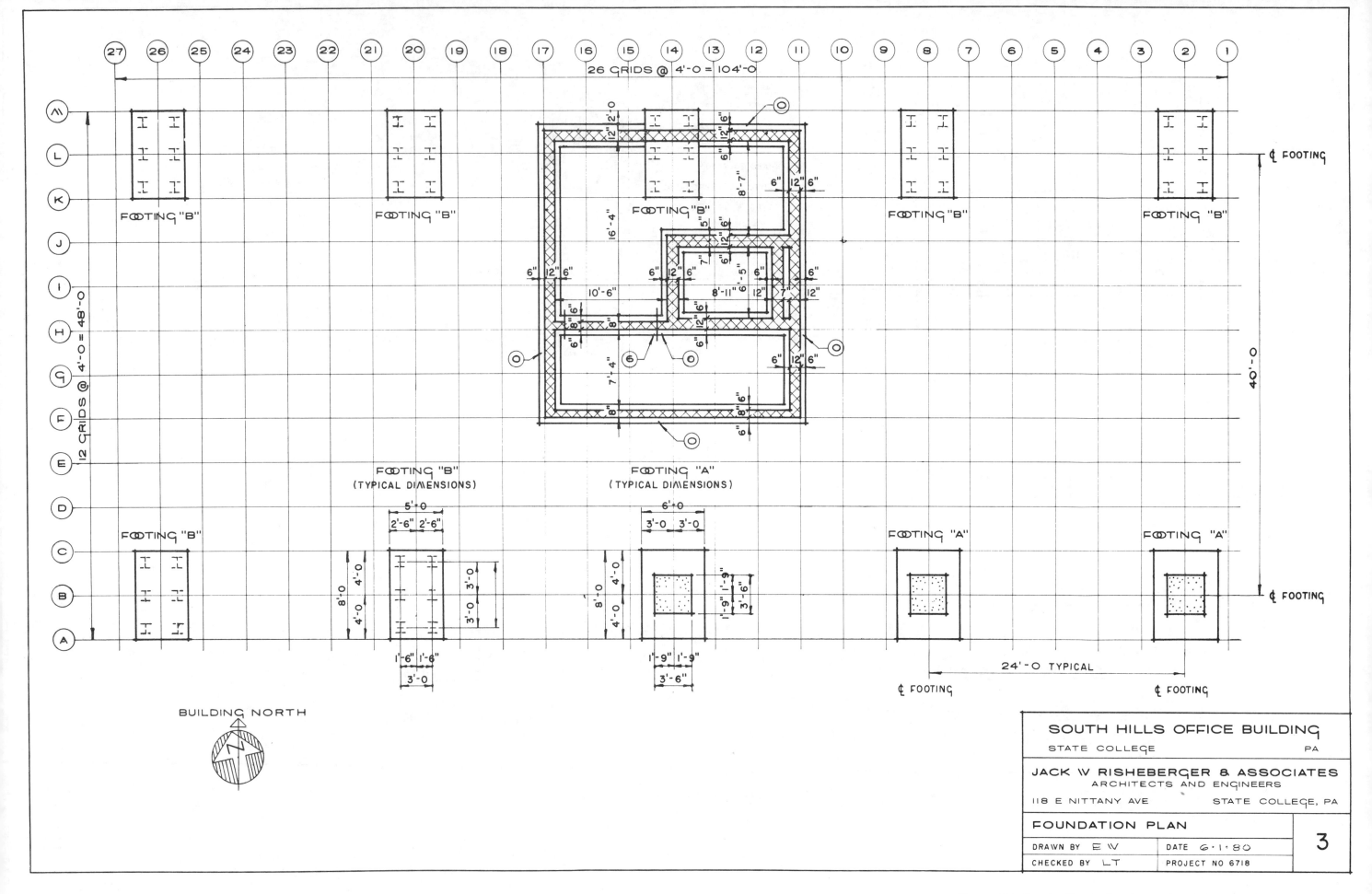

Figure 15. Drawing No. 3. Foundation plan of the South Hills Office Building.

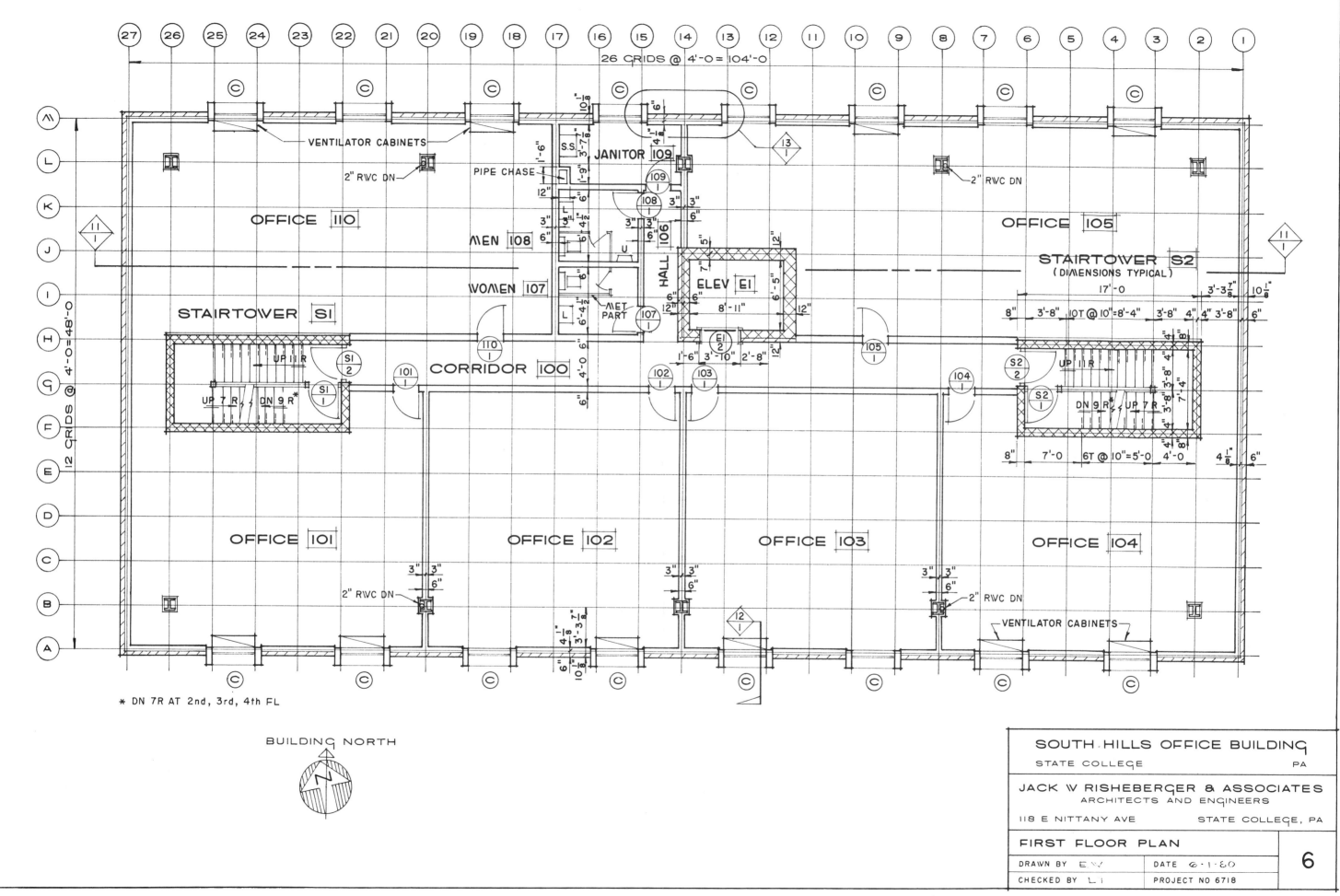

Figure 18. Drawing No. 6. First-floor plan of the South Hills Office Building.

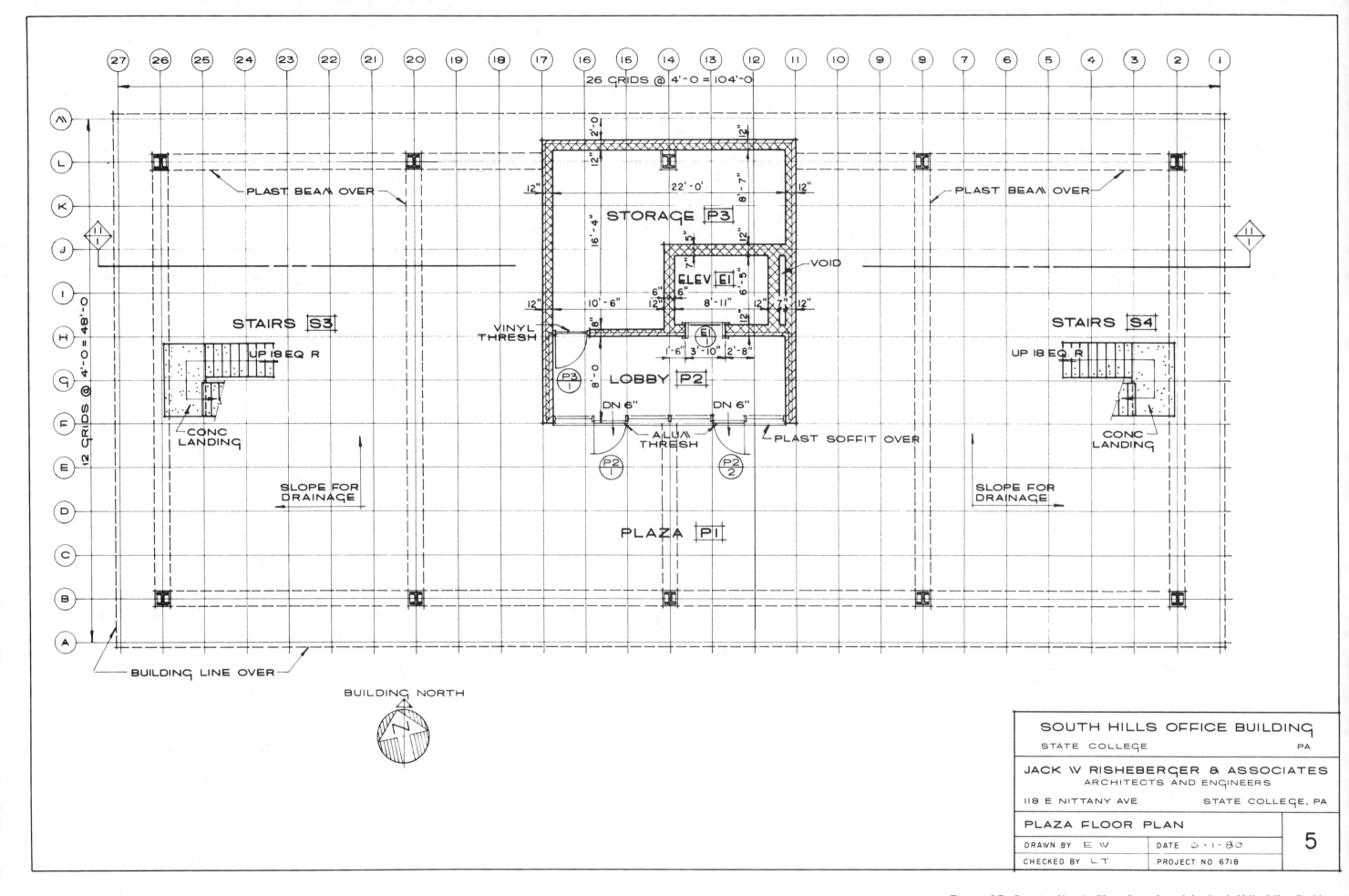

Figure 17. Drawing No. 5. Plaza floor plan of the South Hills Office Building.

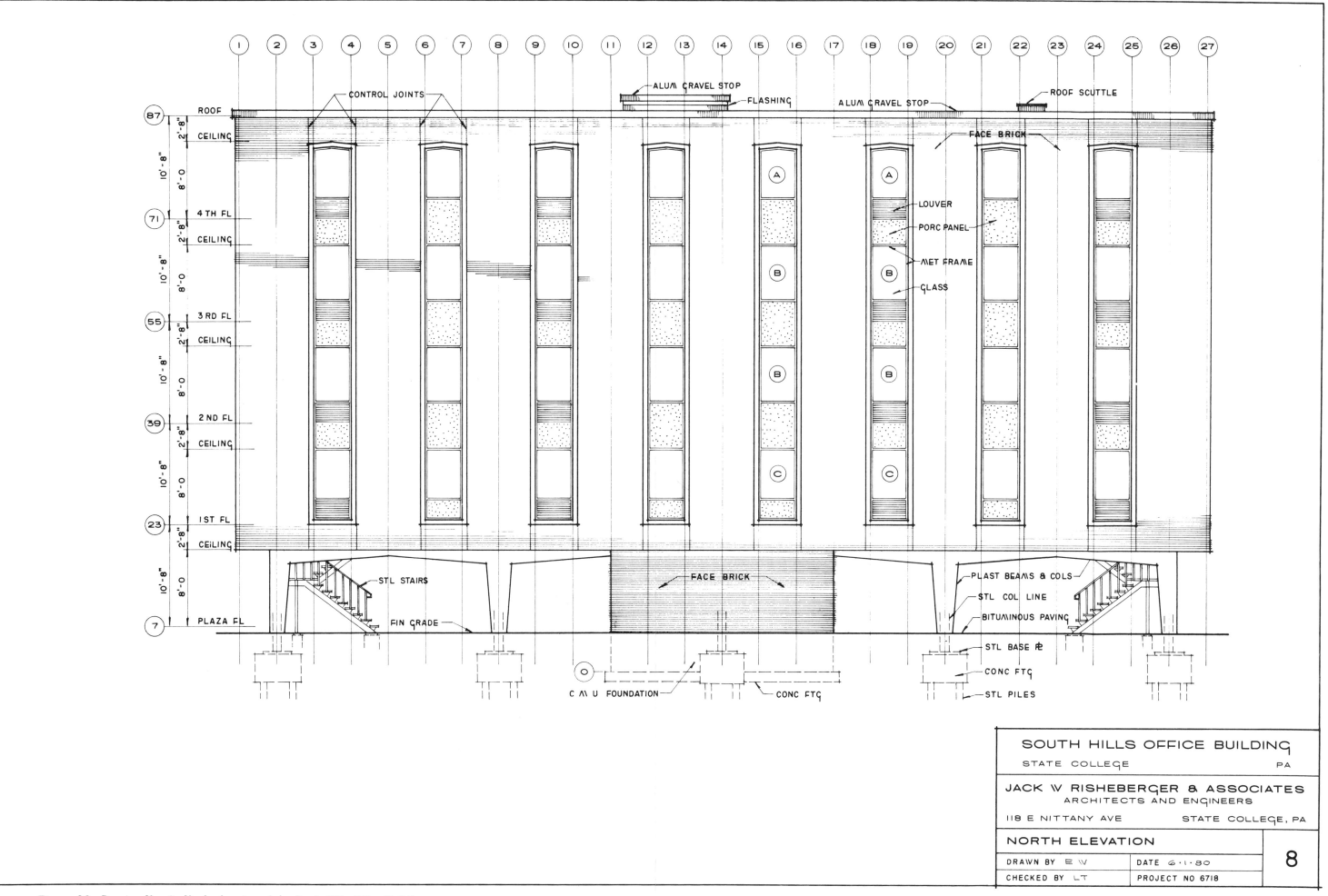

Figure 20. Drawing No. 8. North elevation of the South Hills Office Building.

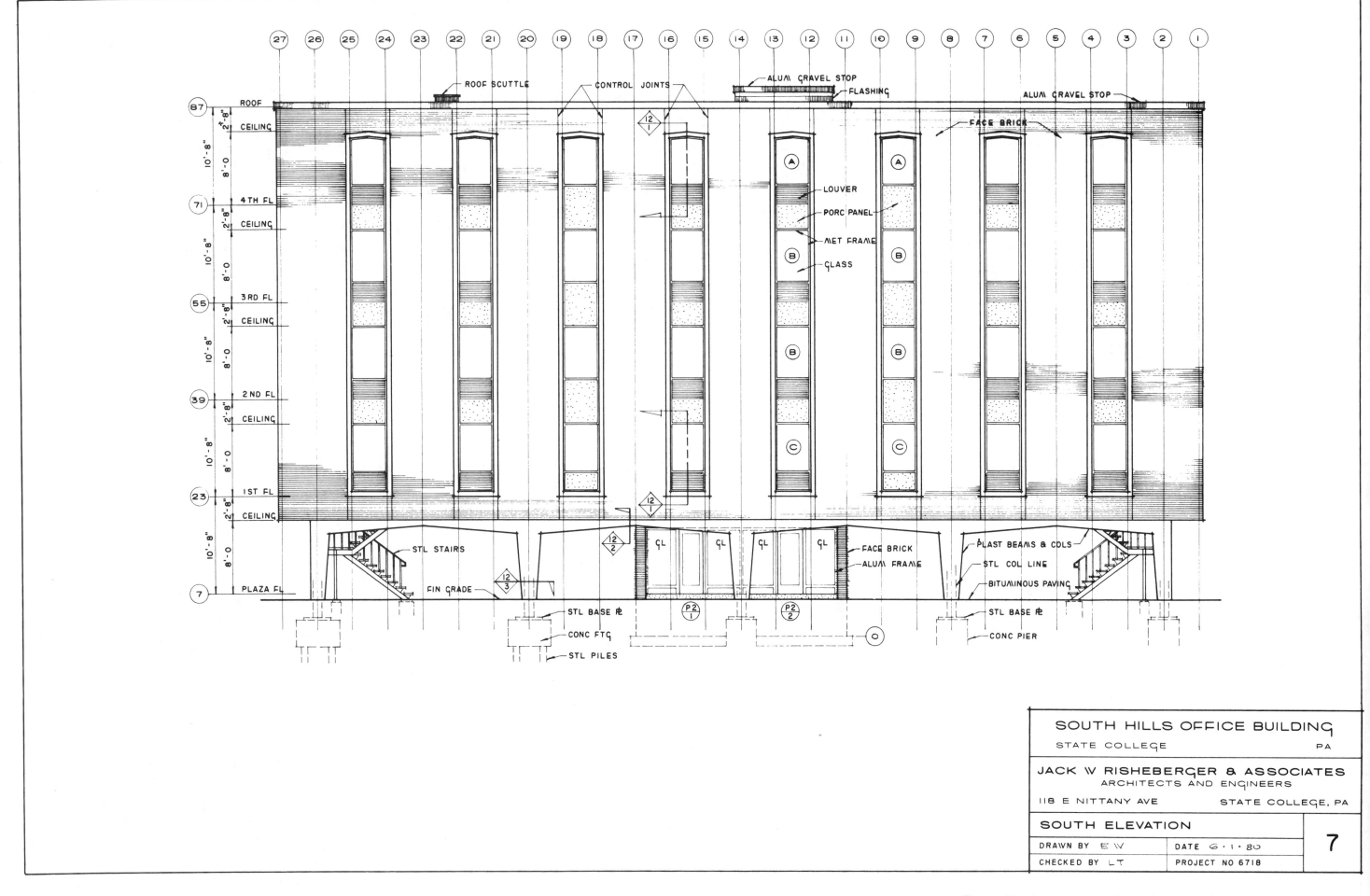

Figure 19. Drawing No. 7. South elevation of the South Hills Office Building.

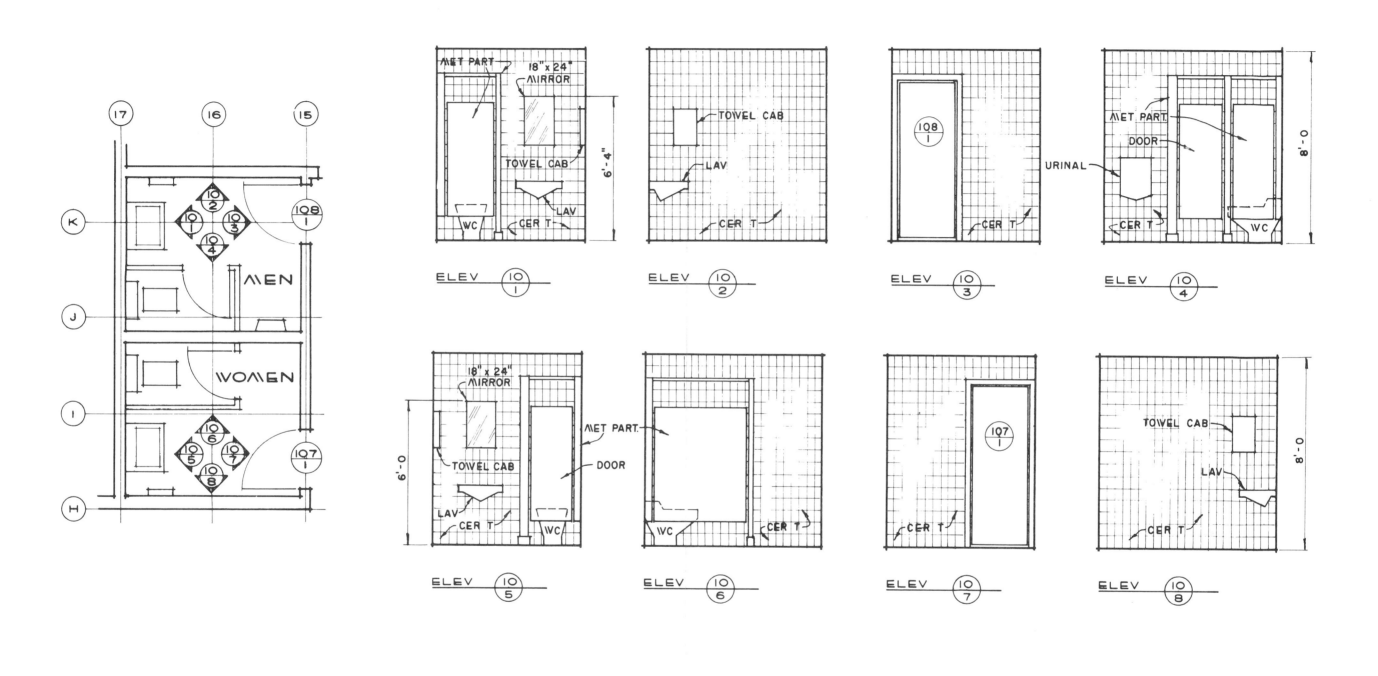

ELEV 10/1 ELEV 10/2 ELEV 10/3 ELEV 10/4

ELEV 10/5 ELEV 10/6 ELEV 10/7 ELEV 10/8

SOUTH HILLS OFFICE BUILDING

STATE COLLEGE   PA

JACK W RISHEBERGER & ASSOCIATES
ARCHITECTS AND ENGINEERS

118 E NITTANY AVE   STATE COLLEGE, PA

INTERIOR ELEVATIONS

| DRAWN BY E W | DATE 6·1·80 | 10 |
| CHECKED BY LT | PROJECT NO 6718 | |

Figure 22. Drawing No. 10. Interior elevations of the South Hills Office Building.

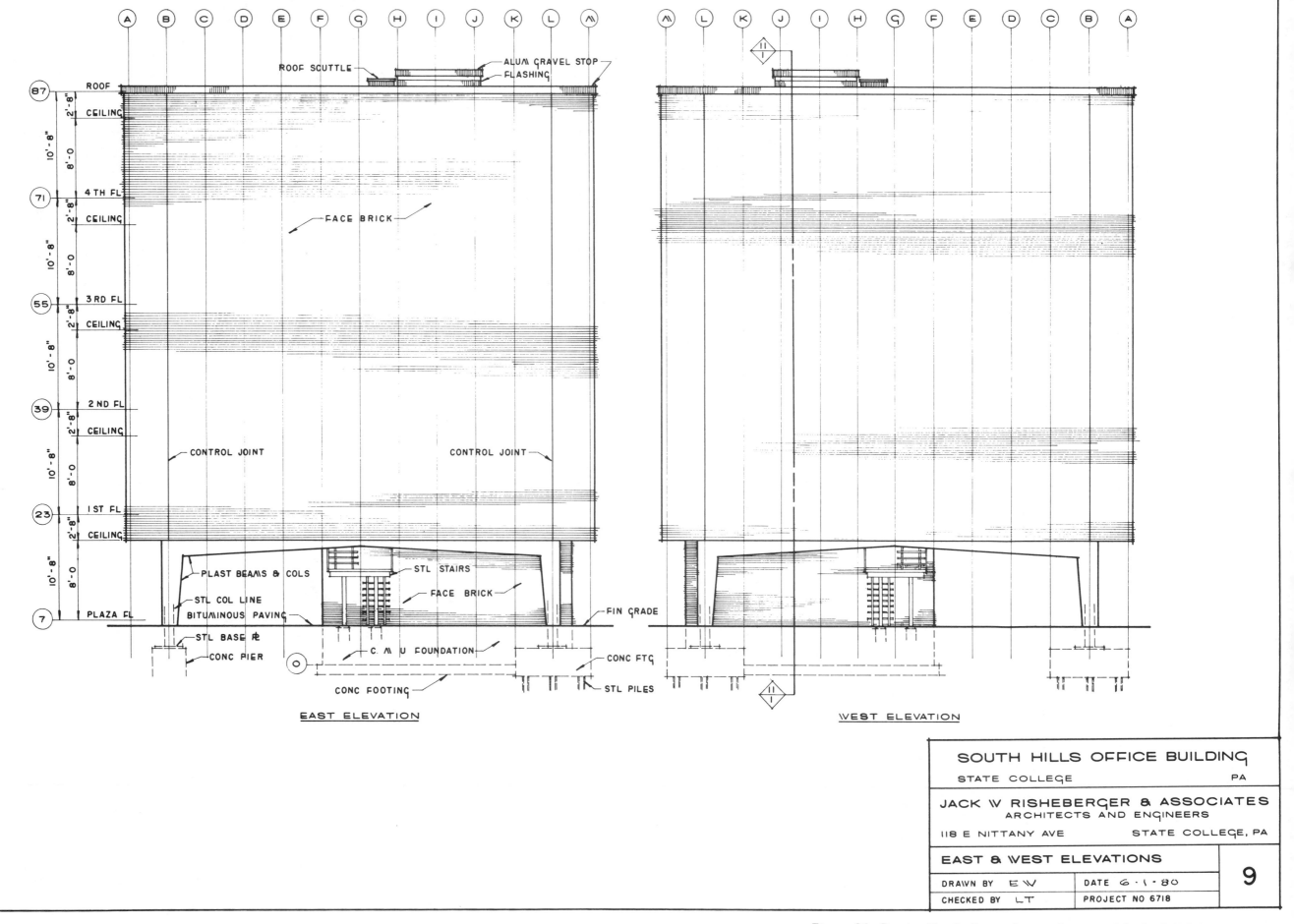

Figure 21. Drawing No. 9. East and west elevations of the South Hills Office Building.

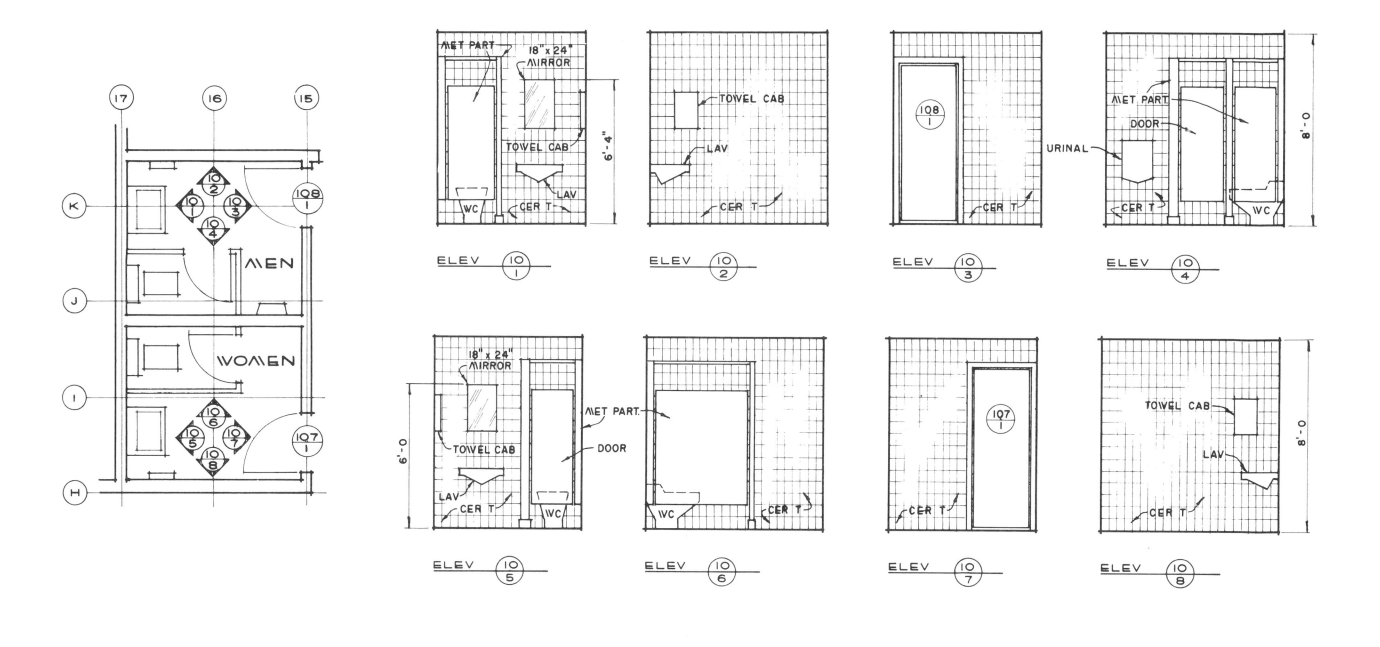

SOUTH HILLS OFFICE BUILDING

STATE COLLEGE   PA

JACK W RISHEBERGER & ASSOCIATES
ARCHITECTS AND ENGINEERS

118 E NITTANY AVE   STATE COLLEGE, PA

INTERIOR ELEVATIONS

| DRAWN BY E W | DATE 6·1·80 | 10 |
| CHECKED BY LT | PROJECT NO 6718 | |

Figure 22. Drawing No. 10. Interior elevations of the South Hills Office Building.

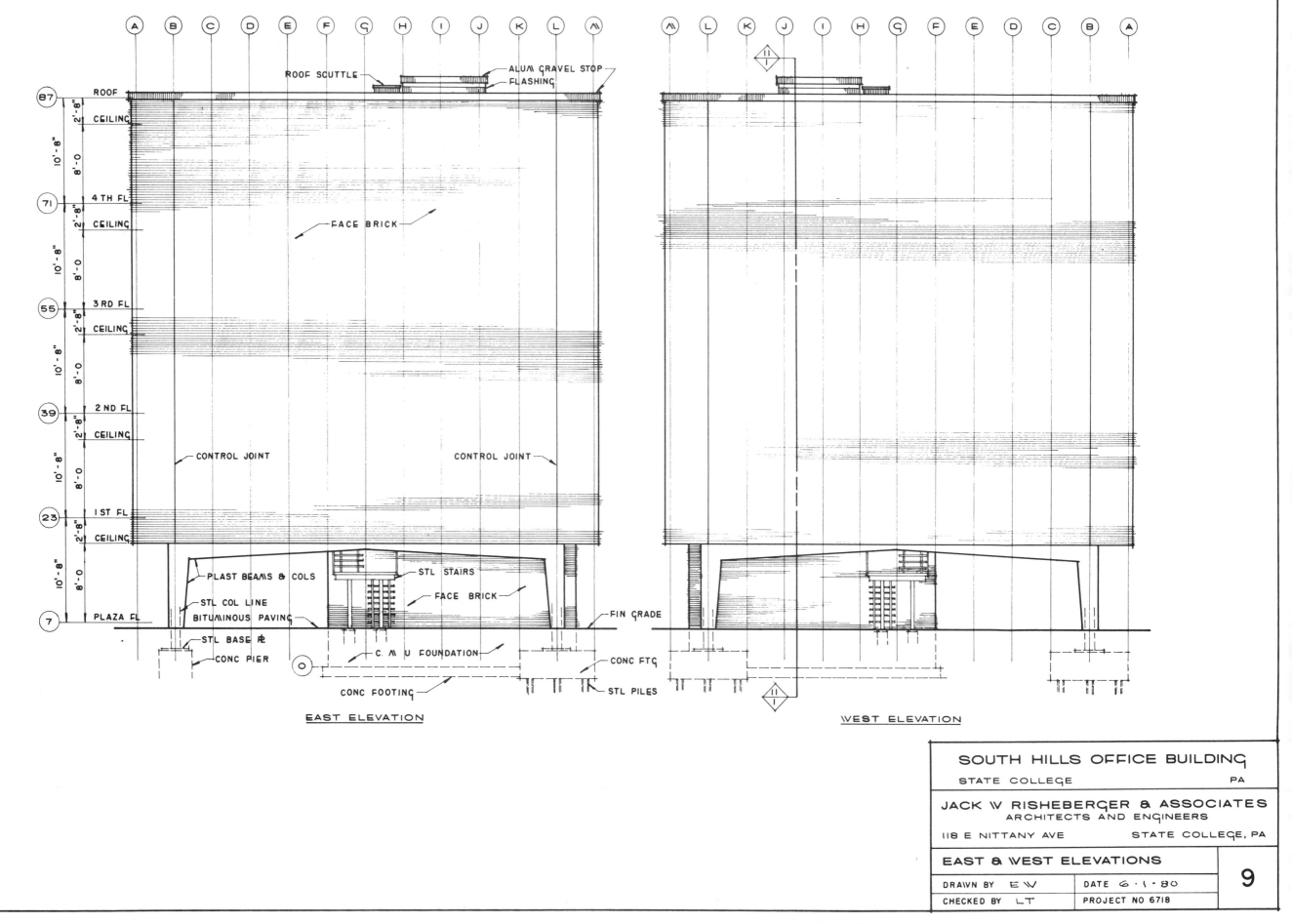

Figure 21. Drawing No. 9. East and west elevations of the South Hills Office Building.

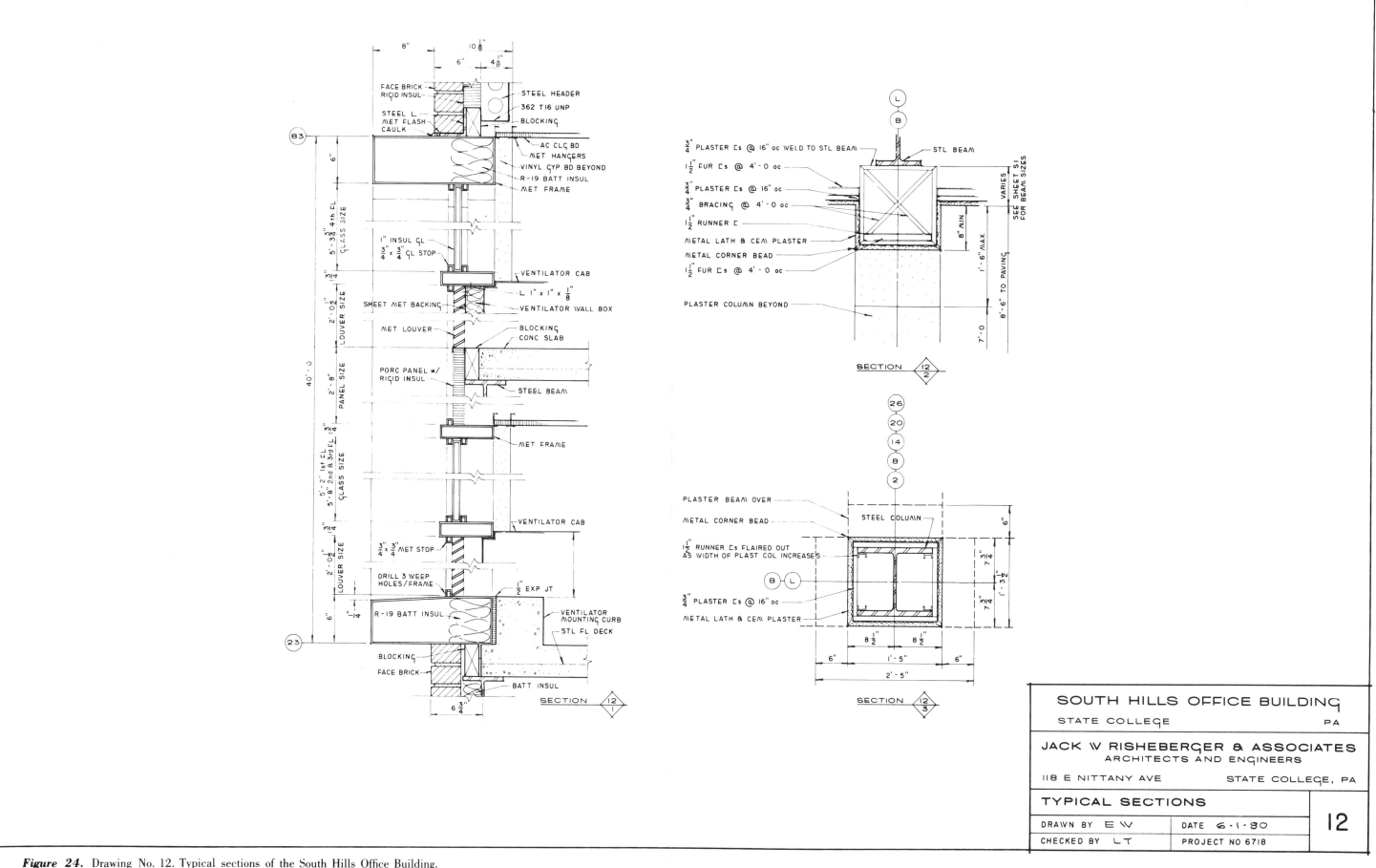

FACE BRICK
RIGID INSUL
STEEL L
MET FLASH
CAULK

8"
10⅛"
6"
4⅛"

STEEL HEADER
362 T16 UNP
BLOCKING

AC CLG BD
MET HANGERS
VINYL GYP BD BEYOND
R-19 BATT INSUL
MET FRAME

83
6"
5'-3¾" 4th FL
GLASS SIZE

1" INSUL GL
¾" x ¾" GL STOP

3¾"
2'-0½" LOUVER SIZE

VENTILATOR CAB
L 1" x 1" x ⅛"

SHEET MET BACKING
MET LOUVER

VENTILATOR WALL BOX

BLOCKING
CONC SLAB

2'-8" PANEL SIZE

PORC PANEL w/
RIGID INSUL

STEEL BEAM

40'-0"

3¾"
5'-2" 1st FL
5'-8" 2nd & 3rd FL
GLASS SIZE
3¾"

MET FRAME

VENTILATOR CAB

3¾"
3¾" MET STOP

3¾"
2'-0½" LOUVER SIZE

DRILL 3 WEEP
HOLES/FRAME

½" EXP JT

6"
3¾"
2¾"

R-19 BATT INSUL

VENTILATOR
MOUNTING CURB
STL FL DECK

23

BLOCKING
FACE BRICK

BATT INSUL

6¾"

SECTION 12/1

L
B

¾" PLASTER Cs @ 16" oc WELD TO STL BEAM
STL BEAM

1½" FUR Cs @ 4'-0 oc
¾" PLASTER Cs @ 16" oc
¾" BRACING @ 4'-0 oc
1½" RUNNER C
METAL LATH & CEM PLASTER
METAL CORNER BEAD
1½" FUR Cs @ 4'-0 oc

8" MIN
VARIES
SEE SHEET S1
FOR BEAM SIZES

1'-6" MAX

PLASTER COLUMN BEYOND

8'-6" TO PAVING
7'-0

SECTION 12/2

26
20
14
8
2

PLASTER BEAM OVER
METAL CORNER BEAD
STEEL COLUMN

6"
7¾"
7¾"

1½" RUNNER Cs FLAIRED OUT
AS WIDTH OF PLAST COL INCREASES

B L

7¾"
7¾"
1'-3½"

¾" PLASTER Cs @ 16" oc
METAL LATH & CEM PLASTER

8½"
8½"

6"
1'-5"
6"

2'-5"

SECTION 12/3

SOUTH HILLS OFFICE BUILDING
STATE COLLEGE PA

JACK W RISHEBERGER & ASSOCIATES
ARCHITECTS AND ENGINEERS
118 E NITTANY AVE   STATE COLLEGE, PA

TYPICAL SECTIONS

| DRAWN BY E W | DATE 6-1-30 | 12 |
| CHECKED BY LT | PROJECT NO 6718 | |

Figure 24. Drawing No. 12. Typical sections of the South Hills Office Building.

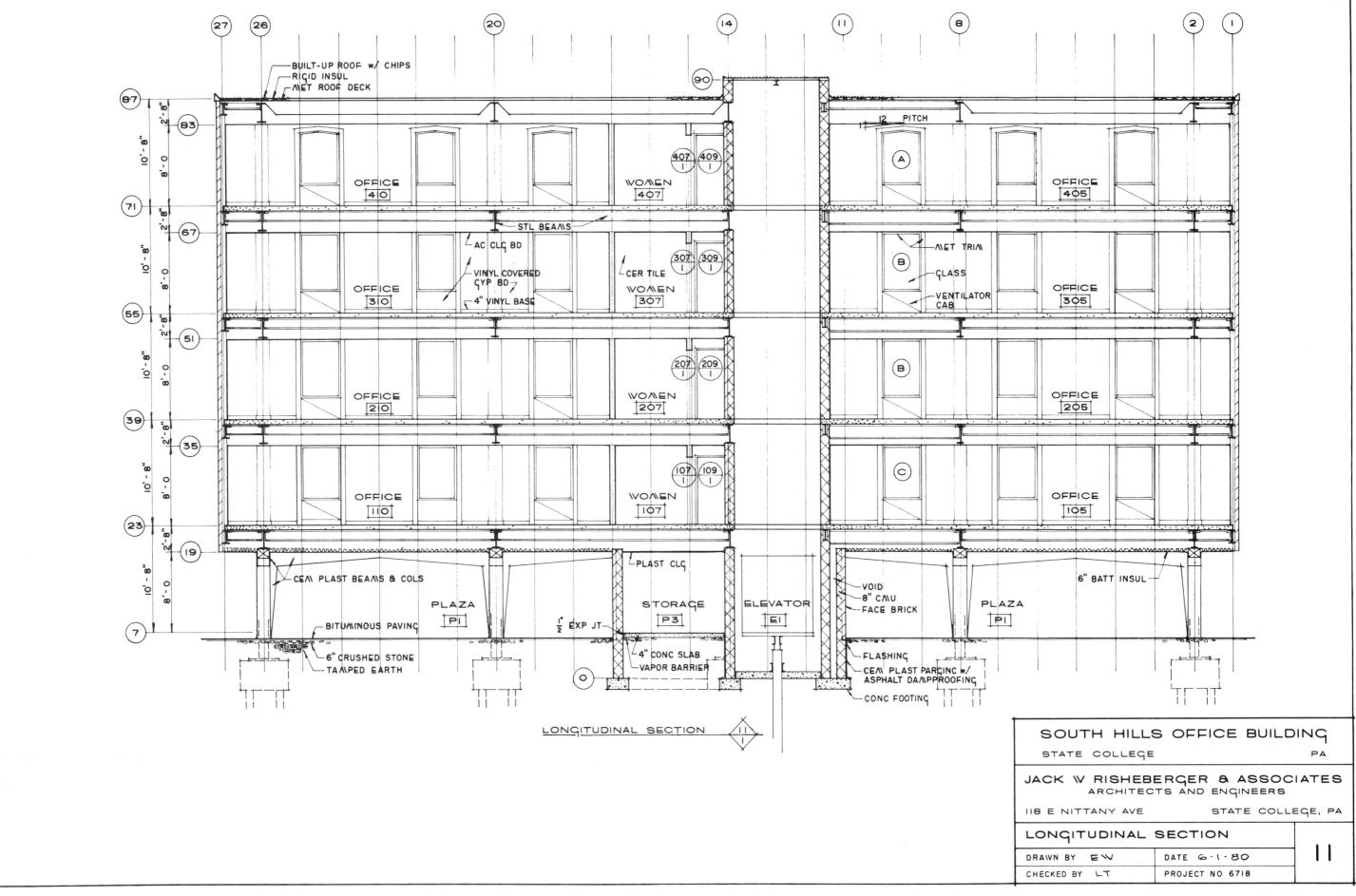

Figure 23. Drawing No. 11. Longitudinal section of the South Hills Office Building.

ROOM FINISH SCHEDULE

NO	NAME	FLOOR		BASE		WALL		TRIM		WINDOW STOOL		CEILING		HGT	REMARKS
P1	PLAZA	BITUM				BRICK	5	ALUM	9			PLAST	11	VARIES	CEM PLAST BEAMS & COLS
P2	LOBBY	VAT	1			"	5	" HM	9/10			"	13	8'-0	
P3	STORAGE	CONC	17			CMU	6	HM	10			"	11	8'-0	
100	CORRIDOR	VAT	1	VINYL	3	VINYL BRICK	7/5	HM	10			AC CLG BD	14	8'-0	NO BASE AT BRICK WALL
101	OFFICE	"	1	"	3	VINYL	7	"	10	ALUM	9	"	14	8'-0	
102	"	"	1	"	3	"	7	"	10	"	9	"	14	8'-0	
103	"	"	1	"	3	"	7	"	10	"	9	"	14	8'-0	
104	"	"	1	"	3	"	7	"	10	"	9	"	14	8'-0	
105	"	"	1	"	3	"	7	"	10	"	9	"	14	8'-0	
106	HALL	"	1	"	3	VINYL BRICK	7/5	"	10			"	14	8'-0	
107	WOMEN	CER T	2	CER T	4	CER T	8	"	10			PLAST	12	8'-0	PROVIDE MIRROR, TOWEL CAB, MET PART
108	MEN	"	2	"	4	"	8	"	10			"	12	8'-0	" " "
109	JANITOR	VAT	1	VINYL	3	VINYL CMU	7/6	"	10	ALUM	9	AC CLG BD	14	8'-0	
110	OFFICE	"	1	"	3	VINYL	7	"	10	"	9	"	14	8'-0	

STAIRTOWER FINISH SCHEDULE

NO	RISER		TREAD		STRINGER		INTERMEDIATE FLOOR		BASE		FLOOR LANDING FLOOR		BASE		SOFFIT		CEILING		RAILING		WALL RAILING		WALLS	
S1	STL	15	VAT	1	STL	15	VAT	1	VINYL	3	VAT	1	VINYL	3	PLAST	13	PLAST	13	VINYL	16	VINYL	16	CMU	6
S2	"	15	"	1	"	15	"	1	"	3	"	1	"	3	"	13	"	13	"	16	"	16	"	6
S3			CONC	17	"	15	CONC	17							"	11	"	11	STL	15			PLAST	11
S4			"	17	"	15	"	17									"	11	"	11			"	11

INTERIOR MATERIAL SCHEDULE

NO	MATERIAL	SIZE	TYPE	FINISH
1	VINYL ASBESTOS TILE	9" x 9" x $\frac{1}{8}$"	SEE SPECS	WAX
2	CERAMIC FLOOR TILE	$1\frac{1}{16}$" x $1\frac{1}{16}$"	CERAMIC MOSAIC	FACTORY FINISH, UNGLAZED
3	VINYL COVE BASE	4" HIGH		" "
4	CERAMIC BASE TILE	$4\frac{1}{4}$" x 6" x $\frac{5}{16}$"	COVE BASE	" " MATTE GLAZE
5	BRICK	3 COURSES = 8"	SEE SPECS, COMMON BOND	$\frac{1}{4}$" CONCAVE JOINT
6	CONCRETE MASONRY UNIT	1 COURSE = 8"	" " " "	$\frac{3}{8}$" " " PAINT
7	VINYL COVERED GYP BD	4'-0 x 8'-0 x $\frac{1}{2}$" SHEETS	" " "	ALUM BATTENS
8	CERAMIC WALL TILE	$4\frac{1}{4}$" x 6" x $\frac{5}{16}$"	WALL TILE	FACTORY FINISH, MATTE CLAZE
9	ALUMINUM		SEE SPECS	" "
10	HOLLOW METAL		" "	PAINT
11	PLASTER		CEMENT	SPRAYED ON WHITE
12	"		KEENE CEMENT	WHITE COAT
13	"		SAND FINISH GYPSUM	PAINT
14	ACOUSTICAL CEILING BOARD	2'-0 x 2'-0 x $\frac{5}{8}$"	SEE SPECS, EXPOSED "T" BARS	FACTORY FINISH
15	STEEL		STEEL STAIR PARTS	PAINT
16	STAIR RAILING	2" x 2" x $\frac{3}{8}$" STEEL BASE PLATE	VINYL STAIR RAIL	FACTORY FINISH, PAINT BASE
17	CONCRETE			SEAL w/ LIPIDOLITH

PANEL D (TYPICAL)

- 31 - 20A - 1P - CB - LTG, REC
- 9 - 30A - 2P - CB - HTG, WTR HTR
- 3 - 20A - 2P - CB - HTG
- 2 - 20A - 2P - CB - SPARES
- 4 - 20A - 1P - SPACE ONLY
- 400A - MLO   3Φ - 4W - 120/208V

PANEL E

- 9 - 20A - 2P - CB - LTG, FA SYS EXH FAN
- 4 - 20A - 1P - CB - LTG, REC
- 4 - 20A - 1P - CB - SPARES
- 4 - 20A - 1P - SPACE ONLY
- 100A - MLO   1Φ - 3W - 120/208V

PANEL EM

- 5 - 20A - 1P - FU - LTG, ELEV JB
- 5 - 20A - 1P - FU - SPARES
- 100A - MLO   1Φ - 3W - 120/208V

MAIN DISTRIBUTION PANEL

- 400A - 3P - SW - W/3 - 300A - FU - PANEL A
- 400A - 3P - SW - W/3 - 225A - FU - PANEL B
- 400A - 3P - SW - W/3 - 225A - FU - PANEL C
- 400A - 3P - SW - W/2 - 275A - FU - PANEL D
- 100A - 2P - SW - W/2 - 100A - FU - PANEL E
- 60A - 2P - SW - W/2 - 50A - FU - PANEL EM SW
- *200A - 3P - SW - W/3 - 200A - FU - ELEVATOR
- *TIME DELAY FUSES (FUSETRON)
- 1200A - BUS 3Φ - 4W - 120/208V

ELECTRICAL PANEL SCHEDULES

ELECTRIC HEATING-COOLING UNITS

NO	MANUFACTURER	HEATING BTU	WATTS	COOLING BTU	WATTS
EK-7S	REMINGTON	8400	2460	6500	1240
EK-10S	"	8400	2460	9000	1520
EK-10M	"	11330	3320	9000	1520
EK-12S	"	8470	2480	11700	1770
EK-12L	"	15300	4480	11700	1770
EK-15L	"	15370	4500	14100	2220

ELECTRIC BASEBOARD HEATING

NO	MANUFACTURER	CATALOG NO	BTU	WATTS
A	ELECTROMODE	8950-D	2560	750
B	"	8950-A	1707	500
C	"	8960-C	4439	1300

SOUTH HILLS OFFICE BUILDING

STATE COLLEGE   PA

JACK W RISHEBERGER & ASSOCIATES
ARCHITECTS AND ENGINEERS

118 E NITTANY AVE   STATE COLLEGE, PA

ROOM SCHEDULES

		14
DRAWN BY E W	DATE 6-1-80	
CHECKED BY LT	PROJECT NO 6718	

Figure 26. Drawing No. 14. Room schedules of the South Hills Office Building.

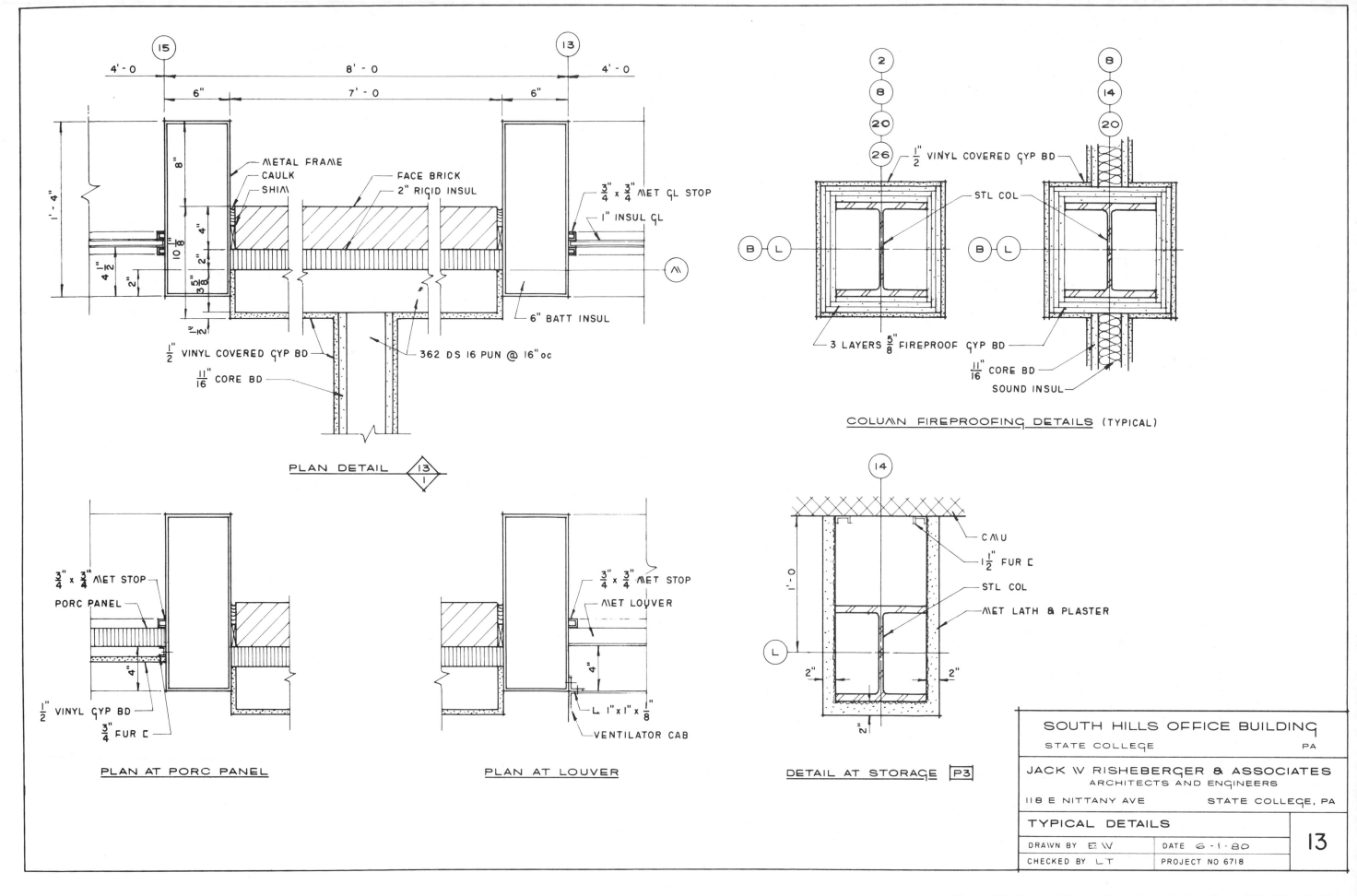

PLAN DETAIL ⟨13/1⟩

PLAN AT PORC PANEL

PLAN AT LOUVER

COLUMN FIREPROOFING DETAILS (TYPICAL)

DETAIL AT STORAGE ⟨P3⟩

SOUTH HILLS OFFICE BUILDING
STATE COLLEGE   PA

JACK W RISHEBERGER & ASSOCIATES
ARCHITECTS AND ENGINEERS

118 E NITTANY AVE   STATE COLLEGE, PA

TYPICAL DETAILS

| DRAWN BY E W | DATE 6-1-80 | 13 |
| CHECKED BY L T | PROJECT NO 6718 | |

Figure 25. Drawing No. 13. Typical details of the South Hills Office Building.

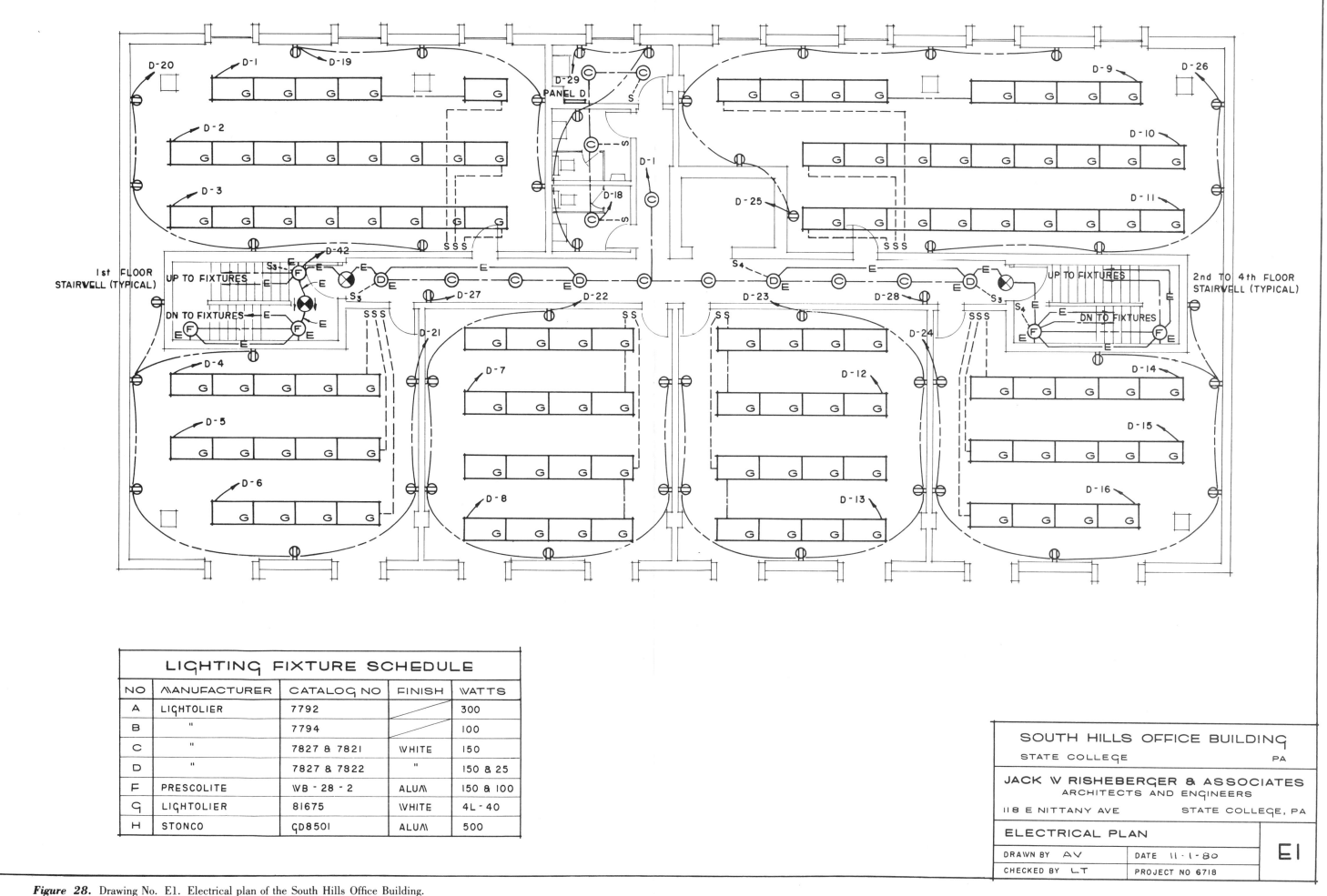

Figure 28. Drawing No. E1. Electrical plan of the South Hills Office Building.

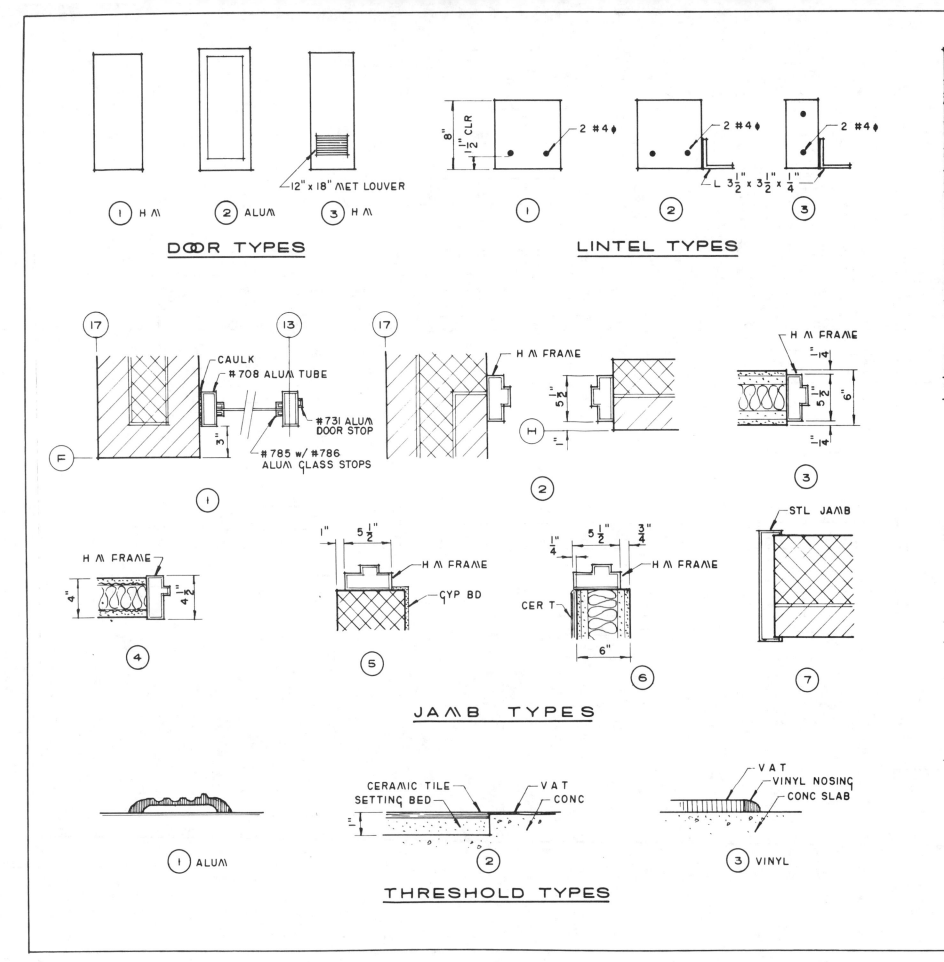

DOOR SCHEDULE

NO	TYPE	MAT'L	SIZE	JAMB		LINTEL		THRESHOLD	
P2-1	2	ALUM	3'-0 x 7'-0 x 1¾"	ALUM	1			ALUM	1
P2-2	2	"	3'-0 x 7'-0 x 1¾"	"	1			"	1
P3-1	1	H M	3'-0 x 6'-8" x 1⅜"	H M	2	CONC STL	3	VINYL	3
101-1	1	H M	2'-8" x 6'-8" x 1⅜"	H M	3				
102-1	1	"	"	"	3				
103-1	1	"	"	"	3				
104-1	1	"	"	"	3				
105-1	1	"	"	"	3				
107-1	3	"	"	"	6				2
108-1	3	"	"	"	6				2
109-1	1	"	"	"	3				
110-1	1	"	"	"	3				

STAIRTOWER & ELEVATOR DOOR SCHEDULE

NO	TYPE	MAT'L	SIZE	JAMB		LINTEL		THRESHOLD	
S1-1	1	H M	3'-0 x 7'-0 x 1¾"	H M	4			ALUM	1
S1-2	1	"	"	"	5	CONC	1		
S2-1	1	"	"	"	4			ALUM	1
S2-2	1	"	"	"	5	CONC	1		
E1-1		STL	3'-6" x 7'-0	STL	7	CONC STL	2	BY DOOR MANUF	
E1-2		"	"	"	7		2		

WINDOW SCHEDULE

NO	MAT'L	WIDTH	HEIGHT	REMARKS	
A	1" INSUL	4'-0	5'-9¾"	SEE DETAILS	12/1 13/1
B	"	"	VARIES	" " "	
C	"	"	5'-9¾"	" " "	

SOUTH HILLS OFFICE BUILDING

STATE COLLEGE   PA

JACK W RISHEBERGER & ASSOCIATES
ARCHITECTS AND ENGINEERS

118 E NITTANY AVE   STATE COLLEGE, PA

DOOR & WINDOW SCHEDULES   15

DRAWN BY E W   DATE 6-1-80

CHECKED BY L T   PROJECT NO 6718

Figure 27. Drawing No. 15. Door and window schedules of the South Hills Office Building.

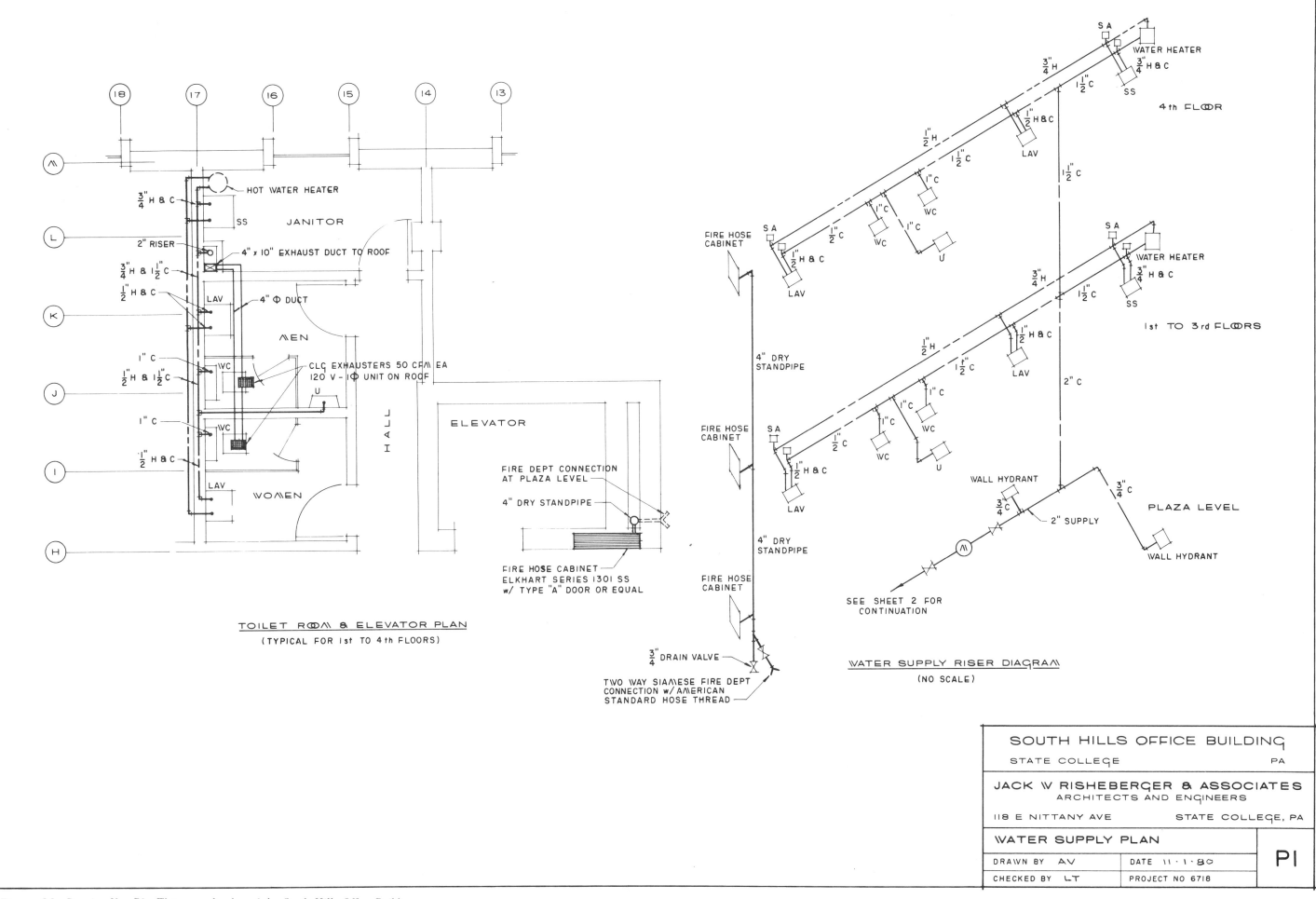

Figure 30. Drawing No. P1. Water supply plan of the South Hills Office Building.

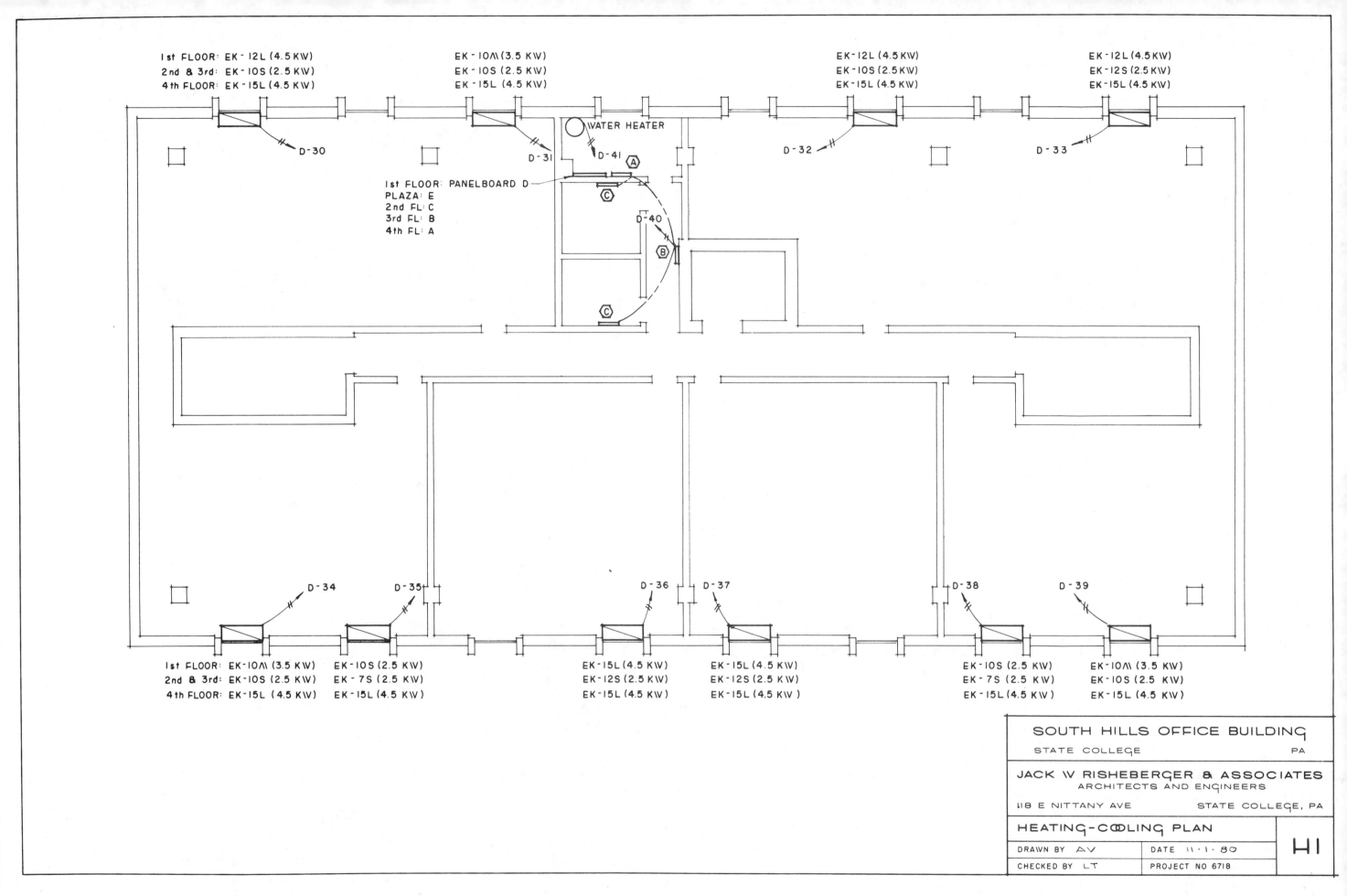

Figure 29. Drawing No. H1. Heating-cooling plan of the South Hills Office Building.

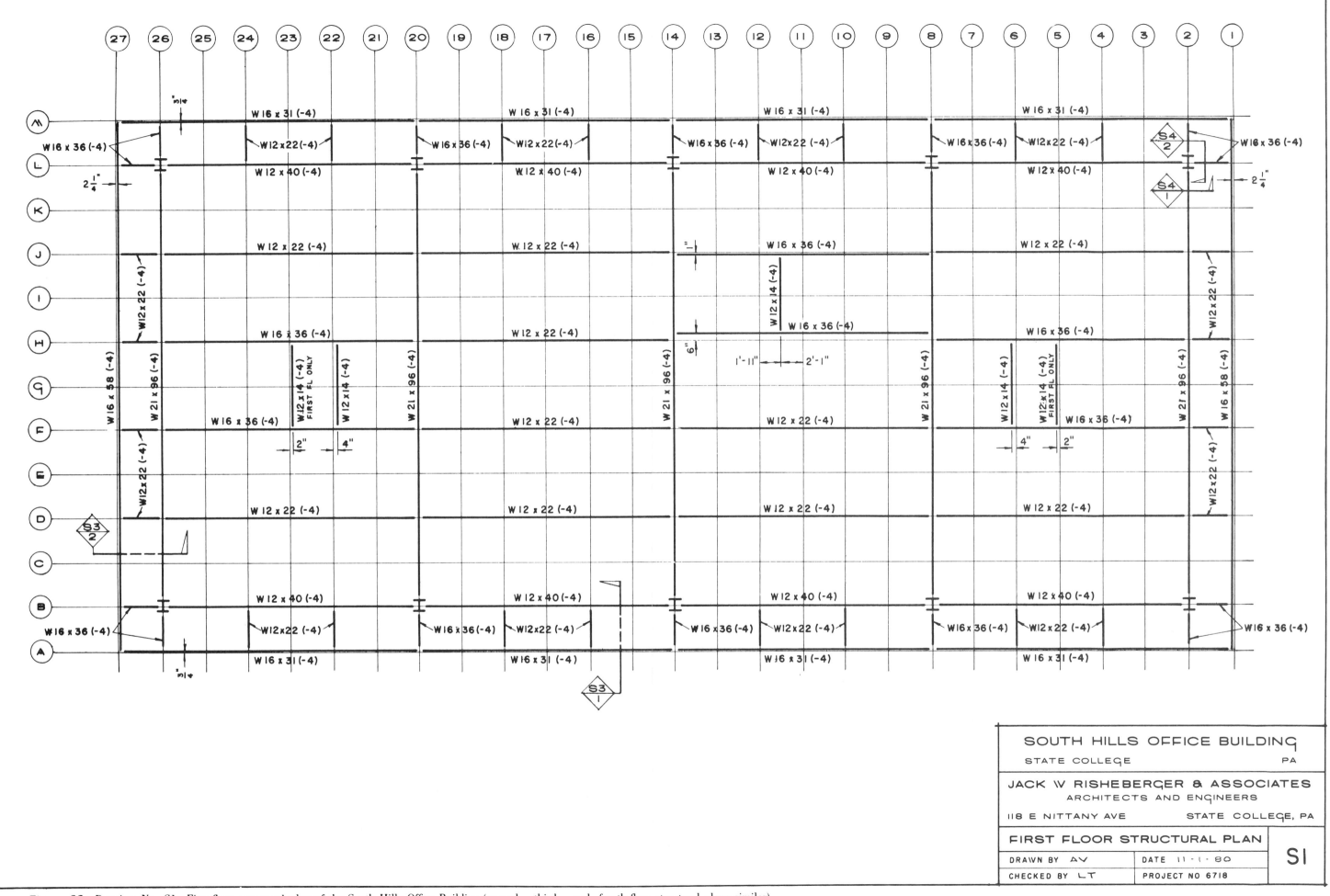

Figure 32. Drawing No. S1. First-floor structural plan of the South Hills Office Building (second-, third-, and fourth-floor structural plans similar).

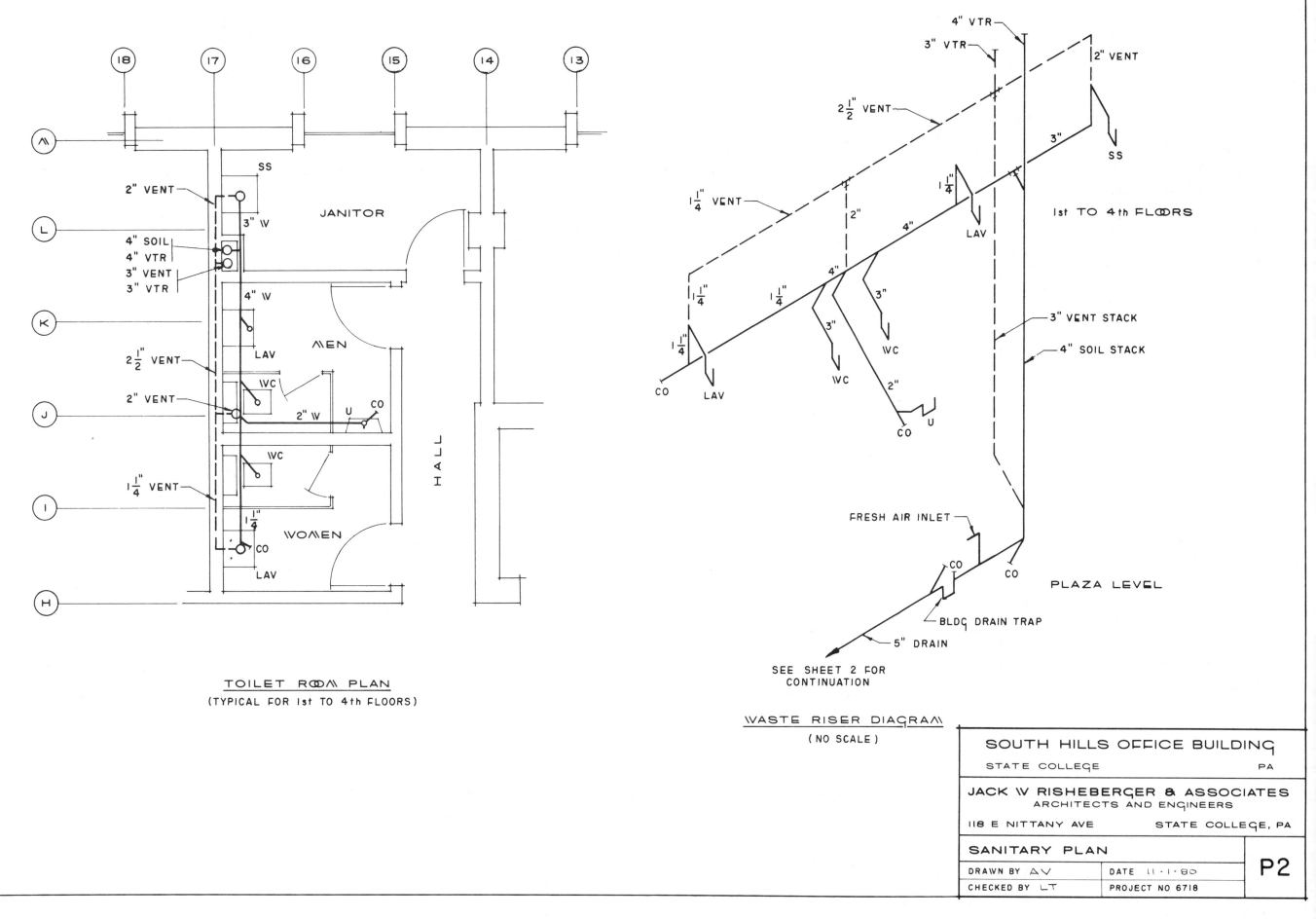

TOILET ROOM PLAN
(TYPICAL FOR 1st TO 4th FLOORS)

WASTE RISER DIAGRAM
(NO SCALE)

SOUTH HILLS OFFICE BUILDING
STATE COLLEGE   PA

JACK W RISHEBERGER & ASSOCIATES
ARCHITECTS AND ENGINEERS
118 E NITTANY AVE   STATE COLLEGE, PA

SANITARY PLAN

| DRAWN BY AV | DATE 11-1-80 | P2 |
| CHECKED BY LT | PROJECT NO 6718 | |

Figure 31. Drawing No. P2. Sanitary plan of the South Hills Office Building.

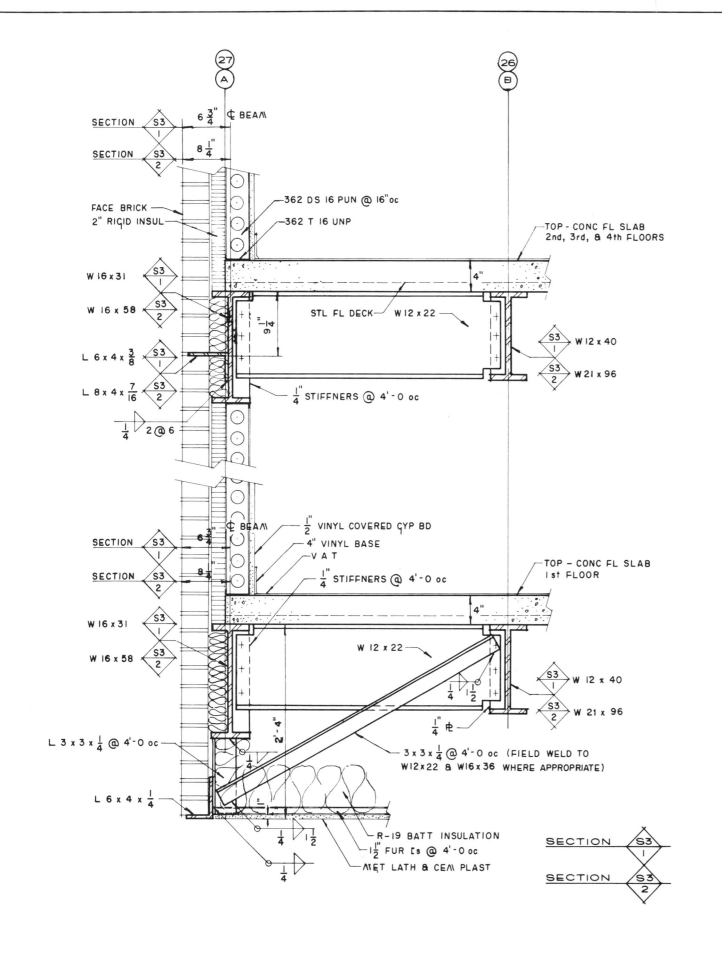

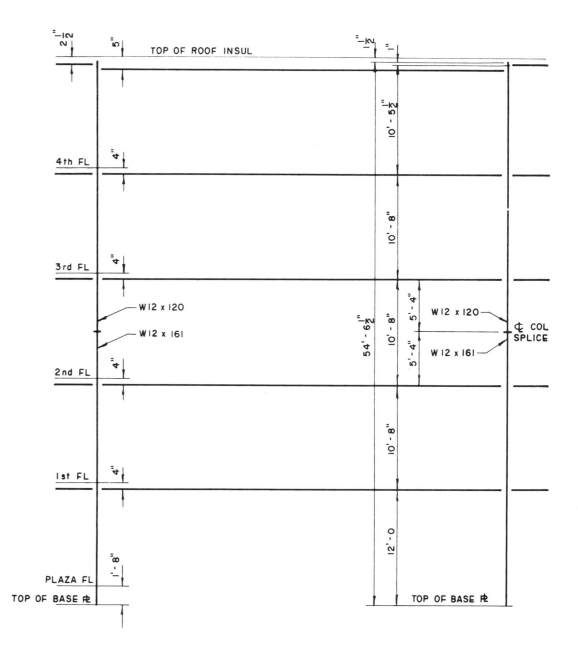

COLUMN SCHEDULE

(TYPICAL FOR ALL BENTS)

SOUTH HILLS OFFICE BUILDING

STATE COLLEGE   PA

JACK W. RISHEBERGER & ASSOCIATES

ARCHITECTS AND ENGINEERS

118 E NITTANY AVE   STATE COLLEGE, PA

COLUMN SCHEDULE

DRAWN BY AV	DATE 11-1-80	S3
CHECKED BY LT	PROJECT NO 6718	

Figure 34. Drawing No. S3. Structural section and column schedule of the South Hills Office Building.

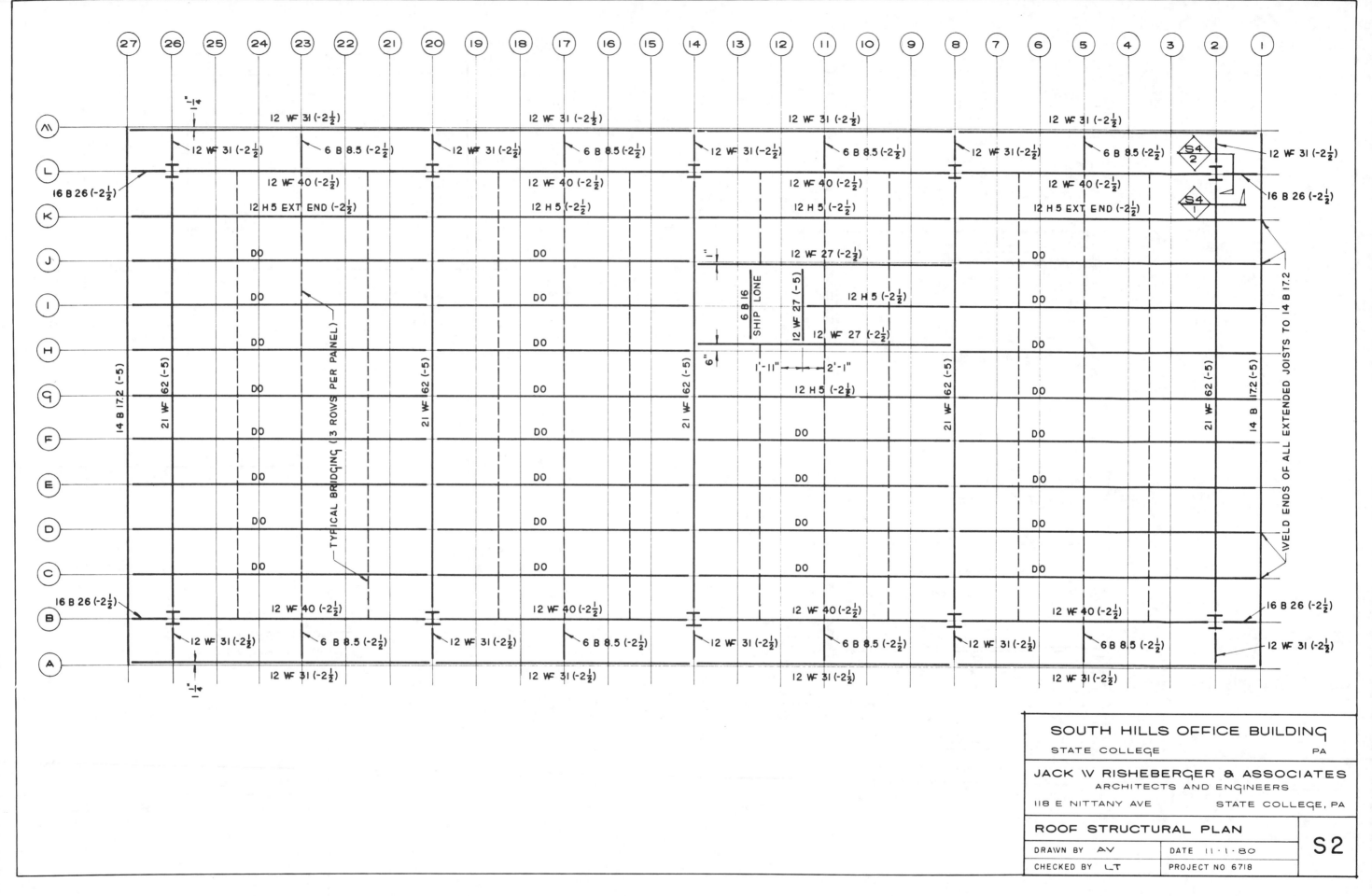

Figure 33. Drawing No. S2. Roof structural plan of the South Hills Office Building (using "old" steel designations).

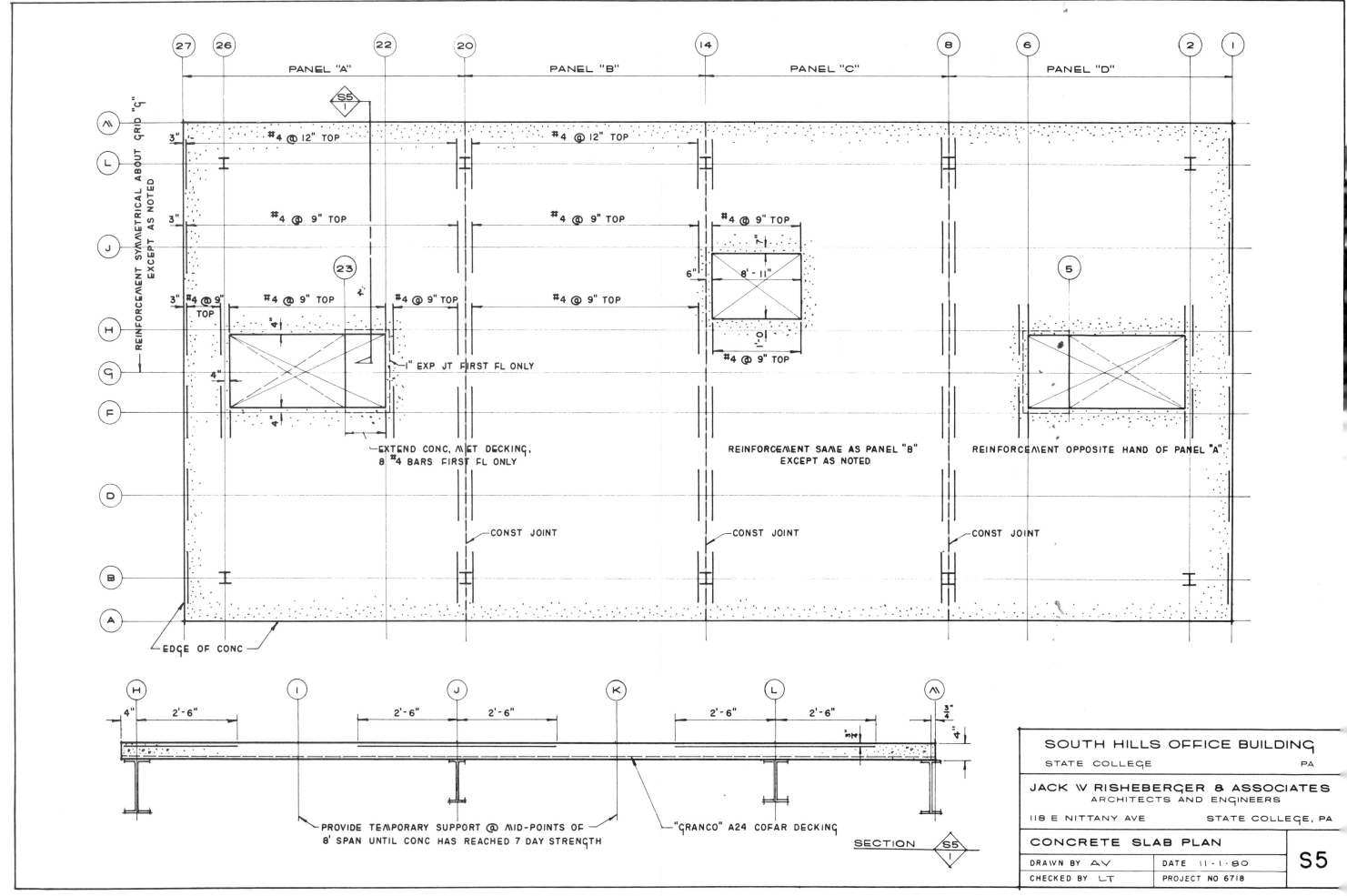

Figure 36. Drawing No. S5. Concrete slab plan of the South Hills Office Building (first, second, third, and fourth floors).

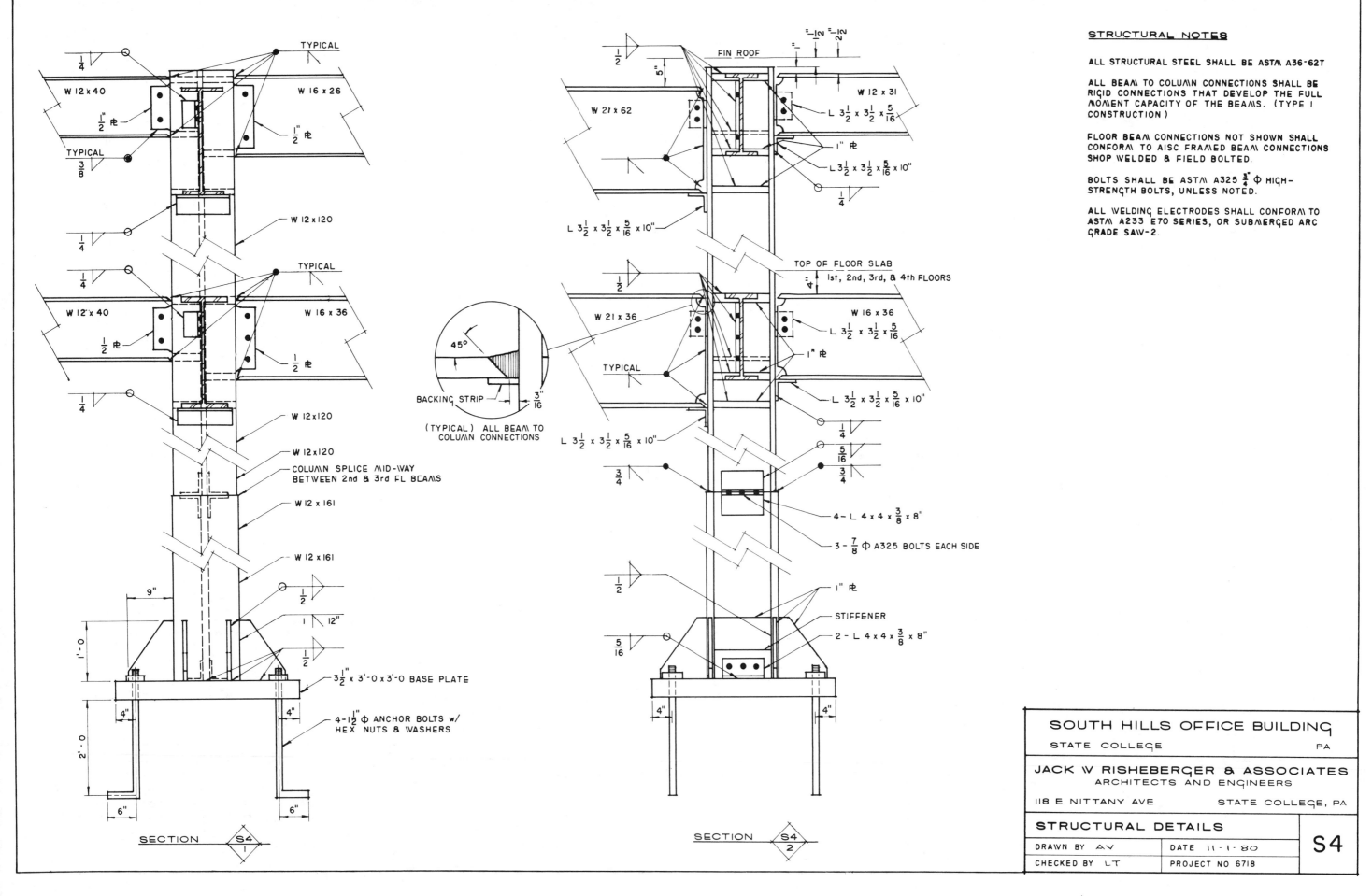

STRUCTURAL NOTES

ALL STRUCTURAL STEEL SHALL BE ASTM A36-62T

ALL BEAM TO COLUMN CONNECTIONS SHALL BE RIGID CONNECTIONS THAT DEVELOP THE FULL MOMENT CAPACITY OF THE BEAMS. (TYPE I CONSTRUCTION)

FLOOR BEAM CONNECTIONS NOT SHOWN SHALL CONFORM TO AISC FRAMED BEAM CONNECTIONS SHOP WELDED & FIELD BOLTED.

BOLTS SHALL BE ASTM A325 $\frac{7}{8}$ Φ HIGH-STRENGTH BOLTS, UNLESS NOTED.

ALL WELDING ELECTRODES SHALL CONFORM TO ASTM A233 E70 SERIES, OR SUBMERGED ARC GRADE SAW-2.

TYPICAL

W 12 x 40

W 16 x 26

TYPICAL

W 12 x 120

TYPICAL

W 12 x 40

W 16 x 36

W 12 x 120

W 12 x 120

COLUMN SPLICE MID-WAY BETWEEN 2nd & 3rd FL BEAMS

W 12 x 161

W 12 x 161

9"

12"

$3\frac{1}{2}$" x 3'-0 x 3'-0 BASE PLATE

4 - $1\frac{1}{2}$" Φ ANCHOR BOLTS w/ HEX NUTS & WASHERS

1'-0

2'-0

4"

4"

6"

6"

SECTION $\frac{S4}{1}$

45°

BACKING STRIP $\frac{3}{16}$"

(TYPICAL) ALL BEAM TO COLUMN CONNECTIONS

FIN ROOF

W 12 x 31

W 21 x 62

L $3\frac{1}{2}$ x $3\frac{1}{2}$ x $\frac{5}{16}$

1" ℞

L $3\frac{1}{2}$ x $3\frac{1}{2}$ x $\frac{5}{16}$ x 10"

L $3\frac{1}{2}$ x $3\frac{1}{2}$ x $\frac{5}{16}$ x 10"

5"

TOP OF FLOOR SLAB 1st, 2nd, 3rd, & 4th FLOORS

W 21 x 36

W 16 x 36

L $3\frac{1}{2}$ x $3\frac{1}{2}$ x $\frac{5}{16}$

1" ℞

TYPICAL

L $3\frac{1}{2}$ x $3\frac{1}{2}$ x $\frac{5}{16}$ x 10"

4 - L 4 x 4 x $\frac{3}{8}$ x 8"

3 - $\frac{7}{8}$ Φ A325 BOLTS EACH SIDE

1" ℞

STIFFENER

2 - L 4 x 4 x $\frac{3}{8}$ x 8"

4"

4"

SECTION $\frac{S4}{2}$

SOUTH HILLS OFFICE BUILDING

STATE COLLEGE   PA

JACK W RISHEBERGER & ASSOCIATES

ARCHITECTS AND ENGINEERS

118 E NITTANY AVE   STATE COLLEGE, PA

STRUCTURAL DETAILS

S4

| DRAWN BY AV | DATE 11-1-80 |
| CHECKED BY LT | PROJECT NO 6718 |

Figure 35. Drawing No. S4. Structural details of the South Hills Office Building.